D1560868

"Katharine T. Carter has been in the business of helping artists find their place in the art world for 25 years. She not only has an intimate understanding of the inner workings of the art world herself, but is also a consummate networker who taps into the expertise of a wide range of respected art professionals. This book is the culmination of her experience and that of her extensive community of artists' advisors. There is not a better book for an artist looking for solid, practical advice on how to make a life as an artist."

Kathryn Markel, Kathryn Markel Fine Arts, NYC


"In *Accelerating on the Curves: The Artist's Roadmap to Success*, Katharine T. Carter & Associates outline an amazingly detailed plan for artists to establish a successful career (including an equally detailed analysis of what 'success' might mean to a particular artist). Carter and her associates take you through specific steps in each stage of achieving a successful portfolio, exhibition history, and individualized goals for any artist who wants more recognition from audiences and arts professionals as well as more financial and professional rewards."

Glenn Harper, Editor, *Sculpture,* Washington, D.C.


"Whatever you call *Accelerating on the Curves* – manual, guidebook or bible of professional practice for the visual artist –  it also offers the wisdom and counsel necessary to achieve true success."

Roland Reiss, Professor of Art and Humanities, Emeritus,
Claremont Graduate University, CA


"As a stand-alone reference or as part of a formal program of study, *Accelerating on the Curves* provides both developing and established artists with an incomparable and comprehensive tool for personal professional development in today's increasingly complex cultural and commercial marketplace. I am eager to share this book with all of our faculty and students!"

Raymond Allen, Vice-President for Academic Affairs and Provost,
Maryland Institute College of Art, Baltimore


"Katharine T. Carter has assisted hundreds of artists with career development over the past 25 years. Now she and her Associates have produced a book on how to make it in the art world. They certainly know how it works and what it takes to succeed. This will be a great resource for all serious artists."

Astrid Preston, artist, Santa Monica, CA

"Having known Katharine since she first began presenting her lectures on how to go about the 'artist's business,' I have watched her accelerate on the curves – growing, adding, and improving her services to artists. She has practiced what she preaches, and her modeling of the thinking, strategies and methods for success demonstrates both their applicability and functionality to a career in the arts. This is a great guide for ruminating about the business of art wherever you are in your career."

John P. Begley, Gallery Director, Hite Art Institute, Louisville, KY

"A whirlwind ride on the highway to artistic success! Thanks, KTC and Associates, for providing a clear, comprehensive, and authoritative roadmap – an invaluable navigational tool kit that every artist should have."

Mallory O'Connor, art historian, author and president of oconnorart LLC, Gainesville, FL

"KTC is a fantastic force not only for any 'new artist on the scene' but for any established practitioner. She has proven herself over and over to be consistent, dynamic and effective."

Ronald Sosinski, Director, The Proposition Gallery, NYC

"Katharine Carter knows what it takes for an artist to become successful. To have her knowledge and expertise in book form will be an indispensable resource for any artist wanting to grow in today's marketplace."

Robert Bissell, artist and owner, The Dreamroads Press, Oakland, CA

"A dream became a successful art gallery in large part due to Katharine T. Carter's astute guidance and encouragement. Her professional approach to laying a solid foundation upon which to build the critical elements of a gallery: artist procurement, interior aesthetics, showcasing art media, mounting one-person exhibitions, marketing, etc., was unparalleled. This essential volume for anyone interested in doing it right is long overdue and will be revisited often."

Denyse McLean, McLean Gallery, Malibu, CA

"*Accelerating on the Curves* is essential to any artist who needs guidance in taking their careers to the next level. Artists: take from this important guidebook and grow."

Robert Melee, artist, NYC

"I have known Katharine T. Carter for many years as a friend as well as professionally and I can certainly vouch that whatever she touches is done with 100% heart and total professionalism. *Accelerating on the Curves: The Artist's Roadmap to Success* is no exception. It takes into consideration both perspectives: what is expected of an artist to have the best opportunities and also what the artist can do to break through the boundaries with the necessary information provided in exceptional detail."

Nadiya Jinnah, artist, NYC

"Katharine T. Carter has drawn upon her considerable experience as an advocate for artists to put together this very handsome and useful book. This book will provide good-humored, valuable career advice for artists for years to come."

McWillie Chambers, artist and private dealer, NYC

"Most artists have never made a business plan and are waiting for their big break, which is like waiting for a lottery win. This book is a useful tool – bringing together many experts to educate artists on the realities of what happens outside the studio."

Susan Shockley, Curator, The Parthenon, Nashville, TN

"What an excellent and comprehensive road map for any artist on the winding, and sometimes bumpy, road to a successful career! Katharine T. Carter & Associates have brought much more than 25 years of their broad marketing experience and expertise to create a clear guide through the maze of marketing, press packets, presentations, exhibitions, and so much more."

Marilyn M. Bassinger, Director Emeritus, The Ellen Noel Art Museum, Odessa, TX

"I have worked collegially with Katharine T. Carter for over 20 years at three respected museums. She is a consummate professional with an excellent eye for talented artists. The services she provides artists are comprehensive and unparalleled in the field. A book like this is long overdue. I only wish something like this was available when I graduated from college with an MFA. They taught us nothing about the art world. We were totally on our own. I think it's still that way."

Tom Jones, Director, Museum of the Southwest, Midland, TX

"Katharine T. Carter has made use of her 25 years of experience in marketing artists to write *Accelerating on the Curves: The Artist's Roadmap to Success.* The book provides information on what professional artists should know, sources for learning it, and how to develop a plan that will guide their careers in the direction they want to go. It is a compilation of practical, reality-based information designed to improve the chances for artists to achieve their goals."

Kevin Dean, Director, Selby Gallery, Ringling College of Art and Design, Sarasota, FL

"Katharine T. Carter's *Accelerating on the Curves: The Artist's Roadmap to Success* is aptly titled. Through her experiences she has filtered out much of the unnecessary and distilled the essential stepping stones of an artist's career."

Stephen Haller, Stephen Haller Gallery, NYC

"*Accelerating on the Curves* provides both a great metaphor and a powerful guide for living the artist's life. Katharine T. Carter offers a powerful and entirely original template for achieving professional success."

Sally Helgesen, author, *The Female Advantage, The Web of Inclusion,* and *The Female Vision*

"I find this to be a well-conceived, practical and highly informative how-to manual for working artists who wish to take control of the business end of their enterprise."

Livio Saganic, artist and Professor of Art, Drew University, NJ

"Katharine is a bold trailblazer helping artists establish their careers. She definitely got mine on track. There are not that many people out there in the artist's corner, which makes her an even more valuable part of our world. Take heed of her and her Associates' wise counsel and you will go far!"

Susan Read Cronin, artist, Manchester, VT

"*Accelerating on the Curves* is a must-read for any artist who aspires to have his or her work seen. Katharine Carter and a host of the best critics, artists, web experts and writers cut through the fog to guide you along the road to success."

Phil Joanou, artist, Los Angeles, CA

"Every sentence is filled with useful information. Most definitely an artist's best guide to protocol and professional practices."

Suzanne Jackson, artist and art faculty, Savannah College of Art & Design, GA

"Katharine T. Carter & Associates does an excellent, conscientious job of analyzing the work and prospects of under-recognized artists, helping to make them more marketable, teaching them how to take charge of their careers, and finding them opportunities they didn't know existed."

Victor M. Cassidy, art journalist and contributing critic for artnet.com,
*Art in America, Black & White*, and *Sculpture*, Chicago, IL

"Katharine T. Carter writes a navigational system that integrates proven points into an effectual menu-driven guide for artists. It is an invaluable resource, which when combined with tenacity, will enable aspiring artists to reach the next levels of achievement."

Ellen Slupe, corresponding critic for *Art Matters*, Lancaster, PA

"Since not all artists are effortless self-promoters, a book like this is needed. Tools for helping artists move ahead with their careers are suggested and provided by Katharine T. Carter and a team of savvy critics. From the practical to the philosophical, the writing is what you'd expect from such an A-list."

Cynthia Nadelman, art critic, poet, and contributing editor for *ARTnews*, NYC

"*Accelerating on the Curves: The Artist's Roadmap to Success* is a great resource for the aspiring artist. For the past 25 years Katharine T. Carter & Associates has been instrumental in shaping artists' careers and continues to have a professional rapport with artists in all levels of their development."

Scott Canty, Senior Curator, Los Angeles Municipal Art Gallery, CA

"In thoroughly walking artists through the ABCs of how to achieve success, Katharine T. Carter offers the all-important *E* for empowerment. *Accelerating on the Curves: The Artist's Roadmap to Success* will be an indispensable guide to artists in finding the steps to take through the maze of the art world, as they embark with the benefit of 25 years worth of knowledge and insight provided by KTC and Associates."

Marcia Wood, Marcia Wood Gallery, Atlanta, GA

"The gulf between what happens inside an artist's head/studio and what happens in the art world is hard to cross. Katharine T. Carter & Associates' new book will be an invaluable guide to that difficult passage. They have the experience and, most of all objectivity, to aid any artist on their career path."

Martin Weinstein, artist, NYC

"This rigorous, detailed, exceptionally thorough treatise on career management for artists reflects the author's (and contributors') years of observing the contemporary art market. Clearly and efficiently, it demystifies self-promotion by providing insights into the expectations of dealers, curators, collectors, critics, and other art-world players."

Stephen Maine, artist and contributing critic for *Art in America*, artcritical.com, artnet.com, *Art on Paper*, and *Artecontexto*, NYC

"*Accelerating on the Curves: The Artist's Roadmap to Success* is an impressive and comprehensive compendium of insights that are vital for any artist serious about following a clear path to career success. Katharine T. Carter & Associates has produced a book that is singular and unique in its vision for providing artists with ideal game plans to follow on their professional journey."

Jude Schwendenwien, critic and writer, Los Angeles, CA

"Sharing professional expertise and guidance through the years, Katharine T. Carter & Associates has been a powerful link bridging artists with museums and galleries. The latest endeavor, *Accelerating on the Curves*, is a comprehensive resource for any artist wanting to navigate a course from unknown to shown."

Deborah Stapleton, Director, The Anderson Center for the Arts, IN

"Fielding artist's requests for 'insider' advice about exhibiting their work and how to professionally advance their careers has always been a real challenge. *Accelerating on the Curves: The Artist's Roadmap to Success* will be required reading for not only the artists asking these important questions, but also for the teachers, professors, gallery directors, and museum professionals they turn to for guidance and mentoring."

Jose Gelats, Leepa-Rattner Museum of Art, Tarpon Springs, FL

"Some time ago in a galaxy far, far away…actually it was in St. Leo, Florida, and later in New York City, and it wasn't that long ago, Katharine T. Carter was kind enough to represent me and to share with me her secrets to achieving recognition in the Art World. She started me on a road that led to shows in art museums and galleries. The secrets she taught me are in this book!"

Michael McWillie, artist, Dallas, TX

"Art-world manuals that are both practical and readable are few and far between. *Accelerating on the Curves* pairs focused reflections by an impressive range of essayists with a precise and detailed guide to making the most of professional creative ambition."

Michael Wilson, independent critic and editor, NYC

"A concentrated collection of advice by art industry insiders, *Accelerating on the Curves* is a valuable guide for artists navigating their own careers."

Andi Campognone, curator and gallerist, Pomona, CA

# ACCELERATING ON THE CURVES

### THE ARTIST'S ROADMAP TO SUCCESS

*By Katharine T. Carter & Associates*

RUNNING HARE PRESS
Kinderhook, New York

**Contributions by Katharine T. Carter Associates**
Henry Auvil
Karen S. Chambers
Kathleen Cullen
Robert Curcio
Peter Frank
Jonathan Goodman
Mary Hrbacek
Ann Landi
Anne Leith
D. Dominick Lombardi
Robert Mahoney
John Mendelsohn
Bill Mutter
Dominique Nahas
Deborah Ripley
Steve Rockwell
Alison Slon
Richard Vine
William Zimmer

**Special Contributors**
Iyna Bort Caruso
Edward Leffingwell

**Editor in Chief:** Katharine T. Carter
**Managing Editor:** Karen S. Chambers
**Senior Editor and Researcher:** Henry Auvil
**Book Design:** Bill Mutter
**Cover Painting:** *Mountain Path*, 1989, 8'x 6', by Astrid Preston
©2010 Katharine T. Carter & Associates
ISBN: 978-0-9845453-0-8
Printed in the United States

*For all those who have traveled the road before us and endeavored to light the way.*

KATHARINE T. CARTER

# TABLE OF CONTENTS

TABLE OF CONTENTS (continued)

*No one can do it alone, no matter how capable or driven.*

KATHARINE T. CARTER (KTC)

ACKNOWLEDGMENTS

### Francis Rothluebber

I have been more than fortunate – blessed really – to have worked with such a wise and loving teacher, and friend, on an ongoing basis over the last 15 years. Francis has taught me how to find the strength to stand in my own truth, and the courage to honor myself in the daily choices I make. Our work together has transformed and emboldened my life; her counsel and encouragement have been a substantive part of my personal growth and professional achievements. I remain committed to realizing my potential as a human being and to help others do the same.

### William Zimmer (1946-2007)

Bill was the Founding Associate of Katharine T. Carter & Associates, a collaboration that began over two decades ago. He was the first prominent art world figure to believe in the concept and mission of the company, and he led the way for other recognized professionals to join our efforts. Much of what I have achieved on behalf of my clients goes back to the moment when Bill and I decisively joined forces to empower and educate artists.

Bill's involvements in discovering and encouraging promising talent were legendary. He was a mentor to many, myself included; he was the toughest taskmaster I have ever known. He introduced me to Ouspensky, Gurdjieff, Nicole, The Fourth Way, and the writings of Vernon Howard in my early 40s, and a process that was life changing. He is a deeply missed colleague, and an ever-present ally and friend.

### The Associates

To all the Associates, including Gerrit Henry, who has passed on, I want to express my enduring gratitude and appreciation for the ongoing support and loyalty I have been afforded over these many years. I want to acknowledge the invaluable contributions made by the Associates to our educational programming and artist support services. When you have been surrounded by a distinguished team of art world professionals who lend their names and talents to your efforts, so much more has been achieved than would otherwise have been possible. No one can do it alone, no matter how capable or driven.

### John Mendelsohn

A special thanks to a dear friend and collaborator from the get-go. John's generosity, patience, and kindness encouraged me as a public speaker and in the realization of my gifts as an advisor to artists. He made significant written contributions to the success of the "Highlights of the New York Art Season" lecture series from 1985 to 1995. His poetic interpretations, revealing observations and insights, and undeniable gifts as a writer gave eloquence to these annual presentations. Today, John's talents enhance and enliven the essays and written support pieces he produces on behalf of our artist clients. This collaboration evolved, in later years, into the professional workshops and seminars offered in New York City and nationally; these ultimately became the scaffolding for Katharine T. Carter & Associates. Without the "Highlights" series, nothing else that followed would have transpired.

### Rick Fisher

A debt of gratitude is owed to Rick Fisher for his substantive contributions; he provided the preliminary blueprint for some of the company's most innovative programs – most importantly, the concept development of Exhibition Placement Services for Artists. In the 1990s, when art world paradigms were noticeably shifting, Rick recognized the need for developing cost-effective exhibitions and educational programming, intended to simultaneously benefit artists, critics, curators, and educators. Rick worked tirelessly to educate art professionals regarding the new role that Katharine T. Carter & Associates was spearheading within the existing structures of the art world. But most importantly, he helped to validate and strategically position the company.

### Karen S. Chambers

My skills are as a public speaker, not a writer, so if Karen had not agreed to take on the enormous editorial challenges presented by this project, it might never have come to fruition. I admire her tenacity, and her ability to get her arms around all the valuable, but shapeless mass of information I wanted to share with artists. Karen brought her extensive experience as an art critic (*Aeqai, Review, American Style, La Révue de la Céramique et du Verre*, etc.), published writer (*Artist's Resource: The Watson-Guptill Guide to Academic Programs, Artists' Colonies & Artist-in-Residence Programs, Conferences, and Workshops, Trompe l'Oeil at Home*, and contributor to *Chihuly: Color, Glass, and Form* and *Object Lessons: Original Art from Guild Artists*, etc.), editor (*Dan Dailey/Linda MacNeil: Art in Glass and Metal, Chihuly: Form from Fire*, and *Frank Herrmann: The Asmat Paintings*, etc.) to the undertaking. She was instrumental in organizing the contributions of everyone involved in the project.

This project began in 1998 in Florida, in a recording studio in Tampa with the production of ten one-hour tapes/CDs based on the information provided to artists during my one-on-one consultations, and expanded information presented during my eight-hour professional development seminars. This verbal approach was later scrapped because it could not adequately illustrate how to properly frame a pitch letter or press release, etc. Realizing that the recordings would only work as an instructional manual in book form, I began laboriously transcribing my recording sessions.

Then I realized that a practical marketing approach would need to be developed, with step-by-step procedures that artists, at any stage of their career development, would find useful. So, for almost another decade, during every vacation, break, and holiday, I hammered out a chapter or two. I was completely overwhelmed, with no sense of how to organize my commonsensical approach into a book.

In 2006, Karen came to my rescue. In 2007, the Associates became contributors to the book. As we all approached the 25th anniversary of the company, I knew we must bring the project to conclusion.

As managing editor, Associate, and friend, Karen has patiently endured the endless stops and starts, adjustments, and perpetually changing deadlines, and erratically available funding for the project. She has helped make this dream a reality, and has given me the opportunity to bring artists a sense of hope, and to share the tools necessary for their professional advancement.

### Henry Auvil

As senior editor and administrative director of Katharine T. Carter & Associates, Henry has shared his gifts as a writer, and his support as a friend. Anyone who can interpret my scrawl, hardly readable handwriting, and translate it into readable form; decipher illegible rewrites and correction codes in the margins, in-between lines, and on the backs of pages; do four, five, six rewrites of the same page – well, he deserves a badge for endurance and patience.

If someone possesses the ability to interpret your often repetitive mantras, enthusiastic and sentimental bantering, translate these into something inspiring by modifying the sentence structure or finding better words to bolster and complement your own – well then you can imagine how lucky I have been to have a wordsmith of high order sitting at my side. Henry and I and our families go back three generations, and there has been a great advantage working with someone who really understands what I am trying to say, and helps me to say it in a more profound and meaningful way.

### Joe Ferrandino

Thank you, fellow traveler, for your guidance and wisdom along the road as I prepared to walk across Spain following the pilgrimage route to Santiago de Compostela, and for helping me bring finality to the Florida chapter of my life. Your words of encouragement, and the inspiring quotes you shared with me – some of which appear in this book – have been a source of continuing strength.

*The road has only two requirements! Begin and continue.*

DR. JOE FERRANDINO

FOREWORD
# Traveler's Information
By William Zimmer

Her house in Kinderhook is painted black, but there is nothing solemn about Katharine T. Carter, who favors flowing garments in rich fabrics and colors, loves adornments of all kinds, and still speaks with her quiet and ladylike Floridian drawl. She's also the "steel magnolia" who founded Katharine T. Carter & Associates 25 years ago, as the first and "still the country's only full-service public relations and marketing firm exclusively for artists," she states with some pride.

The premise of the company is simple: to empower artists to reach their highest potential and gain the art-world recognition they seek. Over the years she has worked with hundreds of artists of all stripes and was a painter herself, so she knows how to get art out into the world.

The founding of Katharine T. Carter & Associates was spurred by the annual lecture series she presented all over the country (from 1985 to 1995), titled "Highlights of the New York Art Season." Inviting her audience to talk with her after the lecture, often audience members introduced themselves by saying, "I'm a professional artist and my career isn't going anywhere…."

After hearing this plaint repeatedly, she became aware that too many artists lacked the basic skills necessary to successfully promote their work. "They all want to be in the Whitney Biennial, reviewed in *The New York Times*, and represented by a blue-chip gallery," she explains.

Realizing there was a common thread, she saw an opening: she would teach artists to manage their careers with a respect for business principles and help them land in the place they should be.

Carter herself has recently landed in Kinderhook, New York, located in the Hudson Valley. But the business began in Oceanport, New Jersey, with the opening of the Whitney Biennial in 1985. It then relocated to St. Leo, Florida, near where she was born and raised. She is from an orange-growing family. Her grandfather LaMarcus Colquitt Edwards was the first to put frozen concentrated orange juice into production.

But she has always had one foot in New York City, making frequent trips there for consultations with artists. Her usual Manhattan meeting place was the fabled Algonquin Hotel, a childhood haunt.

*We have our brush and colors, paint paradise and in we go!*
NIKOS KAZANTZAKIS

In a three-hour consultation with artists, who may have contacted her after attending a professional development seminar or seeing her full-page ads in *Art in America*, Carter prepares an in-depth evaluation of the artist's work, makes specific recommendations, and advises as to how to best promote his or her career. She also loads up the artist with printed information and resource lists that include not readily available materials, such as guides and directories designed to help an artist locate an appropriate venue – gallery or museum – one that is a good fit. Some clients see this ream of information as enough to get them started.

*Accelerating on the Curves: The Artist's Roadmap to Success* is intended to guide artists through a practical, nuts-and-bolts program that breaks down the promotional process into three stages of career development: progressing from the local/state, then regional, and finally to the national level. For those others who don't want to take the do-it-yourself route, they can opt for more advanced services that can lead to exhibitions in small and mid-sized museums nationally through the company's Exhibition Placement Services Program for mid-career artists.

Carter's program teaches her clients how to become strategists and tacticians in order to better advance their careers. "What counts is the quality of your involvements, not the quantity," she tells them with all the enthusiasm of a motivational speaker.

She urges clients to take control of their career development rather than waiting for a fairy godmother in the form of a critic, curator, gallerist, or collector to appear. In preparing them for the reality of the art scene, she takes an unorthodox tack. "Our ideas were almost always counter to the more standard practices and approaches in art," she explains. "We always believed it was in the artist's best interest to exhibit in the not-for-profit institutions (museums, art centers, college and university galleries), before attempting to affiliate with commercial galleries in major cities.

"I've found that dealers want to 'go into business' with a mature, more experienced artist," Carter says in reflection. "They don't want to educate an artist and bring them up through the ranks. It's a matter of time and money for them, as well as a disinclination to do so." She continues, "Artists who have carefully cultivated the interest and support of collectors, curators, and critics, and have an understanding of appropriate markets for their work make the best partners. In this way, two equally capable professionals join forces for mutual success."

Carter's ability to immediately size up the exhibiting and commercial potential of any kind of art is a major asset to her business. Another is her team of Associates that now numbers 18. Mainly based in New York City, they are art editors, writers, critics, curators, and gallerists who possess a variety of insights into contemporary art, and their work with Carter consists mainly of critical writing, studio visits with artists, and presenting lectures on current trends and professional development topics for artists in the Fine Arts Lecture Services division of her company.

A vital element in Carter's program is the creation of a full-color promotional brochure or catalogue. They are used to introduce an artist's work to dealers and curators, and if the artist has a museum exhibition, the catalogues are given away during its run. She still maintains these are much more effective than CDs of digital images that have supplanted the familiar sheets of slides.

Another service offered by Carter is the New York Presence and National Gallery Placement Program, which is available to artists who have gone through the company's museum-placement program or have a strong record of exhibitions (galleries and nonprofit institutions), as well as sales and reviews. Associates make studio visits, provide Carter with a critical assessment of the artwork, and then carefully compile a recommendation list of New York City galleries or other appropriate venues for their work. Making this list requires all of an Associate's imagination as well as a full understanding of the New York City art scene.

Katharine T. Carter & Associates is a unique concept, clear and subtle at the same time. Because of its groundbreaking concept, the company has encountered challenges and misunderstandings about the role it plays on behalf of its artist clients. At first, some observers thought she was just another independent dealer with a stable of artists. Carter responds emphatically that she has no stable. The artists she works with don't "belong" to her, and she never profits from their sales, even though her practice of not "taking a cut" is frequently deemed suspect.

Carter is perhaps closer to her artists than many conventional dealers, and her role might be more analogous to that of a personal manager, executive administrator, or advisor who is paid a salary, than that of an agent who takes a percentage of every deal. She charges an annual administrative fee, plus additional placement fees based on the level and quality of her accomplishments for her clients – when she produces tangible results. She counts it a success when an artist no longer needs her.

Carter discloses that the majority of her work boils down to decidedly unglamorous telephoning. She says, "I guess the toughest part of it all – if I am going to be completely honest and talk about the burdens – is that the majority of artists will never realize that I have contacted over 100 museums for every one exhibition I book," she shares. "And that translates into approximately three calls per museum, an equal number of follow-up e-mails to any interested curator or director before you get a serious nibble, then another 15-to-20 calls before the actual finalized booking of one museum exhibition."

A few years ago, Carter took the advice of a childhood friend who had settled in Hudson, New York, to return north. Instead of trendy Hudson with its charming antique shops, galleries, and restaurants, she chose the more tranquil Kinderhook, several miles to the north.

Carter's Florida house was a kaleidoscope of bright colors inside and out, while her Kinderhook house's interior is painted in various subdued but rich colors. Some Florida possessions came north with her – her black standard poodle, Cézanne, and a cat named Jack; a year-round Halloween Room installation replete with ghosts, goblins, and witches; and an amazing collection of rabbit figures numbering in the hundreds. Appropriately, the collection keeps growing.

Rabbits have special meaning for Carter who has adopted one for her company's logo. But instead of an adorable bunny, she's chosen a muscular and fleet leaping hare to symbolize the strides a committed artist can take.

INTRODUCTION:
# Driver's Manual

For many artists developing a workable plan and finding the resources and courage necessary to reach their destination as a "successful artist" is an almost insurmountable challenge. Some get detoured along the way to success, get stalled before they get there, or wind up at a dead-end. They may be traveling on a side road when the superhighway is only a few miles away. What *Accelerating on the Curves* does is to provide "The Artist's Roadmap to Success."

In the more than 25 years that have passed since I founded Katharine T. Carter & Associates, I've worked with hundreds of artists, helping them to find their way to a professionally rewarding career. *Accelerating on the Curves* describes the journey, which is the culmination of what I've learned, along with the contributions of the Associates and other colleagues, all of whom are accomplished art-world professionals.

*Accelerating on the Curves* is written for artists at varying levels of career development, which I've categorized as Stages One, Two, and Three. There are practical guides and concrete examples to help you navigate through each stage. Mindful attention and careful consideration of each facet and requirement expedites reaching your destination that much sooner.

For purposes of understanding the sequence as well as the integral relationship between each component of activity, you must be fully conscious of where you are in the three stages of career development and related areas of professional involvement. At Stage One, you focus on achieving success at the local – city, county, and state levels – moving on to regional in Stage Two, and finally arriving, properly equipped to compete at the national level in Stage Three. At each stage your success will be measured by the quality of the exhibitions in which you participate, the types of media coverage you secure, and your sales performance.

Several qualifying factors will also help you to identify a level for each of these institutions, nonprofits, and gallery venues nationally. Although each situation/entity must be qualified or assessed on an individual basis, for the purpose of our roadmap and the organization of information and research, we have developed a unique way to profile venues as Level I, Level II, Level III, and Elite. This is based on annual attendance or the estimated number of people that would view your work during the run of an exhibition. (Attendance levels can be found in *The Official Museum Directory* and the *American Art Directory*.) There are

> *All you need is a plan, a roadmap, and the courage to press on to your destination.*
>
> UNKNOWN

*From small beginnings come great things.*
UNKNOWN

many exceptions to this method of profiling, and some venues may have low attendance, but, by virtue of location, exhibit major artists, thus raising their level. The stature of the curator or the quality of exhibition programming also affects the category of the venue.

At Stage One, you need to compete and gain recognition on the local and state level before you can garner regional or national acclaim. Success at Stage One prepares you to participate in progressively larger arenas, extending your professional activities to your region in Stage Two and beyond in Stage Three.

To determine where you are on this journey, and your current stage of activity, it is imperative for you to assess what you have already accomplished in terms of solid, professional value and what areas still need to be addressed.

Recognition and success at higher levels of professional involvement require an honest evaluation of your talent and level of commitment, as there are no guarantees of any kind in the art world. Objectivity – knowing what you can still realistically accomplish – and how effectively and efficiently the desired outcome can be achieved is essential.

The Stage Three pinnacle of success for most artists would be gallery representation in New York City, Los Angeles, Chicago, or other metropolitan and cultural destinations; reviews in major art magazines; one-person exhibitions in mid-sized to larger museums; inclusion in exhibitions at the most prestigious museums nationally; and living solely from the sale of work.

This process ultimately has nothing to do with speed. For example, one artist's goal of affiliation with a gallery, especially in a major American city, may be achieved in less than a decade; for others it may take two or three times longer. This is largely determined by the level at which he or she enters the program of career development and the quality of his or her accomplishments. An artist who has developed a strong history of sales and a solid base of collectors can reach this goal more quickly than someone with no proven track record.

Attention and thoroughness given to each strategic area of your career development is vital to quality results for your efforts. This includes being constantly vigilant and recognizing the delicate balance between exhibitions, sales, awards and honors, and reviews. (In many cases, cultivation of the press and media is largely overlooked, and it is a critical component to every artist's name recognition on the local, regional, and national levels.)

Waiting for others to discover you and to help make you successful, or to write about you and your work, is an absolute, sure-fire path to failure. Acting with dignity and integrity in the professional arena, having an overall sense of what you believe to be appropriate to your professional goals, and the proper timing of your initiatives are crucial pieces to attaining the recognition you deserve and progressing to the next stage.

Doing your very best and never being ashamed of acting on what is in your own best interest is clear productive thinking, and a strategy to follow at all times – without apology.

As artists become educated about the value and importance of investing in themselves through promotion, advertising, marketing research, and public relations, many are questioning whether it is wise to wait for the "possible eventuality" of a dealer or exhibiting institution offering to invest in a catalogue and critic's essay, advertising, and public relations.

Even if this should happen, it is not uncommon these days for artists to assume part of these promotional expenses, even advertising costs in some situations, a paradigm shift that has been occurring for the last decade or more.

In the past, self-initiated publishing projects were considered suspect by some, especially when the printed piece was a brochure or catalogue with an essay for which the artist has paid the writer or critic. Yet the identical practice has long been followed by exhibiting institutions, and galleries. The essays in their publications (catalogues and books, not reviews) are also "bought." So it certainly stands to reason that artists, who are also art professionals and who wish to act as their own representatives, would have the same and equal right to avail themselves of the writing services of a critic or writer.

Nonconstructive and judgmental notions about this or similar initiatives, which involve artists taking the wheel and having more control in the outcome of their careers, have too often been perpetuated in the academic environment, resulting in many talented and deserving artists being under-recognized or unknown – fearful that they will be judged harshly by their own colleagues.

*The rule is: if it really contributes to your best interest, it is right.*
*The other side of the same rule is: if it hinders your self-development, it is wrong.*
VERNON HOWARD

This negative programming and *helpless* attitude, which translates into an ineptness in business, purity in poverty, along with loads of victimization – "poor misunderstood me" – have not equipped artists with the survival tools or dose of reality necessary to succeed in today's art world.

There is no nobility in this limited kind of thinking. Common sense survival modes and the right to happiness and financial success dictate that artists move beyond a role that is professionally crippling and hampers their ability to take advantage of the untold possibilities available to any life.

When you decided to become an artist or just gave into that compulsion to make art, you did *not* take a vow of poverty. The idea that artists can create great art *and* have a mind for business, take well-planned initiatives, and consciously and aggressively pursue certain outcomes through judicious promotional ploys was, and still is, seen by many as selling out, or even worse, selling your soul, when in fact, *it is your salvation.*

I spent ten years on the road educating artists, giving over 1,000 lectures and seminars at universities and colleges, museums, and art centers in an attempt to try to shift these attitudes and perceptions that limit and restrict artists. Katharine T. Carter & Associates has also hosted dozens of Professional Development Seminars during the last two decades: one- to three-day exhaustively informative workshops and lectures on all aspects of marketing and promotion. As a team, we are committed to the empowerment of artists, and our main thrust is to enable them to reach their full potential.

*Accelerating on the Curves* was written to help you reach the highest possible levels of professional achievement and recognition in the art world. I want you to become empowered, and to have a successful and meaningful career – this is the purpose and mission of Katharine T. Carter & Associates.

Your colleague and traveling companion,
Katharine T. Carter

*Accelerating on the Curves:* The Artist's Roadmap to Success

BOOK ONE
Stage One:
Local, County, and Statewide
Career Development

CHAPTER ONE
# Driver Education: Rules of the Road

Getting started properly and doing it right the first time at Stage One insures a successful outcome for your efforts and prepares you for continued success at Stages Two and Three. The knowledge and know-how you acquire during Stage One are unquestionably the most important working tools and template for reaching your professional goals, and they will provide a solid and credible foundation for your future success.

At each stage of the program, the discussions, descriptions, and general outlines are designed to put you on your road to success, and you will acquire a clearer understanding of why each leg of the journey must be completed if you are to reach the next destination. You will also gain the confidence and professional poise that comes as a result of your various experiences, which are the necessary building blocks for attaining desired outcomes. If any aspect of preparation is neglected, your ongoing progress and success at subsequent stages may be compromised.

For example, if you are seriously gearing up for a distinguished artistic career, and you have not yet garnered reviews as a result of participation in solo and group exhibitions, or made sales to patrons of the arts in your community, the likelihood of professional recognition, which can lead to being included in more prestigious exhibitions, is unlikely. Without a base of collectors and loyal following, exhibition credentials, and accomplishments of substance such as reviews and media coverage, curatorial invitations for inclusion in group or thematic exhibitions at museums and educational institutions, or affiliation with a recognized commercial gallery would also be improbable.

Completion of the requirements of Stage One usually requires three to five years, or longer, depending on your situation, and the amount of time given to your efforts. This is not a race to a defined finish line, or against a time clock: it is a process.

To advance too quickly to the next Stage, before you are fully prepared to do so, could lead to disappointment and discouraging setbacks to your future efforts. Also, comparing

*As is the case in all branches of art, success depends in a very large measure upon initiative and exertion, and cannot be achieved except by dint of hard work.*
ANNA PAVLOVA

*Ye shall know them by their fruits.*
MATTHEW 7:16-20

yourself to other artists is a sure way to sabotage your progress and to diminish the sense of accomplishment that comes from overcoming personal and professional challenges that will doubtlessly occur during your unique development.

Trust yourself and your process. We each have a path, stories to tell, and a hand to play.

### Vision Test: Communicating Your Ideas

Museum curators and gallery directors prefer to see work created in the last two to three years, but that may also have evolved over a longer period of time. They want to sense that you have given considerable thought, time, and energy to developing your work, as well as to mastering the method of approach and your chosen material, culminating in a body of work that effectively communicates your ideas. When introducing your body of work to a curator, gallerist, or collector, it would be the strongest work culled from a larger group – ideally 30 to 40 works that are the product of reflection and determination.

So the term "body of work" implies a sufficient number of related works that successfully communicate your ideas, and need only be understood as an ongoing investigation, a continuum or record of experience that resonates with you – and hopefully the viewer.

Another primary consideration is the presentation of a body of work that is both cohesive and thematically linked. This speaks to a persistent focus and approach, an in-depth investigation of a particular concept, which results in a thoughtful evolution of the work. Often it is a group of pieces intended to be displayed together and may, or may not, be a chronological record of formation and development.

There should be an ongoing dialogue that occurs between you and your work during creative progression. A work of art speaks to its creator, providing clues and insights that stimulate continued exploration through growing awareness. This slow and natural growth process allows for the refinement of your ideas with the completion of each piece, as opposed to a superficial investigation or jumping from one idea to another without exploring all inherent possibilities.

How do you select what to present? You ask the advice of art professionals. And who are these professionals? They could be art educators at any level, art historians, collectors, critics and writers, colleagues, or even a trusted friend – anyone you respect with a general knowledge of and appreciation for art.

18

*The reward of a thing well done is to have done it.*
RALPH WALDO EMERSON

Feedback and opinions from others can help you understand how your visual vocabulary communicates to your audience. The context or relationship of your work to current dialogues and prevalent trends in art can also profoundly affect curatorial response and interest.

### Body (of) Work: How Much Is Enough?

Obviously before you even attempt Stage One, you must have created a body of work that you can use to introduce yourself to curators, gallerists, critics, and collectors. There are so many varieties of artwork that it is difficult to speak of a precise number when referring to what constitutes a sufficient amount of work for an individual artist. However, for our purposes, we can identify basic parameters, meaning generally accepted definitions and requirements in the world of art, and which do not necessarily pertain to installation, or to new media and practices.

The established norm of 15 to 20 pieces being the minimum amount of work required was likely established because of the number of frames on a clear slide sheet and the average size of many exhibiting spaces. Through the years this amount has become the minimum required when the term "body of work" is employed.

Also, generally speaking, most commercial exhibition spaces can accommodate approximately 12 to 15 two-dimensional works, depending on their actual size, for an average area with 80 to 100 running feet of wall space. For sculpture, this may be between 8 and 12 pieces.

Commercial gallery situations can vary greatly, but often these spaces are not as large as those in museums. However, exhibition spaces at powerhouse galleries in the larger cities can equal or exceed exhibit spaces in some mid-sized museums. Still, a one-person exhibition at a commercial gallery may require a minimum of 15 two-dimensional pieces averaging 36" in width.

Eighty percent of the nonprofit exhibiting opportunities nationwide (museums, museums and galleries on college and university campuses, art centers, etc.) are small to mid-sized institutions; again, the sizes of these spaces also vary greatly. However, it is advisable to have a body of work that could accommodate between 150 and 250 running feet of wall space, or approximately 1,500 to 2,500 square feet. With two-dimensional work, this would require approximately 25 to 50 available works, and 12 to 24 three-dimensional pieces.

Some museum curators want to personally orchestrate and stage their exhibitions, and prefer to cull their selections from a larger body of work, or even multiple bodies of work. Offering

*Successful people are not gifted; they just work hard,*
*then succeed on purpose.*

G.K. NIELSON

ample choices and plenty of flexibility creates conditions, which are favorable to presenting your work to its best advantage. Their concerns may include audience engagement and participation, educational application or the scholarly discourse accompanying your exhibition, and a plethora of other reasons related to the specific goals of the institution.

A commercial gallery director may be inclined to show your most recent work, and primarily concerned with the interests of his or her collecting base when selecting works for your exhibition.

**Stage One Goals: City, County, and Statewide**

• Requires three to five years to complete

• 25 to 30 group and juried exhibitions at all level institutions statewide; five to six one-person exhibitions at Level I exhibiting institutions (annual attendance 5,000 to 25,000): community/junior college art galleries, college art galleries, art centers, small museums, community centers, organizations and associations, corporate and public exhibition spaces, emerging talent galleries in larger towns and cities

• Media coverage by general press, art writers, and critics in dailies, weeklies, local, and state glossy magazines, internet, cultivation of professional relationships with writers

• Recipient of prizes, awards, and honors from participation in juried and competitive exhibitions

• One or two gallery affiliations; active sales record

• Work acquired for public, corporate, and private collections; possible inclusion in museum and other nonprofit collections through purchase awards and donation

• Private and corporate sales through art consultants, interior designers, and architects

• Studio and direct sales to collectors of $2,000-$4,000 per month; total gross sales annually of $24,000-$48,000

• Investment in advertising and promotion of $3,000-$6,000 annually

• Budding relationships, through initial contact and introduction, with art professionals, collectors, and the press statewide

• Production of color announcement cards in conjunction with exhibitions, or fold-over brochures with short essay by an art writer or critic

CHAPTER TWO
# Carpooling: Who Should You Know and How to Meet Them

Whether we like it or not, the success of nearly everything we attempt comes down to who we know. The art world is no different.

It's all very well and good that you are making fabulous art in your studio, but unless you show it to a fellow artist, curator, or gallerist, it can't be included in an exhibition. Similarly if critics don't see your work in your studio or displayed in a public space, they can never write about who you are and the art you create.

To succeed in the art world, at any stage, requires a broad array of art professionals and collectors rooting for you. You'll need a base of supporters to help you navigate and advance on the road to success. First, you must do your research to identify these individuals and to create an active database (accurate and up-to-date) of all of the people in your community, county, and state (Stage One) that need to be kept apprised of your professional accomplishments and involvements. When you proceed to Stages Two and Three, the categories remain the same, the geographical area simply increases.

This living and breathing database is used to create a master list with all of your contacts – actual and potential – and then more focused lists for nonprofit institutions and for-profit businesses, media and press, community arts supporters, art department heads and faculty, dealers, collectors, and your friends and family.

The nonprofit sector covers institutions that are generally not involved in sales (though there certainly are more and more exceptions, especially at art centers) and encompasses museums, college and university art galleries (including junior and community colleges), art centers, libraries, and alternative spaces.

Their focus is on education and outreach, research, acquisition of works, historical preservation, and archival maintenance of their collections. Supporting the work of local and regional artists may be a part of an institution's mission or purpose; ideally you want to get to know the director and curator or, at the very least, acquaint them with your accomplishments and your work.

It is also important to know university and college fine-art department heads and faculty because not only are they your professional colleagues, they can also tell you about workshop, seminar, and lecture opportunities, and sometimes even teaching positions that are available, as well as providing information about art department and other campus-based exhibition spaces.

*It ain't enough to get the breaks. You gotta know how to use 'em.*
HUEY P. LONG

*The road to success is lined with many tempting parking spaces.*
UNKNOWN

Similarly you need to know the different players in the for-profit sector. Of course, there are the owners and directors of commercial galleries, but there are also art consultants, curators of corporate collections, interior designers, architects, and landscape architects. There are journalists, art writers and critics, collectors, and community supporters of the arts – all individuals to know in order for you to succeed in the statewide arena.

It's likely impossible to meet them all personally, or to personally exchange business cards (yes, you need one), or to have them visit your studio. But it is possible to identify them, and to invite them to your exhibitions.

You must begin to do your research and spend the time necessary to create your master mailing list, as well as specially tailored lists targeted to certain individuals. To insure greater visibility and increased name recognition on the statewide level will require consistent initiative on your part.

Your master list must also be subdivided because different professionals need to receive different materials. A collector would receive an invitation card for an exhibition with a personal note, but not necessarily additional visuals. While the media would receive the announcement card, a press release, and other written and visual support material such as artist statement and biographical summary, CDs with jpegs or PDF presentation of works to be included in the exhibition.

Ultimately, the media list should be categorized by type of outlet and specific requirements. For example, a monthly magazine sometimes requires 90 days or more advance notice, while a daily newspaper may prefer to receive your announcement and e-release only a week or two before the event for a free listing. Media directories often describe the preferred format and lead times for submissions (see *Bacon's Information, Burrelle Luce News Media Directories,* and other media directories under Critics/Media in the "Information Resources," p. 309). A personal telephone call to a newspaper or magazine can help you obtain procedural information, the correct contact name , and electronic address.

### Local Roads: Art Councils
Identifying all the art institutions, professional organizations, and people you need to know may seem daunting, but do not despair. Remember at Stage One you are only concerned with city, county, and state entities.

*There are no gains without pains.*
BENJAMIN FRANKLIN

One way to begin is to contact your state art council to learn if they can provide you with all, or if not, some of this information. (To identify state arts councils, consult the *State Arts Agency Directory*, published by the National Assembly of State Arts Agencies, *www.nasaa-arts.org*, or the *American Art Directory.*) Art councils may serve both the fine and the performing arts, and frequently staff a visual-arts coordinator whose sole purpose is to provide information to help support artists who reside in their jurisdiction.

Your state and local arts councils may produce newsletters or other publications that list current exhibition opportunities in nonprofit and commercial venues, including juried and competitive exhibitions, individual grants, and public art commissions, as well as employment opportunities. Much of this information may also be found online.

Arts councils sometimes make available mailing lists of professional art organizations in your area. They are often provided at little or no cost, and can include listings of directors and curators of college and university art galleries, art centers, and museums; art consultants, corporate collection curators, architects, landscape architects, and interior designers who work with visual artists; and even art writers and critics. Some organizations maintain image registries and/or websites to showcase the work of artists who reside in the area.

Professional artists' organizations, associations, and cooperatives also exist in almost every state and town in America. They can provide a local support structure for the artist. If robust, these groups may offer an exciting exchange of ideas and information, marketing leads from well-developed databases, seminars and workshops designed to further skills, and exhibition opportunities.

At the other extreme, these situations may be limited and restrictive in what they allow or exhibit, and may not encourage mutual sharing, stimulation, and support. These situations depend entirely on the sophistication, artistic level of accomplishment, merit, and maturity of the members.

Additional local exposure for visual artists may also be coordinated with local churches, hospitals and medical facilities, retirement homes, historical societies, and professional service organizations. Each of these groups may be more or less involved with the support of local artists in their respective communities, and their awareness or knowledge of the arts can vary greatly. Due to personnel or geographic limitations, commitment to working with local artists may also be inconsistent.

*Well begun is half done.*
ARISTOTLE

## Getting Directions: Directories

There are also readily available directories that can help you to identify the organizations and people you need to be acquainted with as a professional artist. These directories also supply contact information, as well as descriptions about what the organizations do. Three of the most extensive are the *American Art Directory, The Official Museum Directory,* and the *Art in America: Annual Guide to the Art World Galleries/Museums/Artists* (see "Information Resources," Directories, p. 311).

Your local or college library will undoubtedly have at least some of these reference books available to enable you to assemble a comprehensive database of organizations and art-world professionals. Information from these directories is used to build a mailing list for sending exhibition announcements, press releases, and to contact anyone of importance.

**TEXAS**
**MIDLAND**

M **MUSEUM OF THE SOUTHWEST**, 1705 W. Missouri, Midland, TX 79701-6516. Tel 432-683-2882; Fax 432-684-9151; Elec Mail jeanh@museumsw.org; Internet Home Page Address: www.museumsw.org; *Planetarium Dir* Gene Hardy; *Exec Dir* Thomas W. Jones; *Mktg Dir* Jean Hoelscher; *Develop Dir* Cathy Burgess; *Children's Mus Cu* Karen Winkler
Open Tues – Sat 10 AM – 5 PM, Sun 2 PM – 5 PM. cl Mon; No admis fee; $3 Childen's Mus; Incorporated 1965 as an art & history mus with a separate planetarium providing various science exhibits; children's museum; Six galleries exhibiting traveling exhibts & permanent colls; Average Annual Attendance: 100,000; Mem: 800; dues $20-$1000; board meeting third Wed monthly
**Income:** Financed by mem. contributions and grants
**Special Subjects:** Landscapes, Ceramics, American Western Art, Photography, Pre-Columbian Art, Painting-American, Prints, Sculpture, Drawings, Watercolors, American Painting, Southwestern Art, Etchings & Engravings
**Collections:** Art & archaeological materials of the Southwest; Indian art collection; permanent art collection
**Exhibitions:** The Collection; The Search for Ancient Plainsmen: An Archaeological Experience; Under Starr Skies: Defining the Southwest; Seeing Jazz; Dreamings: Aboriginal
Art of the Western Desert from the Donald Kahn Collection; Crossing Boundaries: Contemporary Quilts; 12-16 rotating exhibitions per year
**Publications:** Annual Report; Museum Bulletin bimonthly
**Activities:** Classes for adults & children; docent training; arts & crafts classes; video showings; lects open to pub & for members only, 204 vis lectrs per yr; concerts; gallery talks; tours; individual paintings lent to other mus; book traveling exhibs 6-8 per yr; mus shop sells books, jewelry, gifts & original clothing

*GEORGIA (Atlanta)*

**FERNBANK MUSEUM OF NATURAL HISTORY, (M),** 767 Clifton Rd., NE, Atlanta, GA 30307-1274. Tel.: 404-929-6300 & 6400 (tickets). Fax: 404-929-6405 & 6406
*Web Site:* www.fernbankmuseum.org
*Founded:* 1992
*Congressional District:* 4
*Key Personnel:* C.E.O. & Pres., Susan E. Neugent; Bd. Chm., Hampton Morris; Vice Pres. Devel., Leslie Marlowe; Vice Pres. Education, Christine Bean; Museum Shop Mgr., Linda Gerber.
*Personnel Profile:* Full-Time Paid 77; Part-Time Paid 30; Part-Time Volunteers 350; Interns 6.
*Governing Authority:* private; nonprofit organization Parent Institution: Fernbank, Inc. Tax-exempt: 501(c)(3)
Natural History Museum.
*Collections:* geology; paleontology; zoology; anthropology; archaeology; ethnography.
*Major Exhibits:* Gold, 11/09-11/3/10; Nature Unleashed: Inside Natural Disasters, 2/6/10-5/2/10; Geckos: Tails to Toepads, Summer and Fall 2010.
*Research Fields:* archaeology.
*Facilities:* 181-seat auditorium; 150-seat café; 60,000 sq. ft. exhibit space; 315-seat IMAX theatre; children's discovery room; facility rentals for private events.
*Activities:* lectures; loan, temporary, participatory & traveling exhibitions; volunteer program; summer camp; summer archaeology educational/research program; school programs; after-school program in partnership with Atlanta Public Schools; Urban Watch Atlanta; children's programming; special exhibitions; Martinis & IMAX ® theatre; facilities rental.
*Hours & Admission Prices:* Mon.-Sat. 10-5. Sun. 12-5. Museum: adults $15, senior citizens & students $14, children 12 & under $13; discount to groups & ASTC members; members no charge. IMAX: adults $13, seniors & students $12, children $11, members $8. Closed Thanksgiving; Christmas.
*Attendance:* 402,412 (accurate)
*Membership:* Individual $60; Family & Dual $85; Contributing $135; Family Advantage $150; Patron Circle $250; Benefactor's Circle $500.

---

## The Official Museum Directory

When *The Official Museum Directory*, published by the American Association of Museums, is used in conjunction with the *American Art Directory*, they provide a complete picture of exhibiting opportunities in nonprofit fine-art institutions and possibilities for exposure in hundreds of other types of regional and specialized museums and exhibition spaces around the country, such as, dog, rock 'n roll, anthropology, natural history and science, automobile, railroad, celebrity, costumes, sports, and children's museums, to mention only a very few.

The entries are arranged alphabetically by state, city/town, as in the *American Art Directory*, but offer more extensive information including an expanded staff list, major exhibitions, research fields, and facilities. Both institutions and personnel are indexed alphabetically.

A Museum Calendar of upcoming exhibitions provides limited information, and can also be accessed at www.omd-online.com.

*You make the road while walking [riding] on it.*
NICARAGUAN PROVERB

*Always do more than is required of you.*
GEORGE PATTON

**3576. Kathleen Cullen Fine Arts**
526 W 26th St. Suite 605  10001
(212) 463-8500
fax: (212) 463-8501
E-mail: info@artekcontemporaries.com
Web site: www.kathleencullenfinearts.com
Wed-Sat 11-6
Dir: Kathleen Cullen
*Emerging and midcareer artists.*
*Advisory services for individuals, corporations and institutions.*  **G/D/P/C**

Artists exhibited: Mark Chamberlain, John Fuller, Frantiska + Tim Gillman, Peter Gerakaris, Nolan Grunwald, Alex Haas, Gail Leboff, Joe Lewis, Peter Maslow, Tom McDowell, Anne Schaeffer, Marc van Cauwenbergh

**3578. curcioprojects**
433 E 9th St  10009
(212) 228-8924
fax: (212) 228-8924
E-mail: curcioprojects@yahoo.com
Web site: www.curcioprojects.com
Dir: Robert Curcio
*Emerging and midcareer international artists working in painting, sculpture, photography, video and performance*
**D**

Artists exhibited: Ricky Allman, Sandra Bermudez, Claire McConaughy, Michael Miller, Matt Schwede, Andre Stitt, Ginna Triplett

## Toll Road: Local Museum and Institutional Memberships

You are strongly encouraged to join local museums and art centers, because they are the very organizations and cultural institutions from which many of your professional opportunities will come.

Actively supporting and participating in the programs of your local museums, as well as contributing time, effort, and money to these institutions is a practical and solid investment in your career and invaluable when it comes to making local contacts.

Contributing to the cultural opportunities in your community, lending physical presence in support of the artists who are offered exhibitions, and also participating in *selected* juried and competitive exhibitions are critical to establishing a professional presence.

Opt for the upper-level memberships, such as associate and/or supporting categories, which are more expensive. These affiliations can provide an opportunity for higher-level networking within the business and artistic communities and visibility at important cultural functions. This more serious level of professional participation is necessary for your continued success.

Upper-level members receive annual reports from the museum or cultural institution that acknowledge the contributions of individual and corporate donors – potentially your collectors, too.

There are also more elite events such as black-tie openings where the movers and shakers of the community, along with other recognized art professionals – curators, writers, educators, and the press – may likely be present, creating a veritable networking extravaganza. Therefore, you should consider this *tax-deductible* opportunity as a solid investment in the future of your career.

### Hitch a Ride: Commercial Galleries

Before initiating contact with an established gallery to discuss possible representation, a solid exhibition track record, reviews, and a base of collectors must be in place. You must do comprehensive research, beginning with various gallery guides, directories, and the internet prior to contacting a gallery – in fact before contacting any art professional or individual in order to ascertain if your work is appropriate for a given situation. There are also independent publishers throughout the US that compile directories of galleries in different regions, states, and sections of states. And there is, of course, always the state arts council.

The first thing you need to know is the aesthetic and focus of the gallery and who they represent. Does the gallery's stable consist of both established and household names in the art world, which would classify the gallery as "blue chip"? Are they representing solid mid-career names mixed with some strong emerging artists? Or are they primarily showing younger talent and less known artists? Some galleries show a mixture.

*You must pay the price if you wish to secure the blessings.*
ANDREW JACKSON

---

### Researching Exhibition Venues on the Internet

Without a doubt, your best tool to augment the wealth of information contained in the *American Art Directory, Official Museum Directory,* and the *Art in America Annual Guide to the Art World Galleries/Museums/Artists* is the internet. The ability to "virtually" visit almost any museum, art center, or commercial gallery nationwide from your desktop is revolutionary. It saves an incalculable amount of time and effort, and the accuracy with which you can hone your target venue database is greatly enhanced. Before the advent of the Web, an artist would have to rely on the "areas of focus" or "collections" included in a museum listing, or peruse recent exhibitions and art magazine reviews to ascertain if a venue would be appropriate. Beyond that (unless the institution or gallery was within visiting distance), the artist could merely take an educated guess and hope for the best. Today, visiting a museum's website, (depending on its scope, ambition, and frequency of maintenance), allows you to view current, past, and, in most cases, upcoming exhibitions as well as gain a clear understanding of the institution's mission and curatorial direction. Additionally, you can often get a feel for the physical space as well.

As you gain experience navigating museum websites, you will notice certain recurring organizational and formatting tendencies that will help speed you toward the information you need. Typically, the institution's home page will offer an "About Us" option where you can learn about the institution and its history. There is usually a "Mission Statement" that is essential reading as it can define parameters that could disqualify you from consideration. Perhaps the focus is limited to local or regional artists or works related to some aspect of the permanent collection. These policies are not always spelled out in the directory listings.

Frequently (although not always), this section of the site will contain a staff directory, which is invaluable for confirming that the contact name and title you have in your database is current and correctly spelled. Staying on top of ever-changing museum staff is one of your primary challenges in maintaining an effective database, and in this respect the Web is a godsend. An annual directory can only be updated once a year — and with only a certain degree of thoroughness — whereas a museum's webmaster will likely update personnel changes immediately. These staff listings are also the easiest way to locate a curator's e-mail address as the directories only list a general e-mail for the institution.

Sometimes the staff directory will be located elsewhere on the site, often under the "Contact Us" section. You may still encounter museum websites that do not list personnel or e-mail addresses, but this is increasingly rare. In such cases, your only option is to pick up the phone.

The "Exhibitions" pages will allow you to quickly learn if the institution is appropriate to pursue. Usually these pages are divided into current, upcoming, and past exhibitions. Look at the exhibition archives first, because this will show you in thumbnail form what the institution has chosen to feature over the past few seasons, and allow you to ascertain the overall curatorial drift. Be honest with yourself in your assessment. Are all the artists chosen here for solo exhibitions of a stature and professional acclaim that you have not yet achieved? What percentage of the temporary exhibitions is devoted to emerging and mid-career artists? Do they even have one-person exhibitions, or only thematic or scholarly surveys? While it is

*Chance does nothing that has not been prepared beforehand.*
ALEXIS DE TOCQUEVILLE

Judging from who is represented (artists and estates), you can ascertain if the gallery is dealing in the primary market (work directly from the artist) or secondary market (works that are being resold by collectors).

Check to see if the gallery's shows are regularly reviewed. This information can be gleaned by an internet search, using the gallery or artist's name.

The gallery may be a co-op, run by artist members. If so, does it also present nonmembers in invitational shows?

It is imperative that you know to whom you would send your materials. Not only must the name be spelled correctly, you may also need to inquire about the gender to determine how to address the recipient. If it's Ms. Dashley Hare, she will not appreciate being addressed as Mr. Dashley Hare.

**Hire a Chauffeur: Art Consultant**

Art consultants are a form of private dealer, meaning that they usually don't maintain a public viewing space. They generally do not function as an agent, but are as close to that definition as any individual in the art world. Also, most consultants do not arrange public exhibitions or provide publicity services for artists.

Traditionally, they have acted in the role of liaison between the artist and corporate or private clients, architects, and interior designers, and they embrace a broad aesthetic to accommodate a wide range of client tastes. Some larger consulting firms represent hundreds of artists because they require the availability of a large selection of styles and media to meet the needs of current and upcoming projects.

Consultants work in a myriad of ways, organizing their businesses to operate in a manner that they believe best serves their clientele and their own business and financial goals. Some art-consulting firms are sizeable, with many employees working on multiple projects simultaneously, but there are many who work in small teams or alone.

Most consultants do not maintain a storefront, but may have offices with storage space for artworks. They may also maintain extensive visual support for the artists they represent. Consultants can arrange PowerPoint presentations for a client, and these could be in their own offices, on site, or via the internet.

28

Today consultants often have arrangements with an artist similar to commercial gallery dealers at 50/50 or 40/60 cuts from the total retail sales price. Consultants may charge certain fees to the artist for representation, or they may simply charge the artist for out-of-pocket expenses when a client or corporate entity is paying them on a per-project basis.

In the high-flying days of major corporate acquisitions, which was at its peak in the 1980s, if an artist directly approached the in-house curator or person responsible for purchasing art for the corporation, he or she would receive 100% of the mutually agreed upon sales price. If the corporation was working with an outside consulting firm or art consultant to develop its collection, then the artist might still receive the full sale price – if the corporation was paying the consultant a finder's fee on a per-project basis, or compensating with an annual retainer or hourly fee. Another equation was for the art consultant to take a fee from the corporation, and a lesser percentage (20%-30%) from the artist, which was sometimes referred to as "double dipping." However, often the fee and commission amounts equaled close to 40% to 50% of the retail sale price. This was not considered unethical, just another way of doing business and creating a successful consulting business.

When there is shipping involved for a client presentation, it is not uncommon for the artist to assume a portion of this expense. If the artist pays incoming shipping costs and the consultant pays outgoing, there is the added incentive for the consultant to sell the work and not incur the additional expense of returning the work.

In some situations, the consultant or client will pay to ship the artist's work to a location where it can be viewed firsthand before the purchase. This is a clear indication of the seriousness of the potential buyer, and some consultants, depending on their status and the reputations of the artists they represent, may even require the client to assume 100% of this expense.

Caroll Michels, an internationally recognized artists' advisor, offers mailing lists of more than 600 art consultants, and has been a respected source of this type

*I do not seek. I find.*
PABLO PICASSO

never a bad idea to reach out to museum professionals to familiarize them with your work, inappropriate submissions could do damage to your chances down the line.

In some cases a museum or website will have a section offering guidelines for artist submissions including policies, deadlines, and qualifications. This is most likely to be found on the sites of regional art centers, which often post specific "Requests for Proposals" or "Open Calls to Artists" for specific theme group shows. It's a good idea to check these websites frequently, as they offer excellent opportunities for exhibition that you would likely only learn of on the Web.

The internet is equally beneficial to your research on commercial gallery opportunities. Every gallery worth its salt maintains a current, up-to-date website as this has become an essential component of commerce, especially in a business dependent on such highly specialized and far-flung clients as collectors of art.

If you are willing to roll up your sleeves and spend three or four days in front of a monitor with a copy of the *Art in America Annual Guide to the Art World Galleries/Museums/Artists* at hand, you can literally review almost every gallery in a region (or if you have a week or ten days, nationwide), and emerge with a clear knowledge of which dealers would be inclined to consider your work. There is no other tool to even remotely make this possible.

Gallery sites tend to be very similar in format and organization. All will have pages for current, past, and upcoming exhibitions. Some may offer brief histories or guiding philosophies, but as these are strictly commercial ventures, this is rare. You want to immediately proceed to the gallery's roster of artists. The most user-friendly sites will have a list of names, which are

*Where there's a will, there's a way.*
UNKNOWN

of information for decades. Her annotated art consultant lists are broken down by state, and the interests and preferred mediums of these consultants are sometimes described.

*Art Calendar* and Art Network are other sources for lists of consultants, architects, interior designers, and corporations collecting art. Always check to see how recently the lists have been updated.

Contact information for these resources and others can be found in the "Information Resources" (see Directories, pp. 311-314; Mailing Lists/Marketing, pp. 330-335).

## The Company Car: Corporate Collections

In the '70s and '80s, corporations worldwide were actively acquiring and commissioning original works of art for their collections. The corporate art world was an enormously lucrative and active area for art consultants, dealers, and artists alike.

However, these wide-ranging opportunities began to diminish in the mid-1990s. Corporations that had retained the professional services of important curators for the development of their collections began to make acquisitions without the assistance of these art-world professionals, or stopped acquiring altogether.

In some cases, if they continued to buy, the responsibility for adding to the collection was assumed by an employee or even the CEO or president of the corporation, none of whom may have had a background or knowledge of art.

Although opportunities in the corporate market have dwindled considerably, there are still opportunities for artists to make sales, either directly to the corporation or through a commercial gallery, art consultant, or corporate consultant who serves as an advisor and resource to corporations, private business owners, and residential clients.

If a company is still developing its collection, an internet search or telephone call may elicit that information, along with a contact name and an e-mail address.

State and local arts councils may have lists of corporations that use original works of art in their corporate offices. The *American Art Directory* also lists some corporations with both collections and exhibition spaces.

Perhaps one of the best sources for information on corporate collections is the *International Directory of Corporate Art Collections*, compiled by Shirley Reiff Howarth of the Humanities Exchange. It provides comprehensive information on corporate collections worldwide. Each is described, with status (ongoing or completed), the name of the person in the corporation who is responsible for selection and acquisition, and indicates whether an art consultant or gallery is involved in the process. Contact information is often provided.

### Professional Drivers: Residential and Contract Interior Designers, Architects, and Landscape Architects

Interior designers are responsible for the decoration of a plethora of spaces, ranging from private homes (residential) to huge commercial and public projects (contract). Although they frequently rely on the services of a commercial gallery or art consultant, some take work on consignment or arrange for more extensive commissioned projects for their clients, while some purchase outright for resale.

Interior designers do not usually work like commercial gallery dealers, taking a 50/50 cut on the final sales price, but are more of a first cousin to the art consultant. Their mark-ups may exceed 50%, and can also include framing as well as additional presentation and installation charges based on the actual time involved on a project. Artists working directly with an interior designer need only determine what they need to "net" from a sale, and not concern themselves with all the various permutations and arrangements the designer makes with the client.

There are two major national professional organizations: ASID (American Society of Interior Designers) and IIDA (International Interior Design Association). These organizations are composed of local chapters in major metropolitan markets or chapters encompassing larger geographical areas.

The ASID divides its membership into two groups by the focus of practice: residential and contract or commercial.

*The work will teach you.*
ESTONIAN PROVERB

## Coverage Outside the Art Press

Phil Joanou is an excellent example of an artist who has garnered impressive coverage, indirectly as a result of his former career in the advertising industry. Phil's paintings are strongly influenced by both mass communications and psychology; his training and historical vocabulary takes "very old stories and makes them new again," according to critic Jonathan Goodman. This style and approach has captured the attention of art critics and general press alike, culminating in reviews and articles in *Art in America*, *d'Art International*, *NY Arts*, *International Economy*, and *The Wall Street Journal*. Noreen O'Leary of *Adweek Magazine* was intrigued by Joanou's story, and felt it would be of interest to her readers.

As the long-standing chief of one of the oldest Los Angeles agencies, Dailey & Associates, Phil Joanou would be expected to retire to the lush golf greens of Palm Springs. But Joanou viewed that time of life as just the beginning. The 73-year-old has wanted to be a painter since he was a teenager. But family money problems while at the University of Arizona forced him to switch from the fine arts school into business. Even while running an agency, he never stopped drawing, painting, taking classes and studying with artists. When he left Dailey nearly a decade ago, he moved to Manhattan and enrolled in the New York Academy of Art to get a masters degree in painting. Working everyday in his

*The day you decide to do it is your lucky day.*
JAPANESE PROVERB

The IIDA breaks down its membership into forums covering contract, education and research, governmental, healthcare, hospitality, retail, and residential.

Mailing lists may be available for purchase through the local and state chapters or the national headquarters of these professional organizations. You are advised to purchase these lists on an as-needed basis, checking to be sure they have been recently updated and are zip code specific. Also, be aware that these lists are often sold as either mailing lists or telemarketing lists, having either an address or telephone number, but not both. You will want both, plus e-mail addresses when available, but you can always consult www.whitepages.com or use a search engine like Google to supply the missing information.

Architects and landscape architects represent two areas of opportunities for artists: the purchase of existing works and commissions.

Architectural firms often specialize in specific project categories of buildings, such as hospitals, hotels, performing arts centers, office buildings, real estate development projects, etc., and some firms maintain an interior design division, which can extend to the realm of art.

On its website, the American Institute of Architects (AIA) has "Architect Finder" (www.architectfinder.aia.org), which allows you to search its database of members by zip code, indicating radius of search. You may also search by country, state, building type, and service type.

American Society of Landscape Architects (ASLA) publishes the online "Firm Finder," which lists member firms and may include individuals not licensed. The ASLA also maintains two members-only directories. The *ASLA Member Directory* allows members to search by name, firm/agency/institution, city, metropolitan area, state, or country to locate individual members and corporate members. The *In Practice Directory* allows members to search by f irm name, city, metropolitan area, state, or country.

Artists who wish to access "trade professional" information would have to identify someone in their community who is currently a member, and who would be willing to share this information. If a sculptor has worked on other public or commissioned projects in the area, chances are good that based on his or her reputation and previous involvements, he or she could connect with such an individual.

## Race Coverage: Media

Detailed information on both print media (daily and weekly newspapers, magazines, and special publications) and electronic (radio, television, and internet) outlets is available in directories that may be divided geographically or by category and/or subject. Statewide media directories are available in certain states so check with your local librarian.

Bacon's Information, which touts itself as the nation's largest media database company, publishes directories for newspaper/magazine, radio/TV/cable, and internet media. These directories are divided into North American Directories and Regional Media Directories (Metro California Media Directory; New York Publicity Outlets Directory) and profile over 125,000 media outlets.

Bowker's three-volume *North American Directories* includes a newspaper/magazine directory, radio/TV/cable directory, and an internet media directory.

The *American Art Directory* lists art magazines and professional art publications, with contact information, subscription rates, and frequency of publication as well as editor's name. There is also a Newspaper Art Editors and Critics section that is arranged by state and then alphabetically by the newspaper's name, but no contact information is provided. What is revealing about this section is actually having a listing of the top cultural cities in the US that have newspapers with art critics and art writers on staff.

*Art Diary International* is an exceptional source for the home addresses and telephone numbers of leading critics and art writers worldwide. Caroll Michels also publishes lists of New York City-area critics and press contacts, as well as regional, national, and international press contacts.

It is wise, however, to go beyond concentrating only on art writers at major publications. Be creative in researching other possibilities for coverage. Don't neglect general-interest writers for the neighborhood weekly. For example, if you gave up your investment-banking career to paint, the business writer at the local paper may be intrigued by your story and end up writing a feature.

Tribeca studio, Joanou turned out complex paintings in a style he describes as contemporary figurative expressionism. Old friends like IPG chief Phil Geier have attended openings and past colleagues like Peter Dailey have bought the former member of the Tuesday Team's work. Joanou admits trading the corner office for the solitude of oil paint and canvas can be lonely at times. The founder of the Partnership for a Drug-Free America encourages others to rediscover early interest. "You have to let go of a lot of things, but it's always nice to think you can recreate yourself," he says.

**"Industry Leaders: Where Are They Now?"** *Adweek*, October 30, 2000.

*Learning is a treasure, which accompanies
its owner everywhere.*

CHINESE PROVERB

**School Crossing: College and University Art Department Heads and Faculty**

Art department heads and faculty are practicing professionals who should be kept abreast of your activities for a number of good reasons. In addition to potential fulltime or part-time teaching positions already mentioned, there may be a visiting artist and lecture possibility, which could be offered to coincide with your exhibition at a local gallery, art center, or museum, or in conjunction with a show at the college or university itself.

The *American Art Directory* also lists art schools with contact data, degree programs, scholarship programs, entrance requirements, and tuition information; schools abroad; state directors and supervisors of art education; and fellowships; as well as other art organizations. It is indexed by subject, personnel, and organization.

The College Art Association's *Directories of Graduate Programs in the Arts* provides current and comprehensive information on art schools, colleges, and universities with graduate programs in studio art and art history. In addition, there is information on faculty and specializations, facilities and resources, financial aid, curricula, and admission requirements.

College and university websites also list faculty by department, such as fine arts, art history, new media, video, etc., and sometimes provide brief biographies.

**Business District: Community Arts Supporters**

Community arts supporters are private citizens who focus their philanthropic interests on the visual arts, perhaps serving on museum boards as fundraisers or underwriting operational or exhibition costs. They also include local businesses that actively contribute to and support the cultural activities of their community.

As previously mentioned, the annual report and newsletters published by most museums list individual contributors and corporate sponsors of the institution. Social organizations, private clubs, business organizations, and service clubs can also be sources for developing your mailing list of community supporters of the arts.

**Fuel Injection: Collectors**

Collectors need no explication. They have either purchased art from you or could and hopefully will. Galleries come and go, but your collectors – if properly cultivated – will stay loyal to you throughout your career, so if you are smart and at all thoughtful, you never need to be solely dependent on sales generated through a gallery.

On average, collectors will purchase three to five works over the course of a career if the artist is willing to keep them abreast of career activities and to rub shoulders on special occasions. Collectors generally feel they are investing in an artist (a "piece" of the artist, so to speak), and are entitled to some personal attention.

Provide collectors with periodic updates. You can send them copies of reviews; press releases and announcement cards for exhibitions; notifications of awards, honors, and sales (private and corporate); and even holiday cards. Invite them to your studio to view new work being sent to an important exhibition held elsewhere. Host an annual cocktail party in your studio or home, in the home of a supportive friend or patron, or even a corporate lobby that has empty walls and good lighting. Make it a memorable event. And always serve something alcoholic – it stimulates conversation and sales!

A handwritten personal thank-you note for a purchase, referral, or a professional introduction to someone is always appropriate and appreciated. A glass of wine or champagne sent to a collector's table in a restaurant or bar is a special gesture of acknowledgment and appreciation for his or her continuing support.

Each and every month commit to identifying a minimum of 50 potential collectors and make at least one sale, even if you have to reduce your price or negotiate a payment plan. If necessary, start with your immediate circle of family and friends, and then branch out to neighbors and old college buddies.

We all know accountants, librarians, bankers, dentists, doctors, and lawyers. And then there is the plumber, electrician, auto mechanic, massage therapist, chiropractor – these are only the tip of the iceberg.

Your spouse has personal and professional friends and acquaintances, and your family and friends can often be seriously appealed to and asked to make a list of anyone they know who might be interested in art or be a potential collector.

In addition to identifying potential clients, get creative. Your realtor may know an architect, contractor, or interior designer, and, in exchange for referrals, may be willing to pass on information on newly built or purchased homes, and on architecture and design projects in the works. Your and your friends' children may attend public or private

*Whatever is worth doing is worth doing well.*
EARL OF CHESTERFIELD

*The first step is the hardest.*
PROVERB

schools with art departments and ample corridors for the display of art. And then there are local merchants you patronize and favorite restaurants you frequent that may want to acquire your work, or at least showcase it. Banking institutions, the health-care sector, and hospitality (hotels and restaurants) almost always display art of some kind, and your local business establishments are no different. Business and professional contacts may also have unused wall space, or their offices may be located in large buildings with lobby spaces. There is also the possibility that these professionals are willing to trade services for art, which constitutes both a sale and a new client. Using art as collateral in exchange for names and leads is another approach you can take.

Try to give out and exchange 15 to 20 business cards per week. Offer your services gratis as a speaker, and exchange your contact information (printed on the back of a color reproduction or on a brochure or catalogue) for their business cards at the end of your presentation. Invite them to a party in your studio the following month. Check into other local professional organizations for other guest speaking opportunities.

Let literally everyone you know, and everyone you meet, know what you do. Carry business cards or color announcement cards for your exhibitions at all times. If you have a casual conversation in a bar, on a plane, or in a queue anywhere with someone who seems sincerely interested in and knowledgeable about art, enthusiastically tell them about what you do, mention a recent accomplishment, etc., and tell them you'll gladly invite them to your next opening or in-studio party. And exchange cards!

In five years time this will probably translate into at least 20 to 30 loyal collectors of your work who you will continue to cultivate during Stages Two and Three. Proven sales performance and a base of collectors gives you leverage and credibility with a commercial gallery, and is a prerequisite accomplishment before attempting affiliation and representation with an established gallery in your state or elsewhere.

Keep in mind that artist-initiated marketing campaigns directed to individuals and corporate collectors as well as art consultants, architects, and designers locally and statewide, which result in sales, can stand in lieu of an affiliation with a commercial gallery as you move from Stage One to Stage Two.

### Going for a Test Drive: Telephone/E-mail Scripting and Establishing Your Contact Plan

When your marketing research list is assembled, create a printout with two columns. Use the left-hand column for the contact's name and contact information, and the right-hand column for detailed notations, which include information obtained during a telephone conversation or an e-mail exchange, the support materials initially provided to the prospective client, and/or any additional follow-up requested.

It is disconcerting for someone you are speaking with on the telephone to hear you tapping on the keyboard of your computer so handwrite your notes, and enter the information after completing your calls for the day.

Utilizing these callback sheets, each call and/or e-mail attempt should be logged and dated with adequate notes for follow-up. Any change in the director, curator, principal/company head, or individual contact should be noted – as well as any change in telephone numbers or e-mail.

Keep a record of what was provided in the original e-mail introduction or contact package, such as résumé/biographical summary, artist statement, promotional brochure, catalogue, 8" x 10" color reproductions, or CD with jpegs or PDF presentation. Should any contact request additional information, you should respond immediately, with a handwritten note, price list, copies of reviews of note, etc., and call back within two weeks. Reiterate that you can also provide a CD with a more complete inventory upon request.

You can pre-canvass your research list by sending an e-mail (when address is available), cover/pitch letter of introduction with a single image of your work, or you may call the sales venue first, try to reach your target, or at the very least, check with the receptionist to make sure the name, address, and e-mail

*Never do things by halves.*
PROVERB

---

## Key Phrases for Assistant Making Calls

Always refer to the artist as "Mr." or "Ms." and yourself as his or her "assistant." If there is possible interest in setting up a studio visit, emphasize that this work, in particular, needs to be viewed in person; that the photographic process and/or digital documentation is an inadequate representation of the actual painting surface. It is essential that you explain to your assistant in great detail the working process, so that in this conversation the listener may be seduced by the description of the process and the desired results are achieved.

"Hello, this is 'so and so' speaking; I am calling on behalf of the artist _____, who recently sent the gallery an introductory package with a catalogue and CD of her current work. I wonder if you received these materials. The catalogue essay was written by William Zimmer."

"I am calling to follow-up on a catalogue and support materials the artist _____ recently sent to the gallery. I wanted to inquire if you received the materials and if I could provide you with any additional information, such as copies of reviews and price list. You would have received these materials approximately two weeks ago." (A verbal description of the work would be appropriate at this time – not lengthy, but enthusiastically emphasizing the unique quality of surface and working process). "I was hoping, if you have several minutes, you would permit me to describe the artist's unique process of creating these paintings."

## Specific Questions for Architects, Designers, Interior Designers

- Are there any projects currently underway or being planned for which this work might be appropriate?

- Are there any clients that you are currently working with who might respond to this work?

- What further information, such as a price list, can I provide to assist you in your efforts?

*All that glitters is not gold.*
UNKNOWN

contact information is correct. State in your introductory e-mail that it is your intention to try to reach so-and-so personally to ascertain his or her preferred method/requirements for submission. Extend an invitation or provide a link to your website.

All efforts in follow-up should be neutral and non-aggressive. Your primary goal is to determine if they recall receiving the initial e-mail or your presentation package; if they have had an *opportunity* to review your CD, visit your website; and if any further information, i.e., additional support pieces, is appropriate at this time.

Communicating with commercial gallery dealers and their assistants will be the most difficult, but it is essential that no matter how they respond, you are always positive and neutral.

### Adding Horsepower: Describing the Work

Trying to verbally describe the visual is always a challenge, and reproductions don't always replace a thousand words. Photographs may not communicate the actual depth of a painting's surface that may have been built up from a three-dimensional clay mold.

Only if the time and situation allows, would I suggest discussing the origins of your unique technique. Be aware of the difficulty of communicating effects such as these and use it as a way to bring someone to the studio, as opposed to confusing them by lengthy discussion on technique.

Write a List of Three Key Descriptive Phrases to Use:

      1) Three-dimensional paintings that are literally sculpted in clay

      2) Surfaces inspired by the landscape and the ocean's floor

      3) Could express a dimension of reality beyond the physical world

Refer to information in the cover/pitch letter sent with the presentation. This letter has all the most pertinent factual information appropriate to a given situation. It includes descriptive phrases and marketing possibilities. Remember your paintings could conceivably work in any interior environment – private, commercial, corporate – or they might also be applicable to exterior spaces if translated into different materials. This could be used as leverage when marketing to commercial galleries who also work with corporations and corporate consultants, architects and interior designers, corporate consultants, and artist reps.

Follow-up calls and e-mails to these professionals must be made to ascertain whether they are a solid lead, if further time and effort should be expended on this individual, and when to follow up with additional information. In some instances, it may be more appropriate to send periodic updates of your involvements, such as invitations to openings, press releases, and copies of reviews. In the case of heightened interest, arranging a studio visit, or even offering to bring work to the interested party may be the best approach.

### Priced to Sell: How to Figure It Out

Before you make that first sale, you must learn how to price your artworks. This task is one of the more confusing and confounding challenges that face the professional artist. Art market prices vary by location. For instance, prices are consistently lower in the Southeast, Midwest, and on the West Coast, than they are in New York.

Although it is counterintuitive, if work is priced too low (an artist undervaluing their own talent), buyers may question its artistic worth, or no one will buy it because they imagine there must be some reason or defect that caused it to be underpriced.

Conversely, when the work is priced above your level of accomplishment and recognition, serious collectors will not even consider such a purchase. They want to know if you have a proven track record, supported by your professional involvements and accolades. Determining your level of accomplishment for the purposes of accurately pricing work would be based on your exhibition record, reviews, and, if possible, by the prices previously paid by collectors.

There are a few exceptions to this rule. Certain works of art, because of the unquestionable level of skill in execution, may be perceived, by some, as requiring no substantive pedigree to command large sums. Some photo-realist

*Mistakes are always initial.*
CESARE PAVESE

---

### Presentation and Perception

An artist I met with a number of years ago was painting remarkable, autumnal landscapes, primarily of trees with highly detailed leaves in rich colors that appeared to shimmer with golden light. When I reviewed her images in reproduction in advance of our consultation, I assumed she was creating exceptionally accomplished photo-realistic works. However, when I saw the actual paintings, I realized she had cut out thousands of pieces of hand-painted cloth, in the shapes of leaves, and individually affixed them to her canvas. Her paintings required literally hundreds of hours to complete.

She was most concerned that her work was not commanding high enough prices. I recall her price range for an approximately 30" x 40" piece was around $15,000 to $18,000. The frames on her paintings really looked cheap — like an afterthought — and the minimal contemporary design of the molding diminished the vibrancy and energy of her images; they were certainly not in keeping with either the quality and accomplishment of the work.

I immediately recommended that she make an appointment with a highly reputable framing company that had worked with institutions like the Metropolitan Museum of Art for well over a century.

I suggested she spend between $2,000 and $3,000 on a single frame and to double the price of the work. I had no doubt she could command $40,000 per canvas. However, this would require the most pristine presentation and museum-quality framing. A true sense of the value of her own time and the dedication required to create these remarkable canvases, and a supreme confidence in her talent and abilities were necessary. It's one thing to deserve $40,000 for your efforts, but another thing to get it.

works might be an example, or virtuosic displays of technique by a glass blower that dazzle. Prices are also affected by the cost of the materials, scale, number of hours required to complete the artwork, unusual use of materials, and other qualities that may distinguish work from other mainstream art forms.

Another part of this equation can be the number of exhibitions, reviews, and/or sales in a given year. If you have had a particularly fruitful year, it would not be in the least unreasonable to increase prices between 10 and 20 percent. The reputation of a collector can also affect pricing of subsequent works; a purchase by a high-profile collector or respected museum raises the perceived value of your work.

Consistency and credibility in pricing must be maintained at all costs, or loyal collectors will feel betrayed if they learn that a similar piece sold for considerably less somewhere else.

Your sales prices should be within 10 to 20% of retail, whether or not the works are sold from a commercial gallery in another part of the country or from your studio.

Operating within a 10 to 20% discount range also accommodates a dealer's need for leeway in negotiating the price of a sale. Given these parameters, you may want to consider building a 20% buffer to your prices. Example: $1,000 retail + 20% buffer of $200 = $1,200.

You must have a price list available upon request. This is not included in your presentation or press kit. However, in a cover letter to certain commercial venues, such as interior designers and architects, a general reference to size and price range is acceptable, for example, $3,000-$10,000. Also, it is never ever advisable to provide images of work in your presentation if they are not available for both viewing and for sale.

The real secret is to price the work to sell through a realistic assessment of what other artists at the same level of accomplishment are commanding for similar types of work, and the maximum of what your geographic market will bear.

*If you would hit the mark, you must aim a little above it.*
HENRY WADSWORTH LONGFELLOW

CHAPTER THREE
# Taking the Wheel: Getting Organized

To get into the passing lane on your road to success, you need to put together your own personal pit crew. In order to start your engine, you need to identify these people, and mailing lists are one effective way to survey the field. Some lists will be compiled by you, putting all of your contacts into a usable database, or researching various directories. But to help you efficiently expand beyond the personal realm, there are lists put together by professionals. They can be purchased or rented, but sometimes are free for the asking from state arts councils and other artist-centric organizations. They may target specific categories, such as commercial galleries or art critics, and can also be divided by geographic area.

Your three most important research publications for purchase and for creating your mailing list are the *American Art Directory* (see sidebar, p. 24), *The Official Museum Directory* (see sidebar, p. 25), and the *Art in America Annual Guide to the Art World Galleries/Museums/Artists* (see sidebar, p. 26).

By cross-referencing entries from all three sources, you can compile a comprehensive and detailed database for your targeted geographic area.

To maximize the value of any mailing list, you must go beyond simply the name of the institution, address, phone and fax numbers, e-mail address, and to whose attention to send your materials. Further research on these venues' websites can give you a more complete picture of possible opportunities that could purposefully connect you.

Notes need to be entered as to what aspect of an institution's mission, collections, and research areas relate to your work. *The Official Museum Directory* offers specifics about each entry's collections and research areas. For example, The Textile Museum in Washington, DC, clearly declares its focus: textiles, carpets, and rugs. Its collection spans 5,000 years, from 3,000 BC to the present. If you are a textile artist, this is a natural venue for you.

Juried competitions, annual and biennial exhibitions as well as previously presented exhibitions are described in many of the entries in the *American Art Directory*, and may provide multiple reasons to approach these organizations.

Do not reject specialized institutions. *The Official Museum Directory* includes aquariums, botanical gardens, children's, decorative arts, general, history, historic sites/houses, natural history, nature centers, science, planetariums, technology centers, and zoos, in addition to

*Plan your work for today and every day, then work your plan.*

NORMAN VINCENT PEALE

art museums. Their subject areas may relate to your work, and they may mount changing thematic exhibitions to complement in-house curated shows developed from their permanent collections, or host rental and/or traveling exhibitions.

There is also the possibility of their acquiring artworks for permanent display. If your work has aquatic themes, it's not a stretch to contact natural history and science museums and aquariums.

Accurate notes along with dates of importance related to all of your specially tailored marketing research will allow for the proper preparation of your presentation materials, timely submissions, and follow-up. This information must be carefully entered into your database.

It is essential that you set up a computer system to organize this information and make it easily accessible, so before you contact a specific organization or person, you can know their particulars and their value to your particular goals.

You must continually update this database. You are unlikely to impress your target if the mailing is addressed to someone, say a curator in a museum, who may not have held that position for many years.

Public agencies, state and local arts councils, and other related arts organizations often make mailing lists available to artists. You must learn which mailing lists are available for purchase or free of charge, and the quality and accuracy of the information.

In addition to mailing lists from these resources, lists can also be purchased. Sometimes organizations sell their membership lists, and there are also companies whose business is to compile and sell mailing lists. There is about a 15 to 20 % attrition rate on most purchased mailing lists as they become outdated so quickly; you will especially find this to be the case with art consultants and designers.

Remember mailing lists are not static. Literally every morsel of information can change at any time. Your job is to keep them current.

### Revving Up: Dealing with the Media

In a way, success in the art world can be likened to that old saying: if a tree falls in the forest and there is no one to hear, does it make a sound?

The art-world corollary is: if you have an exhibition and no one reviews it, have you made a sound?

That sound can actually become a symphony, composed of reviews and articles from local and state art publications, general-interest or niche magazines, and daily and weekly newspapers. You also want coverage on radio, television, the internet, and new media opportunities that may come along. You will want to get to know art writers, art critics, and feature writers, both staff and free-lance. You will also need support from the editors in all areas, for they are the ones who assign and ultimately decide what is published.

Targeted mailing lists for media are essential to getting the word out about you and your work. There is a wealth of information available to assist you in your promotional efforts (see "Information Resources," Critics/Media section, 309).

When you are included in a group exhibition at a nonprofit institution, do not hesitate to ask the curator if there is a list of local press that he or she would feel comfortable sharing. (Curators are more inclined to do so when you live outside their area or are from another state.) Explain that it is your intention to complement the institution's public relations efforts with personal handwritten notes to the press.

In addition, press and media lists are often available through professional artist's organizations, local and state art councils, and may be complimentary or available at nominal cost with membership or proof of residency. Your local librarian may be able to direct you to a statewide media resource or listing. The library also has local newspapers and other publications that you can use to research the different kinds of coverage opportunities, plus they will have up-to-date names of editors and writers.

Colleges and university libraries are also repositories and distributors of local magazines and free newspapers.

Your independent bookstore or national bookseller usually has local publications, newspapers, and shelves with extensive selections of magazines. And they often thoughtfully provide comfortable seating so you can peruse rather than purchase these periodicals.

*Hitch your wagon to a star.*

RALPH WALDO EMERSON

*I will prepare and someday my chance will come.*

ABRAHAM LINCOLN

The internet can be helpful in identifying glossy magazines and special publications unique to your state. These publications may do articles with a cultural slant, and even use original works of art for the cover or to enhance articles or stories.

You are only required to possess a healthy curiosity and determination as you search for what can be abundant coverage opportunities in your area.

## Go Along for the Ride: Courting the Media

Even though one of the most critical components for establishing name recognition is a healthy relationship with the media, it is the component most often neglected by artists in their career development. Establishing a balanced, well-timed, and respectful alliance with the press is vital to your future success. Relying on others to actively promote you to the press is not a "roadmap to success."

Too often the responsibility for coverage is left in the hands of others, for example, the hosting venue for your exhibition. Having an exhibition provides the visibility and credibility necessary for media coverage – and sales – but you must actively exploit these opportunities on your own by reaching out to the media as well as other exhibiting organizations and businesses in that area.

If you are willing to personally complement press mailings generated by an institution or commercial gallery with self-initiated support materials and personal letter of introduction, then the likelihood of attention, whether a mention or a review, is far greater. Persistence is needed to win over the media. In fact, it is also necessary for cultivation of all your relationships with art-world professionals.

To gain media attention, you need to engage the writer, make him or her aware of you and your work, and most importantly, make him or her want to know more about what you are doing and where this may lead in the future. If you can view this process as a "slow seduction" of a critic or writer over a number of years, and you do not expect immediate payoff for your efforts, you can relax into thoughtfully and respectfully developing a professional relationship. This will create an opportunity for the critic to participate in the same slow dance with you – if they are so inclined. What artists often don't understand is that critics want to be in long-term relationships with artists. They want to attend your exhibitions, follow the development of your ideas, watch the work change direction, and they enjoy being kept abreast of your accomplishments and involvements.

Realistic expectations, patience, and consistency over a long period of time, as well as mutual regard and respect for one another, are essential in creating successful relationships with the press.

Rule number one is to exploit your art-world achievements and use them as a reason to contact and re-contact the press. You want to take advantage of any recognition that you receive to maintain continuity in these relationships.

For example, if you are selected for inclusion in a juried exhibition, and you receive commendation from a notable juror, this is the perfect time to contact the press. Winning a purchase award or receiving an honor or accolade may garner media coverage and critical discussion of your work. You may even score a reproduction in your local daily or weekly newspaper; there is also the possibility of the "winning work" becoming the cover image in the arts or weekend section.

Whatever media attention comes your way, it increases the likelihood that your name will be remembered not only by the juror, but also by museum directors and curators, other artists included in the exhibition who may be your entrée to meeting gallerists or other art professionals who can advance your career, and the arts community at large.

Your work may also catch the eye of a local collector, interior designer, architect, art consultant, or art dealer/gallerist. Media acknowledgment of your work in print or on television, radio, and on the internet could elicit offers for other exhibitions and even sales. An art dealer might offer you an exhibition opportunity because the credibility and notoriety to leverage a sale is being handed to them by virtue of the recent media coverage of your work in an exhibition at a nonprofit institution.

An executive from a local corporation, with a space suitable for an exhibition, also may offer you an opportunity to display your work. A copy of the actual coverage can accompany a simple written proposal to the corporation requesting a one-person exhibition at its facility.

If you are exhibiting in another part of the state, you can maximize the impact of your award and coverage by informing the media where you are currently residing, where you were born, or any other place where you may have ties.

Getting media attention insures that when you're shifting into a higher gear in your career, it doesn't go unnoticed.

*A wise man will make more opportunities than he finds.*

FRANCIS BACON

## The Press Package

- Cover letter

- An invitation or color announcement card if promoting an exhibition

- One- or two-page press release

- Artist's statement

- Chronological résumé and/or biographical summary

- Copies of several reviews, articles written about your work (especially if a critic is quoted in the press release), and/or critical essays

- Several 8" x 10" color reproductions of work included in the exhibition and/or CD (with jpegs or preferably a PDF presentation)

- Professionally designed color brochure or catalogue with a critic's essay, if available

*Consciousness of your powers augments them.*

EPICTETUS

### Approaching the On-Ramp: The Press Package

Your body of work is assembled. Writers, critics, and editors have been identified. The green flag is ready to drop, and now you need to put together a high-octane press package.

The press and art professionals are faced with unprecedented challenges when it comes to the careful viewing and assessment of artists' work due not only to differing kinds of presentations and submissions, but also the vast number of competing artists.

A well-prepared presentation package is necessary to effectively promote your work to the media as well as to the nonprofit and commercial sectors. You must consider a number of possibilities because submission policies and procedures vary greatly, and you must find out the *preferred* format by contacting each venue directly.

It's a good idea to have the basic press packages already assembled with the standard contents so you can respond quickly to interest generated through your initial contact. Why not make 20 copies each of every component piece so you can tailor your presentation to the recipient's needs and special requests.

The standard contents of an artist-generated press package are the invitation or color announcement card for your exhibition (ideally with an image of your work), a one- or two-page press release, artist statement, chronological résumé and/or biographical summary. Additional component pieces would be copies of reviews, articles, and/or critical essays (especially if a critic is quoted in the press release), a professionally designed brochure or catalogue (see "Making It to Print," p. 286) if available, or carefully selected 8" x 10" images of several of the works included in the exhibition. You have the option of including a CD with high-resolution images of a far broader selection of work than would be presented in a catalogue or a four-to-six page folding brochure, or even sending a PDF presentation in an initial or follow-up communication.

Your presentation would be assembled in a professional-quality folder with interior flaps designed to hold your thoughtfully orchestrated materials and

*What we have to learn, we learn by doing.*

ARISTOTLE

business card. A cover/pitch letter introducing yourself to the recipient is carefully paper-clipped to the outside of the folder. When the recipient opens the folder, the first thing that he or she would see is an image placed on the right-hand side. If the recipient is a member of the press, the release is usually placed to the left of the image.

**Aerodynamics: The Press Release**

Although anything of note in your career can prompt the dissemination of a press release (see examples in Book Two, "The Press Release," p. 147), an exhibition is the most common. Other reasons may be an award, honor, grant, or the acquisition of your work by a prestigious collection, an institution, or a well-known collector. A press release should be no more than two pages in length: one is preferable. The writing is brief, concise, and non-effusive.

The top of the first page of every press release states who, what, when, and where. It provides contact information: phone, fax, e-mail, and website of the venue.

FOR IMMEDIATE RELEASE

Contact: Name

Firm

Telephone               Fax

e-mail


**Your contact information is on the last page.**

> For more information, contact Fab U. Lous, 123-456-7890 studio or 234-567-8901 cell, e-mail fabulous@fabulousartist.com.


Beneath the basic information about the exhibition is the hook, message, or lead – a phrase or short sentence that will pique the curiosity or capture the attention of the reader – in other words, why the recipient should "take notice." It may be presented as a "headline" or, if there are space constraints, incorporated into the introductory paragraph of the release. This paragraph should be a maximum of 100 to 150 words and reiterate the information presented at the top of the release, followed by a brief and essential

*Every art requires the whole person.*

FRENCH PROVERB

description of the work being exhibited, discussion of the materials, unique approach or style, and whatever else strongly distinguishes the work.

The second paragraph (often at the top of the second page if it is needed) is a brief discussion of your work and its influences, and could include a quote by a notable critic.

The third paragraph is often biographical, noting pinnacle achievements such as significant exhibitions and collections, awards and honors, commissions, etc. The final paragraph is personal information such as education and current place of residence.

An exhibition announcement card, 8" x 10" color prints or CD, brochure or catalogue – something tangible that can be held in someone's hand – are still by far the best introduction to your work.

Including a CD is your professional choice. It could be sent in a follow-up communication, or you can direct the recipient to your website, which can provide more comprehensive support information and visuals. If you elect to send a CD, be certain your name and contact information are written or printed on the disk; never ever use a stick-on label that can trash another professional's computer. Include all press release materials on your website, as well.

**Driver's License: Who Do You Think You Are?**
The first thing you must do in any promotional effort is to tell your audience who you are. There are two completely acceptable ways to do this in an efficient and concise manner: the chronological résumé and the biographical summary.

The chronological résumé format is appropriate when you have had considerable exhibition experience – one- and two-person exhibitions, group, juried, and competitive exhibitions at reputable venues. It is also appropriate when you are included in a number of nonprofit, public, and corporate and private collections; have received notable awards, honors, grants, and residencies; and have been covered by the press (print, radio, television, and internet).

It is acceptable to substitute a biographical summary, in a narrative form, in lieu of a chronological résumé if you do not have extensive experience. It can also be effective if you have come to the art field through other courses of study or life experiences because it can tell your unique story.

## Lookout Point: The Artist's Statement

The artist's statement is your chance to reflect on your work and to convey what you feel about your work, what may have inspired it, and how you came to this form of expression. The statement can place your work in a contemporary context through specific comparisons, and position you on the art historical continuum by acknowledging antecedents who have influenced your work. Ideally it should provide a point of entrance or access into the work for the reader and viewer.

As the artist's statement is the most challenging piece you will ever write, you may seriously want to consider hiring a professional to work closely with you on the development of your ideas (see "Making a Statement," p. 253).

When writing your artist's statement, it is essential that you keep several things in mind. Remember, one-half to two-thirds page is sufficient and never more than one page. The statement should be brief, non-effusive, concise, and clear, without revealing too many of the personal inspirations or analysis of the work from your point of view. If you give too much away by providing too much information, you eclipse or preempt the critic's, curator's, or even a collector's read on the work, and limit the interpretations that may be possible from a critical or scholarly position of experience and knowledge.

You should avoid using "I" and "my", as this can lead to sentimentality. This is not a hard-and-fast rule, but in the long- and short-run, you will hurt yourself by being too personal or too revealing, not to mention that you may risk trivializing or short-changing the work. Hold yourself back when you feel tempted to wax poetic or to explore your personal pain, illness, or hardships.

When all is said and done, your work will always speak for itself far and beyond your own imagined or understood reasons for its creation. Be assured that it has a life of its own. It is essential that you acknowledge this by using restraint when writing your artist's statement for the presentation packet. It might even be advisable to provide it to the gallery only as an item "available upon request" during your exhibition, or at the dealer's discretion.

*I am Mata Hari, my own master.*

GRETA GARBO

---

### The Case Against Slides

Digital formats that provide higher resolution have replaced slides. For reproductions of the highest quality for use on a website or in a video or film, you are strongly advised to seek the services of a qualified professional in the digital realm.

Also, the effectiveness of images on a CD or website can be compromised by a photographer's level of skill, the resolution (dpi) of reproduction, as well as the staging and lighting of the works of art.

When you also consider the costs involved in producing several thousand catalogues or brochures, investing in the best possible reproductions of your work just makes good sense.

## Business Cards and Stationery

You are a professional, and your promotional package must look like you take yourself seriously. Do not underestimate the subtleties that are operating when an art professional sees your stationery or accepts your business card. You have made an impression that may be lasting.

You need attractive business cards, matching stationery, and press/presentation folders in a 9" x 12" format that will fit into a 10" x 13" white mailing envelope. Use quality paper, pens, and folders – stay away from cheap textured tag paper.

In the art world especially, less is more where the design of business cards and letterhead is concerned. Simplicity is always preferable: stay with at least 80 to 100 pound white or cream paper with black or neutral-colored ink. No colored papers, although solid-colored envelopes can sometimes help catch someone's attention, i.e., red envelopes around Valentine's Day or Christmas. Elaborate designs, decorative borders, or fussy, fluffy gender-specific elements should never be used. You must create a consistent look and select visually unifying typefaces for both cards and stationery.

Business cards and stationery with a picture of the artist or an imprint of the work is not advisable or well regarded in the more serious environs of the art world. Elegance and understatement is the artist's best professional choice.

*I know winning, I'm a winner, winning is inside me.*

MARGARET AVERY

### Ready to Roll: Cover/Pitch Letters

Cover or pitch letters (see Book Two, "The Cover/Pitch Letter," p. 125). are necessary for an effective promotional package directed to art-world professionals in the nonprofit and for-profit sectors, and to the press.

Each letter must focus on meeting the needs and interests of the recipient, so individually tailor your letters. A writer or art critic may find it interesting to know where your reviews have appeared and the names of the writers; a museum professional may be more concerned with exhibitions and reviews; and a gallerist would most likely want to know about your sales record, especially your museum collections, recent exhibitions, and recent reviews. One size does not fit all.

First, there are several purposes for a cover or pitch letter, and it is wise to keep copies for your files or in folders on your computer desktop so you will know exactly what you have written and when it was sent. Cover letters are governed by the situation and the recipient. The letter may be generated to extend a personal invitation to the opening of an exhibition, announce a recent accomplishment, or just introduce yourself. They will be successful only if you address it to the proper person, spell his or her name correctly, and get the gender right.

If there are specific dates associated with your reason for contacting the institution, such as an exhibition currently on view or to open shortly, or if you are planning a visit to the city where the gallery is located in the near future, be sure to mention this.

All letters should conform to a basic business format. They should be on your letterhead, which need not be extravagant; in fact, simpler is better. Your contact information – name, address, phone numbers (studio, home and/or cell), e-mail address, and website – can be flush left or right or centered, but the text of the letter itself is flush left, single-spaced with one extra space to separate paragraphs. The salutation is punctuated with a colon – **Dear Ms. Critic:**

The tone is respectful and professional, but use whatever wording reflects your own style of expression. The letter itself follows a rather specific outline.

In the first paragraph, you state the specific reason for writing. The strongest opening sentence, regardless of the target or occasion, is to mention someone who is known to the recipient and who suggested that you write to him or her. For example, mentioning a major artist or an artist already in the gallery's stable or museum's collection, or a respected curator, critic, or collector lends credibility and further validates you and your work – and you want the recipient to read on...

In the first paragraph, it is also appropriate for you to give a brief, one or two sentence description of your work, i.e., "My current paintings are based on the ancestral legacy of African tribal art."

Alternatively you can simply state that you wish to introduce yourself and your work. To strengthen this, mention why you believe that this person or organization may find the work of interest. To do this convincingly, you must first be fully acquainted with the mission, aesthetic focus, and interests of the venue. It may be that your work fits into a nonprofit's mission, such as exhibiting regional artists, or it may be complementary to a gallery's stable of artists, but you've *really and truly* got to know exactly who you are approaching and why.

To summarize, the first paragraph is simply an introduction of you and your work to the recipient. If you are writing to inform him or her of a current or forthcoming exhibition, then provide all the basic necessary information, including name of exhibition, venue and its location, opening hours, and duration. You may certainly send a self-generated press release or copy of the venue's press release, or a color announcement card.

> *Success is not so much achievement as achieving. Refuse to join the cautious crowd that plays not to lose – play to win.*
>
> UNKNOWN

## Chronological Résumé

- Vital Statistics

- Exhibitions: One- and Two-person, Group or Selected (inclusive of both categories)

- Collections: Museum, Public, Corporate, Private (listed in order of importance, beginning with museum collections and not divided into separate categories, a continuous listing, e.g., Gotham Museum, Museum of Canine Art, City of Metropolis, Big City Transit Authority, International Artmaking Inc., Global Vision Corp., John Q. Artlover, Frank Lee, and so forth.

- Bibliography, Selected Bibliography, or Selected Reviews

- Awards and Honors

- Grants and Residencies

- Education

## Pitch/Cover Letter Format

• First paragraph – reason for writing; two to three sentences maximum with a very brief description of the work.

• Second paragraph – pinnacle accomplishments; three to four sentences maximum noting exhibitions, reviews, collections, awards, etc.

• Third paragraph – how do you intend for the recipient to view your work in person; outline your follow-up plan; and close in the last sentence.

*Think things through, then follow through.*

EDDIE RICKENBACHER

### Cover/Pitch Letter to a Nonprofit Organization

Stage One Artist
123 Accelerating Hwy.
Hopeful, GA 12345
Studio Phone: 123-456-7890
Cell Phone: 123-567-8901
E-mail: stageoneartist@settingthestage.com
www.settingthestage.com


Peter T. Lapin, Curator
Greater Atlanta Art Center and Museum
567 Possible Street
Burbs, GA 10009

1 April, 2010


Dear Mr. Lapin:

Having recently moved to the Atlanta area from Tampa Bay, I would like to introduce you to my current paintings and collages, and to apprise you of my professional accomplishments. I was formally trained as a medical illustrator, and have provided a biographical summary for your further information.

My work has been included in juried exhibitions and invitationals throughout Florida and is also represented in numerous corporate and private collections in the state. H.P. Critic gave me the "Award of Distinction" in the "Annual Critics Choice Exhibition" held at the Sewanee River Museum in Safe Harbor, FL, in 2009; subsequently I was interviewed for a feature article in *The Duval Chronicle* by Art T. Writer, and given an exhibition at the newspaper's offices in Jacksonville. In 2008, my work was selected by a statewide panel of museum curators for the Florida Triennial, hosted by The Clear Springs Museum.

Please retain these materials for consideration for any future opportunities, such as thematic group exhibitions, for which my work may be appropriate. I will certainly keep you abreast of any local or statewide exhibition venues where you might view the work.


Sincerely,


**Stage One Artist**

*If the creator had a purpose in equipping us*
*with a neck, he surely meant us to stick it out.*

NORMAN VINCENT PEALE

## Cover/Pitch Letter to a Commercial Organization

Mid-Career Artist
Stage Two Street
Hopeful, AZ  99999
Studio Phone: 123-456-7890
Fax: 123-567-8901
Cell Phone: 123-567-8901
E-mail: mcareerartist@mca.com
www.mca.com

Ms. Bunny Fontaine, Director
EML Gallery (Established Mid-Level Gallery)
201 Halfway-up-the-Hill
San Francisco, CA 12345

1 April, 2010

Dear Ms. Fontaine:

Harry Hare introduced us last month at his opening at your gallery, and during our conversation, you encouraged me to send my materials for review.

My work is included in numerous museum and public collections, and in over 80 private collections. Recently a series of 15 monotypes and four paintings, based on Peter R. Jokester's book, *Courageous Tails of an Ambitious Rabbit*, were acquired by the Global Lapin Corporation for its world headquarters in San Francisco. I have been reviewed by the *Warren Chronicle* and the *Briar Patch Times*. My résumé will apprise you of my professional background and other accomplishments.

I will be in San Francisco from April 15-22 for the installation of my monoprints and paintings at Global Lapin. There will be a private cocktail reception on April 21 at 7 pm, and I would like to extend a cordial invitation to attend. I will call you regarding your interest and availability.

Sincerely,

Mid-Career Artist

PS: I would be pleased to have you as my dinner guest following the reception.

*or*

If the evening of the 21st is not possible, I can arrange for you to see the installation at your convenience, and would be delighted to take you to lunch or dinner, as your schedule allows.

*Any publicity is good publicity.*

### First Sentence Alternatives

I am contacting you at the recommendation of Peter J. Lapin, curator of art at the Greater Atlanta Art Center and Museum.

*or*

I would like to take this opportunity to introduce you to my photographs and collages. I am aware of the Art Center's focus on contemporary artists of the New England region, and as a Connecticut-based artist, I wanted to acquaint you with my background and accomplishments.

*or*

V.I. Artist has recommended that I contact you regarding my most recent paintings, which depict the endangered manatees of Florida's coastal watersand rivers. I have visited your gallery (or museum) on several occasions, and believe the work to be appropriate to your current direction (gallery) or mission/permanent collection/research areas (museum).

*or*

At the suggestion of Connie Collector, I am contacting you. She felt you would be interested in my photographs documenting the studios and workspaces of 100 women artists of accomplishment across America. I believe this work reflects your gallery's (or museum's) commitment to the tradition of black-and-white documentary photography, and I hope you will find the work worthy of serious consideration.

### Merging Lane: Second and Third Paragraphs

In the second paragraph, which is no more than three to four sentences, summarize the most significant achievements of your artistic career: exhibitions (past or upcoming), reviews, collections, or other accomplishments. This is an engaging summary of your professional accolades, usually with specific information expanded to more generalized and encompassing statements. You may enclose a résumé and draw the reader's attention to this fact: "I have also provided a résumé for your further information."

You should highlight the information that will most impress your recipient. For example, when contacting a museum professional, you might write, "My work has been extensively exhibited in the Southeastern United States; recently I was selected for inclusion in 'Name of Exclusive Juried Exhibition' by Enormously Important Critic, held at the Widely Recognized Museum in Atlanta, GA, as well as for the 'Critics' Select for the Southeastern US', presented by the Prestigious Art Center in Birmingham, AL."

*Go and make your luck.*

PERSIAN PROVERB

A gallerist is also interested in your exhibition record and reviews, but be sure to mention your sales history, e.g., "My work is represented in a number of public and private collections, including Big Deal Museum, Lapin Global Corporation, and Super Impressive Private Collection."

Pitch letters are often sent in conjunction with an exhibition that features or includes your work, because this provides an opportunity for the gallerist to view actual work, presented in a professional context, in a venue nearby. Thus, your letter format can be slightly different. Begin with a personal invitation to attend the opening of your exhibition (the title in quote marks) and give all of the pertinent information, just as in the opening paragraph of the press release. That means the name of the exhibition space, its location (including street address, city, and state), phone and fax numbers, e-mail address, and website. Provide both the opening date and the closing (day of the week, then date) and the day, date, and time of the opening reception. Make sure to include the hours and days of operation. If it is a group exhibition, you can also note the curator, critic, or juror who made the selections. Include a color announcement card from the exhibition if available.

## Invitation to the Exhibition

I would like to extend a personal invitation to view two of my large-scale sculptural works included in "Form, Flux, and Finality," a group exhibition curated by Miriam Maas at the Riverside Sculpture Center, located at 2144 Van Dyke Boulevard in the Bronx. The opening reception is on Saturday, June 4, at 2 p.m., and the exhibition will run through August 12. Hours are Tuesday through Saturday, 10-6, Sundays, 12-4.

You can conclude paragraph two, which highlights your accomplishments, by mentioning that you have enclosed a résumé and other support materials, such as an exhibition announcement; brochure and/or catalogue, if available; and, if you know what format the recipient prefers, CD or color prints. You can also direct the recipient to your website.

*Never ever* ask for your materials to be returned; this is the cost of doing business, and it is presumptuous for you to assume this is the responsibility of the gallery or an art critic, especially if the materials were unsolicited.

If you have initiated contact with a more elaborate presentation, or if you are planning to visit the gallery or art center during an upcoming trip, indicate that you have not provided

*A man with wings large enough and duly attached
might overcome the resistance of the air.*

LEONARDO DA VINCI

a self-addressed stamped envelope (SASE) as you intend to stop by the venue to see the "Such and Such" exhibition, and that you will introduce yourself and pick up your materials at that time.

## Exit Ramp: Final Paragraph

The closing paragraph is the most important in the entire letter. Here explain how you are going to make your work available for the recipient to see. You may invite the curator, critic, gallerist, in fact, anyone to meet you at the opening of the exhibition, during the run of the exhibition, or at their convenience. If geography and logistics allow, you can also invite these professionals to your studio at a mutually convenient time to preview the artwork before it is shipped. You should explain how you can be reached – phone, fax, and cell numbers as well as e-mail address and website, and/or tell them you will follow up on this invitation, which relieves your target of the burden of contacting you. No matter which art professional you are trying to reach, make it as easy as possible for them to respond. One does nothing effectively without a plan, so in this paragraph include your plan of action for follow-up and follow-through.

Allow ample time for your target to carefully consider your submission; two to three weeks is usually adequate for a review of your materials. For a studio visit, you can certainly follow up in one-to-two weeks, but it may require several months or longer to set a date and time, and there may be some last minute cancellations before the studio visit actually happens.

You are encouraged to assume the expense of sending a car to pick up the gallerist or curator. If there is an hour or more of actual travel involved, try to schedule your meeting later in the day, and offer to take them to dinner. This demonstrates your respect and that you understand the value of their time.

Ask yourself basic questions. Is it in your best interest to first e-mail, then telephone in follow-up to ascertain how you can facilitate further contact? What is the time frame you are working with, and will you be in their location between specific dates? Do you have original works of art available to view at a friend's loft near the gallery? Can the critic, dealer, or curator see your work in an exhibition setting, and is the exhibition within a reasonable distance and traveling time?

**The Final Paragraph**

I would be pleased to meet with you at your convenience to discuss my work at Riverside Sculpture Center. I will phone next week, or you may reach me at 212-345-6789 or via e-mail at <u>respectful@respectfulartist.com</u>. I would be pleased to provide you with transportation to and from the exhibition. Thank you for your consideration.

An effective concluding sentence when contacting an art critic is "I would appreciate any support that you could extend to me in this endeavor."

So, to summarize, your cover letter is usually three paragraphs, and do not, I repeat, do not go into a lot of detail about yourself, your art, or your life. This is business: be exact and clear, state your purpose succinctly, summarize your professional accomplishments, and indicate how you intend to follow-up. You must be willing to see it all the way through and to do what you have stated – to the letter – in this last paragraph.

One tip from direct-mail advertising pitch letters is to include a PS It is nearly impossible to ignore so use it to emphasize the most important point in the letter. For example, "I hope that I will have the opportunity to meet you at the opening of Important Exhibition" or "I will be speaking about my work at 7 p.m. at the University Art Gallery, 123 College Drive, Schoolton, on February 21, 2011, and I hope you can attend."

**Are We There Yet? Follow-Up and Follow-Through**
The procedures and protocol for follow-up and follow-through remain the same at all stages of career development and for all institutions or persons receiving your material. In the closing of your cover/pitch letter, you always state when and what you intend to do in follow-up, and then do exactly that.

You may indicate that you will call within a specific time frame. For example, "I will phone next week to confirm that you have received my material, and to inquire if additional information, such as a CD or copies of reviews and articles, etc., is necessary at this time."

*Let us train our minds to do what the situation demands.*

SENECA

*Success consists in the climb.*

ELBERT HUBBARD

If you sense it would be appropriate, you could suggest that several of your works are small enough to transport easily, and you would be only too happy to bring them to the gallery, as viewing them in person would reveal their subtle surface treatment, which is impossible to discern in reproduction.

You may also tell the recipient to retain these materials for the files in the event that your work would be appropriate for a future exhibition or project. You can conclude by saying that you look forward to having the opportunity of meeting the recipient personally and becoming better acquainted with the venue. If you do not reside in the vicinity, you may say that you will contact him or her when you have plans to be in the area.

You must keep a record of exactly what you've said and done, what material you have sent, and what follow-up you've promised. One way is to make notes on the hard copies of your correspondence or in your computer files with the date and result of your attempt. If you have sent out a large number of packets, you may wish to make a list of names with their contact information, and provide additional space for notes. Record any pertinent information you have gleaned, such as the person you're trying to reach never gets in before noon or is only reachable Tuesday, Wednesday, and Thursday.

When calling to follow up on a presentation package sent to a commercial or a nonprofit institution, ask to speak to the person who received the package. Frequently the receptionist will ask you what your call is in reference to, and your reply is simply that you are following up on a package of materials you submitted, and you wanted to make sure it was received. This can be a diplomatic and tasteful way to get through to the person.

If you do not reach your target person – actually succeeding on your first attempt is rare – your notes should include who you spoke with so you can remember the name of the receptionist or assistant on your next try. This earns you points: he or she may be your best ally in getting the recipient's attention. It is likely that this person logs in materials when they are received, and can provide you with information as to where they are in the process of consideration. They may even suggest what your next best move would be and exactly when you should call back.

If the person to whom you wish to speak is not available, ask if he or she has voice mail – if you have not been offered this option – and if you can leave a personal message there. Also ask for your target's direct e-mail address for future contact.

*Don't take counsel of your fears or naysayers.*

COLIN POWELL

The nonprofit area moves very, very slowly. It is important for you to fully understand the enormous demands and responsibilities that these professionals must handle on a daily basis. Communications from other artists, curators, galleries, museums, and nonprofits are in the hundreds, and they are all competing for this person's attention.

Following up the press kit with a brief telephone call or e-mail, or sending your announcement card with a personal note in follow-up is also effective. This is a situation where "easy does it" applies. Using basic common sense and recognizing that these professionals are literally inundated with requests for attention is critical for the success of your follow-up. It is almost impossible to reconnect with a critic or any other art professional that you have alienated through too frequent, inappropriate, or poorly timed contacts.

When following up on packets sent to the press, the same general rules apply. Writers and critics are also inundated with press materials, and it is rare for free-lancers to have assistants. Editors and staff writers can be a different story. Depending on their position, they could have assistants, and it is likely that the receptionist will route your call to the assistant. He or she is the gatekeeper for the writer or editor; treating this person with respect and courtesy boosts the chances of your materials being reviewed, and eventually reaching the big kahuna.

If you are fortunate enough to reach your target directly, take a deep breath and calmly say "Hello." Introduce yourself, and ask if your materials have been received. Be sensitive to the voice on the other end of the line. If the person sounds harried or inconvenienced, just gently say that you understand how very busy he or she must be. Ask if your materials have been reviewed; if not, respectfully say that you remain hopeful that he or she will take a careful look when time permits.

It is also acceptable to inquire if any group exhibitions or other projects are being planned for which your work might be appropriate. Asking that your materials be retained in the files for future consideration is also a subtle invitation for the dialogue to continue.

It is not a good idea for an artist to make more than three attempts at follow-up – first by telephone or e-mail, second by vice versa, and the last by another e-mail or personal, handwritten note. This should occur over a three-to-six month period. Too many left messages are not advisable under any circumstance. Sometimes "no response" translates to "no interest."

*Each of us is the architect of our own fate.*

CAECUS (paraphrased)

On the other hand, a follow-up communication may be welcomed if the reaction to your work has been positive and the person has just not had the time to respond.

If you are pushy and don't demonstrate respect for his or her professional constraints and time schedule, you will find it difficult to make inroads into any institution. Changing a poor first impression you have made is a challenge, usually one of futility, and best avoided by being courteous to everyone at the institution, bottom to top.

### Hit the Horn: Promote Yourself

As stated earlier, acting with dignity and integrity in the professional arena, having an overall sense of what you believe to be appropriate to your career goals, and proper timing of your initiatives are the crucial pieces to your professional progress.

Producing your own promotional materials is a smart way to start to take control of your own destiny. As you move through the various stages of career development, you will progress from a simple full-color postcard to a brochure, to a modest catalogue and then a larger catalogue, which may include an art critic's or writer's essay, and eventually to a hardcover book with many pages and color reproductions.

When more substantive support pieces are called for, perhaps in conjunction with a solo exhibition or a major group exhibition that may travel, some are self-generated while others will be published by a gallery or museum.

If it's in print, it must be true. Of course, appearing in black-and-white or color on a printed page is no guarantee of veracity, but it can mean validation. And that holds true, in some respects, whether Abrams publishes it or you do.

### Flashing Light: Announcement Cards, Brochures, and Catalogues

In the early years of career development, most artists produce marketing pieces that are modest – both in scale and cost. Publishing projects and expenditures generally increase in direct relation to the stature of the exhibition venue or opportunity.

The self-generated announcement card is one of the basic ways that you can maintain regular contact with collectors, art professionals, colleagues, and art critics, etc. It is acceptable to produce your own announcement card to augment an institution's marketing and public relations efforts. Be willing to take the initiative and make a modest investment as it could pay off in the long run.

*There is always room at the top.*

DANIEL WEBSTER

Even when you are included in a juried group exhibition, it is a wise marketing strategy to produce a color card with an image of at least one of your works included in the exhibition. In this type of situation, it does one little good to have your name listed with a dozen other artists on a general announcement card, unless the company in which you find yourself is stellar.

If you use a postcard format, the information provided on the back must be accurate, and it must be evident that you are included in a *group* exhibition, that it is not a solo show, and that the work featured on the card was selected for inclusion in the exhibition and not selected to represent the entire exhibition. It must be clear that this is a self-generated promotional piece.

You may wish to expand the information that appears on the address or blank side of a postcard so it fills the entire space, but this requires using an envelope and boosts mailing costs. However, you can also increase the value of the card when you use this space for your artist's statement, biographical summary, or other professional information, and it is also possible to list several exhibitions occurring in the same general timeframe.

### Taking the Wheel: The Value of Brochures and Catalogues

In the advancement of your career, the single most important investment you will ever make is a professionally produced brochure or catalogue, which includes an essay on your work by a nationally recognized critic (see "Making It to Print," p. 286).

Producing a catalogue in conjunction with a significant exhibition at a prestigious institution or in conjunction with a traveling exhibition of your work – or at any other important juncture in your life and career – can be a tactically cool move.

However, you should not be premature in the decision to produce a catalogue or book. It can be off-putting to a seasoned professional to receive an unsolicited, expensively produced publication if the quality and maturity of the work and your accomplishments do not warrant such a substantial presentation.

Rule One is that you should not attempt to design your own promotional catalogue, even when you have a background in design.

Complete objectivity and a working knowledge of the art market is required to select the six-to-eight images that are needed for a four-to-six page brochure or catalogue, which is the appropriate size to consider at Stage One of your career development. The works to be considered for selection would be the most visually arresting and powerful images representing your body of work. Consulting with a professional public relations and/or marketing expert who can advise you about the suitability of an image for your marketing purposes, or with a professional designer practiced in selecting visuals for reproduction, can determine this.

A visually impressive brochure or catalogue can have multiple uses and can serve as an effective marketing tool for several years to come. The larger-picture purpose of investing in this promotional piece is to create a presentation that will appeal to the widest possible audience, from the nonprofit museum professional to the residential or contract interior designer, and all potential sales and exhibiting opportunities in between. It also needs to be effective for introducing your work to the art press and general media.

Typically the essays in a four- or six-page brochure are anywhere from 500 to 1,000 words, but it is important to remember that large reproductions of your artwork are the first consideration, not descriptive verbiage. Unless someone is visually stimulated by your images, they will probably not take the time to read the entire essay; what they will do before they read it, is check the name and credentials of the author.

**Passing Lane: Capturing the Viewer's Attention**
So, bottom line, it happens in the most fundamental steps. First, you've got to grab their attention with the artwork on the cover before they will even open a brochure or catalogue to view the rest of the featured work. Then they will likely glance at the writer's credentials, and if sufficiently interested, read the first few sentences or introductory paragraph. This means you've captured them for 10 to 15 seconds. If engaged by the critic's initial observations, they may possibly continue reading. That means that in 10 minutes, you may be in the "passing lane," speeding past the 50 to 100 more packets on their desk.

On a related subject, critics who have been hired to write an essay do not appreciate having their work tampered with, beyond correcting grammatical or factual errors. I strongly advise against the need to control or change these professionals' observations. How would you feel if someone started altering or changing a piece of your work? This is not a good approach, on any level, and will alienate the essayist.

**Power Windows: Artists' Websites**

Having a presence on the internet (see Book Three, "Anatomy of an Online Campaign," p. 269) is essential today in the successful marketing of your work. You have a number of options where this is concerned: developing your own website, having a page on a number of well-known art sites or even creating a personal blog. Posting your work solely on a social networking site like Facebook.com or MySpace.com will not enhance your stature in the eyes of a professional.

If you choose to develop a website to showcase your work, it must be easy to navigate, updated regularly, and provide all the fundamental elements.

• Biographical Summary

• Artist's Statement

• Essays or reviews (always credit the writer and where it originally appeared)

• Background information

• Listings of upcoming exhibitions

• Chronological Résumé (but only the pinnacle points, between 20 and 30 lines)

• Quickly viewable sampling of your work with titles, dates, and dimensions.

Take the time to do an internet search on successful artists you admire, and view a number of artist sites to cull ideas that may work for you. Discuss your ideas at length with an experienced web designer who specializes in artist's sites, and then trust his or her judgment in executing the site design (see "Do You Need a Website?" p. 273).

Keep it simple. The fashion for long Flash introductions and gimmicky animations has passed. The use of websites to view artwork has become universal, and art professionals have no time for these extraneous effects. You are not serving yourself by distracting the viewer from concentrating on your work. You don't want bells and whistles – just an elegant application of sophisticated design that allows your work to take the center stage.

It is important to have the site built so that the images open instantly – you don't want to test the patience of curators, dealers, critics, and others who may lose interest if there is a

*Talent develops in the quiet places. Character in the full current of human life.*

GOETHE

## Recommended Artist Websites

www.anastasiapelias.com

www.margaretevangeline.com

www.stevenposter.com

www.karensilve.com

www.lynnedgulezian.com

www.sandragottlieb.com

www.astridpreston.com

www.annatomczak.com

www.wendyedwardspainting.com

www.bartgulley.com

www.dudleyzopp.net

*First impressions are the most lasting.*

UNKNOWN

long wait to view images. Low-resolution (commonly 72 dpi) images, which open more quickly, are preferable to higher resolution (300 or higher dpi) images that you can provide upon request.

You can use your site for name recognition and as a research resource for art professionals, or you can use it for e-commerce and sales, but never for both. A curator considering your work for an exhibition or a commercial dealer would be put off if the work on your site had prices and a "Buy Now" button.

If you have two entirely separate bodies of work – one could be bread-and-butter work that provides you with a steady income, and the other more seriously involved with building your reputation – you should definitely consider two separate websites. One should be devoted to sales, and the other for the work you want to direct serious art professionals and collectors to visit.

If you do choose to sell your work on the internet, you must confront practical concerns such as payment procedures (finding a credit card company with the best transaction rates, investigating PayPal, etc.), sales-tax requirements, return policy, shipping procedures, and costs – all these issues need to be carefully considered. Consult with an accountant or tax lawyer first.

Other low-cost alternatives to creating a website include posting your work on some group sites for artists, or even creating a blog to showcase your work. A personal site is by far the preferable approach, but until you are ready to take that step, you can still maintain a Web presence for your work.

CHAPTER 4
# Green Light: Exhibitions

Your exhibition goals at Stage One are to participate in as many as 25 to 30 group and juried exhibitions, invitationals, and annuals and biennial exhibitions at Levels I, II, and III museums, art centers, and college and university art galleries. This is the beginning of becoming known to curators, galleries, collectors, and the press throughout your state.

This process may begin in your hometown or current place of residence, then to your immediate geographic area (county or contiguous counties), and ultimately extend across your entire state as you seek to expand your visibility and reputation. Otherwise, you could find yourself facing a parade of the same faces, participating in the same shows, with the same level of potential outcome, endlessly treading water, bored, and frustrated by the old, safe choices.

Be mindful that not all exhibitions are created equal. It is just not possible or advisable to enter every competition or every show offered. So it is basic common sense at Stage One of your career development to participate in exhibitions held at the most prestigious institutions, with good visibility and the possibility of press coverage.

## Warning Flashers: Are You on the Right Road?
You must learn how to discriminate about whether a particular exhibition opportunity, say participating in a juried or competitive exhibition at the local community center, would really be advantageous to your career. One critical factor in determining which exhibition opportunities will serve your career goals is to understand the style or type of work you create, as this helps you to know where you should target your efforts.

Do you paint, draw, photograph, make prints, or sculpt? Does your work have broad audience appeal? Do you create still lifes, landscapes, florals, animal subjects? Are you a painter or a photographer specializing in portrait work? Is what you produce appropriate for either interior or exterior locations, public or private spaces, or both? Is your subject matter suitable for the corporate context? If so, your work may be appropriate for some commercial galleries, banks and financial institutions, the hospitality sector, entertainment industry, health care and medical professions, or real estate development projects.

On the other hand, does your work, because of the subject matter, have limitations in terms of viewing audience? Is it politically volatile in nature? Are the concepts and ideas so esoteric, intellectual, or theoretically based that only the larger colleges and university

*What good is running if you are on the wrong road?*

GERMAN PROVERB

*Man is man because he is free to operate within the framework of his destiny.*
*He is free to deliberate, to make decisions, and to choose between alternatives.*

MARTIN LUTHER KING, JR

museums, galleries, alternative spaces, and larger city markets offer the possibility for exhibition or critical dialogue? Are you working with new media and leading-edge practices such as video, installation, time-based work, or the internet? Are you more concerned with exhibitions and reviews in the nonprofit arena and less concerned with sales?

You must have the answers to these questions to appropriately and correctly evaluate exhibition opportunities. This may require the outside services of an advisor or consultant to assist you in making these determinations. You must have an understanding of the best geographic audiences and markets for your work. Identifying the jurors (often curators, gallerists, or critics) who are interested in certain kinds of work and/or specific mediums will provide the most successful outcome of your efforts.

**Avoid Detours: Evaluate Opportunities**

Many nonprofit institutions host juried and competitive exhibitions, invitationals, annuals, biennials, or present thematic exhibitions, produced in-house or guest curated. To determine if you wish to enter such competitions or participate in these exhibitions, you must bring a high degree of discrimination to your participation choices.

Some qualifying factors are the professional status of the juror, the size and location of the institution, the possibility of a review, and the opportunity for your work to be viewed by potential clients in the vicinity.

For each group exhibition you are considering, carefully research the qualifications, professional affiliations, and reputation of the curator or juror. Ideally he or she should have national prominence or, at the very least, regional or statewide stature.

**Power Seats: Evaluating Exhibition Opportunities**

You must carefully evaluate competitive exhibition opportunities. If the juror is a museum director or curator from a bona fide museum (member of the American Association of Museums), you are on the right track. The larger and more significant the museum that a juror hails from, the better for you professionally.

If the juror is the director of a nationally positioned art gallery, you must familiarize yourself with the focus of the work presented before deciding whether participation would be to your benefit. Going to the gallery's website and looking at the work of the artists represented is an excellent way to reach a decision.

If the juror is an art critic or writer, it is certainly in your best interest to participate if they are on the editorial staff of, or affiliated with, national art publications such as *Art in America* or *ARTnews*, or leading regionals such as *Art New England* or *Art Papers*.

When a well-known artist is invited to jury an exhibition, one of two things can occur. The artist will select work similar to his or her own sensibility, style, or theoretical approach, an obvious and natural inclination. Alternatively, the artist may also be an educator and base his or her decisions on the most serious, informed, and open-minded criteria imaginable.

Suffice it to say, it is a good idea to do an internet search on your jurors to learn about their backgrounds and interests, so you can make a well-informed decision as to whether you want to invest the money, energy, and time to participate in a juried exhibition.

Your ability to discriminate must be exercised at all times when deciding whether or not to ultimately participate.

**Parallel Parking: Alternative Venues**
Venue opportunities for your work are broader and more abundant than you may initially think. Museums and educational institutions often have several exhibition spaces, one of which may even be set aside exclusively to present the work of artists from the state or region. On college and university campuses, there are often auxiliary exhibition spaces, as in the theater, student union, library, restaurants, etc., in addition to the university art museum. There may also be multiple gallery spaces attached to the department of fine arts.

Beyond such nonprofit organizations, there are other public venues such as visitors' centers, libraries, government buildings, corporate spaces (lobbies, naturally, but there may also be opportunities in less public spaces, e.g., the board room), real estate development projects, hospitals, banks, churches, private and public schools, theaters, and mass transit. All offer you the chance

*Don't let adverse facts stand in the way of a good decision.*
COLIN POWELL

---

**Navigation: Career Advancement**

Before making a tactical decision to participate in an exhibition opportunity, ask yourself the following questions:

- In this situation, what are some of the tangible results for your career development and the building of your reputation as an artist?

- Can you make new and significant contacts? Is there a good chance that "movers and shakers" will see your work in this context?

- Are there commercial sales opportunities, such as dealers, art consultants, interior designers, and architects who may have clients or projects appropriate to your work in this general geographic area and does this offer the perfect introduction to your work?

- Is the juror in a professional position to assist you in furthering your career?

- Is this exhibition venue/opportunity of greater significance than your most recent involvement and achievement?

## Exhibition Fact Sheet

You must develop an Exhibition Fact Sheet to accompany your presentation materials. It provides the institution/venue with a summary of the basic components of and conditions for your exhibition. An Exhibition Fact Sheet is usually two pages and includes a 100-150-word description of your exhibition and information in the following categories.

- Number of objects

- Size

- Space requirements

- Installation requirements

- Insurance

- Promotional materials

*Life is either a daring adventure or nothing.*

HELEN KELLER

to exhibit with the possibility of garnering professional exposure and getting reviewed, which helps to develop a following in your local community, and, importantly, potential sales opportunities.

### On the Road: After the Exhibition Is Booked

After all of your preparation and hard work, you've finally done it – you've secured a one-person exhibition.

Regardless of the venue, it is a personal and professional achievement that presents a rare opportunity to explore media and sales opportunities for your work in a well-defined geographic area.

Valuable opportunities surround each and every exhibition. To find these sales and other opportunities requires in-depth research in that geographic area. You need to identify museums and other nonprofits, commercial galleries, art consultants, corporate collection in-house curators and consultants, interior designers, architects and landscape architects, the media, and educational and professional institutions that can help to advance your career.

The success of your exhibition rests with you. Your artistic talent may have secured the exhibition, but its success depends on your practical business skills. And the career momentum created from it will be in direct proportion to your professionalism, efficiency, thoroughness, and follow-through. It is imperative that you work diligently to maximize the impact of the exhibition.

### Watch for Falling Rocks: Check All the Fine Print

A letter of confirmation from the exhibiting venue finalizes the dates of your exhibition, the day of the opening, and the terms of your agreement with the institution, organization, or gallery.

There are numerous details that must be addressed and questions you need to ask that will clarify your responsibilities, as well as those of the hosting institution. Not dealing with these concerns during your initial discussions only leads to confusion and complications further down the road. You want to avoid as many bumps as humanly possible so the experience will be positive for all parties involved.

It's a good idea to make a list of all your questions prior to the execution of the final letter and discuss each point with the curator. If it is a museum, it's also smart to ask for a copy of its annual report, so you can familiarize yourself with the institution and its community supporters. It's easy to explain that your primary concern is that the exhibition be a great success, and that your purpose in asking these questions is to avoid any unforeseen circumstances.

Once your exhibition has been scheduled, and you have the letter of confirmation from the exhibition venue, make an appointment to speak with the curator by telephone, or in person, if possible.

First, remember to be courteous, never demanding or needy when dealing with the exhibition venue. It is not a good idea to seem overbearing in your expectations with curators, or to convey in any way that dealing with you will be a "high maintenance" ordeal. Word travels quickly among these professionals; a "difficult artist" label is hard to shake once acquired.

Conduct yourself in a considerate and patient manner in all dealings with the exhibiting institution. Prompt responses to any requests, attention to details, and a willingness to cooperate set you apart in the eyes of these professionals. With severe budget constraints affecting much of the art world, these professionals are often asked to assume the role of two or three people in their organization. If you can make their jobs easier with efficient communication and professional decorum, you will be remembered with respect. Preserve and advance your professional reputation by exceeding expectations.

Express your intention to work with the institution in making this an event that garners print, electronic, radio, and television coverage, and that will provide a strong educational component, including a lecture for students in local college art programs or for the museum's audiences. Be clear about your desire to

*Always bear in mind that your own resolution to succeed is more important than any other one thing.*

ABRAHAM LINCOLN

*God is love, but get it in writing.*

GYPSY ROSE LEE

complement their efforts, and ask what public relations support is normally extended to an exhibitor, indicating that it is your intention to complement those efforts only as is deemed appropriate.

Calmly communicate that you want everything to go smoothly and that you want to be of assistance in any way that can be helpful. Inquire about timelines, and what is needed to make their jobs easier. Unnecessarily complicated and draining artists only alienate curators and museum staff, so remain flexible, accommodating, open to suggestions and possible changes. Hopefully you have already learned this through your experiences in the many group and juried exhibitions you have participated in prior to your first one-person exhibition. Professionalism and consideration are what lead to a successful exhibition and are the ingredients that make it a positive experience for all involved – this is what can be built upon in the future.

Museum directors and curators speak among themselves. They may attend statewide meetings several times a year. Some institutions think competitively, and some like to work together to bring high-quality programming to their audiences. It is in their interest to share exhibition ideas, and sharing shipping expenses between venues can be appealing. This may pique the interest of a curator who was undecided about scheduling an exhibition of your work. Also, they could share promotional costs, such as producing an announcement card, brochure, or even catalogue that may be more expensive and impressive. This creates a true win-win-win situation.

Remember once a venue is scheduled and your exhibition dates finalized, this is your excuse to contact other curators who may have retained your materials for future consideration. When another venue in the same state has booked your exhibition, a telephone call or e-mail from you about this new development may, at long last, turn the key, and initiate a *traveling* exhibition hosted by several state nonprofit venues.

Also, although it may be almost impossible to believe, artists have been known to cancel shows, leaving a museum or gallery in the lurch at the last minute. Your continued, appropriate, and well-timed attempts could actually lead to a completely unexpected exhibition opportunity. Respectfully keep your name and your work present in their thoughts without becoming a pest.

To help capitalize on the momentum of an exhibition and to secure the greatest advancements for your artistic career, there are some guidelines to follow to insure that the exhibition proceeds as smoothly as possible.

**Right Turn Only: 90 Days Prior to Exhibition**

It is customary to provide, in writing, a complete list of works to be included in the exhibition – full title and series title (if germane; both in quote marks), date of execution, size (height x width x depth), medium, description, and retail price. Insurance value for works is calculated at 50% of the work's retail value.

CDs or jpegs must be provided to the institution for the color announcement card and other promotional pieces that may be produced in-house. The image for the color announcement card must feature one of the works in the exhibition and a work mutually agreed upon by you and the curator.

If you have produced your own brochure or catalogue, you can send a modest number to meet the institution's basic press needs (25 to 50). They must be sent well in advance of your exhibition (60 to 90 days) so the organization can use them for pre-exhibition promotion.

You can also suggest that the institution purchase at cost additional copies, say 100 to 200 catalogues, to use during the run of the exhibition, or you can offer to provide additional copies gratis if they are sent to important patrons and local collectors. The balance can be sold at your exhibition, especially if it is an expensive promotional piece.

You are encouraged to attach a label to the catalogues with your name, address, telephone and fax numbers, e-mail address, and website so interested parties can contact you directly.

**The Sticker Price is Always Negotiable: Sales**

Although a nonprofit institution does not represent artists or act as a sales venue – and a director or curator cannot ethically act as your selling agent – you are encouraged to provide the organization with a letter indicating your desire to sell works from the exhibition.

Give the exhibiting institution a strong incentive to work closely with you in providing sales leads, should there be inquiries about purchasing your work, by offering a percentage

*Any fact facing us is not as important as our attitude toward it, for that determines our success or failure.*

NORMAN VINCENT PEALE

*This is your victory.*

WINSTON CHURCHILL

of the sale as a gift to the museum's educational or other outreach programs (if this percentage arrangement is not already part of the original exhibition agreement). Some smaller museums and art centers may receive a percentage of the sale price, ranging from 10 to 30%.

Another "sweetener" is offering to donate a piece from the exhibition to the institution's permanent collection if area collectors are identified. This also has the added benefit of having your work represented in a respected institution's collection.

There are several strategies that can be employed to encourage sales during the exhibition. If the museum is featuring paintings, providing drawings or prints is the perfect way to maximize the potential for sales. Similarly a related series of works on paper, prints, and/or smaller paintings could be made available to a dealer or consultant in the area.

Practical considerations and financial necessity stimulate many artists to consider creating complementary bodies of work, often smaller in scale, to be made available during their exhibition at lower price points, perhaps in the $1,000-$2,000 range depending upon the prices of their major works.

You may produce a major body of museum-quality works, but additionally one or two other bodies of related works for increased sales opportunities: an exhibition at a commercial gallery, corporate space, or even for sale through the nonprofit institution itself. You could speak to the curator or director and ask them if they have some private collectors in mind for your work, and that for every work purchased at full price, you will donate a second piece to the museum's permanent collection.

While you can act as your own sales agent, it is preferable to have a commercial venue, private dealer, or consultant acting on your behalf. Ideally, this individual would represent your interests not only during the run of your exhibition, but also after it concludes. A sustained presence in the same general geographic area as your museum exhibition is clearly in your best long-term interest, and that of a dealer or another commercial representative.

**Pedal to the Metal: 30 Days Before the Exhibition**

It is vital for the institution to receive all of your support materials in a timely manner. They must be professionally prepared and assembled. All correspondence, lists, résumés, and written materials must be typed, not handwritten, and most institutions will request these be forwarded electronically.

Approximately a month before the opening day, the exhibiting institution must have complete instructions, in writing from you (verbal agreements *do not count* in the world of business), for the pick up of the work. This includes the complete address and telephone numbers to be able reach you (should there be a last minute snafu), and you'll also need numbers to reach whoever is doing the actual pick up. The curator should also have your cell phone number. Make note of any pertinent details needed to facilitate the process. How does the trucker access the studio building? What are the dimensions of the door to the building and the studio door? If there is an elevator, is it freight or passenger? And what are its dimensions? Are there stairs? How many flights? Are there tight corners to navigate? Are the works in wooden crates, cardboard boxes, or soft-wrapped? And what are their sizes and approximate weight? Will additional help be needed to load the truck?

**Auto Detailing: Framing and Presentation**

As you begin to be accepted into juried exhibitions, invited to participate in thematic group exhibitions, or offered solo shows, the framing, presentation, and archival preservation of your work needs to be seriously addressed.

Have you ever carefully considered why most frames look like an afterthought? The selection of an appropriate frame or molding is one of the most important, but frequently overlooked, aspects of framing a two-dimensional work of art. The challenge is how your selected presentation will complement and enhance the work of art.

In a sculptural or three-dimensional piece, the presentation base or pedestal must be an extension of the sensibilities operating in the actual work as well as a unifying concept. When the base and the work seem unrelated, or even worse, at odds, the viewer will be left with a sense that your presentation is unresolved.

*Failure to prepare is preparing to fail.*

JOHN WOODSEN

*One can present people with opportunities.*
*One cannot make them equal to them.*

ROSAMOND LEHMAN

If the ephemeral nature of time itself is part of the concept being expressed in the artwork, permanence would not be a concern. However, if you are making work with the dream that it will someday be acquired by museums or sold at auction, then the materials you choose must stand the test of time.

Likewise, if sales, commissions, and commercial applications are part of your thrust as an artist, it is best to utilize materials that, at the very minimum, will last through your lifetime, or your valuable time in later years will be spent dealing with irate collectors and dealers who may demand that you repair or replace the pieces they purchased. So, investing in the highest quality framing and archival presentation materials is a basic prerequisite.

### Packing for the Trip: Shipping

When you are accepted into a group show or offered a one-person exhibition, you may be responsible for delivering the work to the exhibition site and back. Packing, crating, and shipping can be the most formidable expenses surrounding an exhibition.

Whatever the type of work you make – photographs, prints, drawings, modest-scale paintings, or different kinds of three-dimensional work – as long as the size and weight are reasonable, using commercial companies can be cost effective and practical. (By the way, it's never a good idea to ship works framed with glass.)

The number of professional shipping companies, both fine art and commercial, is extensive. In most areas there are local pack-and-ship companies, both independent and affiliated with UPS, Federal Express, and other leading shipping firms. The range of costs is also enormous, so you are well advised to get multiple quotes; and you will save money if you can do the packing and crating yourself.

Depending upon the fragility of your artwork and shipping method, cardboard containers can be a relatively inexpensive yet durable solution, although these types of materials are not intended to be reused more than a few times. A range of grades and densities is available to fulfill your needs. Fragile sculptures can be shipped in triple-wall cardboard boxes with lots of styrofoam peanuts and bubble wrap.

*Happiness lies in the joy of achievement
and the thrill of creative effort.*

FRANKLIN DELANO ROOSEVELT

You can also use two or more packing boxes, which fit inside one another, with an additional layer of packing material between each to act as a buffer. When the outer box becomes damaged or worn from repeated use, it can simply be replaced. Plan for this when purchasing containers. Costs can be reduced by ordering in larger quantities.

You may wish to investigate packaging suppliers, such as ULINE, one of the largest, as they can provide virtually any size box, heavy-duty or triple-wall thickness corrugated containers, interior packaging, oversized bubble envelopes, and just about anything you would need to create durable and secure packaging for your work (see "Information Resources," Shipping/Crating/Packing Materials, p. 253).

Large-scale and heavy works of art, or materials that are fragile or easily damaged, present a major challenge for shipping. They may require wood crating, which is expensive for two reasons: the cost of the materials and labor – if you cannot do it yourself. And wood crates are heavy and thus, more expensive to ship. One plus is that they are very sturdy, reducing the risk of damage to the artwork, and can be used repeatedly.

Fine-art shippers, which abound, will also transport soft-wrapped or blanket-wrapped art when appropriate, but these companies often charge more for the specialized handling.

You will also need to protect your artwork by insuring it. Large-scale and heavy works of art or materials that are fragile or easily damaged, present a major challenge. Most shipping companies offer insurance options at an additional charge. The United States Postal Service provides up to $25,000 insurance. For artwork, Federal Express offers a maximum of $500 of insurance per box for air and $100 for ground shipments. Both FedEx and UPS will not ship original art (one-of-a-kind items) by their standard means, so you can simply say the boxes contain "exhibit materials," knowing you carry your own insurance or that this represents a risk you are willing to assume. Maintaining a wall-to-wall (from the time the artwork leaves your studio until it is returned) insurance policy may resolve all your concerns.

CHAPTER 5
# Crossing State Lines: Poised for Stage Two

There will be a juncture, a moment in time, when all your efforts to reach the next Stage seem to converge. A number of important factors in your career developments will bring the activities specified in Stage One to a close.

- You have competed in and been accepted by the most important juried or competitive exhibitions in your state, and been recognized with awards and honors on multiple occasions by significant jurors.

- You have been invited to participate in a number of major group exhibitions organized by museums or institutions in your state or beyond – exhibitions that have traveled to several other venues of importance in the state. Catalogues may have been published in conjunction with some of the exhibitions.

- You have had at least five or six one-person exhibitions at Level I – better college or university galleries, small museums, art centers, alternative spaces, or important corporate spaces.

- You have garnered media coverage on a number of occasions, and have been reviewed by a recognized art writer or critic in your state.

- You may be a recipient of a visual arts grant in your state, or participated in a residency or visiting artist program.

- As a result of your successes and recognition, there is curatorial interest in your work by Level II and Level III museums in your state. They have been made aware of your work either because of your involvement in a group exhibition, or you have formally introduced yourself in the context of your accomplishments and accolades.

- One or two gallery affiliations are solidly in place, and several consultants are working to place your work in corporate and private settings.

- You have made contact with many noteworthy professionals, some of whom have offered to assist you by way of introductions to an important curator or dealer – in your state, region, or beyond.

- You have a base of 20 to 30 collectors – nonprofit, institutional, corporate, private – and you have made repeat sales to a number of these patrons. You have cultivated relationships with your serious collectors.

*I do not know anyone who has gotten to the top without hard work. That is the recipe.*

MARGARET THATCHER

- Collectors and art professionals alike are beginning to watch with interest to see what may be coming next in your artistic and career development.

- You are thinking strategically as you make your professional choices. You have clarity of purpose, and realize that this kind of awareness – ABC – About Being Conscious – is taking you closer to your goals.

If you have met most or all of these conditions, then you are now poised and positioned to move on to Stage Two. Along the way you have gained a greater working knowledge of how the puzzle pieces of career development and promotion fit together. Here you will be as successful as the performance level you attained in the first three to five years of Stage One.

It is important not to go on to Stage Two until you are sufficiently convinced, no, *truly* convinced, that you have achieved the best results possible from your efforts. This is not about meeting the minimum goal requirements, but rather excellent professional performance throughout your state in meeting all the requirements of Stage One.

At the next Stage, the competition will be even keener, and fewer artists will have the commitment and talent necessary to successfully maneuver at this level of activity. This is where the road clearly divides. Anyone with a modicum of ambition, drive, and average talent can perform at Stage One, but it requires another kind of stamina and perseverance to be successful in regional career development.

Establishing realistic sales goals each year is part of an organized approach to tracking the results of your promotional efforts. In a location where there are few successful or established commercial galleries, it is incumbent upon you to actively develop your base of collectors and to determine when you are ready to move to Stage Two.

To progress to Stages Two and Three, you must have a respectable plan of action and the experience to proceed with certainty and confidence, before running headlong into a situation for which you are unprepared. Not only do you need talent in making your work, you also need a fundamental understanding of the mechanics of business and promotion to take the checkered flag.

*Don't cross the bridge 'til you get to it.*

PROVERB

# Stage Two:
# Regional Career Development

CHAPTER 6
# Interstate Commerce: Going Regional

Your career development is an ongoing process, moving from one orbit of activity to another. In Stage One, you acquired all the tools necessary for your future success and the strategies for continued progress at Stages Two and Three. But you cannot move to Stage Two, which can take five to ten years to complete, until you have successfully navigated through Stage One and achieved its goals (see Chapter 1, "Stage One Goals: City, County, and Statewide," p. 20).

As you extend your radius of activity, decisions about who you approach, and why, must be more focused and well defined. As in Stage One, and aided by the quality of your research, you will be ranking exhibition possibilities in terms of quality of programming, prestige of the institution, visibility, and levels of exposure. You are still playing a numbers game, but as more people learn about your work and accomplishments, your probability of securing quality exhibitions will increase.

Stage Two's requirements are fundamentally the same as at Stage One, but you have expanded your sights beyond your home state boundaries to the region. Your primary focus will be on the regional level and securing 12 to 15 one-person exhibitions at higher Level I (more prestigious and more substantial venues with larger attendance – 15,000 to 25,000 – and with serious exhibition programming) as well as at Level II (25,000 to 100,000 annual attendance) institutions including museums on college and university campuses, better university and college galleries, and high-ranking art centers.

Level III and Elite museums may also be approached with your basic introductory package, but your aim is to merely introduce your work to the curator and to learn if there are any exhibitions – group, thematic, or guest-curated – being planned for which your work is appropriate.

Keep in mind that it is best to have a one-person exhibition scheduled at a Level I or Level II museum before introducing yourself and your work to a Level III or Elite curator. Using one venue to catapult you to the next venue of equal or greater importance creates momentum.

*Every great human achievement is preceded by*
*extended periods of dedicated, concentrated effort.*

BRIAN TRACY

*I will strain my potential until it cries for mercy.*

OG MANDINO

It is premature to approach Level II and Level III institutions in your state about a one-or two-person exhibition at this point in your career. As a general rule, the Level II museums in your state will not offer a one-person exhibition so early in your career, and it would be unrealistic to expect otherwise. Securing significant exhibitions in the nonprofit and for-profit areas regionally or nationally, and receiving coverage from critics who contribute to regional, national, and international art publications are prerequisites to achieving that recognition. You will likely find it to be far more difficult to get the attention you deserve in your state, than it is to garner recognition elsewhere.

This being said, it is still vital for your progress to keep curators and media at home abreast of what you are doing. Remember that these individuals are evolving in their career process, too. A curator may accept a position at a leading exhibiting institution or move into the commercial sector. An employee may be promoted to the directorship of an important gallery. A critic who has previously written about your work could affiliate with a major-league international art publication. As these art professionals reach more influential positions, they may be willing to offer a helping hand to you in future years as you also advance in your career.

There is also the ongoing challenge of maintaining your relationships with collectors, galleries, consultants, designers, and architects statewide while cultivating new business relationships and developing additional sales contacts in the region. Even when you do go national at Stage Three, you must keep in regular contact with Level I, II, III, and Elite curators in your own region. It pays to stay in touch.

In Stage Two, set a goal of three one-person and three group exhibitions per year. If there are eight to ten states in your region and, even though it is imprudent in Stage Two to include Level I (smaller college or junior college venues, local art centers, or any juried competitive shows), there could be close to 400 to 500 possible exhibition opportunities, encompassing all levels, including commercial galleries, alternative venues, corporate spaces, and high-visibility public spaces.

Another goal at Stage Two is to affiliate with at least one commercial situation (gallery, private dealer, or consultant) in each state of your region.

However, you must have enough work to accommodate these opportunities.

**Interstate Access: Regional Research**

As in Stage One, you must develop a database covering the region; this may take three to six months to compile. But remember, the better the quality, the better the results. Making and taking the time to do thorough and accurate research can lead to a successful outcome for your efforts. Reviews, sales, and gallery affiliation are the measurable results, so superficial leads and hurried entries will not ultimately serve your purposes.

To determine the scope of your region, you can use the American Association of Museums' regional divisions as a guide: **New England** (Connecticut, Maine, Massachusetts, New Hampshire, Rhode Island, Vermont), **Mid-Atlantic** (Delaware, District of Columbia, Maryland, New Jersey, New York, Pennsylvania), **Southeast** (Alabama, Arkansas, Florida, Georgia, Kentucky, Louisiana, Mississippi, North Carolina, South Carolina, Tennessee, Virginia, West Virginia), **Midwest** (Illinois, Indiana, Iowa, Michigan, Minnesota, Missouri, Ohio, Wisconsin), **Mountain Plains** (Colorado, Kansas, Montana, Nebraska, New Mexico, North Dakota, South Dakota, Oklahoma, Texas, Wyoming), and **West** (Alaska, Arizona, California, Hawaii, Idaho, Nevada, Oregon, Utah, Washington).

You would begin with in-depth research for exhibition opportunities, media, sales, grants, fellowships, and residencies. Regional art councils and foundations can help you identify possibilities, and tactically speaking, gallery affiliation should also be in the forefront of your mind.

You will use the same resources to create your database as in Stage One: *American Art Directory, The Official Museum Directory,* and *Art in America Annual Guide to Galleries/Museums/Artists* (see Chapter 2, "Getting Directions: Directories," p. 24) and the internet (see "Your Presence on the Internet," p. 277).

Depending on the size of the state, there could be anywhere from 25 to 50 nonprofit venues at all levels per state. Some will have fewer, but states like California and New York may have a hundred such institutions.

*Work is much more fun than fun.*

NOEL COWARD

*Genius is one percent inspiration and 99 percent perspiration.*

THOMAS EDISON

For example, if there are approximately 300 nonprofit exhibition venues at all levels in the 12 states of the Southeast, then it could require several months to complete the research. This entails visiting the individual sites on the internet, and entering the pertinent data (contact name, title, institution type, address, phone, fax, and e-mail with additional notes applicable to your situation and their interests, i.e., "artists of the region," "strong focus on women," "experimental new media," etc., into your database).

The most effective way to start your regional research is to target the state universities that have graduate studio and art-history programs. To identify these institutions, there are the directories previously mentioned. The *American Art Directory* lists art schools by city and state, as does the *Art in America Annual Guide to Galleries/Museums/Artists*. In addition, the College Art Association publishes *Graduate Programs in the Arts* directories for both fine art and art history.

Venues in the larger cities are always more desirable because there are usually one or more newspapers with art critics or contributing art writers who regularly review art exhibitions and cultural events. This substantially increases the possibility of garnering coverage. Art audiences also tend to be more sophisticated because of the exposure they have to leading-edge practices, new mediums, and trends in contemporary art.

Carefully peruse the school's website to be certain it is appropriate for your work and your goals. Check to see who is on the faculty, how they have distinguished themselves professionally, and then consider how they may also positively affect your career. Use Google to supplement the information.

Rather than tackling the entire region at once, you might begin with several contiguous states. However, if you market yourself state by state, or even in just a few of the neighboring states, this process will take much longer, and it will severely limit the number of opportunities you can build upon simultaneously.

Approaching all the high Level I and Level II venues in your region is manageable. When introducing your work in the region, it makes more sense to contact all the higher Level I venues first, and then to build on these successes, before approaching Level II.

Scattershot marketing is expensive and the percentage of return is low, so build on existing opportunities and the credibility and status they provide.

One-person exhibitions and inclusion in significant group exhibitions in the region lend validity to your work and enhance your status, and they can be leveraged and parlayed into other exhibition bookings.

Once a one-person exhibition is scheduled in any state, it is the ideal time to introduce your work to other curators at any level. In Stage Two, when you secure a one-person exhibition at a Level I institution, you may proceed to a higher Level I or Level II institution.

If you are included in important group exhibitions at a Level III or Elite institution and also have a one-person exhibition traveling to small and mid-sized museums, this is also your entrée to curators at all levels in the region.

Use your upcoming exhibition as the "mothership" or your "command center," and expand out geographically from that point. For example, let's say you have secured a one-person exhibition at a higher Level I museum in the panhandle of Florida, but you reside in St. Louis, Missouri. To capitalize on this booking, identify all the higher Level I (15,000 to 25,000 attendance) and lower Level II (25,000 to 50,000) institutions along the probable shipping route, but do not consider any venues within a 150 to 200 mile radius of your exhibition site because this may pull on the same audience, and would be counterproductive.

You can even recontact the higher Level I institutions in the region again unless they have already definitively said no. Your upcoming exhibition may stimulate these nonprofits to revisit the possibility of mounting an exhibition of your work prior to or following your scheduled show.

It is also advantageous to the exhibiting institution for you to secure additional bookings. For small- to mid-sized venues, shipping costs are often the biggest impediment in scheduling exhibitions, so sharing these expenses can be an attractive proposition. Institutions may also want to split promotional costs. A color announcement card can list two or more venues, and dividing the cost of a brochure or catalogue with several venues may allow for a more elaborate and costly piece to be produced. Advertising in magazines is more likely when multiple venues share these expenses.

*Actions speak louder than words.*

PROVERB

*There is no security in this life. There is only opportunity.*

DOUGLAS MACARTHUR

When reconnecting by phone or e-mail with an institution to discuss your recently confirmed exhibition, you could indicate that a new body of work is currently underway, and inquire as to whether it might be suitable for any upcoming group exhibitions being planned by the curator. You might also inquire when the exhibition committee will next convene.

At the end of the conversation, if nothing concrete has been decided, you might tell the curator that you will send a CD for review when the new body of work is completed. It's often appreciated, and appropriate, to tell a curator or gallerist that you will keep them abreast of your professional involvements by sending periodic updates of your activities.

Even if a curator still does not offer you an exhibition opportunity for whatever reason – a scheduling conflict or having already booked an artist with similar work – each contact increases name recognition, and keeping curators regularly informed about career advancements will enhance your standing. Persistence may pay future dividends.

Curators can be generous and helpful, even recommending that you contact a colleague who might be interested in your exhibition proposal. It is not beyond the realm of possibility that a curator at a Level I institution knows a curator at a Level II institution, and the two have wanted to collaborate on a project for some time. In this situation, they may be willing to discuss your exhibition proposal with other colleagues, who could also do the same.

If you use this strategy in every state, it is plausible that after three to five years of building opportunity upon opportunity, you will be in the position to be considered for a one- or two-person exhibition at Level II institutions throughout the region.

Timing is everything, but opportunities are usually the result of persistence and hard work.

**Getting in Gear: Implementing Your Plan**

Once you have identified your targeted institutions and created your database, another month might be required to prepare all the components of your presentation, pack, and mail it. Then begins the process of follow-up, which is painstaking work requiring both patience and determination.

You can complete sending the first follow-up e-mails in a matter of days, but you will need to wait three weeks to see if you receive any response – e-mail, formal correspondence, or phone call. Your first e-mail is to confirm whether or not the package has been received and to request that the curator give your submission careful consideration.

Then you would wait several more weeks before making contact by telephone.

Arts professionals are swamped with requests, so it is imperative that you allow them enough time to review the submission and to respond. Chances are that you will have to leave a message with the receptionist or in the voicemail system before ever having a conversation with someone in the curatorial department. If no feedback is forthcoming after another four to six weeks, you may follow up with another e-mail, telephone call, or even a handwritten note.

There are several scenarios that can prolong this process. The curator to whom you addressed the package has left, and the new curator, assuming one has been appointed, cannot locate the package, and so you will need to send a new package, and on and on you will go.

Even if an institution is interested, it may take another few months for the curator to take your proposal to the exhibition committee and, if approved, finalize your exhibition dates. This must be confirmed by written agreement from the hosting venue.

All this is for a four-to six-week exhibition one to two years, or even further, into the future.

Be certain to take timing subtleties into consideration before mailing out expensive presentations. Museum professionals vacation during the summer months, and it is difficult to assemble an exhibition committee meeting during July and August. Programming at university and college art galleries and museums runs parallel to the academic year. Because selection committees are traditionally made up of faculty, and sometimes by students with faculty advisors, they are often called together for a joint review of submissions in the late spring (April and May) or in the fall (October and November).

Never ever mail a new submission or something of consequence to anyone after Thanksgiving or before the beginning of the New Year, unless someone has specifically requested your materials, or you are following up on materials sent previously.

**Planning the Itinerary: Strategies for Regional Success**

When you move beyond your statewide promotional activities, some aspects of your involvements, out of practicality, must fall away. As your sights will be set higher at Stage Two, exhibiting at community or junior college art galleries, smaller art centers, or with professional art/artist's organizations will not be conducive to professional advancement.

*Fortune favors the brave.*

TERENCE

*I am the greatest believer in luck, and*
*I find the harder I work the more I have of it.*

STEPHEN LEACOCK

The purpose of these activities at Stage One was to become known by the media, curators, and art professionals through exposure in 25 to 30 exhibitions in your home state.

Participating in juried exhibitions regionally will actually be counterproductive to your long-term goals. The energy, time, and expense you devote to participating in competitive exhibitions only deters your progress as you raise the bar and increase the challenges at Stage Two. However, as long as you are willing to be highly discriminating, there are some exceptions.

For example, if a juried exhibition is being held at a major museum in a metropolitan area (Level III and Elite, 100,000 to over a million annual attendance), and the juror is a recognized and prestigious art-world figure, such as an important New York City-, Los Angeles-, or Chicago-based gallery dealer, museum curator or director, or a highly respected art critic, then an exception can be made. Otherwise your participation in these kinds of exhibitions should taper off at Stage Two.

"Emerging talent" galleries will not be a part of the regional equation unless they are well established, have excellent reputations, feature the work of mid-level/mid-career artists in the mix, and are located in larger cities.

When you decide to go regional, it is tactically prudent to suspend your home state activities for a period of time. Give your colleagues several years to observe your advancements as they occur elsewhere. Involve them in your triumphs by keeping them informed of new developments – exhibitions, copies of reviews and other media coverage, and news of upcoming exhibitions (when they have been finalized in writing).

After several Level II one-person exhibitions are scheduled regionally, you are positioned to reapproach Level IIs on your home turf again. Being celebrated there as one of the "best and brightest" could require two decades or more of consistent and determined promotional effort, before returning home to enthusiastic applause and acceptance. Be aware that seeking recognition and respect from where you hail sometimes has more to do with feeling you did not get the acceptance and respect you felt you deserved when you were growing up. However, wanting to prove yourself can also be a mighty powerful motivator in the game of life and art.

**Regional Connections: Research**

Scheduling an exhibition at a nonprofit venue in proximity to a large city with major cultural institutions is a serious accomplishment. Confirmed exhibitions will lend credibility and provide leverage as you approach new opportunities surrounding your exhibition.

The aims of your promotional campaign should include obtaining media coverage, identifying local arts supporters and collectors, making a local gallery affiliation, and pursuing sales in the immediate area (50 to 100 mile radius).

One of the positive outcomes of an exhibition is that curators from other organizations can become better acquainted with your work. On the commercial side, dealers can see your work in a professional setting, and, if interested, even retain some pieces following your exhibition. Also consultants and designers can bring their clients to meet you and see the artwork.

Often the more desirable gallery affiliations occur when you have secured a nonprofit exhibition in the immediate area. They can be located in the same city or nearby the exhibition venue, or even further afield. Approach a few carefully selected galleries in the immediate area proposing that they consider acting as your commercial representative during the run of your exhibition. This may be a very appealing arrangement for a local dealer or consultant.

However, the gallery must be appropriate for your work. Your overall success is dependent upon cold calculations about the marketability of your work and identifying your prime audience. Don't expect an environmentally conceived, site-specific installation created with ephemeral materials to generate a large number of sales. However, drawings, watercolors, or small studies of carefully selected landscapes of the region with site-specific installation proposals might create a reliable revenue stream. Christo and his late wife, Jeanne-Claude, created a steady income from drawings and prints of both realized and unrealized projects.

If there are no suitable commercial galleries near your exhibition site, build a selling component into your exhibition. Identify other possible sales opportunities, such as consultants, designers, and architects. For example, if your exhibition venue is near a tourist destination or a playground for the rich and famous, consider contacting high-end hotel gift shops and restaurants, even retirement communities for the well-heeled.

*One never notices what has been done,*
*one can only see what remains to be done.*

MARIE CURIE

*It takes 20 years to make an overnight success.*

EDDIE CANTOR

When you fully understand the importance of cultivating a variety of commercial relationships – both the conventional and the non-conventional – and the synergy that can occur when exploring different marketing strategies, you will see that it is a blessing that these nonprofit exhibition opportunities are often scheduled an average of one-to-two years in advance.

Once you have secured an exhibition, and the dates are finalized in writing, shift your focus to scheduling presentations, lectures, workshops, or seminars. In addition to the obvious opportunities in conjunction with the exhibiting institution, there are other possibilities: The American Society of Interior Decorators (ASID), International Interior Design Association (IIDA), American Institute of Architects (AIA), the American Society of Landscape Architects (ASLA) chapters, and other professional organizations. Educational institutions and business groups in the community offer possibilities for lectures and making new contacts locally.

**Feed the Meter: Covering Costs**

Your research and promotional marketing costs increase at Stage Two. Because your professional activities encompass a much wider geographic area and there are more connections to be made, an administrative assistant is essential for the success of your promotional efforts in Stage Two. Additionally, maintaining a studio assistant will allow you to maximize your efforts and not compromise your time in the studio.

You will need to consider investing in advertising and more costly promotional materials. To accomplish all of this, annual revenue from sales should be between $50,000 and $100,000. Establishing and meeting realistic sales goals each year is a way to track the success of your marketing strategies.

To continue to make consistent sales to offset your expenses, you must engage in ongoing, long-term dialogues with both institutions and individuals. Staying in touch with dealers and consultants in your home state will help to secure ongoing sales and commissions, both public and private.

If you find yourself in a location where there are few successful or established commercial galleries, it is incumbent upon you to develop a base of collectors on your own. Other sources of income will need to be identified, and their viability confirmed through careful research. Some possibilities are art fairs; auctions; alternative sales venues; grants and fellowships; and commissioned projects through consultants, architects, designers, etc., in the private, corporate, and public sectors.

*Learn to wish everything should come
to pass exactly as it does.*

EPICTETUS

Outcomes cannot be controlled and events never unfold in some perfectly planned way, especially when you consider all the challenges, and personalities involved in each exhibition situation. The effectiveness of these activities can only be measured in quantifiable outcomes such as media coverage, sales, and new contacts generated, but what is the most rewarding aspect of this process is *knowing* you exercised all available options, and that you used your time and resources in an advantageous manner.

**Stage Two Goals: Regional**

- Requires five to ten years to complete

- 12 to 15 one-person exhibitions at higher Level I and Level II exhibiting institutions (annual attendance 5,000 to 100,000) and mid-level gallery venues

- Participation in major curated group and thematic exhibitions at Level II, Level III, and Elite institutions

- Relationships with respected museum directors and curators in your state and in your region and with other professionals who will champion your work regionally and nationally

- Media coverage by regionally recognized and respected art writers and critics with publication affiliation or associated with major newspapers in larger cities; coverage in glossy magazines with regional or national circulations; and internet coverage

- A minimum of three gallery affiliations in larger cities regionally (plus active contacts with galleries in your state)

- Private and corporate sales and commissions through art consultants, interior designers, and architects

- Studio and direct sales to collectors; $4,000-$8,000 gross sales per month; $50,000-$100,000 annually from all sources

- Administrative assistant one to two days per week and studio assistant one to two days per week (may alternate weeks)

- Invest $6,000-$9,000 in advertising annually

- Produce brochures and catalogues for promotional purposes, either self-published or through an exhibition opportunity

---

**Other Lecture Possibilities for Artists**

- Women's Clubs and Organizations

- Music Guilds

- Antique Guilds

- Interior Decorators

- Architects

- Professional Groups

- Junior League /Junior Service Leagues

- Sororities

- Fraternities

- Business Associations

- Country Clubs

- Corporations

CHAPTER 7
# Roadside Assistance: Getting the Help You Need

When you branch out into your region, your workload will increase exponentially. Since your artwork must continue to develop and mature, and because production and output must be steady and uninterrupted, it is imperative that you get the administrative support necessary for continued progress. With a capable assistant, you can implement a thorough regional marketing effort in about five years' time.

Whatever your financial abilities, the first and best investment is an administrative assistant. At Stage Two, artists generally do not require a full-time assistant, so you may wish to employ someone only part-time (one to two days per week) with his or her duties determined by your needs and your budget. It would also be beneficial to have a studio assistant one to two days per week. If you cannot afford to have them both every week, have them alternate weeks.

Even if you can only afford $500-$750 per month for an administrative assistant, this is a necessary investment. It is virtually impossible for you to handle all the administrative and promotional responsibilities, in addition to the production of work. Without this type of ongoing support, your work could suffer.

To finance this expense, you may want to consider a five-year small business loan of $50,000, which will give you breathing room. Knowing you must pay back $1,500 each month, you would have the additional incentive to make steady sales.

You could offer a base salary of $6,000 ($30,000 for five years) plus commission on all sales generated by your assistant – for a real incentive offer 20 to 25% commission. The balance of the loan would be spent on postage, promotional materials (including CDs), advertising, more elaborate brochures, and even a catalogue.

The reality is that you have to spend money to make money.

### Assembling a Pit Crew: Administrative Support
When hiring an administrative assistant to help with marketing and promotion, list your requirements. Think of what tasks keep you out of your studio so you can identify the skills needed. In general, look for someone with strong organizational abilities as they will be able to get more accomplished in a limited amount of time. This type of person can help you reach your goals, whether you are seeking to advance your career by building your art-world reputation, to increase sales, or desire to do both.

*Many hands and hearts and minds generally contribute to anyone's notable achievements.*

WALT DISNEY

## The Ten Most Important Skills of an Administrative Assistant

1. Highly motivated and organized

2. Enjoys research

3. Excellent management skills

4. Proficient with computer programs, including word processing, internet navigation, Excel, Filemaker Pro, and grasp of graphic design applications such as Quark XPress, InDesign, and Photoshop

5. Capable of handling art professionals and client/collector correspondence

6. Detail-oriented approach to long-term maintenance and quality control of databases

7. Telephone and retail sales experience – able to "close a deal"

8. Marketing background

9. Familiar and comfortable with basic language of art, or, at the very least, a sincere interest in art

10. Website management – handling of all changes, updates, etc.

*Success means only doing what you do well; letting someone else do the rest.*

GOLDSTEIN S. TRUISM

Finding someone with clerical skills is essential. Research abilities and database management experience would be a plus. It is invaluable if your prospective assistant also has telephone skills or basic sales training. A background in art history or commercial gallery work would certainly be ideal. You may wish to hire someone to do only research and database entry. This person might also prepare your presentation materials and assemble them for mailing. Then, at least initially, you could still do the follow up by e-mail and telephone yourself. You must establish a regular mailing, e-mailing, or telephoning pattern on a daily, weekly, or bi-weekly basis in order to succeed in reaching enough contacts to make serious inroads.

You will want to identify an individual who can bring all – or at least some – of these qualities to the table.

Under no circumstances should the person you hire be another studio artist or undergraduate student in a liberal arts program. The exception is if they have returned to college later in life or during retirement. Students are not a good investment for the long term as they often relocate after graduation. Retraining someone new every year is time-consuming and financially draining.

A mature individual with strong ties to the community, who owns property, and has held positions of responsibility is ideal. Retirees wishing to modestly supplement their income may be your best choice.

Once you have hired this person, there are dozens of permutations and possibilities for orchestrating your work situation. Regardless of how experienced, it is unlikely that you can just sit your assistant down at a desk and expect him or her to carry out specified duties without instruction or supervision. Early in the relationship, you must carefully train and direct your assistant's daily activities. Even working alongside this person one day per week, it could still take several months before you feel confident enough to permit independent promotional activities.

### Promotional Materials at Stage Two

During Stage Two, you will need to invest in the substantive support materials appropriate for a higher level of professional activity. You are encouraged to produce larger format, and thus, more costly brochures and catalogues with six to eight images and a 600 or 750 word critical essay. Your presentation must be elegant, attractive, well organized – in a word, perfect.

As in Stage One, you must use a professional graphic designer to assist you with production of your catalogue or brochure. You may also want to seriously consider bringing in professional writers for the standard support pieces: artist statement, biography, cover/pitch letters for exhibiting institutions and press, introductory essay and/or longer essay, press releases, and radio and television spots.

For your more elaborate promotional pieces, commissioning a renowned critic to write a critical essay is an important investment in shaping how you will be perceived. An essay by an important writer is a way to gain greater recognition and wider acceptance as well as credibility.

When a stunning catalogue or brochure, produced in conjunction with a museum exhibition and featuring a critic's essay, is included with your introductory presentation, you'll be sending a clear message that not only do you take your work very seriously, but so do other professionals who are willing to lend their name to your efforts.

## Billboards: Advertising and Press Coverage

Advertising is a luxury, no question, but at Stage Two, there are situations when this level of investment and expense is warranted. Depending on the prestige of the institution(s) and number of exhibitions you have scheduled a full-, half-, or quarter-page of advertising may be appropriate.

Sometimes these costs are shared with the dealer or the nonprofit exhibition venue, but most often, until you are better known and established, you may have to shoulder these expenses alone, and advertising in the leading art magazines represents a hefty investment.

Still, if you have exhibitions booked at several nonprofits, these institutions might see the mutual benefit of sharing advertising costs equally; in this way regional or national advertising surrounding the exhibitions can be made more affordable for everyone involved.

Advertising and promotion on the internet are time and cost effective, and offer the enterprising artist a chance to throw a very wide net. Research your possibilities and be informed as to which opportunities offer quality exposure at an affordable price. An intelligent, well-timed virtual campaign can target hundreds, if not thousands, of prospects with very little expense involved.

An internet campaign is even better when done in conjunction with print advertising and promotional materials created to complement an exhibition.

*Advertising is the most fun you can have with your clothes on.*

JERRY DELLA FEMINA

Make suggestions to whoever can use this information to promote your show – the institution's curator, public relations professional, student assistant, etc., or the gallery's owner, director, receptionist, etc.

Balancing a marketing campaign between general interest audiences and carefully selected professional contacts is the right approach.

In the case of the former, the chances of piquing the curiosity of someone like your doctor, dentist, therapist, etc., certainly always exists. However, the greater expenditure of time and money (research, production of promotional materials, mailing preparation, implementation, and follow-up) must be directed toward your professional audience base within a 50 to 100-mile radius.

But as effective as advertising may be – many readers peruse the ads before tackling any of the articles in some prestigious magazines – nothing beats editorial coverage. That means having your work reviewed, featured, or included in a magazine or newspaper article. If the exhibition does get editorial coverage, your name and images may be seen by thousands of people who may not regularly visit galleries or museums.

No matter what the museum's public relations professional or a gallery director is doing to promote your exhibition, it is imperative that you personally initiate your own press effort in conjunction with your one-person exhibition. Suggest partnering with the gallery or museum to produce a comprehensive and aggressive press campaign. Offer to handle whatever aspects of promotion they do not normally undertake. Nothing beats a handwritten note or even a brief personal telephone message from the exhibiting artist – it supercedes anything generated by a dealer or curator – as long as it is done tastefully and graciously.

Most art writers are flattered to receive a personal call from an artist from outside their region when he or she is exhibiting at their local museum or art center. Offer to provide any further information that they may require, and make yourself available for a telephone or face-to-face interview when you arrive in town. Your mission is to interest them in knowing your work and you personally.

Expanding beyond your local confines is exciting and challenging. Its rewards go beyond the tangible – exhibitions, reviews, and sales. Knowing that you and your work are connecting with a broader audience is not only satisfying, but exhilarating. It propels you to Stage Three – the national arena.

# Stage Three:
# National Career Development

CHAPTER 8
# Coast to Coast: Going National

Once you have achieved your goals in Stage Two, this is not the time to switch over to cruise control. You are ready to progress to Stage Three of career development: expanding your efforts into the national arena.

After a decade, more or less, of statewide and regional career development, you certainly understand the importance of maintaining your engine properly. You know all the highway attractions in your state and in your region. And with all the valuable lessons learned in your travels, you are also more self-assured and confident.

No one entirely escapes bruising when competing for higher professional stakes. Urban myths and horror stories about galleries are a curious, but predictable phenomenon in the art world, and are usually generated and perpetuated by artists with rather naïve and unrealistic expectations. While the art world certainly has its share of unscrupulous individuals, other professions do as well. There are financial disasters and victims of injustice everywhere, which is why it is imperative for artists to become better informed in their business dealings.

These are the harsh realities of the art business. Take this information to heart so as to not be disappointed and disillusioned down the road.

So what's next? It's a big country and opportunities abound.

## High Gear: Crossing Time Zones
The step-by-step procedures for success at Stages One and Two were designed to help you establish a credible track record of exhibitions, garner reviews, develop a collecting base, and build a strong sales record.

With the goals of Stage Two completed, unlimited choices and options lie before you. In the past, you have operated within a structured plan to reach specific goals. Before taking the on-ramp to the Interstate Highway System – national recognition – you should pause, reflect, and ask yourself some important questions about what you have already achieved, and what remains to be done in Stage Three.

*If you don't know where you are going, you will
probably end up somewhere else.*

LAURENCE J. PETER AND RAYMOND HULL, *THE PETER PRINCIPLE*

## Strategies in the Commercial Sector

- Suspend exhibiting in the nonprofit sector until you have secured gallery affiliations in larger cities throughout the country. At that point you can approach Level II and III museums.

- Approach leading galleries in larger cities based on your track record at Stages One and Two if, and only if, your performance has been exceptionally strong. The galleries that decide to represent you may then introduce your work to select museum curators at Level II, III, and Elite institutions locally, regionally, and nationally as part of their promotional efforts on your behalf.

- Do not contact galleries in the major metropolitan markets like New York City, Los Angeles, and Chicago until you have at least one Level III museum exhibition to your credit, reviews in regional and/or national art publications, and established gallery affiliations in other competitive markets nationally.

- Approach artists with desirable gallery affiliations, visit their studios, and invite them to yours in the hope that they may introduce your work to their dealers.

Have your professional goals changed? Do you wish to continue using the same strategies you used in Stages One and Two? Are they still relevant to your life? Or do you want to make some adjustments?

Are you seriously considering a geographic move? Do you want to relocate closer to a major metropolitan art center? Or are you inclined to retreat to a more remote area because the reduced cost of living will give you more time in your studio and, thus, provide you with additional resources for continued promotion?

Do you want to suspend your involvement in the nonprofit sector for several years, and focus on generating as much income as possible through your activities and affiliations in the commercial arena?

The key to success at Stage Three is knowing where you want to go, why you want to go there, and what you'll do to sustain yourself after you arrive. Short cuts and tactical maneuvering will be at your discretion and inclination, but maintaining a clear vision and sense of purpose throughout must be an integral part of your strategy.

Because you have successfully completed the requirements of the earlier Stages, you already have an impressive record of accomplishments, one that will be taken seriously by curators at the larger institutions, dealers at mid-level (and above), galleries, critics, collectors, and your colleagues – other artists.

Before you shift into high gear, it is essential you evaluate your available options, make some choices, and then commit fully to your goals. This is an adventure that will be long and arduous. It will require real endurance. If you undertake an itinerary that is too extensive to be realistically accomplished, you could lose both your enthusiasm and momentum along the way.

If you "put the pedal to the metal" before you are familiar with the road, you could take a curve going too fast and spin totally out of control. Identifying the real points of interest and major attractions one leg of your trip at a time and maintaining a steady speed, helps you enjoy the scenery while reaching your destination.

## Directional Signals: Know What Your Goals Are

Each leg of your journey must be undertaken for a well-defined reason. The direction you choose is directly related to what you want to achieve in the immediate future. Knowing why you don't want to go somewhere can be just as important as knowing where you do.

You may choose to build slowly outward from your current region of activity to contiguous states. To expand nationally, you may wish to continue to use Stage Two strategies and systematically take one region at a time. Or you may prefer to mobilize your energies for a non-adjacent area in another part of the country. This may be to achieve a bi-coastal presence focusing on the East and West Coasts, or for two cities, such as Atlanta and Chicago.

If you are an artist residing in Ohio seeking to make inroads into the Mid-Atlantic states before advancing on the New York City galleries, and you have met the previously discussed requirements for the conclusion of Stage Two (see Chapter 6, "Stage Two Goals: Regional," pp. 91), you might consider approaching mid-level galleries in Baltimore, Philadelphia, Pittsburgh, and Washington, DC; and Level II museums in Pennsylvania, Maryland, and New Jersey. You could even extend your sights into western New York State.

If you are an artist from a much more centrally located state, such as Missouri or Arkansas, you may want to consider approaching Level II museums in the Mountain Plains and Midwestern states. Perhaps your work is landscape imagery or you create with craft media and would fare better with audiences in the contiguous Mountain Plains states (Texas, Oklahoma, Kansas) and Midwestern states (Illinois, Indiana, Ohio). Museums in these states should be contacted prior to approaching leading galleries in Dallas, Houston, Tulsa, Kansas City, or in Chicago, Indianapolis, and Cincinnati.

If you are an artist residing in Virginia, your next arena of activity may be Pennsylvania, Maryland, New Jersey, and Washington, DC – along the Eastern Seaboard – as you prepare to make your marketing assault on New York City.

*An idea is a beginning point and no more. If you contemplate it, it becomes something else.*

PABLO PICASSO

---

### Strategies in the Nonprofit Sector

- Contact Level II and III museums in other regions of the country when you have affiliated with galleries in their area, have had one-person exhibitions, garnered reviews, and made sales.

- With the active support of your dealer, invite curators to your gallery exhibitions. This may lead to one-person exhibitions at Level II and III institutions, and could also be an entrée into areas of the country where you are not yet known.

- After you have been successful in securing one-person exhibitions in two or more Level II venues, approach select Level III museums in and beyond your region. You could also approach Level III and Elite museums for group exhibition opportunities in multiple regions.

- Explore opportunities along the shipping route from your studio to the exhibition venue where your work will be seen.

- Approach Level II museums simultaneously with approaching galleries in larger cities.

- Ask museum curators and directors that you already know (also art critics and collectors) to introduce you to curators and other professional colleagues outside your region.

*In my beginning is my end.*

T.S. ELIOT

If you are based in San Diego and have a solid track record in the Western US, you may look to the Level II museums in the Mountain Plains states and in metropolitan centers such as Denver, Houston, Dallas, and north to Oklahoma City, Tulsa, Kansas City, Sun Valley, and Ketchum. Or you may decide to focus solely on obtaining a show in New York City for the ultimate purpose of giving yourself enough clout to land major gallery representation in Los Angeles.

If something materializes from the initial approach to the nonprofits, it can facilitate a gallery connection.

### Extended Road Trip: Level II Museums Nationally

Your plan could be to approach museums and/or galleries at Level II (mid-level) nationally, and let your journey unfold based on responses to the work. Begin by identifying all of the approximately 400 Level II museums outside your region. Eliminate from your database any that have criteria that preclude you, for example, some may focus solely on artists from their region.

Then approach these curators about considering you for a one- or two-person exhibition. Once you have scheduled a Level II museum in the region, you can approach other Level IIs nationally, especially those on the shipping route from your studio to the institution, or in contiguous states.

If you book a second one-person exhibition at a Level II venue, you could then consider yourself ready to approach Level III museums and better galleries. Once you have scheduled two Level IIs and one Level III, this is a possible segue into other Level III institutions.

### Open Road: Expanding Your Horizons

If you have secured a one-person exhibition at a Level I or II institution, you can feel confident when approaching an established mid-level gallery. If the institution has a regional or national reputation, the exhibition can be your entrée into a better commercial gallery situation.

The prestige of a museum exhibition can be used as the rationale to contact again, or for the first time, galleries where you reside. You will never have more clout with a commercial gallery than when you have a one-person show at a well-respected institution.

102

*Strategy is a style of thinking, a conscious and deliberate process, an intensive implementation system, the science of inspiring future success.*

PETE JOHNSON

For example, if an artist based in New York City is without gallery affiliation, but has an exhibition scheduled at a museum in southwestern Texas, it is good strategy to approach four commercial areas simultaneously: 1) galleries within a 150 mile radius of the museum; 2) in larger metropolitan areas within the state, such as Dallas, Houston, San Antonio, and Austin; 3) within the region, i.e., Denver, Santa Fe, Oklahoma City, Tulsa, etc.; and 4) New York City.

**Twin Carburetors: Nonprofits and Commercial Galleries**

Most curators at Level III museums would hesitate to host a one-person exhibition for an artist unless he or she has high-powered gallery affiliations in major cities, received reviews in regional and/or national publications, and secured important nonprofit exhibitions. Alternatively an important collector or several collectors, who are patrons and supporters of the museum, might need to personally introduce your work to the director or curator, and/or donate your work to the museum's collection.

Most established mid-level or above galleries in major metropolitan centers would not consider exhibiting an artist unless he or she has had a one-person exhibition at a Level II museum. A one-person exhibition in a Level III museum could lead to making a high-level gallery affiliation.

Perhaps the Level III institutions in your region have included you in thematic exhibitions or smaller group shows. If so, it might be worth setting up an appointment with the director or curator to inquire how they decide to offer an artist a one- or two-person exhibition. What are the qualities they look for? Level of accomplishment? Recognition by respected critics? Are there other personal attributes that can factor into the decision-making process?

It may just come down to actual road experience. Some Level III curators may feel that ten years of professional involvement is way too early in the game for a one-person exhibition, and may only consider artists with a national exhibition record established over several decades. Find the answers to your questions so you don't waste valuable time pursuing a situation that is years from being realized.

It is important, when preparing for a meeting with a director or curator, to remember that you would never have been included in a group or thematic exhibition if the curator did not respect your work.

## Profiling Whitney Biennial and Carnegie International Participants

The following represents the venues and some major exhibitions in which Whitney Biennial and Carnegie International artists have exhibited:

Aldrich Contemporary Art Museum, Ridgefield, CT

Art in General, New York City

Art Space, San Antonio, TX

Atlanta Contemporary Art Center, GA

"Prospect. 1, New Orleans," Contemporary Art Center, New Orleans, LA

Contemporary Arts Center, Cincinnati, OH

California Biennial, Orange County Museum of Art, Newport Beach

California College of the Arts, Berkeley and San Francisco

CEPA Gallery, Buffalo, NY

Corcoran Gallery of Art, Washington, DC

Hirshhorn Museum and Sculpture Garden, Washington, DC

Institute of Contemporary Art, Boston, MA

International Center of Photography, New York City

List Visual Arts Center, Massachusetts Institute of Technology, Cambridge

MASS MoCA (Massachusetts Museum of Contemporary Art), North Adams

Mattress Factory, Pittsburgh, PA

Museum of Contemporary Art, Chicago, IL

Museum of Contemporary Art, Los Angeles, CA

Institute for Contemporary Art, Philadelphia, PA

P.S.1 Contemporary Art Center/Museum of Modern Art, Long Island City, NY

SECCA (Southeastern Center for Contemporary Art), Winston-Salem, NC

SITE Santa Fe, NM

Wexner Center for the Arts, Columbus, OH

Williams College Museum of Art, Williamstown, MA

---

*Opportunities are usually disguised as hard work, so most people don't recognize them.*

--ANN LANDERS

It also helps to recognize the complex dynamics that may be operating in a given situation – between the director of the museum and the curator, the director and/or curator's role on the exhibition committee, and their respective relationships with board members and patrons. All these dynamics factor into any decision-making process.

**High Octane: Choosing Competitive Exhibitions**

Another approach to developing a national exhibition record is to identify the most important annuals, biennials, and invitational exhibitions held at Level III and Elite institutions in the largest cities nationwide. These are not the same mid-level juried and competitive exhibitions that you did in Stage One – and in a limited way – in Stage Two. In Stage Three you are systematically identifying the most important competitive opportunities across the country, at the most prestigious, high-powered venues.

Inclusion in one of these exhibitions constitutes a major career accomplishment. There are almost always catalogues, which include a juror's or curator's statement. Curators and dealers throughout the state and region use these catalogues for reference. You can also use the catalogue for your own promotional purposes.

It is almost guaranteed that these exhibitions will be reviewed in the local papers and regional publications. Also, when included in an exhibition, you can contact art critics and the press in your own city, state, and region to keep them informed of your activities.

To judge whether you are ready for consideration, study the career high points of the artists who have been included in major group exhibitions in Level III and Elite museums around the country. Study the Whitney Biennial or Carnegie International catalogues from the last decade to see the accomplishments of the participants. Review coverage in the major art magazines to see what characteristics may be common to these artists and the professional experiences they may share.

**Getting on the Race Team: Participating in Group Exhibitions Nationwide**

To be considered for these prestigious exhibitions, begin by contacting the institution through e-mail to ask for more information about the exhibition. Inquire if a prospectus is available and about the proper guidelines for submission.

You could also send an introductory package to the museum with a CD, indicating your desire to have your work considered for appropriate thematic or invitational group exhibitions.

A panel of three or more professionals often makes selections for shows like these. Not being chosen for a specific exhibition does not preclude inclusion in others. A curator on the jury may find your work engaging, but other jurors may not share his or her enthusiasm. However, he or she may be planning another group or thematic exhibition, and wish to retain your submission for consideration and possible inclusion.

**High-Performance Engines: What Attributes Are Galleries Looking For?**

To an established and seasoned dealer, your most valuable accomplishments are your museum exhibitions, inclusion in museum collections, and your sales history. In many mid-level and above galleries in New York City, it is a prerequisite for representation to be included in both museum collections and/or have one-person museum exhibitions. In terms of importance, this would likely be followed by inclusion in important public, private, or corporate collections. Where your work has been reviewed is also a factor in gaining a dealer's and/or collector's confidence. Reaching these milestones validates your status and helps to establish the value of your work.

These achievements are the dealer's selling tools. Without verifiable credentials, it is difficult to determine the actual worth of a piece of art or to convey that to a collector. Even if the dealer believes your work has exceptional promise, without a track record, you may represent little more than a financial risk that he or she may be unwilling to take.

---

## Establishing Your Bona Fides

Usually by the time artists get into the important biennials, they've already been showing regularly in well-known galleries. They may, however, get a big boost from new exposure in key events, like the Whitney Biennial, the Carnegie International (every four years or so), the New Museum's Generational (every three years), SITE Santa Fe, and P.S.1's "Greater New York Roundup."

Then there are all those satellite fairs that cluster around the Armory Show in New York City and Art Basel Miami: Scope, Pool, Bridge, Red Dot, Pulse, and Volta (maybe the best), etc.

Residency programs can launch an artist with studio visits from professionals and group shows at their conclusion. Some notable programs include Core at the Museum of Fine Arts, Houston; Art Omi International Artists Residency, Ghent, NY; and the International Studio & Curatorial Program, Brooklyn.

Richard Vine

---

*Doing is better than saying.*

UNKNOWN

## The Ideal Artist Client

- Experienced and mature

- Operates in reality

- Conveys goals clearly

- Plans ahead

- Has reasonable expectations

- Exhibits professional and considerate conduct

- Steady and dependable

- Confident, not needy or over-anxious

- Low-maintenance

*Satisfaction lies in the effort, not in the attainment. Full effort is full victory.*

MAHATMA GANDHI

There are a few dealers who focus on emerging artists (see "The 'E' Word," p. 193) and who work with collectors who thrive on the excitement of bringing new talent to the forefront, but this is the exception, not the rule. (To be an "emerging talent" in a prominent New York City gallery usually means you've already come up through the ranks elsewhere.) It takes a very smooth operator to convince a serious collector to invest in an unknown regardless of promise or potential, unless, of course, the risk is the thrill.

### Track Record: Demonstrating Sales Potential

If you do not reside in the area, it is unlikely your collectors and other contacts will frequent the gallery, attend openings, and purchase work. These are reasons why dealers prefer to partner with artists who live nearby, have extensive exhibition experience, a strong sales record, and important contacts with collectors and the press.

You have more leverage in securing gallery representation outside your region if several of your collectors commit to making a purchase from your exhibition in advance of the opening. Although this may seem like a tall order, having the power and connections to insure the sale of several works from your exhibition could alleviate some of the dealer's concern about representing an out-of-towner, and make the risk a little more attractive.

If you've carefully cultivated your collectors, given them price breaks when they've referred buyers to you or made important introductions for you, and you've invited them to tangentially participate in your career successes (preferably for a decade or more), some may go the extra mile to support you.

This begs a number of questions about your collectors that require serious consideration. Who of your core base of perhaps 20 to 30 collectors would fly from Los Angeles to New York City to attend your first Manhattan opening? Who of these collectors has the resources to come to New York City for the weekend, and also to purchase a work of art from your show? Who has the power and the motivation to put together a contingent of people – personal friends and business contacts – to attend your opening, and to purchase a piece of art? How many of your collectors do you actually know well enough to sit down and strategize for a successful exhibition?

A strong sales record goes hand in hand with your ability to ask your collectors for their ongoing support, including recommendations and suggestions of who may be an important contact or potential buyer. You must be willing to ask the home team for its support if you ever hope to generate significant income from the sale of artwork. And like it or not, in the early years of affiliation, or the first few shows with a gallery, the success of your relationship with a dealer will either succeed or fail based on the loyal support of your collecting base.

Artists have difficulty believing what is actually required of them to succeed. On some level it is natural for everyone to wish for someone to take care of him or her and to be provided with financial security. But it is incumbent upon artists to assume full responsibility for making personal sacrifices and taking professional gambles. Acting in your own best interest is not selfish.

**An Experienced Traveler: Maximizing Trip Efficiency**
Any trip you take can advance your career. Approach each journey as a fact-finding and contact-making mission. National travel can set the stage for cultivating relationships with movers and shakers operating at higher levels within the art world.

You already know what needs to be done in advance from Stages One and Two, and you will begin this process long before your arrival by doing thorough research prior to making personal contact. Identify the steps needed to accomplish specific tasks when you arrive at your destination. Your goals represent your "plan of action."

Careful orchestration of your plans, made well in advance, will help to motivate and direct you, and lead to unexpectedly exciting results from your trips.

If your trip is predicated on a specific outcome, it should be realistically within your reach. You'll be expending time, energy, and money – tax deductible – so maximize your efforts.

Even if you are visiting family, friends, or other artists, there are opportunities to gain first-hand knowledge about the area – organizations and people who can advance your career. Traveling to see an exhibition or attend the opening of a friend's exhibition also offers opportunities for your own career advancement.

*The person who asks for little deserves nothing.*
MEXICAN PROVERB

*Grab a chance and you won't be sorry for a might have been.*

ARTHUR RANSOME

### Geared for Success: Plan of Action

Even if you are making a short trip, the same preparations are required to make the best and most productive use of time away from your studio.

Make a pact with yourself to schedule at least three formal appointments. Pursue all the contacts – curators, dealers, consultants, designers, architects, collectors, critics, and others – that will be advantageous to you.

Schedule studio visits with at least one local artist during your visit. Start by meeting with artists you know or who may be part of your gallery. They may suggest other artists to contact in the area.

If you are attending an exhibition of your work, invite the local art elite to meet you at the gallery or museum to discuss your work. Offer to take them for drinks or dinner. As it is preferable to remain in town during the run of a commercial gallery exhibition, you may wish to seek a temporary or extended stay situation.

Always take advantage of your upcoming one-person exhibition to introduce yourself to other important curators, and do the same when you have been included in a major group exhibition at a Level III or Elite museum.

Keep appropriate galleries in mind that are located in metropolitan areas surrounding these exhibitions because dealers nearby could easily see your work. Inviting a museum contact from a Level III or Elite museum to view your gallery exhibition may lead to inclusion in a group exhibition.

There may be a unique professional situation in the area that is necessary to the execution of your work and ideas, such as an atelier or master printer that you prefer to make contact with in person.

As a recipient of a grant for a residency elsewhere in the country, you can use the opportunity to create new work and to make valuable professional contacts on location.

A promising situation exists when a consultant expresses serious interest in your work. An appointment with a corporate consultant may lead to a major commission, which would bring you back to the area for a longer period of time.

Positive outcomes for your trips may include a soirée given by your collector, which provides the opportunity to meet other collectors, and/or perhaps an important art critic. A collector may invite you to install your work and concurrently host a party on your behalf.

An artist may tip you off to a living/studio space that will become available in three- to four-month's time, which is perfect for your plans if you are seeking to relocate permanently or just make an extended visit.

Even actions that do not achieve the desired outcome can be a positive experience. For example, learning that a gallery is not the right fit may be as valuable as making a gallery contact that leads to an affiliation. It is just as vital to your future plans to know where you do not belong.

### Reconnaissance: Relocating

At Stage Three, you may be considering a major geographic move to advance your career. Having visited the area to get a feel for the opportunities that await you, your trips will become reconnaissance missions. You will be making a life-changing decision so a comprehensive understanding of the desired locale is crucial. Nothing beats having firsthand knowledge about any situation to ascertain if a move will benefit you.

While visiting the area, check real estate options for work and/or living space. Evaluate opportunities for professional development. You may be able to interview for employment, such as a teaching position or some other job that is compatible with your artistic endeavors. You might even begin to interview for potential administrative and/or studio assistants.

Your ultimate success rests on your determination and diligence. However, what is the most rewarding aspect of this process is *knowing* you exercised all options available in a given situation, and that you used your time and resources in a truly advantageous manner.

Arriving someplace worthwhile will not occur by chance or luck alone, coincidence or happenstance. Being deserving doesn't count. No one can rise on talent alone, and genius guarantees nothing in the world of art.

*A moment's insight is sometimes worth a life's experience.*

OLIVER WENDELL HOLMES

**Stage Three Goals: National**

- Administrative assistant three days per week; studio assistant three days per week, or alternating weeks

- Investment in advertising and promotion of $10,000 to $15,000 per year

- Supported primarily from the sale of your work, repeat purchases by collectors, gallery sales, consultants, commissions, direct sales to corporate, and public and private sectors in the range of $100,000 to $200,000 per year or higher

- Average two-to-three one-person exhibitions annually at Level II and III institutions

- Participation in major thematic curated group exhibitions, invitationals, annuals, biennials, etc., at Level III and Elite institutions in the largest US cities

- Works acquired by museums for their collections through direct contact and sale or through mid- to high-level gallery affiliations

- National media coverage by leading art writers and art critics with affiliation to national and international magazines and newspapers; personal relationships with leading critics and writers

- Established and budding relationships with museum directors and curators nationally, continued contact with professionals in your state and region who will promote your work to other museums, collectors, and the press

- Gallery representation by major, high-level or blue-chip galleries in the cultural capitals of the US

# Conclusion: Reaching Your Destination

CHAPTER 9
# Conclusion: Reaching Your Destination

*The pilgrimage to Santiago de Compostela, Spain, began in the ninth century. The Apostle St. James (Santiago) was the first apostle to be martyred, and the only of the Apostles to be buried in Western Europe. Beheaded by Herod in 44 CE, his disciples eventually transported his bones by ship to Spain and buried the remains on a hill (Compostela). Then, no word of Santiago for nearly 750 years. In 813, a Christian hermit by the name of Pelayo saw lights over a small cave on a hill in the woods. Digging on the site, he found the bones of the Apostle and two of his disciples; the Cathedral of Santiago de Compostela was built on this site.*

*In 852, at the decisive battle between the Muslim and Christian armies near Logrono, Santiago appeared mounted on his white horse, and led the Christian army to victory. He became Santiago the Moorslayer.*

*The Way of St. James – El Camino – was the most significant spiritual pilgrimage of the Middle Ages. Supposedly El Camino follows the earth's ley lines, beginning in France, across the Pyrenees, northwest to the site where the bones of St. James were found buried. A spiritual journey and quest, and a physical test (of close to 500 miles) of endurance and commitment, traveling El Camino represents, for many, the transformational experience of a lifetime.*

● ● ●

In closing, before you proceed to the chapters by the Associates and other contributors, I wanted to give you something to fuel thought, and just a few more bumper slogans to reflect upon. I hope you will find these observations reassuring as you encounter the various curves, detours, and roadblocks along the way.

If you are willing to anticipate encountering an occasional obstacle, and can remain open to making adjustments and modifications to your roadmap when necessary, you will not only master the road, but yourself as well. Any setback can present an opportunity, so train your mind to desire the best possible outcome from any challenge – then your journey can become what you have decided it will be.

For myself, I had a long-held dream to walk the El Camino from Roncesvalles, near the French border, across Spain to Santiago de Compostela. When I was finally able to make the time in my personal life to fulfill this dream, the journey was not all I had hoped. I planned and planned, and prepared physically for months on end. I left my business for more than six weeks to make the pilgrimage; even so, it was by no means a perfect crossing – far from it. It was fraught with challenges and frequent disappointment. But

*As you master the road, you'll master yourself.*

KTC

*There are an infinite number of permutations*
*to the meaning of success.*
                        KTC

I was determined I would press on to completion, regardless of the situation in which I found myself. It was my commitment, in spite of the unforeseen difficulties, that transformed the experience for me.

We should all be willing to define our success in a number of ways: personally, professionally, spiritually, physically, mentally, emotionally, and financially. If you can establish priorities and decide where to focus your attention, you will transform the meaning of your encounters along the road. There will be times when your priorities will need to be reevaluated, and you'll decide to take another route. Or you may even elect to leave the road while you temporarily shift your attention elsewhere, but in doing so, you might revitalize your desire and enthusiasm to continue. Positive and constructive thinking will definitely contribute to your sense of purpose and clarity, and are necessary for reaching your desired objectives.

I am still goal oriented, but much more driven towards personal fulfillment; my goals have changed, as has my definition of success. In my early years, I was a less flexible, no-nonsense person traveling directly toward a point on the horizon. At the end of each year, I put down my goals in writing, and compiled long detailed lists of my intended outcomes in a host of categories that I promised myself I would complete the following year.

This system worked well for about a decade, between 1994 and 2004. I was able to review my goals on a regular basis, and as the year came to a close, I could assess what I had accomplished and if my goals had been achieved. I knew what still remained unrealized, and, if appropriate, I would bring these tasks forward into the next year. On New Year's Eve, at around 2:00 pm, I would meet up with my administrator, Dudley MacKinlay, at my offices, and we would work on the next year's roadmap. This became an annual tradition and was invaluable to the progress I made on my journey – as was Dudley's friendship in this rather tedious process of unfolding.

I listed financial and business goals, personal, emotional, spiritual, and physical goals, and long-range goals. I had a mission, an ultimate goal, and hoped-for outcome. This was the most critical component, and defining my mission helped me to better clarify my other goals because it gave a larger, more meaningful rationale to my efforts.

*"No" only means "Not right now."*
                        KTC

*Luck is not a lady, and some maiden voyages have been disastrous.*

KTC

For example, my mission under physical goals was self-care – to put my physical well being first and foremost. Then it would follow that my ultimate goal was increased energy and the ability to focus on personal and professional achievement, as well as financial security. In retrospect, and to put this in some kind of context, it did require enormous physical endurance to travel 200 days per year giving lectures and workshops nationwide.

My ultimate lifetime goal was, and still is, peace of mind. My journey on the El Camino was the ultimate road to physical and spiritual well-being. After I made the crossing in 2004, I decided not to make lists anymore because I felt my life purpose was no longer ambiguous. Nevertheless, these carefully stated goals were invaluable to my progress during that decade of my life.

There is a famous quote, "Fall seven times, stand up eight." I don't remember who said it, or where I read it, but it has stayed with me, part of my ongoing quote collection started in the beginning years of the company. You can decide to come away from any experience on the road with greater understanding. There are always other opportunities, and the next time you can be better prepared, more thorough with planning, and, consequently, a lot more confident going into the situation. Regardless of what happens, you must get back behind the wheel and keep driving – so don't confuse a flat tire or fender bender with serious engine trouble. Think of it as just another bump along the road. Endurance is born out of your willingness to soldier on no matter what.

I can still remember with genuine mortification a particular experience I had during the decade I spent on the road presenting the "Highlights of the New York Art Season" and "Marketing and Promotional Strategies for the Professional Artist." I had received an invitation from the chair of the art department at the University of Wisconsin, Madison, to present my lecture and workshop to students, faculty, university and general audiences. At this point, I had already been on the road as a public speaker for nearly four years. My policy was to never have any alcohol until my speaking responsibilities were fulfilled. In this instance, I left the house for Newark International at 5:00 am, arrived in Madison late morning, had lunch with faculty and staff from the museum and art center, which was followed by a tour of the current exhibition at the Elvehjem Museum (now called the Chazen Museum of Art). The chair then invited me to a local pub to share a pitcher; it

*Nobody gets it right all the time – nobody.*

KTC

was only 3:00 pm, so "no problem," or so I thought. I returned to my room by 5:00 pm for a short nap and shower before the 7:00 pm presentation.

Arriving at the auditorium of the Elvehjem Museum, I found the podium was set midway on the stage and in front of a huge screen. The slide changing mechanism for the carousel was stretched taut from an electrical outlet at the front of the stage to the corner edge of the podium. Well, that damned thing flew off the podium no less than three times during my "Highlights" presentation. I could never really regain my composure and although I did get through the lecture, I cannot, even today recall a more unnerving situation in the close to 1,000 public lectures I presented in over 200 venues.

It was probably the stress of travel and length of day. Maybe if I hadn't had those two beers and taken a nap, I might have had the presence of mind to request a more manageable set up on stage. Anyway I swore my speaking career was over. I had three more weeks of engagements in the Midwest, and I intended to come in from the road and retire – that was in about 1988 or 1989.

Of course, I felt I had let my host down, and far worse, myself. I returned home to the Jersey Shore, rested physically, and reflected. I read a slew of self-help books and got over it. I'm not sure what my life would be like today if I'd stopped trying. I surely would not have this company or the company of Associates I have today, which calls to mind another favorite quote: "Failure is nothing but success trying to be reborn in a bigger way."

Developing your intuition and inner compass can help you avoid potentially hazardous situations in the future. Being in control when taking a curve is crucial to successful navigation.

Regularly exercising your inner decision-making muscles, being awake and aware, is a better plan than constantly needing to ask the advice of others. But when you do encounter circumstances for which you are totally unprepared, there is nothing wrong with seeking counsel. However, never lose sight that in the end, you must be willing to own your decision and the outcome. Selecting the most direct route to your destination while steering clear of problematic situations, and seeking solutions to your problems from informed professionals is just good, basic common sense.

*Success is (A)about (B)being (C)conscious.*

KTC

*Not counting on anyone other than yourself is the best idea
going, but asking for help when you need it is just smart thinking.*

KTC

I never quite understood why someone else with a critical and/or scholarly background had not developed an annual slide lecture giving an overview of the museum and gallery exhibition season in New York City. To my knowledge it appeared nothing really comprehensive was being offered by anyone else.

It was the mid-'80s in New York City, an incredibly exciting moment in the art world, and everyone everywhere seemed to want to know more about what was going on. I realized developing the lecture would involve attending hundreds of exhibitions, obtaining visual documentation, researching the 50 to 60 artists I chose for inclusion, writing the lecture program, and then marketing it nationally. It was a tall order, which was perhaps why no one else had wanted to undertake it, but it was the only idea I could conjure since I was no longer interested in college-level teaching.

Maybe it was a combination of blind ambition and naiveté, or my sheer force of will to survive, but I tackled all of the above and developed a mailing list of over 3,000 museums, art centers, professional art organizations, colleges, universities, community centers, and private schools. I did all the research, hired a hotshot computer programmer from Princeton University, Jay Lieske (who was trained at Stanford), to enter all the data, produced a very basic marketing brochure, collected and assembled the reviews and coverage on the artists selected, and wrote basic descriptions of the work. I also included other anecdotal or corroborated hearsay and gossip, because I knew this would give the lecture some color.

I knew I was not a writer. I was a studio artist with only the required undergraduate and graduate courses in art history to my credit. Under no circumstances was I equipped to fine-tune the presentation. What I needed was someone who could help me rev-up the presentations and polish the content – a historian and wordsmith. John Mendelsohn was that person – a close friend who was not only knowledgeable, but whose writing talents helped give wings to this series; John made the descriptions of some of the work pure poetry. This was actually the beginning of Katharine T. Carter & Associates.

We all have different talents – mine were as a public speaker and marketing intuitive. Hard work and commitment are my forte. However, a writer, scholar, and art critic I am not. I asked for help when I needed it, and as an artist you should do the same.

*Everyone takes their cue from you.*

KTC

*No one has the answers so you will want to find your own.*

KTC

If you don't know what to do next and you need help, make it a point to get the advice and assistance you need to reach your goals and live out your dreams. Do whatever it takes to get the job done – without excuses or apologies. Not counting on anyone other than yourself is the best idea going, but asking for help when you need it is just smart thinking.

I often reflect on a puzzling "condition of mind" that I have encountered fairly frequently over the years. I have met, known, and worked with some highly intelligent and capable individuals. Some were excellent facilitators, geared toward tangible outcomes, and others were trapped in the labyrinth of their own minds – unable to take action that corresponded to their mental capacities.

I also came to another conclusion a good while back regarding mental gymnastics and acquiring useless information in the service of posturing and careerism. If you really want to accomplish something of value, it is imperative to get out of your own way and just do what needs to get done. In short, you can think and think, and still sink, so just get to work.

Yet I always maintained that where artists are concerned, they are actually more balanced between left- and right-side functions and capacities of the brain than we realize. For example, I imagine that an artist could not conceive, create, formally compose, or resolve a work of art without both lobes firing off signals, if not simultaneously, then at least occasionally or coincidentally. I have no background in science or psychology, but I'm quite certain that artists can be creative in business. My take on the standard excuse is that it is an avoidance mechanism because no one enjoys rejection, or it could be a refusal to accept full responsibility for outcomes – or just preferring to assume the mythical maladjusted role associated with artistic types.

My late Associate, the critic Gerrit Henry wrote, "The paradigm of the moody and childlike artist no longer holds professional water. Today's artist must be, to a large degree, self-generated, self-motivated, self-determining, and with the right help, today can be."

I can still remember what William Zimmer said to me in the lobby of the Algonquin Hotel the last year of his life. We were having drinks together, as we often did when I was in New York City. He turned to me and said, in an off-handed way, that he had reached

*Knowing and believing aren't even in the same galaxy.*

KTC

*You can think and think and still sink, so just get to work.*

KTC

the conclusion that all the extensive information he'd acquired had little value or meaning. St. Thomas Aquinas also once said, "All my works seem like straw after what I have seen."

Although both statements clearly refer to a level of enlightenment where such intellectual trappings become meaningless, I do think it a good idea to reserve your energy for the truly important "thinks" and create your life by doing the work you were meant to do – and to endeavor to share those unique gifts with the world as was very likely intended.

During the last 25 years, I'd venture to say I've done close to a thousand studio visits and one-on-one consultations, and I've witnessed and listened to a surprisingly large number of artists who want to opt for confusion and lack of direction, instead of clarity of purpose.

There are three or four stumbling blocks that artists repeatedly encounter on the road to becoming. The first is the refusal to choose a clear direction from multiple areas of investigation. This is necessary in order to pursue, in depth, a unified body of work, and to actually develop the courage needed to see where this will lead over a period of time. The second difficulty lies with committing to a timeline of actions, and the third, and total clincher, is failing to implement a promotional plan.

Each one of these components of activity must be dealt with head on if an artist wants to end his or her confusion and inertia. Without the ability to create a structure within which a serious investigation can occur, a serious body of work may never evolve.

About 15 years ago, I met an artist who was talented, brilliant, well read in endless subjects relating to art, science, and music. At the time of our meeting, he was well into his span of life, somewhere in his 70s. I went to his loft studio where he had lived some 30 years or more. There were over a thousand works on canvas and paper, but he had never had a New York City show of consequence. He was completely out of touch with the art world, and had his share of disappointing stories to tell. He had withdrawn into his own world, a life in the studio, and the relationship he shared with his work.

Then, all of a sudden, he decided the work was deserving of inclusion in the Whitney Biennial. Now he was ready to connect with museum and gallery directors. It was as if

*Most people need to think they know more than you do, so let them; reserve your energy for the truly important "thinks."*

KTC

he believed this was a business where you could suddenly determine "your time has come" and be offered fame entirely on the merit of the work. Of course, this was not reality, and although I knew I could be of some assistance, without a track record, it would be very difficult.

It is farfetched for artists to imagine that they, in the twilight years, will somehow be miraculously discovered, that everyone important will take an interest in their work, and that, in very short order, they can rise to great heights of professional recognition. Although at certain times the economic, cultural, and critical stars have aligned to create an atmosphere that allows for the sudden emergence of a wave of "art stars" (the aforementioned New York City in the '80s being a strong example), this is far from the norm in my 32 years of experience since inclusion in my first major exhibition in New York City in 1978 at the New Museum.

We are already equipped to accomplish great things – all that is needed is to commit yourself to it. Why is it so difficult for artists to understand that a curator or gallerist would choose to work with an artist who has involved his or herself in the thick of the struggle? Why would they choose an artist who has refused to participate, take any risks, or share his or her gifts in the spirit of possibility?

There are thousands of artists in the New York City environs, with enormous bodies of work to their credit. Many are artists who have entered into the flow of professional life full-force, who exhibit when and where they can, sometimes in small galleries off the beaten path or alternative spaces, in group shows in the ongoing struggle to obtain greater exposure for their work. These are artists who share their work with as many people as possible, who do endless reciprocal studio visits, who never stop giving to their life's work, and sometimes even more to their teaching responsibilities. These artists have taken the risks in spite of the odds – and as a result, they have had unanticipated opportunities and surprises. Unexpected circumstances have presented themselves, and they have extended their sphere of influence beyond what even they imagined to be possible. And remarkably they continue to survive with hope intact.

I will never devalue thorough planning, developing an extensive and detailed itinerary, and defining goals, as this approach has served me well over the years. But our best-laid plans

120

*You paint a masterpiece the same way you botched the previous piece; you try again.*

KTC

must often be adjusted or altered, sometimes even abandoned. The outcome can astonish, and even shock, but there can be untold value in turning failures into opportunities and creating positive outcomes for growth and transformation – a stepping stone for future professional achievement.

As I traveled most of the Camino alone, I became less fearful of outcomes; even my physical safety seemed almost entirely beyond control. Remarkably, I settled into a more accepting way of being in my life on the road. I would sometimes walk until close to 10:00 pm, as it stayed light during the summer nights until a later hour than in the States. I would, on occasion, see other pilgrims; I would get familiar with some faces, and we would nod as we passed each other during our travels. There were very few Americans, mostly Europeans – Spaniards or Germans.

It was the final 180 kilometers into Santiago that were the most magical for me, but what I am really discussing here is continuing on to your final destination. When I entered the city at 10:00 am, it was on the Feast of St. James, one of the holiest days of the year for Catholics (of which I am not). It never occurred to me that there would not be ample time to reach Santiago's statue and kiss his head, a tradition practiced by pilgrims of the Camino for more than 1,000 years.

To my complete astonishment, there were literally hundreds of people in line. Unbeknownst to me, the Spanish consider anyone who walks the last 100 kilometers to be a pilgrim, and they were all in the queue. It was nearly noon, and as I reached within a few yards of the statue, a priest stopped the line with me. It was unbelievable. To have walked hundreds of miles to have my journey end like this – I did most certainly begin to dissolve into tears. Then, a man I had seen along the road a few times turned to the priest and said something in Spanish. He then looked at me and said, "I told him you were a true pilgrim, and to let you pass." I reached my destination that day at high noon.

Life is nothing more than an opportunity – one right after another – so move forward with conscious deliberation and allow the magic of your own road to unfold. Reaching your destination is very possibly assured the moment you will commit yourself to it.

*It is your commitment, in spite of unforeseen difficulties, that will transform your life.*

KTC

*Accelerating on the Curves*

BOOK TWO
Mapping It Out:
Templates and Examples of the Elements of
Press Kits and Presentation Packages

*by Henry Auvil, Katharine T. Carter, Karen S. Chambers, and John Mendelsohn*

**The Cover/Pitch Letter**

Even in the age of e-mail and texting, an actual letter (presented on thoughtfully designed letterhead, printed on a paper that is attractive in its own right), accompanied by tangible support materials – photographs, announcement cards, brochures, catalogues, copies of published reviews, résumés, artist statements, etc. – remains a highly effective way of reaching your art-world target. Also it requires the least effort on the recipient's part, which is always a consideration. In many cases, an assistant may even open the package.

This sort of package is much more likely to receive careful attention than an e-mail with attachments that must be downloaded, opened, and then viewed on a monitor that most likely is not calibrated to accurately reflect the artwork's color. This being said, curators and gallerists increasingly cite cost and environmental concerns as argument for artists to present electronically, so you should strive to make your hard copy packages streamlined and highly personalized. Never give the impression that it is part of a random mass mailing.

These introductory letters are called "cover," meaning they accompany a package of information, or "pitch," which promotes a specific proposal or your work in general.

You do not need to reinvent the wheel and compose a completely unique letter to every museum curator, gallerist, designer, architect, consultant, etc., you wish to contact. Each of these represents a category, and you can write a generic letter for that category that can then be customized for each individual case. Here, the more specific information that you can include, the better. If you're writing an architectural firm, name it rather than merely say "your firm." If your works are part of a series, include the title. It gives the recipient more information in an economical way. For example, if your recent series of woodcuts is called "SoHo Nocturnes," the reader immediately has a sense of your direction.

We have provided templates to guide you through the writing process, but do not follow them slavishly. Actual examples show you how the basic elements can be elaborated. Feel free to mix and match paragraphs from the various examples (from the commercial gallery outline to architects) to suit your and their particular needs and audience.

While it is important that you write in your own "voice," avoid a too informal or casual tone. Conversely, never pontificate or self-analyze your work. Although the letter is all about you, try to avoid beginning each paragraph with "I." In general, avoid using 14 words when 7 will do. For example, you can write, "I would like to take this opportunity to introduce you to my work," but the same information is conveyed by "I would like to introduce my work."

You must use the name of your recipient. "To Whom It May Concern" really doesn't concern anyone. Confirm that the name is correctly spelled. Too often your eye glides over the name when proofing, and the misspelling doesn't register. You can have a hair-trigger response to Spell Check's suggestion, so "Hiltope" suddenly becomes "hilltop." Even if you've gone over the spelling with a receptionist, "Ryan" does sometimes become "Brian." And don't trust your memory: "Rockwell" just might morph into "Stonewell" or "Rockman."

Check and double-check because nothing puts off your recipient more than getting the name wrong. And don't forget to make sure you have the gender correct. An extreme example is "Evelyn." It's obviously a feminine name, except in Great Britain.

The first paragraph is a polite introduction, reinforced by the reason you believe the person or institution would be interested in your work. It may be because a respected art-world professional has suggested you write. Or your work may fit into the organization's mission. If you're from Connecticut, an art center dedicated to showcasing New England artists should be approached. The connection may be your medium – drawings for The Drawing Center. This can be followed by a succinct physical description of your artwork, which can include the medium, technique, and influences as well as your intent – one to two sentences maximum.

Next bolster your bona fides by highlighting key accomplishments in your career. Refer to prestigious exhibitions you have participated in, mention writings (your own catalogue or other publications) about your work by respected critics, note awards you have received, prestigious collections, and so on.

Detail what support materials you have included or can provide upon request. Ask that they be retained for the recipient's files for future projects, and suggest ways for the recipient to view your work. There may be an exhibition currently on view and conveniently located, or extend an invitation to visit your studio. You may also suggest making an appointment to meet at the recipient's institution or gallery. And you should explain how you will follow up this communication.

Conclude with a respectful thank you for the recipient's time and attention.

A strategy used in direct-mail letters is to add a PS to reiterate the most important point of your letter. For example, "I look forward to meeting you" or "I hope you have the opportunity to view my exhibition at Art Stadium."

For maximum impact, the letter should be no longer than a single page. More than that almost guarantees a superficial glance by the time-challenged art-world professional reading it. You can elaborate on your career in support materials that are included, such as a chronological résumé or biographical summary; printed matter like announcement cards, brochures, and/or catalogues; a press release; copies of press coverage; photographic prints and/or a CD of images. This is your introduction, with hopefully more substantive exchanges to come, so do not inundate your recipient with more information they may want at this stage. Never combine two bodies of work in one presentation. A messy and overstuffed presentation indicates a lack of discipline and focus. Everything should be coordinated, refined, and pared down to quickly convey the essence of your work and who you are as an artist.

## Business Letter Format

The content is, of course, the most important thing in your letter, but how it is presented constitutes your "first impression." Although there are several accepted formats for business letters, a standard one is as follows. The letter is written on your letterhead, which is simple and elegant. Choose a classic, understated font, and use it consistently in your letters and support materials. It can be either serif or sans serif, but never use a gimmicky font such as a cursive or faux "handwritten" script.

Your name
Your address
Your telephone number/s
E-mail address
Website


Date


Dear Mr./Mrs./Ms. Name:

The first paragraph of the letter gives the reason for writing. It provides a very brief description of the work. *It is two to three sentences maximum.*

The second paragraph relates pinnacle accomplishments. It notes exhibitions, reviews, collections, awards, etc. *It is three to four sentences maximum.*

The third paragraph says how do you intend for the recipient to view your work in person. Outline your follow-up plan specifically. *It is two to three sentences maximum.*


Sincerely,


Your name


Enclosures

## Letters to Directors and Curators of Museums, Art Centers, College and University Galleries, Alternative Spaces, and Other Nonprofit Exhibiting Institutions

### Sample Letter to a Museum Curator

Ms. Beatrice Smith-Colby
Curator
Snyder-Cartwright Institute of Contemporary Art
2400 Southern Boulevard
Dobson, GA 39713

Date

Dear Beatrice:

At the suggestion of Sam Jefferson, contributing editor of the *Southeast Arts Review*, I am forwarding a packet of materials on my mixed media works; Sam felt the work might be of particular interest to the Snyder-Cartwright Institute of Contemporary Art, and mentioned my name to you. The current series refers to layers of history and personal experience, and is directly influenced by my ongoing study of Italian frescos, ruins, and ancient walls.

My solo exhibitions include the Susquehanna Art Museum, PA; Duke University, Durham, NC; the Palazzo Ferretti, Cortona, Italy; and the Franz Meinhof Gallery in Washington, DC. Recently my work was included in the group exhibition "Linked to Landscape," which traveled from the Corcoran Museum, Washington, DC, to the Parthenon, Nashville, TN, and to the Gibbes Museum of Art, Charleston, SC.

I have enclosed written support along with color reproductions of my work. I hope you will retain these materials for your files, and would be pleased to send further information and a CD containing additional available work at your request. I will contact you in the near future to discuss any possible exhibition opportunities at the Snyder-Cartwright.

Sincerely,


Melanie Harrington


Enclosures

**Sample Letter to a Museum Curator**

Ms. Penelope Phelps
Director & Chief Curator
The Wharf Artspace
32 Clementine Street
Norfolk, VA 24005

Date

Dear Penelope:

It was a pleasure to talk with you after your enlightening museum presentation here in Savannah last Tuesday. I am most interested in and impressed by the challenging and diverse programming you are doing at the Wharf Artspace, and, as promised, I am forwarding a package to acquaint you with my work and professional accomplishments. All of this work is a response to "memory experiences": growing up in Alaska, traveling, and moving from place to place – a symbolic retracing of the paths of the ancestors.

As you can see from the attached résumé, the work is in numerous public and private collections, including those of the Indianapolis Museum of Art and the Palm Desert County Museum of Art. I have exhibited extensively in the US and internationally, have been in exhibitions at the Carnegie Institute, the Hirshhorn Museum and Sculpture Garden, the Studio Museum in Harlem, and the Internationale Biennale fur Bildende Kunst in Austria. I received an MFA in scenic design from Yale School of Drama.

I have enclosed support materials including an artist statement, a CD of my most recent work and some recent reviews. I will contact you in the near future, and would be delighted to arrange a studio visit. Thank you for your time and consideration.

Sincerely,



Rebecca Warren


Enclosures

## Sample Letter to the Curator of an Art Center

Mr. Archibald Butler
Curator
Fairfield Hills Center for the Fine Arts
221 Mill Pond Road
Fairfield Hills, CT 01634

Date

Dear Mr. Butler:

I am writing to bring my work and professional accomplishments to your attention. I am also including a brochure to apprise you of the recent direction of my paintings, which contains an essay by Hare Lapin of the *Hartford Courier*. I feel the work may be of interest because of the regional focus of the Center's mission.

My work has been shown in group and solo exhibitions, most recently at the University of Connecticut, Dreyfus Gallery, and James Furnace Fine Art in New York, and the Barrett Fine Art Gallery, Utica College, NY. The work is included in both museum and public collections, including the National Museum of Women in Art, Washington, DC, and the Municipal Institute of America, Dayton, OH. I received an MA from Wesleyan University, and I live and work in Greenwich, CT.

I have enclosed an artist statement, résumé, and a CD of current available work; I will call in follow-up to ascertain if additional information is necessary. I will keep you abreast of my future involvements, and look forward to speaking with you in the near future.

Sincerely,


Anastasia Connors


Enclosures

## Commercial Galleries, Private Dealers, and Art Consultants

The thing that differentiates letters to commercial galleries, private dealers, art consultants as well as other sales opportunities, from other letters you may write is that the reader's primary concern is "Is your work saleable?" Have you already established a base of collectors?

A corollary to that is: are you a professional who can be counted on to continue making saleable work? Galleries are not interested in one-hit wonders.

Nothing grabs a dealer quicker than a recommendation from another artist in the gallery's stable or another respected artist or art-world professional, such as a curator, critic, or collector. So this is included in your opening sentence.

If you don't have that entrée, then you should elucidate why you believe this particular gallery would be interested in your work. Contacting a gallery known for representing abstract painting, when you do realist sculpture, wastes everyone's time. Do your research, which is ideally backed up by actual visits to the gallery.

To summarize, the first paragraph is simply an introduction; use whatever wording reflects your own style of expression.

In the second paragraph, which is no more than three to four sentences, highlight the most significant achievements of your artistic career: exhibitions, reviews, collections, upcoming exhibitions of note.

In these letters, you want to emphasize that you are a seasoned professional with career achievements – exhibitions, media attention, and sales to your credit.

The closing paragraph mentions that you've enclosed a résumé and other support materials, and can provide additional information upon request; you can mention that the recipient can retain all of this for future consideration. You outline your plan of action, what your intentions are for follow-up and follow-through. Do you want to arrange an appointment in the gallery or a studio visit? Is your work currently in an exhibition nearby? Conclude by thanking the recipient for his or her consideration, but never close passively – always indicate that follow-up will be forthcoming.

Your target is in business, and your approach must be businesslike – exact, clear, and never florid or overly personal.

**Sample Letter to a Gallery Director**

Ms. Choire DeLaplaine
DeLaplaine Contemporary Fine Art
410 Mission Drive
Santa Barbara, CA 95612

Date

Dear Ms. DeLaplaine:

At your request, I am forwarding a presentation on my paintings, recently exhibited in a one-person exhibition at the Bakersfield Museum of Art. Sam Sheehan, critic from the *Los Angeles Tribune* suggested I contact you, as the gallery has a focus on representational work by California artists.

The work has been widely shown in both group and one-person exhibitions including Memorial Union, University of Wisconsin, Madison; State University of New York, Potsdam; DeVos Art Museum, Marquette, MI; Ellen Noel Art Museum, Odessa, TX; Walton Art Center, Fayetteville, AR, among many others. The work is in numerous corporate and private collections, many in Southern California. For your review I have enclosed a résumé with a separate listing of collections, as well as a CD containing several related bodies of work.

I will contact you in the near future to discuss possible representation or exhibition opportunities at Delaplaine Contemporary Fine Art. I would be delighted to arrange a studio visit if you plan to be in the San Francisco Bay Area. Thank you for your time and consideration, and I look forward to speaking with you in person.

Sincerely,

Paul Stephano

Enclosures

## Sample Letter to a Gallery Director

Mr. Wayne Sinclair
Director
Sinclair Fine Art
216 Ferry Lane
Atlanta, GA 39713

Date

Dear Mr. Sinclair:

I am forwarding a packet of materials on my mixed media works, which will be the subject of a one-person exhibition at the Snyder-Cartwright Institute of Contemporary Art in Dobson, GA, in the spring of next year. I have reviewed your stable of artists, and feel my work could be a good fit within your current lineup. I am most interested in securing representation in Atlanta to coincide with this retrospective exhibition, which will likely garner several reviews in regional publications.

I am a resident of Annapolis, MD, and have exhibited extensively in the Mid-Atlantic and Southeast regions; solo exhibitions include the Huntsville Museum of Art, AL; Duke University, Durham, NC; the Palazzo Ferretti, Cortona, Italy, as well as the Franz Bader Gallery in Washington, DC. I was included in the group exhibition "Linked to Landscape," which recently traveled from the Corcoran Museum to the Georgia Institute of Contemporary Art. My work is in many private and corporate collections, including those of the Lapin Corporation and the National Institute of Health. Reviews have appeared in *Art Papers*, *ARTnews*, and the *Atlanta Constitution*.

I have enclosed written support and color reproductions, as well as a CD featuring several bodies of work. I will be traveling to Georgia on several occasions prior to the opening of the exhibition and would welcome the opportunity to meet with you. Thank you for your time and consideration.

Sincerely,

Melanie Harrington

Enclosures

## Sample Letter to a Gallery Director

Mr. Ryan Montgomery
Montgomery Contemporary
267 Chase Avenue
Chicago, IL 60614

Date

Dear Mr. Montgomery:

I would like to introduce my work and professional accomplishments. I have long followed the artists you represent and felt, that with your strong commitment to abstraction, my mixed-media paintings and monoprints might strike a chord. I have been exhibiting nationally since 1972, and I am especially eager to have representation in Chicago.

As you can see from the attached résumé, my work has received extensive media coverage and is in numerous public and private collections, including the Indianapolis Museum of Art and the John D. Rockinghorse Collection. I have exhibited extensively in the US and internationally; most recently in group exhibitions at the Carnegie Institute, Cleveland, OH; the Hirshhorn Museum and Sculpture Garden, the Studio Museum in Harlem, and the Internationale Biennale fur Bildende Kunst in Austria.

I have an extensive inventory of works on canvas and paper, including monoprints. Enclosed please find a CD/PDF with written support materials and currently available works. Thank you for your time and consideration and I will call in follow-up to this submission.

Sincerely,

Rebecca Warren

Enclosures

**Interior Designers, Architects, Landscape Architects, and Art Consultants**

What differentiates letters to interior designers, architects, landscape architects, and occasionally art consultants, is the potential for commissions. It is preferable to cite specific works that you have created and placed. Alternatively, make it very clear that you welcome the challenge of commissions.

If you are offering completed works, include images of available pieces, with a price list upon request, and indicate a general price range.

It is the client's taste that matters and this is who you are seeking to accommodate. This can operate in your favor if you indicate that the work you create can be translated, for example, into tiles or other materials that could be used in large-scale murals or other site-specific applications in corporate venues.

**Sample Letter to an Art Consultant**

Ms. Susan Fredericks
Susan Fredericks Art Consultants, Inc.
3556 SW 14th Street
St. Louis, MO 63104

Date

Dear Ms. Fredericks:

I would like to introduce you to my large-scale watercolor paintings and my professional background. I have provided a brochure and CD to acquaint you with the direction of the recent work, which has proven to have a broad appeal to a range of corporate clients and private collectors.

These works have been exhibited widely in solo exhibitions regionally and nationally and are included in numerous private and corporate collections. Recently, a suite of 12 watercolors was selected for the lobby entrance of the High Priced Hotel in Little Rock, AR. I will be adapting these images into tile for O'Hare Airport in Chicago. I have enclosed a CD with installation shots of these projects and a selection of currently available work. The works are generally in the ?"x?" range and are priced from $? to $?.

Kindly retain these materials for your files, and I will contact you in the near future to learn if there are any projects being planned for which my work may be appropriate. I would be pleased to keep you abreast of my activities in the future.

Sincerely,

Dudley Higgenbothan

Enclosures

**Sample Letter to an Art Consultant**

Ms. Renee Schlesinger
Schlesinger/Pratt & Associates
745 Harrison Avenue
White Plains, NY 13429

Date

Dear Ms. Schlesinger:

It was a pleasure to meet you at the Affordable Art Fair, and thank you for encouraging me to contact you about my work. As I mentioned, I trained as a sculptor, and these paintings are created on built-up clay beds, and then molded onto the canvas. I am confident the work will have a broad appeal to corporate and institutional clients, as well as to private collectors with discriminating tastes.

The work has been exhibited extensively in the Northeastern United States, and is included in major corporate collections such as Engulf & Devour Corp., Better Products, Holstein, Inc., and Max Mutual Life Insurance. I have lived, worked and exhibited in the greater New York City area since 1979; the attached résumé will attest to my various accomplishments and professional involvements.

I have enclosed additional support materials including an artist statement, résumé, a CD of all available work, and a pricelist. I encourage you to retain these materials for your files, and hope that you will consider my work for upcoming projects. I will contact you in the near future.

Sincerely,

Inez Ramirez

Enclosures

**Sample Letter to a Corporate Art Consultant**

Ms. Shelly Summers, Director
Art Solutions, Inc.
2047 Corporate Drive
Albany, NY 12345


Date


Dear Shelly:

I would like to introduce you to my work, which will be the subject of a one-person exhibition this November at the Metropole Opera House in Fredonia, NY. I feel the work would be appropriate to any number of commercial, institutional or residential situations, and I am hopeful that it may be a good fit for upcoming projects you may be planning.

I have exhibited widely, with numerous one-person exhibitions since the late 1960s. I am included in many museum, university, public, and corporate collections such as Virginia Museum of Fine Arts, The Long Beach Museum of Art, Manhattan Bank, Concoction Bank (London & New York), Total Insurance Company, Better Products, Inc., AB&C, American Fargo, and National Bank & HMT Communications. Additionally, the work has been reviewed in *The New York Times, Arts, Artforum, Arts & Antiques, The Village Voice, Art in America* and *ARTnews*. Please see attached résumé for complete collections list and bibliography.

I have a number of bodies of interrelated work, including works on paper, painted collages, and acrylic on canvas; works on paper range in size from ?"x?" and are priced at $??; acrylic on canvas paintings (size range) are priced in the range of $? to $?. I invite you to retain the enclosed CD for your files, and am happy to supply periodic updates on new work upon request. I look forward to the possibility of developing a mutually rewarding business relationship.


Sincerely,



Jack Ronson


Enclosures

**Sample Letter to a Landscape Architect**

Mr. Dimitri Palenberg
Palenberg, Kravis and Smith, Landscape Architects
2700 Skyline Drive
Midland, MA 10423

Date

Dear Mr. Palenberg:

I would like to introduce you to my bronze sculptures, specifically the large-scale commissioned projects that have been created for performing arts centers, municipal parks, and other locations. Suitable for both indoor and outdoor environments, my pieces can be freestanding, monumental works or placed on stands that echo a gesture in the sculpture. The whimsical humor of the work invites viewers to interact with the sculptuer.

My work has been shown in numerous one-person exhibitions. Commissions include the Waterfront Concourse, Chicago; the Performing Arts Center of Dubuque, IA; the Children's Museum of Indianapolis; the Shopping Mall of America, St. Paul, MN; and the Fly Fishing Hall of Fame, Billings, MT. I am a graduate of New Hampshire College, and studied ceramics and bronze sculpture with Elizabeth C. Gibbons and Walter Granda at The Foundry Complex, Bangor, ME.

I have also enclosed written support materials, a CD of all available work, and color reproductions, which I hope you will retain for any future project opportunities. I will contact you in the near future to learn if you require any additional materials, or if any projects are being planned for which my work would be appropriate.

Sincerely,

Jane Bickell

Enclosures

**Sample Letter to an Interior Design Firm**

Ms. Bunny Fontaine
Fontaine/Robertson Interior Design
5900 Cartwright Way
Los Angeles, CA 90052


Date


Dear Ms. Fontaine:

I would like to introduce you to the "Dream Hare" series of sculptures, and I have provided a catalogue to further acquaint you with my recent work and background. These paintings would be suited to a large range of corporate clients, and individual collectors seeking to enhance an office or private residence.

I recently worked with a Los Angeles-based designer on two projects – one for a children's hospital in Bakersfield, CA and the other to enhance the lobby space of the Cezanne Hotel on Wilshire Blvd. My work has been extensively shown in group and solo exhibitions, and is included in many private and public collections, including the National Museum of the Hare, Washington, DC and Municipal Monument, Warren Hole, NY. I received an MA from Brown University, and I live and work in Greenwich, CT.

I have enclosed a pricelist of available works, written support materials, and a CD of currently available work. I invite you to retain these materials, and I will contact you in the near future to learn if there are any projects suited to my work being planned.


Sincerely,


Anastasia Connors


Enclosures

### In-House Corporate Curators

As mentioned previously, corporate collections no longer represent the opportunities they once did, but they still exist. The purpose of such collections may vary from interior decoration of corporate offices to the more ambitious aim of creating a world-class collection.

In the heyday of the 1980s, it was customary for corporations to engage the services of professional curators to oversee their collections. Not only did they acquire or recommend purchase of works, but they may have also been responsible for the installation (in some cases, employees could select pieces for their workspaces) and care of the collection. In many cases, these curators were full-time employees of the company.

For collections that are still actively on-going, a corporation may use a part-time consultant rather than maintaining a staff curator. Alternatively, an employee, quite likely the head of the corporation, may have assumed responsibility for acquisition.

These collections generally have specific points of view, so when approaching a corporation, do your research beforehand to make sure your work is appropriate.

**Sample Letter to an In-House Corporate Collection**

Ms. Belinda Carlson
Curatorial Director for Collections
Northeastern Mutual Insurance Co.
245 Atlantic Avenue
Hartford, CT 06105

Date

Dear Ms. Carlson:

I wanted to bring my paintings to the attention of the Northeastern Mutual Collection. Having recently visited your Hartford headquarters, I believe the my paintings would be a compatible and enhancing addition to your collection. I am based in Connecticut, and the helpful receptionist I spoke with described the regional thrust of your collection as well as your focus on large-scale abstraction.

My work has been extensively shown in group and solo exhibitions, including those at the University of Connecticut College of Fine Art Gallery, and the Bridgeport Gallery and Excellent Fine Art in New York, and Yale University. The work is included in many public and corporate collections, including the National Museum of Art, Washington, DC, the Engulf & Devour Corp., and HARE, Inc. I received an MA from RISD, and live and work in Greenwich, CT.

I have enclosed written support pieces and a CD of all available work along with several color reproductions. I can provide a pricelist upon request. These paintings would not only be enjoyed by your employees, but would also stimulate client interest in your firm. I look forward to discussing possible acquisition.

Sincerely,

Anastasia Connors

Enclosures

**Critics, Art Writers, and Editors**

There are several reasons to write to critics, writers, and editors, chief among them announcing an exhibition and inviting them to attend (see pp.42-48). If there is not a specific exhibition or event to announce, you may simply wish to introduce your work to the critic, writer, or editor, with the hope of obtaining future coverage. In this case, your letter can follow the general outline of one addressed to a nonprofit exhibiting organization, with a few modifications.

The best reason for writing a letter to a critic is to invite the recipient to your one-person exhibition or group exhibition. The mere fact that your work is on public display immediately validates it.

## Sample Letter to Critics, Art Writers, and Editors

Ms. Lauren DiGiacomo
Senior Art Critic
*Atlanta Times-Union*
2200 Peachtree Street NW
Atlanta, GA 39713

Date

Dear Ms. DiGiacomo:

I am forwarding an introductory package featuring my mixed media works, along with an invitation to the opening of my one-person exhibition at the Snyder Cartwright Institute of Contemporary Art in Dobson, GA, on April 4th at 8:00 pm. The exhibition will run through June 10th. I will also have an exhibition of recent works on paper running concurrently at Sinclair Fine Art in Atlanta.

I am a resident of Annapolis, MD, and have exhibited extensively in the Mid-Atlantic and Southeast regions. My solo exhibitions include the Gertrude Herbert Institute of Art, Augusta, GA; Museum of Arts and Sciences, Macon, GA; the Banana Factory, Bethlehem, PA; Knoxville Museum of Art, TN; and the Franz Meinhop Gallery in Washington. DC. I was included in the group exhibition "Linked to Landscape," which traveled from the Corcoran Museum to the Jacksonville Museum of Modern Art last year. I have enclosed written support materials and a CD containing several bodies of work.

I am most hopeful you will be able to attend and would be pleased to meet with you to discuss the work. I will be in Georgia for the opening, departing on the 8th. I would greatly appreciate any support you can extend in these endeavors.

Sincerely,

Melanie Harrington

Enclosures

## Sample Letter Extending Invitation to an Exhibition

Ishmael Sanderson
44 Mott Street, #2A
New York, NY 12345

Date

Dear Mr. Sanderson:

I would like to extend a personal invitation to view two of my installations, included in "Meditations on a Hare," a group exhibition curated by John Warren at El Bodega ArtSpace, 399 Flatbush Avenue in Brooklyn. The opening reception is Saturday, June 4, from 2 to 6 pm, and the exhibition runs until August 12. Hours are Tuesday through Saturday, 10 am-6 pm, and Sundays 12-4 pm.

Enclosed is the announcement and reproductions of my installations. Also provided is a biographical summary to further apprise you of my accomplishments. In March of this year, my work will also be exhibited in a two-person exhibition at the P. Shark Gallery.

I would be pleased to meet with you at your convenience to discuss the work. My website is www.buzzfleischman.com and my e-mail is buzz@buzzfleischman.com. I would appreciate any support that you could extend to me in this endeavor.

Sincerely,


Buzz Fleischman


Enclosure

**The Artist Generated Press Release**

Following are four examples of press releases an artist would generate for an exhibition. Try to keep it to one page if humanly possible, but certainly no more than two pages, and be sure to include all pertinent factual information such as dates, times, venue hours, and all contact information.

The top of the first page of every press release states who, what, when, and where. It provides contact information: phone, fax, e-mail, and website of the venue.

Beneath the basic information about the exhibition is the hook, message, or lead – a phrase or short sentence that will pique the curiosity or capture the attention of the reader – in other words, why the recipient should "take notice." It may be presented as a "headline" or, if there are space constraints, incorporated into the introductory paragraph of the release. This paragraph should be a maximum of 100 to 150 words and reiterate the information presented at the top of the release, followed by a brief description of the work being exhibited, discussion of the materials, unique approach or style, and whatever else strongly distinguishes the work.

The second paragraph (often at the top of the second page if it is needed) is a brief discussion of your work and its influences, and could include a quote by a notable critic.

The third paragraph is often biographical, noting pinnacle achievements such as significant exhibitions and collections, awards and honors, commissions, etc. The final paragraph is personal information such as education and current place of residence.

**Standard Two-Page Press Release**

# FOR IMMEDIATE RELEASE

Contact: Name:
Firm
Telephone          Fax
e-mail

### THE PERSONAL AND THE POLITICAL COLLIDE:
### THE PAINTINGS OF DAN FARRILL

New York – Dan Farrill will exhibit a survey of paintings and bas reliefs from the past twelve years at the Excellent Art Gallery, from May 1-June 5, 2011. Gallery hours are 11am-6pm, Tuesday-Saturday. Farrill's work spans the spectrum from impassioned political allegories to portraits that examine identity as a social performance and as a private experience.

Farrill has described himself as a "figurative expressionist," and this applies equally to his intense narratives and his boldly colored paintings of single large heads. He paints directly, inventing dramatic scenarios that symbolically describe the interplay of power and money and their effect on the psyche and the politics here and abroad. Farrill's portraits, whether painted in acrylic and oil or formed with paper mache, become studies of the emotional lives of their subjects.

In this survey exhibition Farrill, who is based in upstate New York, will exhibit twenty-five major works. On display will be the painting *Political Council*, a gathering of a general, a gambler, a gun-toting thug who seem to embody all our doubts about who is really calling the crucial shots for all of us. In *Company of Fools*, a similarly untrustworthy cast of characters has been assembled, this time aboard an ocean liner. They include a patriarchal captain, two possible spies from the Third Reich, a martini-drinking Bible reader, and assorted others. In the center is the ingenue, ready to be exploited or willingly corrupted – the outcome is left up to the viewer, as it is in many of Farrill's paintings.

In *Fawning with a Fan*, the female in question is a fallen Statue of Liberty, tempted by a forked-tongue angel, accompanied by a dissolute clown, a portrait of a corrupt politician, and a monstrous head, the embodiment of a foreign war gone wrong.

Farrill paints his narratives with a fragmented attack, the figures angled and hallucinatory. Rich color glows against the darkened atmosphere. Abstraction and exaggeration become ways of depicting the moral failings that permeate these dramatic works.

page 1 of 2

The artist has acknowledged his roots in German Expressionism, particularly in the work of Max Beckmann, who he learned about as a student in Boston in the 1940s. He also was influenced by the Boston Expressionists, a group of painters of the period, including the social realist Jack Levine, Hyman Bloom, and Karl Zerbe. Their example of combining progressive politics with painterly figuration still informs Farrill's practice.

In his Portraits, Farrill focuses in on one single individual at a time. The looming heads, whether painted or sculpted, have an unsettling immediacy. This impression is strengthened by the faceted or topographic surface, which makes the viewer feel as if the facade of the self is an unstable structure, barely holding in place. *The Pulpit* depicts a priest with a curiously clenched smile, literally trying to put a good face on things. *The Operator* is a nattily-dressed man in a tropical setting, whose shifting eyes alert us to a slippery imperialist ready to work his worst.

John Mendelsohn has written that, "The portraits are social and psychological, each distinctively personal, yet all sharing both a bold presentation of the self and inadvertent exposure, as well... Upon these vain-glorious, melancholy, brave, and introspective faces, the artist lavishes a raw attention, a kind of ambivalent, fevered love..."

For further information, please contact Christina Jones, Excellent Art Gallery, 1018 Madison Avenue, New York, NY 10234, (212) 332-1616, christina@excellent.com.

page 2 of 2

149

# FOR IMMEDIATE RELEASE

Contact: Name
Firm
Telephone            Fax
e-mail

## THE PERSONAL AND THE POLITICAL COLLIDE:
## THE PAINTINGS OF DAN FARRILL

**New York – Dan Farrill will exhibit a survey of paintings and bas reliefs from the past twelve years at the Excellent Art Gallery, from May 1-June 5, 2011. Gallery hours are 11am-6pm, Tuesday-Saturday. Farrill's work spans the spectrum from impassioned political allegories to portraits that examine identity as a social performance and as a private experience.**

Farrill has described himself as a "figurative expressionist," and this applies equally to his intense narratives and his boldly colored paintings of single large heads. He paints directly, inventing dramatic scenarios that symbolically describe the interplay of power and money and their effect on the psyche and the politics here and abroad. Farrill's portraits, whether painted in acrylic and oil or formed with paper mache, become studies of the emotional lives of their subjects.

The artist has acknowledged his roots in German Expressionism, particularly in the work of Max Beckmann, who he learned about as a student in Boston in the 1940s. He also was influenced by the Boston Expressionists, a group of painters of the period, including the social realist Jack Levine, Hyman Bloom, and Karl Zerbe. Their example of combining progressive politics with painterly figuration still informs Farrill's practice.

In his Portraits, Farrill focuses in on one single individual at a time. The looming heads, whether painted or sculpted, have an unsettling immediacy. This impression is strengthened by the faceted or topographic surface, which makes the viewer feel as if the facade of the self is an unstable structure, barely holding in place. *The Pulpit* depicts a priest with a curiously clenched smile, literally trying to put a good face on things. *The Operator* is a nattily-dressed man in a tropical setting, whose shifting eyes alert us to a slippery imperialist ready to work his worst.

For further information, please contact Christina Jones, Excellent Art Gallery, 1018 Madison Avenue, New York, NY 10234, (212) 332-1616, christina@excellent.com.

# # #

**Variation on Two-Page Press Release**

# FOR IMMEDIATE RELEASE

Contact: Name
Firm
Telephone          Fax
e-mail

## MELINDA O'HARA'S ANIMALS:
## THE REAL AND THE IMAGINED

New York–Melinda O'Hara will exhibit mixed media paintings from the past three years at the Excellent Art Gallery, from May 1-June 5, 2011. Gallery hours are 11am-6pm, Tuesday-Saturday. O'Hara's layered, richly colored paintings are populated by real and imagined animals who are often stand-ins for human beings and their inner lives.

O'Hara combines painted and photographic images, fabric, wood, safety glass, and found objects in works that plunge the viewer into dream-like scenarios. In her highly textured paintings, she uses objects and images of personal significance, such as fabric from her childhood home, her son's drawings, and her pet dogs. O'Hara's work looks both inward, expressing the artist's hopes and fears, and outward, embracing the world in its beauty and environmental damage.

In this exhibition O'Hara, who is based in Richmond, VA, will exhibit forty pieces, which represent the major developments of her recent work. On display will be *Songs of Loss*, the 2006 installation that alternated paintings with sculptural fabric animals. Also on view will be the 2007 installation *Enough is Enough*. At the center of the piece is a large fabric sculpture of Louis XIV as a horned animal, surrounded by fantastic paintings inspired by O'Hara's European travels.

In her work, O'Hara explores themes of the self and close relationships, the melding of past and present, loss and memory. Throughout her oeuvre, the artist explores how meaning can be found in the broken and the castoff, with unexpected beauty permeating our daily life. Feelings of vulnerability and ephemeral loveliness are embodied in the recurring images of flowers, bubbles, paper boats, and autumn leaves. In O'Hara's paintings, heartfelt emotion coexists with humor, whimsical wit, and a feeling of affection for her animal subjects.

O'Hara has described her process as intuitive, with a kind of visual poetry emerging from the layering of images and materials. She creates her animal figures from fabric and clay, and uses them as models for painting or photographs them and collages the resulting pictures. By combining paint, images, words, and objects, a piece develops in ways that are often surprising.

More...

John Mendelsohn has written that, "O'Hara is a prolific artist who delights in a constant flow of creative invention, but throughout her work is a feeling of fleeting beauty, of holding on to yesterday and today, and the recognition of the impermanence of it all....This feeling of embracing what is vulnerable and what is loved and keeping it whole at least for a while is at the heart of her artistic vision."

Melinda O'Hara has exhibited her paintings extensively with her solo exhibitions including those at Cronin Contemporary, Nashville; Murray Fine Art, Atlanta; Sanders and Bacon Fine Art, Atlanta; Georgia State University, Atlanta; and the Last Station, Augusta, GA.

For further information, please contact Christina Jones, Excellent Art Gallery, 1018 Madison Avenue, New York, NY 10234, (212) 332-1616, christina@excellent.com.

**Variation on One-Page Press Release**

## FOR IMMEDIATE RELEASE

### HEIDEMAN'S POETIC PHOTOGRAPHS CAPTURE
### THE SEA AND SKY WITH ABSTRACT PURITY

**New York – The Excellent Art Gallery will present the exhibition "Seascapes 1996 thru 2006" by Sarah Heideman from Jan. 15–Feb. 15, 2011. Gallery hours are from 11 am-6 pm, Tuesday-Saturday. The exhibition features Heideman's striking color photographs that focus on the skies and waters of the Atlantic Ocean.**

The exhibition features fifteen photographs from Heideman's series *Seascapes 1996 thru 2006*, which in its entirety consists of forty images, each 30"x40". With an observant eye for the shifting phenomena of clouds and light, she has vividly realized images that range from the abstract, to the painterly, to the highly dramatic. Her poetic work conveys the sense of constant change in the natural world.

Heideman's process is a direct one, and when looking through the viewfinder, she sees the final work. All colors are natural and unaltered, and the image is never cropped. Each day's photographic session produced a single image, whether it took just one shot or many rolls to capture. She has said about her work that, "The process was one of focused awareness of the delicate changes in the light and the clouds. Being centered and mindful of the moment is the attitude that allowed these pictures to be made."

Heideman has shown her work in solo exhibitions at Equator Fine Art Gallery, New York, and Hill & Brown Gallery, Palm Beach, FL. Group shows include those at the Miller (PA) Museum of Art; Banyan Gallery, Boca Raton, FL; and The Center for Fine Art Photography, Ft. Wayne, IN. Upcoming exhibitions include those at the Armory Center for the Creative Arts, Fredericksburg, VA, and the High Plains Museum of Fine Arts, TX.

For further information, contact James Jones, Excellent Art Gallery, 1018 Madison Ave, New York, NY 10021, (212) 311-4356, james@exgal.com.

# # #

**The Chronological Résumé**

Artists must extrapolate the most impressive information to present in their résumés. You must settle on an arrangement that presents your accomplishments and involvements in the best possible light.

The information at the top of any chronological résumé includes your vital statistics: name, mailing address, and always your telephone numbers (studio, home, or cell), e-mail, and website address. This information is usually top left or centered.

Annie Artist
123 First St.
Studio City, CA 99999
Studio: 123-456-7890
Home: 123-456-8910 (if you do not have a cellphone)
Cell: 123-456-9101
E-mail Address: AnnieArtist@AnnieArtist.com
Website: www.AnnieArtist.com

The first section of a chronological résumé should be your exhibitions, and can be divided into "One- and Two-person Exhibitions," followed by "Group Exhibitions." However, if you have fewer than five or six one- and/or two-person exhibitions, combine all exhibitions into a category entitled "Selected Exhibitions" to create a meatier, more substantial résumé. Your most recent exhibitions come first and then continue in reverse chronological order – 2010, 2009, 2008, etc.

The year of an exhibition is listed on the left side of the page. All exhibitions that occurred in a particular year are listed under that year, but the year is listed only once, not with each new entry, and do not include the actual days and months of your exhibition, just the year.

The preferred format for each listing is the title of the exhibition in quotation marks (note comma comes before the final quote mark), name of institution, and location. If the curator or juror is of note, this can be added in parentheses or italics, or may be included under the "Awards and Honors" category with the name and credentials of the juror, after the exhibition entry. One-person exhibitions without a title would list location and place only. A two-person exhibitions may be indicated in parenthesis at the end of an entry.

## One- and Two-Person Exhibitions

2009    "John Artist: A Retrospective," Institute of Retrograde Art, Looking Back, LA

2008    "A Pair of Observations," Scientific Gallery, Comprehensive Institute of Technology, Experimentation, ID (two-person exhibition)
        Blue Cheese Gallery, Brie, Ohio

## Group Exhibitions

2009    "Happy Hunting," Weapons Museum of America, Rifle, NM
        "Annual Juried Cattle Call," State Fairgrounds, Roundup, NE (Juror: Angus McCoy, Curator of Contemporary Art, Mountain Plains Museum of Art, SD)

2008    "Dogs of War," Museum of the Dog, Canine, KY

2007    "Passing Time," The Clock Museum, Greenwich, CT

2006    "Seeing Nature," Institute of American Landscape, Woodland, CA (Purchase Award. Juror: Forrest Mapleton, Director, Museum of Traditional Art, Rolling Hills, NC)

Stay away from listing too many entries noting juried shows that you have participated in regularly for a number of years. For example, if you have been selected for an exhibition like "35th Annual Statewide Juried Artist's Competition" repeatedly, take out the "35th," and limit the number of citations. Alternatively, enter the first year, then place the subsequent years in parentheses at the end of the entry: (2005, 2006, 2007...). You may be able to find ways to alter the title, making it sound more distinguished and accomplished without being untruthful.

The last thing you want a professional to conclude is that most of your exhibition experience is in juried competitions that occur every year or every other year without fail, which will ultimately communicate that you are not really challenging yourself or raising the bar.

### Alternative Format/Variation

2009    Annual Statewide Competition," Same Faces City Museum,
        Treading Water, FL

2007    "Statewide Exhibition," Same Faces City Museum,
        Treading Water, FL (2008, 2009, 2010)

### Collections

The section listing collections is organized by museums and other nonprofits, followed by public spaces funded by public money, then corporate and any business, and lastly, private collections – in that order hierarchically and then alphabetically within each category. Listing the year is not important; however, often the city and state where the collection or collector is located or where the corporate headquarters is based are included.

Include only collectors of note – no personal friends or relatives (unless Charles Saatchi is your cousin). If this list is particularly strong, you have two options: include it as a listing in the chronological résumé or list your collections on a separate page entirely, titled "Collections."

**Gotham City Museum, Gotham City, NY**
**Landscape Institute, Woodland, CA**
**Mass Transit Authority, Subway, MA (Commission)**
**Public Library, Reading, PA**
**Relief Sculpture Gardens, Granite, ND**
**Success University, Secure, AZ**
**Avaricious Oil Company, Offshore, TX**
**Socially Conscious Ltd., Philanthropy, PA**
**V.I. Collector, Self Absorbed, NH**
**Good E. Buyer, Blind Basin, SC**

On the chronological résumé, separate categories can be created for "Awards and Honors" and "Grants and Residencies" and are formatted in the same way as exhibitions are listed – year, award name, presenting organization, and location – followed by the juror's name and professional affiliation in parentheses.

Important juried exhibitions held at prestigious institutions with a notable juror are included here, and follow the same format as in the "Exhibitions" section. If you received an award of distinction in a juried or invitational exhibition, do include this as it further validates your work. The name of the juror and professional affiliation can be provided in parentheses.

## Awards and Honors

2009    Hang the Moon Award, Significant Astronomical Organization (SAO), Saturn Rings, CA (Juror: Star Gazer; Editor, *All the Stars in the Sky Magazine*)

2008    Better Than the Best Award, "The Best Darn Artists of 2008," Middlingtown, MN. (Juror: Goody Eye; Director, Superior Art Gallery, Elite, IN)

2007    Purchase Award, "Critic's Choice Exhibition," Striving, SD. (Juror: *Super Picky*; Editor, *Superlative Art Directions Magazine*, Big Pond, MN)

2006    Lifetime Achievement Award, National Association of Realist Painters, Classical Training, Paris, TX

## The Bibliography

Your bibliography includes all citations about you and your work that have appeared in print or other media. It includes every feature article, review, free listing, radio or television interview, internet coverage, monograph, one-person exhibition and group exhibition catalogue, book or calendar cover, event poster, etc. In other words, anything in print where attention is given to you and your work, especially by those who can "speak intelligently" about art. This category can also include published work by you, both written and visual.

The bibliography is sometimes entitled "Selected Bibliography" or "Selected Reviews" when you have culled from a large number of entries. (You can also use "selected" for any section that includes a number of different categories, e.g., one-person and group exhibitions.) Naturally the most prestigious are chosen.

Bibliographies are alphabetical arrangements of writer's name (last name first), or in lieu of the writer's name, the name of the publication (underlined or in italics), title of article (in quote marks), the name of the publication (if not used as above), date of article, volume (Vol.), number (No.), page numbers (pp. xx). If there was a reproduction of your work – cover reproduction, reproduction, or reproductions, as appropriate – can be placed in parentheses at the end of the listing.

## Alphabetical Bibliography

Artists of New Jersey State Calendar, published by State Art Council of New Jersey, 2009. (February reproduction)

Critic, Enormously Important. "Insightful Review," *Major Art Magazine*, June 2007, Vol. 10, No. 6, pp. 10-20. (reproduction)

*Living With Art Magazine*, December 2007, Vol. 12, No. 12. (cover reproduction)

Make a Note. "Big Artist's Exhibition Opens at Superior Gallery," *Elite Daily News* (Indianapolis), January 1, 2009, p. 10. (reproductions)

Another acceptable arrangement can be chronological, as done in the exhibitions section, starting with the most recent. The format remains the same as the alphabetical listing.

## Chronological Bibliography

2010    "Artists and Their Art Calendar," State Art Council of New Jersey, 2009. (February reproduction)

2009    "Big Artist's Exhibition Opens at Superior Gallery," *Elite Daily News* (Indianapolis), January 1, 2009, p. 10. (reproductions)

2008    Critic, Enormously Important. "Insightful Review," *Major Art Magazine,* June 2008, Vol. 10, No. 6, pp. 10-20. (reproduction)

2007    *Design for All Magazine,* December 2007, Vol. 12, No. 12. (cover reproduction)

Traditionally the artist's educational background came first on résumés; however, it is now preferable to list such information at the end of the chronological résumé. The reason is that you do not want to communicate that your education is your most stellar accomplishment, unless, of course, you went to Yale or Cal Arts.

## Education

| | |
|---|---|
| Rigorous Art Academy, Excellence, VA, Bachelor of Fine Arts | 1999 |
| Color Field University, Hue, CA, Master of Fine Arts | 2001 |

**The Biographical Summary**

A concise one-page biographical summary can serve either as a supplement or an alternative to a formal chronological résumé. This is a narrative recounting of the artist's life, touching on the basic facts – place of birth, education, formative experiences. While personal struggles, illnesses, and tales of overcoming hardships are not appropriate here, a good biographical summary will enlighten the reader about the experiences and influences that shaped the artist's work. It is perfectly acceptable to discuss earlier careers and pursuits apart from your art practice, as people are often intrigued by the arc of an artist's personal life, and the twists and turns that brought them to their current situation. Philosophical positions and beliefs may be included if used to illuminate the decisions that have shaped the narrative of the artist's life history.

## ANASTASIA CONNORS

Anastasia Connors has created a series of paintings of horses that are both physically dynamic and poetically evocative. Connors' paintings are tactile experiences, from whose often dense surfaces the images seem to emerge. The horses that the artist depicts are immersed in the natural world, yet they seem timeless. These are dream horses, capable of flight and independent, even when they carry a rider on their back.

Connors grew up in Oklahoma City, in a family that encouraged her early interest in art. Her involvement with painting deepened on trips with her parents to Europe and to Asia, where her father pursued his work as a professor of art history. While living in the Philippines and Hong Kong in the 1980s, Connors studied traditional Chinese calligraphy. The aesthetics of Chinese art, with its sense of space, devotion to nature, and abstract suggestion of form, was an important formative influence on the artist's vision.

Having moved to the East Coast in the early 1990s, Connors began studying art at the New School for Social Research in New York City with the painter Raphael Boyer. From his classes, Connors gained an appreciation for the sensitive handling of paint and for the layering of color, concerns that have remained prominent in her process. She continued to develop her involvement with art during a fifteen year period when she worked as a representative for her husband, a fashion photographer. In 2001, Connors resumed her art education, first at New Hampshire College, and then at University of Massachusetts, where she received an MA in 2005. During this period she produced a series of sepia prints based on botanical forms, including plants and insects.

A decade of living on an Oklahoma farm with horses proved to be crucial in Connors' work. She both drew the animals from life and imagined their presence in the current series of emotive paintings of horses in the landscape, using oil glazes on highly textured surfaces. These paintings have been widely exhibited in group and solo exhibitions, including those at the University of Texas, Austin; Museum of the Southwest, Midland, TX, Rocky Mountain Museum, Golden, CO, the Louisiana Art and Science Museum, Baton Rouge; Deland Museum of Art, FL; also she has been included in numerous exhibitions at cultural and visual art centers, college and university galleries nationwide. Her work is in many private and public collections, including the National Museum of Women in Art, Washington, DC. Connors today lives and works in Greenwich, CT.


## PAUL STEPHANO

Paul Stephano took an interest in art while still very young; this involvement would stay with him throughout his life, from his small-town upbringing in South Carolina to the raising of four children and a move to Atlanta, where he had a successful career as an art director. His interactions in life and business predisposed him to exploring the excesses of contemporary culture – he wanted to face, as he puts it, the "events and ideas in media and entertainment."

Interestingly, Stephano's realism is not constrained by his choice of figuration; instead, it enables him to work out the signs and symbols of Western art history, in which he quotes the great modernists, Italian Renaissance art, and, perhaps most important, German Expressionist works. This historical filter allows Stephano to develop an allegorical range, in which the imagery stands for a symbolism that, despite its historicist ties, looks very much at such contemporary topics as mass media and advertising. His experience in advertising has left him with a sharp understanding of our wishes and desires, which in the case of his representation may not always be sanguine.

Stephano started his art education in the mid-1960s at the University of North Carolina in the fine arts program. He went on to continue his studies once he moved to Atlanta, taking night and weekend classes with various artists at Atlanta College of Art and the Savannah College of Art and Design and elsewhere.

He devoted his spare time to his own painting, but he also became involved with reading history and philosophy. Additionally, he studied the lives and methods of the great artists in history. The old masters became a focus so that he could learn their techniques. In 2000, his children now finished with college, Stephano moved to New York, where he took an MFA in painting from the School of Visual Arts. After living a few years in New York's Chelsea, he returned to Atlanta; his studio is now located in Marietta.

Paul Stephano has been the subject of numerous one-person exhibitions including those at the Florida International Museum of Art, St. Petersburg; Isaac Gallery, Davis, CA; Peter Gallagher Contemporary Art, New York; Malone Art Museum, TX; University of South Carolina, Columbia; University of the Midwest, Indianapolis.


## JANE BICKELL

Jane Bickell commenced studying sculpture with noted sculptors Elizabeth C. Gibbons and Walter Granda in the mid-1990s, quickly developing a sense of the tradition and craft involved in working in bronze. Bickell works in her home studio in Exeter, New Hampshire, and fabricates her bronzes at foundries in Maine and Long Island.

In addition to mastering the compositional demands of traditional figural sculpture, Bickell has brought to her art a playful sense of humor, which has remained at the core of her work in design and art throughout her career. In a world where most art is to be looked at and not touched, Bickell has a unique point of view. She seeks to engage and amuse the viewer, argues that art should be lived with, and even played with, as she often does herself when devising new compositions and groupings for her work. Bickell's philosophy is exemplified by the fact that she has begun to design wrought iron stands for some of her work. Solid wooden pedestals, Bickell has said, leave her with heaviness in her solar plexus. She, therefore, came up with the idea of designing stands that pick up on a gesture in the sculpture and become a part of the interactive experience of the piece as a whole.

Jane Bickell first exhibited her bronze sculptures, with interactive stands, in a solo exhibition at the Schick Art Gallery at Plymouth State College, NH, in 2005. Prior to that, and subsequently, Brickell has included her playful bronze sculptures at the prestigious Peninsula Art Center on Long Island. She has exhibited her work in both solo and group exhibitions in numerous venues both regionally and nationally.

Jane Bickell was educated at the Marsala School, in Virginia, and is a graduate of New England College (BA, English), Henniker, NH, where she claims to have developed her passion for art design because the reading was minimal and no papers were due. She is married, with three sons.

## The Artist Statement

The artist statement, discussed at length in "Making A Statement," pp. 253-256, is an artist's chance to reflect on his or her work and to convey what may have inspired it, and how the artist came to this form of expression. The statement can place the work in a contemporary context through specific comparisons, and position it on the art historical continuum by acknowledging antecedents who have influenced the work. Ideally it should provide a point of entrance or access into the work for the reader and viewer.

The statement should be brief, non-effusive, concise, and clear, without revealing too many of the personal inspirations for the work or analysis from the artist's point of view. We strongly recommend avoiding the use of "I" and "my" – instead we prefer the use of the third person to lessen the risk of the statement becoming too personal, pompous, or sentimental.

## Example One

The current body of work falls into three categories: narrative paintings, portraits, and bas reliefs. Each group has its own subject matter, and all have a spirited directness of execution.

Most of the narratives are political, dealing with the current state of this country and the world, particularly the relationships of power, money, and democracy. These paintings usually have a cast of many characters who interact with each other, often in theatrical ways. And while there are some recognizable personages, most of the figures are symbolic or fictional. The narratives are anything but straightforward – they are complex, allegorical, and sometimes cryptic. The viewer is rarely supplied with a specific message, but rather the opportunity to create their own interpretations.

The portraits and bas reliefs all share the same subject: the human face that fills the pictorial space. The portraits are painted in a combination of acrylic and oil, often with a textural ground of fabric such as cheesecloth, sand, and gesso. The bas reliefs are made with paper mache, fabric, and other assorted materials. Each of these modes of working affords the possibility of both depicting the outward appearance and suggesting the inner person. The fragmented or topographic quality of the faces, along with the vivid color in the paintings, further emphasize the character of the individual. The titles often suggest a social identity that a person maintains, while at the same time making it impossible to conceal their real selves.

The approach to this work is direct, with never any preliminaries. The process is an intuitive one, working from memory and imagination, with some works developing over a number of months or even years. The style of these paintings can be described as figurative expressionism, with roots in the challenging modern art created in pre-Hitler Germany.

**Example Two**

The current mixed media paintings are textured memories, visual responses to a range of personal experiences. The series *les couleurs du Mandé – The Colors of the Mandé* – was inspired by a recent trip to West Africa, my childhood home. *Mandé* refers to the traditional homelands of the Mandingo people. The paintings evoke both the landscape and the culture through the abstract use of color, form, and collaged materials.

These works embody both fresh impressions and early memories: the beauty of the land, the colors of mud brick and indigo sky, the heat of the sun, the essence of the place in all its contrasts. These contrasts can best be summarized as "the beauty in the harshness" – beauty in a desert, happiness in poverty, gracefulness manifested in a materially raw environment.

The series relates to work from the past fifteen years, reflecting my formative years in Africa and the experience of living in contemporary multi-cultural Canada. As a whole, this oeuvre is an expression of cultural bridging, creating opportunities for bringing people of contrasting cultures together.

Creating mixed media paintings has become a way for me to investigate layering and texturing in relation to the subject matter. Layering is accomplished by overlapping paper, leather, netting, cheesecloth, textiles, photographs, and family documents. Additionally, texturing is achieved by using gels, modeling pastes, and other acrylic-based media. Except for commissioned works, there is no preconceived concept or study. Rather, the work mostly arises from my subconscious, the process being intuitive and spontaneous.

**Example Three**

In this current body of work, figures, household objects, and architecture push and shove, jockeying for space. Images of daily life pile up and become entangled. In the prints, drawings, and paintings, dense visual fields record personal observations of how human beings interact and affect each other. The urgency of expressing these relationships is embodied in the vigorous use of materials and the intuitive quality of the mark-making.

Life's stuff, both the physical evidence and the emotional baggage we all carry, is the raw material of these paintings. At the same time, the work is a way to make sense of the world, and of the ever-shifting balance of chaos and order in both our private and social lives.

The layering of image and material is critical in these works. Paint or other media are layered, letting color and images show through in places, allowing the materials to build up in others. Images are continually moving and bumping into each other, causing an action and reaction on the part of the second image. Bits of the background emerge, suggesting the past and the passage of time. The surface becomes visually energized with the presence of dissonant layers.

The process of this work is both immediate and subject to considerable change. At times, a piece will begin with an idea that evolves into something quite different. Or it may begin with no idea at all, and the pencil or brush is used like a divining rod. When a composition has tipped into chaos, a semblance of order is created by defining certain shapes, or repeating a specific image in regimented formations.

This work uses humor and metaphor to engage the vagaries and challenges of being human. The scuff marks in the work imitate the marks we leave behind. These are pictures of happy intimacy, and of the complexity of finding the right kind of fit with people and work.

165

*Accelerating on the Curves*

# BOOK THREE
# Hare Pen Curves: Essays by Associates

The title, *Hare Pen Curves*, is a play on words alluding to the written contributions (pen) of all the Associates – critics, authors, editors, curators, educators, dealers, and public relations professionals.

# Commitment

# A Life in Art

By John Mendelsohn

As an artist who writes about art, I have a special perspective. I see things from both sides – as a painter involved in my own work, and as someone who reflects on other artists and their development. As I thought about my particular viewpoint, the phrase "life in art" came to mind. These words uttered by a fellow artist have the same effect on me today as when they were first spoken: feeling both an opening out of possibilities and of settling into where I should be.

"A life in art" can mean many things, some of which I will explore here, but it implies, fundamentally, that the field of one's activity as an artist expands, manifesting in many forms, filling one's life. I want to stress that this is a process without borders. I don't have a precise set of procedures for you to follow, although there are some practical tips below. Rather, I hope that my words will be a reminder to you as an artist about the impetus that has always mysteriously moved you to make your work, and has allowed you to imaginatively relate to everything around and within you. And I hope that my words will suggest ways in which those impulses can energize how you relate to the world.

It occurs to me, that in order for this essay to be helpful, it really must relate to your own spirit as an artist, to be translated into your own personal frequency. To recognize that distinct and never-to-be-seen-before-or-again sense of yourself is an important step in making your work as deep and true as you can. This unique artistic character is not something that you can figure out in advance, but emerges over time from your work.

"A life in art" is your creation. It is as individual as each person. You can be as reclusive as Emily Dickinson or as social as Andy Warhol. Or as esoteric or democratic, rigorous or anarchic as you need to be. You can make this life out of scraps and hard times, like Alice Neel, or out of inheritance and psychic dislocation like William S. Burroughs. You can make your life in art an expanding nexus that begins with your work, and your love for art and grows from there, bringing in more of yourself and more of the world. Therefore:

**Keep working**, in your own way, but keep working – staying in touch with your art and with what sustains it. By this regular contact, doing and being become more closely identified. In the word of the Buddhist teacher Maezumi Roshi, your work becomes "nothing special," rather it's naturally what you do. Many people become stressed about the time they don't have to work. Use the time you have, like the artist I know, who while worrying if she had enough time, kept painting in the hours she had each day, and at the end of a year surprised herself with all the marvelous work she had done.

**Keep looking and learning about art**. Remember what it was like when you were first discovering art that moved you? Don't stop absorbing the art and the whole world of sensations that can nourish you. This can be art close to your own or work that might at first appear tangential to your immediate concerns. And it can be nature, science, music, or some other pursuit that keeps enlarging the dimensions of who you are. Artists are among the few who can choose their own ancestors, by who they look at, cherish, and keep returning to. At the same time, it always stirs me when I see a well-known artist of an earlier generation out on a Saturday afternoon looking in galleries at the new art that is happening today.

**Start from where you are**. This place, this time where you are is where art matters. Sometimes people think they are at a real disadvantage being removed from a center of art. And sometimes they are. But at the same time, it really is good to be from somewhere, and to realize that your path, either geographical or psychic, starts from there. Art matters in your own studio, in your immediate circle of artists, and in the community you find yourself in today.

**Reach out beyond your studio**. In the studio, everyone makes their own world, but let the world out there sustain you too. Some people find this easy and some find this hard. The trick is to find your own way of doing it. When I started writing about art, I found my own relationship to the work around me shifting. At first, each exhibition I wrote about strangely reflected my own inner reality at the moment. I realized I was connecting with art in a new way that revealed even more than I knew. Writing continues to be an important aspect of my life in art. Yes, artists want their work shown in galleries, museums, public spaces, and a myriad of other venues. But, I want you to consider one or more of these other activities to reach beyond the axis of studio and exhibition space.

Share studio visits with artists and other interested people, look at art with other artists, trade work, make art in a small collective, collaborate with a dancer or a poet, participate in residencies, work in another country and culture via a travel grant, organize and curate exhibitions, arrange for lectures by artists, interview artists or write about their work, publish a magazine, start a blog, teach anyone from the very young to the very old. These or parallel activities have long been part of artists' lives, but in the present, there are evermore opportunities and streamlined means of connecting to them.

**Realize that as an artist you give something to the world**. This awareness that your work and your involvement does enigmatically touch and change the world can manifest itself subtlety or in direct action. Either way, your work has a worth beyond the price put on it. The artist Bruce Nauman's neon piece that reads, "The true artist reveals mystic truths to the world" may be irony or not, but it serves as a challenge to realizing exactly what your art is revealing to the world.

**Allow things to change**. One's work and the context it exists in keeps changing. Sometimes people resist these alterations with great difficulty. However you do it, recognize that there are things, both inner and outer, that are beyond understanding and control, and that is the very nature of what we are working with. To view this whole process with curiosity, rather than just reinforcing an embattled position can help. In a recent interview, the sculptor Richard Serra noted that artists in their 40s or 50s often experience a shift in how their work is received. His solution was to keep working on one's own, focusing on developing what you have been given to do as your art.

**Stay true to your own vision**. Stay in tune with your own frequency, follow the currents of your experience, keep faith with your vision as an artist. Keep going, keep immersing yourself. In my experience, each connection that you make between your work and the world just beyond it reveals yet another potential connection, an underground root system of intuition and awareness that can allow you and your art to keep growing.

A life in art is not the same as recognition, success, or acceptance. It exists independently of any of these, but makes any of them possible. Now that you have read this essay, take what you need and forget the rest, or better yet reinvent it in the way that feels right. Good luck to you.

**John Mendelsohn** is a painter based in New York City who has written articles and reviews on contemporary art for *ArtNet, Sculpture, d'Art International, Cover Magazine,* and *The Jewish Week,* as well as essays for exhibition catalogues. He has contributed to the forthcoming book, *A Book of Images: Reflections on Symbols,* to be published by Taschen in conjunction with the Archive for Research in Archetypal Symbolism at the C.G. Jung Institute, New York City. He teaches in the Studio Art Program at Fairfield University, CT.

## First You Must
By Dominique Nahas

The art profession is unlike any other animal. One must use singularly distinctive terms and approaches in describing its configurations. Thus, the use of the words *first you must.*

*First you must* arrive at the realization that internal considerations such as intelligence, talent, and resourcefulness, and external circumstances, such as health, location, contacts, and resources, together form the basis of professionalism for the artist.

Firstly, the phrase *first you must,* used throughout this chapter, is a reminder to layman and artist alike that a persistent giant *Artistic Id* is always making its demands on the psyche of the professional artist. How the artist deals with those demands is what we will explore here. Later in my text I have used the word *mindfulness* and *self-monitoring* as a way of referencing productive manifestations of internal and internalized prioritizing.

Secondly, the words *first you must* convey the instructional/conversational tone of this chapter on professionalism in the visual arts.

Thirdly, the repeated phrase *first you must,* distributed throughout this text, offers a paradoxical challenge. Placing it in various places throughout this narrative makes it impossible for the reader to take it all in at once as the imperative tone insists you do. This annoying predicament analogizes artists' positions as they respond to the often-conflicting simultaneity of cross-purposes and mixed intentionalities of public and private demands. The quality of the response to such stimuli inevitably affects the outcome of a creative work or of a life devoted to the imagination. The artist is aware of these mixed agendas, which are part of the often-frustrating demands of living creatively.

To keep the big picture in mind (whatever that might be for you as an artist) while focusing on the issue(s) at hand is paramount. The phrase *first you must* also reminds us to reflect on the nature of priorities: that something that is urgent is not necessarily important. And that the reverse is also sometimes true: something important may have no urgency, necessarily, attached to it. The professional artist has to recognize the difference in order to get creative work done on time and on a regular basis.

I mentioned *internal considerations* and *external circumstances* at the onset of my remarks. This might lead you to believe that my account will be divided into *practical* considerations for the artist (time management, studio considerations, promotional and sales techniques, etc.) and *non-practical* or *mental* or *theoretical* aspects such as mental conditioning, frames of mind, attitudes, the *philosophy* of creativity or of the imagination. While the internal and external metaphor remains cogent, the extrapolation that there is a difference in importance or value between the *practical* vs. the *mental* factors in the field of professional artmaking is simply not true. In fact, this non-separation of powers is what makes the professional art field different than all the other professions.

Artmaking used to be a calling. Now it claims to be a profession that follows some of the codes of all professions (consistency, performance, decorum) while obviously disregarding others as not relevant. In my brief comments, I will be touching upon the contiguous areas of the *practical* and the *mental/theoretical* in the professional art world.

Let me express that *first you must* see the role that internal dynamics have in the shaping of the professional fine artist. In this métier, character, mon ami, is destiny. Informed mindfulness is the great agitator.

It was once said that to become successful in art you have to take into account mistakes, mis-strikes, mis-cues. It gets embarrassing, humiliating after a while. But Bruce Mau, the graphic designer, goes one step further. He claims that artists have to love their mistakes. *That's* how strong a professional artist has to be in order to succeed and flourish. Learning to love, even trust mistakes, takes self-wisdom and rigor.

Fact is, you can't be creative without making a mistake. Creating, systematically, with vision in mind, is hard work. The task requires time, playfulness, planning, willfulness, ambition, and stamina. This means that *first you must* see yourself as on your own, the shaper and creator of your own destiny. This implies being able and willing to develop your own system of micro-directed prioritizing.

What does this entail for the pro? It means that *first you must* be your own expert on self-monitoring. Artistic achievement has its price, takes its time, and takes its toll. It is a serious endeavor that takes a lot out of you because it is predicated on the taking of oneself seriously and knowing when not to get into one's own way (meaning, your creative process's way). The underlying premise is that if you don't take yourself seriously, no one ever will (or should).

To be a professional artist is to be a cultural producer. It takes a finessed skill to do this. Artists are individuated, by definition. They are engaged in this creative field as a means to an end. That end, more often than not, is clarity of purpose and vision. I have never met a professional artist who did not know when to take himself seriously, and when not to.

Such an outlook affects output. It demands mental as well as physical energy, a great deal of psychic reserves. Professional artmaking demands that *first you must* have strong balance and an equally rigorously well-defined sense of self. Humor helps. It demonstrates that a) you have a sense of proportion about things, and b) that you have detachment as well as passionate introspection about yourself and your work, the two requisites for high cultural achievement.

Humor comes in handy, particularly when things don't work themselves out or work out the way you had hoped/anticipated they would. It generates resourcefulness. Such resourcefulness requires (and creates) vibrancy. Humor allows you to grow. Growing up through humor means participating in a self-inflicted descent of dignity, withstanding unblinking self-scrutiny, and rising taller and stronger afterwards because of it. To be a professional artist means that, *first you must* develop fully a sense of humor about your seriousness, your primary serious motivation, which rests upon the commitment you have made to the attempt of making the best work that you know how.

*First you must* get into the routine of it. Labor and crafting become a dual-meditation. After a while you start to notice that no repetitive task is exactly the same even when it occurs over and over again. Rigor sets in over time through mindfulness. Once this occurs Flaubert's words ring true and strong: "Be regular and orderly in your life. Like a good bourgeois so that you may be violent and original in your work. "

Rigor is *de rigueur*. It inspires inspiration.

The professional artist is creative because he knows the nature of the beast called inspiration.

The writer Jack London once remarked, "You can't wait for inspiration. You go after it with a club." This means that, *first, you must* actively engage your imagination, even when there is seemingly nothing noteworthy happening, and hope that in doing so something will be brought to the surface of consciousness. Inspiration often comes after surrendering to what the non-artist might view (from the outside) as "boring routine."

*First*, then, *you must* take into account that professional artists take little for granted. They go into the thick of it. Artists review all their options and create new ones as they go along. The pro knows from trial and error that great faith comes from great doubt. True artists invest their time wisely in self-care. Importantly, the professional artist has humor, as humor is like a shared prayer of commonality. Being able to step back and see themselves with clear-eyed glasses, professional artists go about their tasks with the utmost commitment.

*First you must* see that the character and quality of commitment is the biggest factor for the professional artist.

This means taking measured risks, being resourceful and thinking, as a way of life, *outside the box*. It means finding the resources to continue making the work. It means paying the bills and doing so on time. The professional artist is a man or woman of the world. Not beyond or above it. *In it*. Pros have made the distinction that while money has to be kept in mind, they are not driven by it. Furthermore, productive professional artists are organized, have a sense of completion, and take satisfaction in meeting obligations. Professional artists have learned to become introverted extroverts and extroverted introverts. They can socialize as comfortably in the smartest tea or cocktail party, and also sit and be comfortable in their own skin when alone. Professional artists trust their own instincts. The artist acknowledges the importance of self-promotion and is not ashamed of doing so in the right way at the right time. This means being actively social, going to openings, attending dinners, hosting dinners, participating in the social life of the artistic community. That community is one of the benefits of being a professional artist. Enjoy it and use it. It comes with the territory, just as the spirit of competitiveness does.

*First you must* consider the positive as well as the negative aspects of competitiveness. Competitiveness is part of careerism, part of the ambition of being a professional artist. I think that careerism is a model that has its place while having both advantages and limitations. It can be a form of entrapment, engendering a type of conformism to expectations. Careerism can be a legitimate, yet not necessarily self-justifying, path to greater success and exposure. It means that, as in all things, being a professional artist doesn't mean that you lose your humanity. It means that the pro is able to harness the humanistic drives to the professional drives. It means focusing, prioritizing, and making the right decisions on how to husband or harbor your resources and internal expenditures, your psychic expenditures, your energy.

Being competitive in the professional art world means being competitive with yourself above all things. Keeping your eye on your game, *not on the scoreboard,* will make you a better player, and allow you to play with other good players in a field of mutually respectful adventurers of the spirit.

**Dominique Nahas** is a critic and independent curator based in Manhattan. A newly elected member of the board of AICA-USA (Association International des Critiques d'Art), Mr. Nahas has written for *Flash Art, Review, Paris Photo, Sculpture, Art on Paper, Handmade Paper Magazine, d'Art International,* and *Trans,* among numerous other magazines, and is a regular contributor to *Art in America* and *Art Asia Pacific.* Currently the Interim Director of the Hoffberger Graduate School at Maryland Institute College of Art, Nahas is the former director of the Neuberger Museum and former curator at Everson Museum, Syracuse, NY, and has curated many shows nationally and internationally, and serves as an advisor to many arts organizations. He served as associate curator at the Palm Beach Institute for contemporary Art (PBICA) between 2001 and 2004. Exhibitions include "BROOKLYN!"(2001) and "JAPAN:RISING" (2003). Nahas is concurrently a regular faculty member of Pratt Institute, New York City, and The New York Studio Program where he teaches critical theory.

# Defining Success

# Building a Profit Portfolio

By D. Dominick Lombardi

With all the emphasis on material wealth, evidenced by a big home, luxury car, exotic vacations, and the imperative to keep up with ever-changing fashion, it is easy to equate success with financial gains. This is a trap for the artist.

It is nearly impossible to support yourself solely on the sale of your art, and it is something like a one-in-a million chance to find wealth in this field. So why pursue this vocation? You do it because you have to, because you were born to be an artist, to be creative, and you find it impossible to picture yourself without the creative outlet.

To reinforce your commitment to the artistic life, I suggest that you redefine success. Then develop your networking plan for achieving that goal, for building a "profit portfolio."

When I think of success in the art arena, I prefer to look at how an artist affects the art world around them – whether it be locally, nationally or globally. It does not matter how far your reach is. If you look at all the ways you have a positive affect on the art world, and less at how much you are selling and for what price, it is a far more manageable and healthy way to judge your success as an artist.

Now this is not to say you should not want to sell your work. You should sell when you can, and try to get in the best collections possible. This can only help further your career. But because the appeal of any new or under-recognized art is limited, this should be only a part of your "profit portfolio." It is self-defeating for you to base your success solely and primarily on what you make in terms of dollars from the sale of your art.

To clarify, when I talk about profit portfolio, I mean recognition or personal sense of accomplishment garnered from reviews, curating, lecturing, making connections, building important relationships, and the like.

What you should seek to do is to positively affect the art world in as many ways as possible. And I also believe the more you put in, the more you get back.

This is what I have endeavored to do in my own career as an artist. I have built a very solid local base in my immediate art community by working in a number of art-related fields. This multiple approach has made it easier for me to broaden my scope of influence as an artist.

This is why I find a formula that incorporates the largest variety of art endeavors to be most helpful. We all have an agenda, a goal, ideas to set forth and spread somehow – and this can be done in many different ways in addition to your art-making. Just make sure your art remains a big part of your larger plan.

Let's look at some of the ways of achieving success and building your profit portfolio.

First, a good networking approach is key. When you make a solid, face-to-face contact with someone important, interesting, or helpful, keep in touch. Personal e-mails take little time, and they keep you connected for future projects.

### Making a Show: Curating

When you curate or organize a show with 20 artists, you have made, potentially, 20 new workable relationships, of which, perhaps two or three will develop. Later on, one of the artists you worked with on your show could curate a new exhibition and involve you in some way (as an artist) or perhaps as an essayist for a catalogue. This is more likely to happen if you keep in touch with e-mails about your projects or send announcement cards of exhibitions you are involved in, as participant or instigator.

Also, curating can be most helpful, since it places you in a position to express concepts and ideas outside the scope of your work. In fact, I often curate shows that have nothing to do with the intent of my own work. And when you become successful as a curator or writer, you become more interesting as an artist. It may sound obvious or clichéd, but it gets your name out there.

### Put It on Paper: Writing

Many new opportunities opened up for me when I began writing over a decade ago. This primarily helped to elevate me to equal status with gallery directors and museum curators. Once you give an opinion that is heard, you are respected as a viable participant in the overall dialogue of the art world. And in this situation, you, as you have seen in curating, meet individuals in the field that could one day make a big difference in your art career – if you keep in touch. Under these circumstances, you gain credibility, that merely approaching any institution as just another artist, cannot equal.

**Sound Off: Lecturing**

With writing comes opportunities to lecture. Lecturing can also be a substantive part of the curatorial or exhibiting process. It was very hard for me to speak publicly in the beginning – and still is – but if you stick to what you know, and perhaps start with panel discussions where you are one of several speakers, it is easier. Then, the more you do it, the more confident and relaxed you become.

**Getting Together: Collaboration**

One of my recent endeavors as an artist is called the Intelligent Design Project. Working with Michael Zansky, who is also an established artist, we are attempting to reorganize history, through an artist's vantage point, by creating our own timeline. This timeline, which includes both historic and fictitious "facts," is an ideal vehicle for a score of artists to weigh in on their thoughts about how religion, politics, and science clash and interact. While doing this in various institutions throughout the US, we select other artists along the way to join our cause, whatever their stance.

This type of alliance, where a hot topic fuels a controversy, can put you in touch with some like-minded artists with similar ideas that could further the project's success and your impact on the art world, thereby advancing your and their careers. These projects need not be overtly political or controversial; they could be based on a genre like landscape painting, style like Neo-impressionism, or a medium like watercolor. It is the linking, the networking that comes into play here.

And one great plus is that all of the artists I come in contact with, especially those who have a similar mindset to mine, have proved invaluable as a sort of intellectual support system. You are linking up with others who want to, or who are already working on or responding to similar elements, so it is natural and helpful to all to pool resources.

So with all or some of these activities, you are meeting more and more people in the field. You begin to stand out from the crowd as a curator, a writer, a lecturer, or collaborator. Just be sure to always maintain your commitment to being an artist. Keep track of your studio hours. Make sure you are getting your time in, whether that happens to be 15, 20, 25, or 50 hours a week.

## Some Strategies for Building Your Profit Portfolio

- NETWORK

- CURATE

- WRITE

- LECTURE

- COLLABORATE

- GO BEYOND THE EXPECTED

### Go Beyond the Expected: Be Creative

No matter what you are working on or what your level of involvement is you must remember to always keep your thoughts open and flowing. Don't be afraid to think "outside the box," beyond the gallery walls.

When I was a curatorial advisor for three years at the Lab Gallery in New York City, my partner, Matt Semler, and I hosted dinner parties and openings for each exhibition. We were doing about 25 shows a year, and we kept the dinner guest list lively so everyone could network casually, without the strains and awkwardness found in the gallery system as a whole.

The dinner parties included New York City art critics, curators, gallerists, and collectors who came to eat, drink, and meet the exhibiting artists, who may have come from as far away as the Pacific Rim. The dinner parties put a friendly face on the New York City art world. This, in turn, helped me to find a platform to offer my curating and writing skills to other cities.

And when you travel as a curator or writer, you meet many others who are working hard to branch out so it is only natural, again, to pool resources and perhaps work together on exhibitions that travel to multiple sites.

So take a step back, look at your community, and size up the opportunities you have. Then, seek out good spaces where you could curate shows. Write. Start blogs. Travel. Network. It all adds to your profit portfolio.

**D. Dominick Lombardi**, as an independent curator, has placed shows in a variety of galleries and museums such as The Shore Institute of Contemporary Art (SICA), Long Branch, NJ; Broadway Gallery, New York; Castle Gallery, College of New Rochelle, NY; Pelham Art Center, NY; and the Choate House Gallery, Pace University, Pleasantville, NY. He has written over 200 features and art criticisms that have been published in *The New York Times, Sculpture, Sculpture Review, d'Art* (US editor), *Art Papers, Art Lies, ARTnews, Art New England, NYARTS* magazine and others. He is a member of AICA-USA (Association International des Critiques d'Art).

## Some Observations on Becoming Successful in Today's Art World

By Jonathan Goodman

At present, the pursuit of success in the New York City art world carries with it a feeling of dread, in large part, because of the intense competition here.

There are only so many openings emerging artists can go to, so many CDs that they can send out, and so many invitations for studio visits they can offer to critics before a tiredness sets in, and individual self-esteem is damaged or even destroyed. But it is clear that artists must work as hard at mobilizing support for a career as making the art itself.

But there is a danger here: artists may become more interested in careerism rather than creating a challenging body of work.

Finding a gallery to show with, which of course, is key to a visible career, proves increasingly difficult. This is true despite the huge number of commercial spaces in Chelsea and other art enclaves in Manhattan, and the myriad not-for-profit spaces in Brooklyn and elsewhere in the metropolitan area.

Young artists priced out of Manhattan have settled in the outer boroughs or crossed the Hudson in the hope of benefiting from New York City's reputation as center of the global art world.

In truth, however, New York City's status as a cultural capital seems a little tattered on the edges. Many people are disappointed with the lack of serious, or even competent work, in Chelsea, supposedly contemporary art's most significant neighborhood. Of course, there are good shows by good artists who do stand out, but the feeling about new art is decidedly lackluster.

It is hard to fix such a recalcitrant problem, because the difficulties are woven into the experience of art itself. Despite the promise – some would say onslaught – of hundreds of galleries, sympathetic journals, and ever-increasing numbers of artists themselves, achieving the goal of making good art appears to be as elusive as ever.

Gone are the assumptions of a common culture, whereby artists and viewers both might agree on a shared background. In New York City, with its remarkable diversity of people from around the world, the artist simply cannot make work that will be understood by everyone.

Moreover, there is pop culture's increased dominance. In traditional mediums, such as painting and sculpture, we see that attachments to cultural precedents have often been waved away as examples of elitism. Instead, we find an embrace of popular imagery, whose extended appeal acts as a social leveler and common domain.

As a result, the artist is placed in a position that does not allow him to expand upon preexisting courses in art; a hip resourcefulness, almost always bordering on irony, has become the cultural currency of the day.

While I think it beside the point to judge or decry a tendency in culture that has been going on for decades, it makes sense to be aware of the implications of kitsch as it occurs within the embrace of the avant-garde.

The kind of success that kitsch has brought about in contemporary art results from an attitude that can only be described as satirical – witness the absurdities of Paul McCarthy's videos, which convey a savage contempt for current American culture by emphasizing its materialism and vulgarity.

This is an endgame in which social and political anger serve as the basis for travesty, which accounts for a considerable amount of the new art in New York City. Sometimes, as in the case of McCarthy himself, we find the sharpness of the satire hugely entertaining and focused on real weaknesses in the American way of life.

At the same time, however, artists in search of authenticity will find little to remind them of the sincerity that is concomitant with a genuine legitimacy of outlook. Such attributes as sincerity and authenticity mark a process whereby the superficial is rejected in favor of a deeper ambition, without which we are hard pressed to build a sense of integrity.

The situation affects all of us, especially those of us who are new to the vagaries of the contemporary art scene. The struggle to remain aware of who you are in circumstances that regularly challenge the sense of a unified self remains exactly that – a great effort made to develop an authentic self.

Inevitably, success is based upon the public recognition of achievement, without which many artists would surely feel isolated, too much alone.

Even so, I would claim that there are positions to be taken that do not evade appreciation so much as make the acknowledgment of the artist slightly lesser in importance.

What counts above all remains the territory of a confident artist, who takes upon himself the task of maintaining integrity over the course of a career. This most often would result in a pose whose development takes precedence over the other elements of success, without which we cannot establish ourselves, but which may become a bit marginalized.

The notion of virtue – what a 19th-century word! – seems embarrassing in its embrace of the emotionally authentic, but we are hard pressed to speak otherwise about art's moral force. In fact, we have transferred notions of integrity from private to public concerns, so that our outrage is saved for broader, less individualized matters.

That this happens is neither wrong nor right; it is simply the situation we face today. As a result, the pursuit of a successful career may well be hemmed in by, on the one hand, an overly politicized sensibility and by, on the other, a disturbingly narcissistic approach to expression.

The boundaries aren't quite fair in the sense that the two extremes I describe come close to a caricature of positions that once had genuine force. Certainly, it makes sense to condemn the reactionary forces – the persistence of racism and sexism – in our culture, just as it makes sense to celebrate the artist's own sense of expression.

The point is that these issues push to the side the more mundane aspects of gaining recognition for one's work, without which it seems hard to gain a foothold in the cycle of making art, and hosting exhibitions, that is so much a part of the successful career of the artist.

Yet, even so, it is wise to incorporate some of the concerns mentioned above because the success of a career does not necessarily reflect the power of a moral discourse, the likes of which may seem anachronistic, but which accurately underline what we all are in need of: the sense that art means something beyond the simple circumstances of its making and the often jaded practice of its circulation.

The last thing I would want to do would be to hang on, hard and fast, to a moralizing attitude – this simply won't do in a culture that rejects such a preoccupation as antiquated and beside the point.

Success in art brings with it a series of openings, which can result in genuine progress for the artist in the course of his or her career, and it can result in a give-and-take with the audience, whose reaction to and commentary on the artist's accomplishments form two of the major pleasures realizable in a response to contemporary art. So it becomes important to know that the drive to success does, in fact, have advantages, among them the sense of a communication between the artist and the viewer.

Such an exchange is basic to the practice of art, which needs a theater in which its expression can be performed. Without the infrastructure of support, artists find themselves neglected, isolated within circumstances that do not do justice to the public responsibility they must take on, in order to develop and move on to the next level of his or her achievement.

So, then, it proves impossible to simply wait for recognition; the artist must take it upon him – or herself to enter into a dialogue, which will hopefully result not only in edification, but also in an appreciation of the work's success.

The tension existing between the demands of integrity and the need for recognition tends to balance out in the career of the artist, whose output reflects a long journey toward an apotheosis of self.

Currently, the interest in politics can be indicated, as noted critic Arthur C. Danto has written, as an attempt to realize the political sublime. In consequence, the artist moves in the direction of satirizing public mores, which serve as the material of a political sensitivity that underscores the morality of an entire generation.

The trick is to see success as both a hoped-for goal and a danger – in the sense that sometimes artistic triumph results in false feelings of optimism.

Sincerity and authenticity seem to me to be qualities that are realized over time; success can damage one's access to these attributes. At the same time, we must attend to the psychological needs artists have, needs that are easy to make fun of, but which remain within the provenance of personal as well as public success. It is important, then, to balance psychic pleasure with a sense of communal responsibility toward the practice of art in general.

Success is much to be desired, but must be seen within an environment of shared meaningfulness, in which the altruism of the imagination receives equal billing with the enjoyment of an evident career. We must remember that art cannot continue in a vacuum; it is instead the culmination of private effort and public context. These attributes, so central to art practice, are intertwined more than they would initially seem.

**Jonathan Goodman** is an art writer and editor who has published extensively on modern and contemporary art for such publications as *Art in America, Sculpture, Art Asia Pacific,* and *Art on Paper.* He has written extensively on Asian art for several publications, and has written exhibition catalogues for art venues throughout the world. He currently teaches at Pratt Institute, New York City.

Navigating the Art World

# The "E" Word
By Kathleen Cullen

My career in the art world has focused on "emerging" artists in the marketplace. But how does one define an "emerging" artist? Is it determined by age? Can someone in their 70s be an emerging artist? What about his or her exhibition record? Does it have to be shown at a really alternative space, like a coffee shop? Does having a show in an established gallery disqualify the candidate from "emerging" status? Is there a price limit on artworks for emerging artists?

Even among renowned art professionals these are questions without clearcut answers. There is no consensus among them about what classifies an artist as emerging, or even what the term really means for all involved parties – artists, collectors, dealers, etc. In reality, the term is probably a commercial construct useful for selling art with little significance to the artists, although there are situations where it can be meaningful.

Let's assume that an emerging artist is just being recognized and has little or no exhibition experience. Because of the nature of the business of art, taking on an emerging artist is a gamble. As a dealer, you are betting on the artist to not only continue his or her career and constantly develop their work, but you are also betting on yourself and your ability as a dealer to recognize art that the public will ultimately appreciate.

It is the challenge of recognizing these individuals and providing them with the environment to transform from "emerging" to established artists that draws me to this business. My job is to build a market for the work of an emerging artist, based upon an intrinsic belief that the art will be deemed significant when others – reviewers, dealers, and collectors – have expressed their approval.

As an art dealer, the first thing that I look at in an artist's work is the strength and originality of his or her ideas. In addition, I try to discern the artist's expectations and the potency of his or her ambitions. Are those expectations in line with his or her talent, responsibility, and discipline? These qualifications may seem simple, but it is sometimes difficult to find a reliable measure to gauge an artist.

I have discovered, in my 20 years of doing studio visits, that the artist's studio is the best environment in which to view his or her art. I can tell a lot about the artist's seriousness from the state of the studio. How is the work treated? Is it more important than his or her lifestyle?

I also find it helpful to prolong the process of taking on new artists; it is important for me to bring an artist's work into the gallery and live with it for a few months. By looking at and studying the work for a period of time, I can determine if it will have lasting appeal beyond an exhibition.

In truth, the artist's talent and the dealer's abilities alone are not enough to facilitate the transformation of an emerging artist into an established artist. It may be that a single, adventurous collector, willing to toy with promising but untested work, will play a critical role in an artist's success. For those who are willing to take a chance on emerging artists, there can be an added dimension to the acquisition. After all, every artist was once "emerging," and the thought of being the first to have recognized new talent propels many collectors to support "emerging" artists.

### The Emerging Artist's Natural Habitat
Where do I find these emerging artists? I go to undergraduate and graduate school shows at the various New York City art schools; Cranbrook Academy of Art, Bloomfield Hills, MI; Alfred University, NY; The Chicago Art Institute, etc. Though I have found new talent at these institutions, I think there is a danger in taking on work by students or recent graduates as they may have yet to make a true commitment to their art.

In New York City there are alternative spaces that showcase emerging artists. P.S.1 in Long Island City, Queens, now affiliated with the Museum of Modern Art; White Columns; Artists Space; and Creative Time projects are also great venues for sourcing international emerging artists. There are also lesser-known foundations, such as The Marie Walsh Sharpe Foundation and the Elizabeth Foundation for the Arts Studio Program; they provide artists (national and international emerging talents) with studio space in Brooklyn.

In addition, The Drawing Center, which has been a unique and dynamic part of New York City's cultural life since 1977, has also proven to be a good source for young talent. As the only not-for-profit institution in the country to focus on the exhibition of drawings, it frequently juxtaposes work by master artists with work by emerging and under-recognized artists.

The Brooklyn-based, not-for-profit Smack Mellon's Summer Exhibition is coordinated by an emerging curator and includes artists selected from Smack Mellon's Emerging Artists Exhibition Program. I have also had the good fortune to sit on the NYFA (New York

Foundation for the Arts) panels as a judge for a corporate sponsorship prize awarded to under-recognized artists, and have found it to be a fantastic place to observe the recognition of new talent.

Another source of emerging talent are the various art fairs around the world, and I try to attend as many as possible. The benefit of art fairs is that in addition to the participating galleries, there are usually unofficial offshoot venues that run concurrently in other spaces. This diversity of involvement allows a visitor to experience a multitude of emerging artists.

For example, during Art Chicago, the Art Institute has both its Bachelor and Masters of Fine Art students exhibiting in alternative spaces, and the show is highlighted in the VIP program of the fair. At Art Basel in Switzerland, which is undoubtedly the most prestigious of all art fairs, Liste, a Dutch not-for-profit organization showing student work (generally under the auspices of a government program), has a place to exhibit promising talent.

Additionally, at the Art Dealers Association of America Art Show held at the Seventh Regiment Armory on Park Avenue in New York City, White Columns, Artists Space, Art in General, and a few other established not-for-profits present newcomers. While not featured alongside established dealers, the work is still displayed under the same roof.

The significance of supporting emerging artists is clearly visible in art schools. There is currently a program in connoisseurship, offered by the education department of Christie's auction house, where students are required to make PowerPoint presentations about emerging artists and to speculate about their future success. Similarly, there is a course in New York University's Department of Art and Art Professions in appraisals that examines emerging artists to determine the value of the art produced. It is an interesting balancing act to determine the appropriate value of an artist's work when it has yet to find a market.

Over the years I have found that dealing with "emerging" talent provides an amazing challenge. Although at times it can be frustrating, working with promising young artists that have yet to be discovered is extremely exciting and rewarding.

## A Cautionary Tale

A number of years ago, I curated a large group show of drawings. All of the artists had gotten their work in on time with one exception. On the day of the installation, the delinquent artist arrived, after the hanging had been completed; his excuse was that it had taken days to frame his work. The result didn't seem to have warranted such labor – it seemed cobbled together from salvaged materials.

He insisted that we move everything to accommodate the placement of his work. When the installer (who is an artist in his own right) chided the artist about his behavior and disrespectful tone, the artist countered with "What does it matter to you?" implying that he was "only" an installer.

Needless to say, I will never include that artist in another exhibition because of his overinflated sense of self-importance.

Having a successful working relationship with a gallery necessitates that the artist respect the gallery owner, other artists, and anyone else who might be involved along the way. I encourage artists to cultivate friendships with other artists, and to develop mutually cooperative relationships with other professionals because a well-established network of artists, curators, and dealers can allow for significant advancement of an artist's career; an over-inflated ego has no place in healthy gallery-artist relationship.

## What's Age Got to Do with It?

The idea of supporting new, innovative work doesn't have anything to do with the age of the artist. There's nothing wrong with today's emphasis on youth as long as professionals are also willing to recognize older artists when they are doing something new and remarkable. Shouldn't an artist be judged by the quality of work he or she is producing at a particular time?

Still there are legitimate concerns about longevity – the length of an artist's career. With a promising young artist, who is 21, there is the potential of a long career in the spotlight, but remember the late-blooming artist Willem de Kooning who didn't become a successful and well-known artist until he was well into his 50s, and he died at 93.

With talent, innovation, hard work, and the help of dealers, curators, and collectors willing to take the gamble on a yet-to-be established artist, it is still possible to witness the incredible transformation of "emerging" talent into an established name.

**Kathleen Cullen** is director of Kathleen Cullen Fine Art in New York City and has held that position at leading New York City galleries including Ramnarine Gallery, THE Gallery, Althea Viafora Gallery, Stuart Levy Gallery, and the Sandra Gering Gallery. Cullen has independently curated some of the most controversial exhibitions in New York City during the 1990s in spaces such as P.S.1, the Postmasters Gallery, Barbara Toll Fine Arts, and Ramnarine Gallery.

# Gallery Roulette
By Ann Landi

To the young or emerging artist, the art world may seem like a forbidding maze, a complicated circuitry of inside contacts and arcane codes almost impossible for the newcomer to crack. How can the artist without affiliations approach a dealer? What's the best way to find representation? And what are some steps to take to assure a long and fruitful association?

The number of galleries has been shrinking in recent years because of an uncertain economy, so you will need to do your homework carefully. And the first step is to canvass the territory. Get to know the galleries in your area or, if you have your sights set on making a career in Los Angeles or New York City or Chicago, cruise the dealers in different neighborhoods and buildings to become familiar with their aesthetic. Study dealer websites to understand what kind of work they represent.

"Young artists think there are so many galleries, there has to be one for me," says Mary Sabbatino, vice president of Galerie Lelong in Chelsea. "It's really like love. There probably is one person for you, but you have to find that person the hard way. You can't just speed date."

Networking can also be critical to getting your work looked at and your name and face known in the community. When she first moved to New York City, armed with a law degree to ensure her support while she found her way as a painter, Ellen Harvey went to as many openings as she could. A naturally gregarious and outgoing person of considerable warmth, Harvey had little trouble making friends and finding a support system while she was still in her 20s. A decade later, she now has a long list of commissioned work behind her in addition to a book on her "New York City Beautification" project.

If you've found a couple of galleries that seem a good fit for you, take the time to get to know them better. "Come to openings, get to know my artists. At the very least look at the website," says Kim Foster of the Kim Foster Gallery in New York City. "I can think of a couple of artists who came to be affiliated with me in this way. It wasn't like they just walked in cold to the gallery."

Art fairs can be a good way to review a number of dealers all in one fell swoop, but they're terrible places to approach the personnel. "Do not try to corner a dealer at an art fair," admonishes Margaret Thatcher of Margaret Thatcher Projects in New York City. "Our time and energy there is devoted to selling art, and when you've got more than $25,000 invested to show at an art fair, the last thing you want to do is talk to an aspiring artist."

Most dealers say they are motivated to look at new work because of recommendations from artists they already know and respect, collectors whose taste they trust, museum curators, and even other galleries. "I'm most intrigued when an artist affiliated with the gallery says to me, 'You really should see this work,'" says Sabbatino.

Foster says she decided in part to take on one of her newer artists, Sydney Blum, because of a recommendation from Petah Coyne, who is not part of her stable but has a long and respectable track record of museum shows and critical notice. (For this reason, even if your star is not rising as quickly as you'd like, it's wise to stay in touch with colleagues whose careers may be on a faster trajectory than yours.)

As for approaching a dealer for the first time, some say it's fine to come into the gallery with a piece of art in hand. "If you have a representative sample of your work that's small enough to carry around with you, first make certain that the dealer is not busy – wait for a moment when the telephone's not ringing, when she's not involved with other people – and then make your introductions," says Nance Frank, owner and director of the Gallery on Greene in Key West, FL. "Some might immediately say, 'You'll have to make an appointment,'" she continues. "But if you've got a piece of work in your hands, most are going to look at it."

Others, however, discourage this tactic. "Definitely not," says Katharina Rich Perlow of the eponymous New York City gallery. "Most galleries are usually very busy, and it's embarrassing if you have to reject someone on the spot."

And others are somewhat on the fence. "Last year we picked up one painter who just walked into the gallery," says Andrew Liss, assistant director of Gallery Henoch in New York City. "He actually had the work in hand, and it was terrific, but I wouldn't generally encourage people to make an approach that way."

In the days before digital photography, most artists dropped off or mailed a packet of slides with a cover letter and perhaps a biography. Now dealers say they will look at CDs and sometimes images sent via e-mail. "But have a printout of the images," says Liss. "I don't mind looking at a CD, but I really like to have a few digital printouts first before I go through a disk full of work."

Liss never looks at e-mailed images that require downloading because of the number of viruses out there. "But if they're already in the body of the message or if the sender can direct me to a website, I will generally be tempted to look."

The subject line, Liss adds, is important: don't say you're part of some ephemeral or nonexistent movement, like "Transient Post-Expressionism," but if you can find a way of catching a dealer's eye – "Richard Serra Recommended I Get in Touch" or "Intriguing Portraits in Stained Glass" – you stand a better chance of getting your missive read.

Some dealers, though, say they don't want to be bothered with e-mail at all. "It feels intrusive to me if I get an e-mail submission from someone I don't know at all," Sabbatino claims. The best way to find out how a gallery prefers to be approached is to stop by and ask the assistant at the front desk or make a phone call. "Don't be intimidated, but don't be pushy," says Liss.

And if you're told a gallery is not looking at new work, move on. It's nothing personal, but most likely just an indication that an establishment already has a full roster of artists and has already scheduled shows for more than a year in advance. For that reason, most dealers advise that young artists look for young galleries, places where both can grow together.

Virtually everyone in the business says that it's critical for artists to maintain a website, particularly at the outset of their careers. It's a kind of calling card, a sign of professionalism and seriousness. "I simply expect young artists to have a website as part of their portfolio. It's just like slides were at one point mandatory," explains Liss. "We're also looking for people who are not trying to leave all the attention-getting up to us."

Once an artist has established a relationship with a gallery, and has images on that dealer's site, maintaining a separate site becomes a more delicate proposition. "I think it's important for galleries to have the artists' work on their websites," says Frank. "I always say that an artist's website is competition for me, and I hate that."

But if the dealer's site and that of the individual artist are linked, the playing field is not only level but also wider and more equitable since most reputable dealers ask for a percentage of the sales an artist makes on his or her own.

After you've submitted examples of your work, be patient. Galleries may take months to look at work, but most will eventually check you out. "I try to set aside one or two days a month to review material that comes in," says Liss.

Wait a couple of weeks before following up and do so by phone; an e-mail is likely to get overlooked. When a gallery is truly interested, someone will most likely ask to make a studio visit or to see samples of your work. The usual procedure is to put an emerging artist in a group show and see how collectors and critics react. And don't be devastated if you're turned down.

"'No' doesn't mean you're a bad artist," says Foster. "It more often means your work may not be right for this space, or it doesn't mesh with my sensibilities."

And when you've determined that a dealer is seriously interested in you and your work, look out for your own welfare. "Once you get that important interview, be sure you're doing an interview of your own," advises Frank. "There are some questions you should ask. Do you have insurance? When and how often can you give me a show? How often do you pay, and what is my percentage of sales? How much of my work will be exposed? What can you do to advance my career?" She continues, "You also need to know what responsibilities are yours. If you will be asked to shell out for advertising, announcements, and other 'extras'." This is always a warning sign that a dealer may not be as serious as you'd like.

In addition to your confidence in your work, how you present yourself at all times may determine how much respect you can claim in the end. "When you walk in the door or send an e-mail or drop off your work, think about how you would like to be treated," says Frank. "Try to present that to the person in charge."

**Ann Landi** is a freelance writer and critic who writes frequently for *ARTnews* and *The Wall Street Journal*. She has published articles on art, architecture, reviews, and criticism in *Architectural Digest, Art & Antiques, The New York Times,* and other publications. She has served as editor on a variety of specialty publications and published articles and essays in numerous national magazines. She has curated exhibitions at the Delaware Center for Contemporary Art, Wilmington, and Kim Foster Gallery in New York City. In addition to writing many artist catalogue essays, Landi is the author of the four-volume *Schirmer Encyclopedia of Art* (Gale Group, 2001).

## The Five Quickest Ways to Lose a Gallery, or How To Not Even Get in the Door in the First Place
By Robert Curcio

### 1) Blindly Send Your Packet to a Gallery

You just spent many days and a good amount of money producing your promotional packet of materials, either for e-mail or regular mail, with images that are in focus, properly color balanced, and clearly labeled; a succinct artist statement; a couple of glowing reviews; and an impressive résumé.

Everything is professional and looks great, except that your cover letter starts with "Dear Sir or Madam" or "To Whom It May Concern."

To make matters worse, you send it to the most inappropriate gallery possible for your work. This packet would not last one minute with an assistant, let alone be given to the director or owner. There is no quick or easy way to find gallery representation other than spending your time doing your homework.

As with everything else in today's world, start with the Internet and review the gallery's website. Besides looking at the artists they represent, take a close look at "Other Artists" or "Works Available" to have a fuller understanding of how the gallery conducts business. If this section lists 30 blue-chip artists and only a few artists as represented, most likely the gallery is focused on the secondary or resale market.

See if prices for the works are listed (usually not, but sometimes they are), because if the majority of works are $50,000 and your price is $5,000, it isn't the right gallery for you.

Read its "About Us" and "Contact" sections so you know the gallery's history, the type of art represented, and the name and proper spelling of the person to whom you will address your packet. Specific submission procedures might even be posted, and you want to follow those guidelines.

After finding an appropriate gallery, Google its name to see what pops up. Maybe an article or a blog will say great things about the gallery, or that the artists are charged exhibition fees, or that other artists have had bad experiences getting paid.

While going online will tell you a great deal, there is nothing like going there in person. In addition to attending the gallery's opening receptions, stop by in the middle of the week and talk to some of the staff to get a better feel. And, do not go to the gallery's receptions only to drink and eat because that will be what you are remembered for.

## 2) Host a Bad Studio Visit

The way to avoid a bad studio visit is to first think of it as a job or school interview mixed with a casual visit between acquaintances getting to know each other. Not only is the gallery interviewing you, but you should be interviewing the gallery. Both of you should leave the visit saying "That was great and I want to work with them," and, not shaking your head mumbling "What a waste of my time. This person is totally wrong for me."

As with any good interview, there are many basic commonsense things to keep in mind. Don't be late or forget to even show up. You and your studio should be presentable. Don't fumble around looking for work – have the work you want to show readily available. Turn your cell phone off or have it on vibrate; only answer if it's an emergency. Put the answering machine on the landline. Get a baby – and/or pet sitter. If your significant other is not significant to your art, he or she should not be there. In a nutshell, eliminate anything that will distract the visitor from seriously looking at your work.

You might be thinking that all this doesn't matter, and that it is only about the art. But, would you want to exhibit at a gallery that has poor lighting with haphazardly hung work on cracked walls, or to sit on a broken chair while waiting an hour to meet the director who looks like he or she just got in from a very long night while constantly arguing on the cell with a partner (business, personal, or otherwise), and all this combined with a dog that won't stop barking?

The casual part of this visit is getting to know one another, which is far more enjoyable, but it's tricky to achieve. Since this is a social mixer, you should consider having some refreshments. Keep it simple: water, coffee, or juice, and maybe fruit, cookies, or chips. You want to offer this after talking for a while, to refresh the conversation, and keep the good time going. Also, it's just being a good host to an invited guest.

This might seem silly (it's only about the art!), but my former partner in a gallery would grumble about how inconsiderate the artist was if there had been no refreshments just when we were deciding whether or not to include the artist's work in an exhibition.

It's important to talk about your work, but don't lecture or explain everything down to the tiniest detail. Give the other person time to think, ask questions, and make observations.

Listen to his or her interpretation of your work regardless of how far off it is, then try to tactfully adjust his or her way of thinking to your own through an engaging conversation. This way the gallerist can learn how you view the work, mix this with his or her own interpretation, and then distill it all. Remember this is the person who will be talking about your work to potential clients, museums, curators, writers, etc., and you want him or her to understand your process and ideas.

If, during the studio visit, all signals are moving in a good direction, you can discuss business issues. Ask if there is an upcoming exhibition planned that you might participate in. Discuss pricing and ask about the typical commission agreement. You might also inquire if you could leave a few pieces on consignment.

### 3) Be Unreasonable
You did your research, had a successful studio visit, and now the gallery wants your work to be included in an exhibition. Since this will be the first time you and the dealer have worked with each other, the experience will determine whether the relationship continues or ends. Having an exhibition is great, but the goal is an ongoing relationship with the gallery that represents you. Remember that you are trying to create a win/win situation; it isn't all about you and what you want, forgetting the needs of the gallery.

I recall one artist that my partner and I felt was very good, although he had a bit of a "you-should-be-so-lucky-to-exhibit-me" attitude. Still we decided to overlook that and include him in a group exhibit of new gallery artists. At first he was hesitant because he didn't know any of the other artists – reasonable. But he also expressed his opinion that the other artists probably weren't as good as he was – unreasonable. Only after seeing the other artists' work, which he deigned to be acceptable, did he agree to be in the exhibit.

The onslaught came on installation day: demands about where his work was to be hung and what should hang next to it – unreasonable. The wall behind the work had to be a specific color, different from the rest of the gallery – unreasonable. And the work required a particular type of lighting – unreasonable.

I asked the artist to come back after the hanging was finished, so we could talk – reasonable; he returned only to give a half-hearted approval of the installation.

The opening reception was well attended, and we sold a few works, including one by this artist. Selling a piece at an opening is a very good sign, however; this artist would not step away while we were conducting the sale; later he proceeded to criticize the way it was handled – unreasonable.

In spite of his behavior, we offered this artist a solo exhibition the following year – reasonable. The artist then demanded it be scheduled at the beginning of the season with no room for discussion – unreasonable. We postponed further negotiation and discussion until the end of the group exhibition.

In the interim, an invitation that had been sent out by this artist was returned to the gallery because of an incorrect address, with a personal note stating that he was the only good artist in the current exhibit, and the gallery left a great deal to be desired – unreasonable and unprofessional.

When the artist returned after the close of the exhibition and wanted to discuss his pending solo show, we politely said we had changed our minds, and returned his work with the returned invite and obnoxious note visibly attached to the back – reasonable.

### 4) Micromanage the Gallery

Maybe it's the excitement of your exhibition, or a previously unpleasant experience, or just a different way of doing things, but you must let the gallery do its job. Don't call the gallery every day asking endless questions, and pestering the assistants to do favors for you. If you are calling, e-mailing, or dropping by every ten minutes, each day of your exhibition (and even when your work is not being exhibited), you are keeping the gallery from conducting business, which, by the way, is to further your career. In other words, you are actually being disruptive to your own progress.

Just imagine how you would feel if you were in the studio ready to spend the day creating a masterpiece, but instead you are constantly interrupted by your cell phone ringing, your beeper beeping, people dropping by to say "Hi" and staying an hour, or your computer continually telling you "You've got mail." You would not be able to accomplish anything.

When you are having an exhibition, keep in touch with the gallery by e-mail or telephone. Once a day is fine, dropping by occasionally is a good thing, but call the gallery and coordinate a day and time that would be best. A gallerist wants you to be involved, and to help them help you, as long as it is not overbearing. Just as you don't want someone mixing your paints or picking parts of your assemblage, the gallerist doesn't need you to chat with the receptionist or ask for an accounting of sales at the end of every day.

Be obsessive making your best work and leave the gallery to do what it can do best – promote that work.

## 5) Do Things Behind the Gallery's Back

So that everyone wins, have any inquiries about your work go through the gallery, and let the gallery decide how to best manage you. If someone is interested in purchasing a piece or a writer wants to interview you, let the gallery do the work of representing your interests so you can spend more time in the studio.

Once the gallery is acting on an opportunity or lead, do what you can to assist them, but this does not mean interference, it just means being supportive. And don't launch a phone or e-mail blitz or make promises that the gallery can't fulfill.

By letting the gallery handle the orchestration of an opportunity, you both win. For example, with a museum exhibition, the gallery may get a "courtesy of …" credit on exhibition labels and other written materials. The gallerist could be interviewed with you for a magazine article.

Also, depending upon your agreement with the gallery, the museum may pay for reproduction fees for photographic or written materials, sales tax, shipping expense, and other costs that otherwise you and the gallery might have to incur.

When both sides of a partnership fulfill their obligations in a mutually respectful manner, it becomes the proverbial "win-win" situation. It's no different in the art world.

**Robert Curcio** is a private dealer, an advisor to collectors, and co-founder and producer of the Scope Art Fair, Inc. Scope is an international contemporary art fair, which was launched in New York City, 2002. Curcio has been an arts professional in New York City since the early 1990s, during which time he has been the owner of a contemporary gallery (Curcio/Spector), director of a nonprofit arts organization (Ward-Nasse Gallery), independent curator, dealer, and writer. Artists he represented have been included in exhibitions at Artists Space, Art Resources Transfer, Art in General, New Museum, OK Harris Gallery, Robert Miller, and Throckmorton Fine Art.

# The Art Fair Phenomenon

By Robert Curcio

Somewhere before the turn of the new millennium, the art world began to experience a perfect storm, but one that would generate great power and riches rather than a destructive force. Within little more than a decade, the international art fair has gone from being an experiment in marketing to an unavoidable phenomenon – and a huge marketing success.

The rise of the art fair, which has now become a major topic of discussion throughout the art world, began with the resurgence of the contemporary art market in the mid 1990s and a wave of do-it-yourself exhibitions in cities across the globe. These conditions made it possible in 1994 for four young galleries to organize a fair, with some 20 dealers on a couple of floors at Manhattan's Gramercy Hotel, creating what would become one of the leading international contemporary art fairs. The immediate success and popularity of the fair led them to move to the much larger Armory on East 26th Street, which also happened to be the site of the groundbreaking 1913 Armory Show, and the new venue lent its name to the fair. Now located on the West Side Passenger Ship Terminal Piers, the 2010 Armory Fair boasted of hundreds of exhibitors, 60,000 visitors, and millions in sales.

In addition to the Armory Fair, other well-organized exhibitions and fairs began to spring up in many cities across the globe in alternative spaces including hotels, warehouses, storefronts, and commercial-photography studios, adding to the momentum. Soon new works by emerging artists were selling furiously and bringing respectable prices from noteworthy collectors and museums, accompanied by a great deal of general media attention, which was something new. And, as with anything new and booming, everyone wanted to capitalize on the action simply by focusing on the commerce that was being generated; this led to the birth of what we might call the "Art Fair Marathon."

The momentum came to a virtual standstill in the wake of 9/11, when global jetsetters and serious art-world travelers alike stayed home, auctions sales went flat, museum attendance dropped, and galleries were forced to cancel their participation in fairs. A few fairs canceled and rescheduled for the following year attracting smaller crowds. But by the spring of 2002, the art world was on the rebound, and with the start of a new art season in the fall, the marathon was suddenly back to full speed with many new participants.

Originally scheduled to launch in December 2001, Art Basel Miami Beach was postponed until the following December. The American sister event of Art Basel in Switzerland, arguably the most successful and, after 37 years, the oldest such fair, Art Basel Miami Beach proved that the combination of an international art show, Art Deco buildings, and the white sands of South Beach in December was irresistible.

Everything a successful fair needs could be found in Miami: an active, growing collector base; contemporary museums expanding their collections; an international airport; a city willing to cooperate fully; a crossroads for some of the wealthiest people in the world; and, of course, beaches, nightclubs, luxury shopping, and glamorous restaurants. The first week of December seemed a perfect time, not only because warm, sunny beaches are most appealing in winter, but also because not much else of import is scheduled in the art world just prior to the holidays.

Now the week of the Miami Beach fair is one of the busiest and most expensive events of the year for that resort city. In addition to the main fair, there are numerous satellite fairs ranging from the established (Nada, Scope, Pulse) to hotel-based fairs, such as Bridge, Flow, and Art Now. One of the newest is SeaFair, held aboard a specially designed luxury ship. Ten or more do-it-yourself exhibitions were organized by artists, curators and galleries that were not accepted into any of the fairs – a sort of multiple *Salon des Refusés*.

The art-world global pilgrimage begins long before the Miami Beach extravaganza, however, with fairs such as Art Cologne, Art Forum Berlin, Berliner Liste, and Preview Berlin in Germany during September. October follows with major fairs including Frieze in London and FIAC in Paris. And then there are Art Copenhagen, Contemporary Istanbul, Gulf Art Fair in Dubai, Art Verona in Italy, ShContemporary 2007 in Shanghai, MACO in Mexico City, Art Fair Tokyo, and Toronto International Art Fair, to name a small fraction of the international fairs willing to introduce the established or novice collector to what they believe to be new in contemporary art. If you prefer staying closer to home, you can visit Chicago; Washington, DC; Portland, Oregon; Los Angeles; Santa Fe; Savannah; or Boston, all of which have their own fairs.

The commercial appeal of these events is clear: a city hosting an art fair can go from business as usual to becoming an international hot spot in less than a year, gaining prestige, media attention, and a sizable revenue boost.

But what about the appeal to denizens of the art world? Certainly something can be said for the chance to visit booths representing hundreds of galleries and thousands of artists, one-stop shopping for everyone from collectors looking for bargains to curators wanting to put together new exhibitions of the latest artists in a short period of time. Competition is so fierce that some galleries have been known to tell potential buyers that they will hold a work for only 10 or 15 minutes. But you don't have to be a buyer or seller to get in the swing. The fairs are also a feast for researchers, journalists, networkers, and celebrity watchers.

At their best, these fairs can also be a bonanza for artists at any stage of their career. An emerging artist with little or no exposure can make a first sale to a major collector, get name recognition in art publications, discover international exhibition opportunities, and much more. For an established artist, a fair could set a new price level or breathe vitality into a lagging career. Above all, though, artists should view a fair as an opportunity to do research, seeing which galleries might be most disposed to their work, what comparable pieces are selling for, and which gallery is generating the most buzz. These are places to make contacts with curators, media, and museum directors as well as dealers and collectors. But a word of caution is in order. Visiting artists should approach a gallery booth carefully, gauge the temperature of the booth, and then proceed slowly, rather than insisting that the gallery must come for a studio visit while handing them a CD loaded with images. The pace of activity around the booths can verge on the frenetic, and you might make more connections at one of the many parties and dinners that take place in the evenings.

Perhaps the art world sector most concerned about the fairs are the gallerists. They strive to make sure the collectors, curators, writers, consultants, and all the other major players come directly to their booth, stay awhile to schmooze, and buy. Sales can be so phenomenal at fairs that some galleries have been known to generate a quarter of their annual sales there. So even though participation and expenses can run anywhere from a few thousand for a regional or satellite fair to $50,000 or more for a major international event, the return can be significant. This is especially true for a new gallery without a large collector base or a big budget; a sold-out or even moderately successful booth with good media attention can launch them onto the international circuit, get their artists into important exhibitions and collections, and develop a valuable "waiting list" of collectors wanting to buy their artists' works.

And while these fairs continue to pop up in what seems like almost every city in the world, we still have biennials, auctions, museum galas, gallery openings, benefits, and other significant events happening regularly, which can create major scheduling headaches. Indeed, the art world is starting to show signs of what can be called "art fair fatigue."

Whether as a collector, gallerist, or die-hard pilgrim, you simply cannot keep the pace going from fair to fair, month after month, without running down. A Grand Tour of art in Europe could include the Venice Biennale, Art Basel, Documenta, Prague Biennale, and Sculpture Projects Münster, one opening right after the other, often with just a day or two in between.

As a result of all the overlap, collectors are starting to be more selective about which fairs they attend, taking into account the quality of exhibitors and the range of services offered. Some serious collectors are even going to fairs before they open, while exhibitors are unwrapping art, buying what they want, and then leaving before the VIP opening and the crowds arrive.

Exhibitors are also being more selective in which fairs they participate. One gallery owner I know took part in year-round international fairs with just a brief holiday break, rarely stepping into his own gallery. After two years of continuous fair-going, he had had enough and just wanted to stay at home and work.

Now gallerists are comparing costs and services as a collector might, or opting for more regional fairs because those open a whole new area of the country to the gallery. They may also find it useful to participate in a fair that has a specific focus, such as works on paper, photography, or outsider art.

None of which is meant to imply that art fairs will go away anytime soon. But with so many galleries still wanting to participate in just about any fair they can, many fairs are forgetting the "art" part and focusing on the business of having a trade fair. The trade-fair mentality means stuffing as many exhibitors as possible into ever smaller booths, simply because the galleries will pay just about any fee to participate. The galleries, in turn, feel the need to cram their booths from floor to ceiling with sellable art to cover those fees. In situations like this, the vetting or selection process is often done away with, turning the fair into a "pay-to-play" situation. When this happens, you end up with a hodge-podge of mediocre art that lacks any vitality or inventiveness. Exhibitors and collectors alike go with what they know to be safe and reliable, rather than taking chances. The result is that quality artists, regardless of the stage of their careers, are overlooked.

Additionally, artists cannot produce work fast enough in the quantities needed to supply their dealers with exciting new pieces for each fair. And the best, most commercially successful artists can't risk diluting the quality of their work just to keep their dealers happy. And if the art is not good, why bother going to an art fair in the first place?

So to continue succeeding, the fairs will have to cool down the pace and find a middle ground where business can still take place, and artists can advance their careers and get their work to a wider audience, without feeling like they're trapped in a garish Fellini movie. One hopes that wiser minds will prevail, and that the fairs will find a way to keep both quality and interest high.

Reprinted (with updates) by permission from the *Hudson River Museum & Gallery Guide*, Fall 2007.

# Print Matters

By Deborah Ripley

My first encounter with prints was when I purchased a poster of a Modigliani nude on a special textured paper that resembled canvas to decorate my college dorm room. I put a fancy walnut frame on it and considered it an artwork.

It wasn't until years later when I started working in a print gallery that I became aware of all the different kinds of prints there are. In fact, the sheer number of different printing techniques can be overwhelming.

But the fundamental question becomes why should you consider making prints at all? Prints can serve you both creatively and commercially. Let's start with the creative side.

Printmaking allows you to translate original works onto paper using a variety of reproduction methods. If you have not worked on paper before, this might be a creative shortcut to achieving different effects such as collage, or changing the scale of a work, or even its color or texture. The ability to work quickly to print multiple copies in sequence can lead to new creative possibilities, which can then be fed back into the original work.

This was certainly the case for Jasper Johns, who considered printmaking a medium through which he could experiment easily and quickly, allowing him to cross-pollinate ideas in his paintings. His interest in repetition is certainly based in printmaking. He once observed, "I like to repeat an image in another medium to observe the play between the two: the image and the medium."

Even if you have never made prints, or are unsure of your technique, you can engage a fine-art printer (called a "contract" printer) to help you make prints. This could be done at a university press or by a commercial fine-art press that takes on outside assignments. The ability to work with fine master printers at their atelier is another way to expand your creative reach. Master printers can point out new techniques and possibilities. A consultation with a master printer will aid in discovering which printing technique would best suit your work and creative process.

## How's That Done?
## Printmaking Techniques

• Intaglio, incised marks on a metal plate achieved by dry point or acid etching, is usually best suited for a drawn line. The plate is inked and the paper is pressed on top, resulting in printed relief lines and a plate mark.

• Aquatint is another intaglio process resulting in a more brush-like surface, perfect for creating shadows or different textures against the etched line.

• In a silkscreen, a stencil is secured in place on a nylon screen. The ink goes through the screen onto the paper, but is blocked by the stencil, thereby making the required image. This technique is perfect for laying down blocks of color to build up an image. A recent silkscreen by photorealist artist Richard Estes, entitled "Kentucky Fried Chicken," 2007, published by Marlborough Graphics, used 110 colors, which entailed using 110 different screens!

• Lithography is a perfect medium to achieve a smudged pastel or charcoal-like line. Traditional lithographs are made on limestone, but grained plates can also be used. The artist uses a greasy substance to draw on the surface of the stone or plate; only these greasy areas will accept ink. Once the plate is inked, high-quality paper is laid over it and run through the press.

• One of the earliest forms of printing, dating from the 12th century, is woodcut printing. Woodcuts are made by cutting an image into a block of wood, which is then inked and the paper pressed onto it to transfer the image. The grain of the wood leaves a textured surface on the paper that is very immediate. This technique is wonderful for sculptors who are comfortable with the physicality of carving.

Whether it's iris printing, silkscreen, monotype, lithography, or intaglio, the particular technique you wish to use determines which printer is best suited for you. Unlike the solitary work in the studio, printmaking is a group process, and the collaborative effort is creatively stimulating. Artists have often credited printers with jump-starting a new idea that may eventually be realized in their other work as well.

Printmaking can enhance your creative process, but there is also a commercial side: prints can supplement your income. One of the main reasons for making prints comes from the collector side. A very high number of beginning collectors start by acquiring prints, both because of availability and the lower price, compared to unique or one-of-a-kind works. In trying to acquire one-off works, collectors may be stymied by galleries who are holding works for their favored collectors. Beginning collectors are rarely on that list. So they will naturally gravitate toward buying prints.

It's also a way for a collector to "practice" making a commitment to an artist. Susan Hall, an accomplished printmaker and painter in California, often makes lower priced giclée prints and even cards. Although she makes very little on her framed giclée works, her reasoning is that the prints can be the appetizer that may one day lead to the main course – the sale of painting.

She considers her cards to be little advertisements and always includes her phone number and website address on each one. She has made numerous painting sales this way, when a collector has found her number and made a studio visit to purchase a unique work later on.

There are other less obvious benefits to printmaking. You may have an exclusive arrangement with a dealer or agent with regard to representing one-off works, but are not contractually bound in the making and selling of prints. This enables you to sell prints to a variety of different sources, widening your distribution base, and also allowing for new relationships.

Another benefit of prints is that they act like messengers, sending your work out into the community beyond your gallery and your studio. When working

212

with a new gallery or agent that you are unsure of, you might feel more comfortable consigning prints, until you see how the relationship is developing. This might also be true of Internet sales, which might be devoted entirely to prints.

By the same token, galleries may be more inclined to take a print or two on consignment from a new artist they are trying out, rather than unique works. Prints are also useful for traveling, when taking original works may be prohibitively expensive. Also if you are running out of original material, (perhaps you work very slowly, or happily you can't keep up with the demand for your work), you can supplement a show or a sale with prints.

There is another benefit of working with an experienced printer or fine-art publishing house. They can use their established sales network to distribute and sell your prints for an agreed upon portion of the proceeds.

There are several excellent resources to help you find the right printer or publisher, as well as a venue to show your prints. In New York City's Chelsea area, the International Print Center of New York was established in 2000 as the only nonprofit institution devoted solely to the exhibition and study of fine art prints, through exhibitions, publications, and educational programs. The Center keeps a database of graphics for galleries and art professionals who are looking for new work, as well as notices of open calls for prints in galleries and museums and lists of scholarships and workshops especially for printmakers and of different printers and ateliers. It also has an open examination period, when you can bring in your prints for review for possible inclusion in upcoming exhibitions.

At the Print Center of the New York Public Library, which actively acquires prints, you can make an appointment to have your work seen by the curator.

Most museums with print departments are open to the public for private viewings. If you wish to see a particular print, you can call and make an

- A more recent technique is linocut. An artist carves into linoleum rather than wood. Picasso was one of the first artists to utilize this technique and used it for his most famous color prints such as the brilliant "Buste de Femme au Chapeau," 1962.

- Monotype is one of the simplest forms of printing, and doesn't require a master printer or a whole studio to get started. An artist paints with paint or ink directly on a plate of glass or metal, and then a piece of paper is laid onto the still wet surface. The image is transferred by hand with the use of a spoon or with an etching press. There is usually only one impression made, although a second or "ghost" impression may be pulled.

- Iris or giclée printing utilizes high-quality digital printers. This process began being used in the late 1980s, and each new generation of computer printer is even better. One of the benefits of digital printing is that you only print what you need, rather than an entire series (edition) of works. Another benefit is that the set-up costs are much less, compared with lithography or even silkscreen. One of the drawbacks is the resulting flat surface, which may lend itself well to photography, but may look dull and lifeless when reproducing original drawings and paintings.

appointment. It's often a way to meet the curator personally when you visit the department, and might open an avenue for showing him or her your work.

The print world is completely different from the painting/sculpture world, and is an active, though smaller venue where you can make a much bigger splash. Due to the democratic nature of printmaking, the collectors tend to be more impressed by the work, rather than your pedigree or what gallery you show in.

I hope you are inspired to try printmaking both for the creative possibilities as well as the commercial opportunities.

**Deborah Ripley** has been an acknowledged print expert for over 20 years. She has been a private print dealer in New York City and a monthly contributor to *Art on Paper*. She was the director of the Print Division of Artnet.com and has written on prints and collecting for *Artscribe*, *The Print Collectors Newsletter*, *New West Magazine* and *Artnet Magazine*. Prior to joining Artnet.com she worked at Pace Prints, New York City, and Christie's New York Print Department.

## Criticize This

By William Zimmer

Art critics have a reputation for being tough, but that toughness must be backed up by being rough and ready. We're always getting ambushed: "You're a critic, then criticize this." This is usually said by some inebriated soul at a party or someone who thinks artists are pulling a fast one. Well, the history of "criticize this" is pretty interesting; I like to think as interesting as the criticism itself.

Art criticism has a long history, and it would benefit you as an artist to familiarize yourself with it. If critics need know the history of art, why should it not be mutual? You should know the fascinating personalities that have presumed to criticize your kind. You'll find it's at least good literature.

In the leadoff position is the Italian Giorgio Vasari (1511-1574) who covered 500 art stars of the Renaissance years in his *Lives of the Artists*. He couldn't have known all the personalities he profiled, and so used hearsay and anecdotes for those he didn't. He wrote about his contemporaries from personal experience, but sometimes created accounts that were as fictional as the profiles of those he didn't know. Art is essentially a fiction so there is no reality. What is important for you to see is that the bedrock of art criticism has always been storytelling and with a romantic leaning toward the beguiling.

The next slot historically belongs to the French. Denis Diderot (1713-1784) who compiled an encyclopedia during the Enlightenment (an 18th-century Western philosophy that advocated reason as the primary basis of authority and criticized traditional institutions, customs, and morals) – a mean feat in any era. He combed the annual academic salons, which may be taken as the Whitney Biennials of the 1700s.

Charles Pierre Baudelaire (1821-1867) followed a century later. The Frenchman's great sanction for art critics was that their major aspiration should be to write a piece every bit as good as what is turned out by the painter he's writing about.

A homespun critic near to my heart is Henry McBride (1867-1962), an American writer who wrote during the first half of the last century, contributing to *The New York Sun*, as well as *The Dial* and *The Art News* magazines. He is a good reminder that a regular column in a newspaper of note is the best forum a critic can have. More remembered is an intellectual like Clement Greenberg, but the essential throwaway nature of an art review that McBride excelled at is remembered, too, by those who appreciate McBride's wit.

Closer to our day and mightily influential – as both critics as poets – are Frank O'Hara and John Ashbery. They were leaders of the New York School of Poetry. They were the urbane counterparts of Abstract Expressionist painters who, it must be admitted, were largely depressives.

Up until now, I have given you pretty much background of the practice of art criticism. But like everything in *Accelerating on the Curves*, there is a practical application. Remember that the term "art critic" doesn't have to designate something forbidding or remote beyond your wildest dreams. I am advising you to just take the plunge in trying to meet critics.

Invite a critic to your studio, to get acquainted with you and your work. You will find an art critic near at hand, in your local paper or even your local giveaway paper. He or she is that person who writes about art at the local gallery or community space with a certain enthusiasm.

I used to put artists through some elaborate dance before I could be enticed to their studios. The artist had to be recommended to me by an artist, someone we both knew. In a tight-knit community (this does not imply any necessary affection), the chances of you knowing someone who knows me are pretty good. It was a form of insurance for me, guaranteeing that I wouldn't have to spend a couple of hours with someone with no talent or who made work that I had no affinity for.

But now I am swayed by persistence, regardless of who you know. Any artist who would ask a critic to the studio has to have a glimmer of something. But I may not agree to come right away; this is not playing hard to get. Such visits are not done on the fly, and I want to have a block of two hours free, plus time afterward at home with nothing pressing, in order to recuperate and seriously collect my thoughts. Good or bad – but especially a good one – a studio visit is an exhausting experience.

All right enough navel-gazing. I'm just going through some chilling reminiscences of studio visits I have made. In truth, such a visit is very easy, commonsensical, and, just like life, with some twists.

You as an artist are inevitably eager. This critic may not have seen your work before, so you're anxious to show him or her everything. The temptation is to show a lot of work. I really don't know about other critics, but I suffer from visual burnout and my eyes will soon glaze over. I will become irritable, and hurry you along. The pain is intensified when I can see the amount of work stacked up: I'm going to be here until midnight. By the way, schedule your visit during the day when the light is good, common sense again.

Select your most recent work, a dozen paintings at the most. There is a vogue for the newest thing anyway, so that is what I'm the most interested in. After you've pulled out the paintings, you can lead me to a stack of drawings, works on paper, or prints. Let me rifle through these myself. A critic likes nothing better than to instinctively be in charge.

By then I may have gotten hooked on your work. This doesn't mean that I will bypass my rules just for you. I am still tired, perhaps as exhilarated as tired, but exhausted none the less. I will suggest coming back in a month or so (let's not ruin this romance), when I can see your whole career as a slide show.

Although this should seem easy enough, there are still the logistics of the encounter. You can't play it by ear. How you conduct the visit has a lot to do with the critic's perception of you. The matter of refreshments, for example. Should you serve tea and biscuits, what you might serve a proper English critic? Pretty bland, pretty obvious. Wine is nice. If you present a whole array of fare, alcoholic and non-alcoholic, the lack of clear choice might mirror your wider confusion. I would suggest coffee or tea, not very exciting but businesslike, and maybe have a soft drink or water waiting in the wings.

If I like your work, I'm yours, and there's a tacit understanding that I'll do something for you. This means contact a dealer – not bring a dealer over to your studio – but speak to him or her and say, "I visited the studio of (your name)

## The Zimmer Guide to Writing a Press Release

Learning how to write a press release might seem a jump, far from the relationship of critic and artist topic at hand. It might seem prosaic, beside the point, but it is very relevant.

A press release is essential because it links you up with the world at large. It is the vital link between you and the press. The press doesn't have time to ponder your prose or the details of your art, so that old saying "Just the facts, ma'am" is key.

A press release is a short, one-page document that advertises you and your exhibition. It has three paragraphs. The first is a short description of the upcoming show with your name, date of the opening, and place. But what most people overlook is the closing date. Artists are so eager to announce the show that they forget to say when it closes, which is as crucial as the opening date. Critics have to make up their schedules, and work from back to front; the show that closes soonest has priority. If I am not informed when a show closes, its chances of getting covered at all are simply diminished.

The second paragraph is a description of the work. If the first paragraph is rather cut-and-dried, the second can be creative, even playful.

The third describes the artist's career. This paragraph may seem like ending with a whimper instead of a bang, but it helps the critic understand your back-story. Just remember that art criticism is storytelling but it's up to you to provide the story.

The press release can be accompanied by a brief, handwritten note outlining what you hope to accomplish and what you will do in follow-up, ie.: you'll call or e-mail in a specific time frame or you wish to invite them to your studio prior to the opening of your exhibition. Always thank him or her for their attention and hope he or she will support you in your endeavors.

Remember that a critic is inundated with press releases, so make it short, clear, and enticing.

and found the art pretty good." That is the extent of my obligation. After all I'm not an agent, such people exist and they make good money for the contacts they make. But I keep track of your career and as they say, "Hey, you never know."

**William Zimmer**, Founding Associate, was an art critic who achieved international status through his catalog essays, which were published by museums all over the world. He retired as contributing critic to *The New York Times* after over 20 years. His career began with *ARTS Magazine* in 1975; in 1977 he was hired by *The SoHo Weekly News*, a paper published in Lower Manhattan. By virtue of the paper's location in the burgeoning SoHo district, Zimmer was the first critic to review Julian Schnabel, David Salle, Keith Haring, and many other artists who became major art world figures of the 1980s. Zimmer's catalogue texts include essays on Donald Sultan, Brice Marden, Catherine Lee, Benny Andrews, and Richard Bosman, to mention only a few. Zimmer passed away in September of 2007, and the Zimmer Prize in Art Criticism was established that same year by Larry Powell Management and Katharine T. Carter & Associates.

# Getting Lucky, Getting Reviewed

By Richard Vine

Congratulations. You've done the hard part. You've gotten your studio art degree, probably to the despair of your family and the bafflement of your oldest friends. You've hung in there as a working artist long enough to develop a style and a body of work that some astute dealer or curator now deems worthy of public display. You've struggled for months to produce just the right work for the event, and wrangled with the gallery staff to give it an advantageous installation. At last, the show is up.

So have a drink, maybe two, because now comes the nearly impossible part – getting critical notice in newspapers and art magazines.

Why should this be? The short answer is: it shouldn't. Thoughtful response to one's work from insightful, well-informed individuals with good judgment and a knack for engaging prose is something nearly every artist longs for, and many deserve. Reviews – in print, not just on the lips of good chums and casual gallery-hoppers – are also essential to the health of your prices and the furtherance of your public reputation. Making art for art's sake, with no regard to who notices or how they respond, may be all well and good for the soul, but it doesn't get you into the worldwide critical discourse – or the minds of important collectors, art historians, and exhibition organizers. That feat is largely a matter of having your works talked about, especially by the cognoscenti. The goal, after all, is not just to be seen once, but to be seen again and again. In purely professional terms, to be reviewed is to exist.

Yet there is a great difficulty in getting your show written about, which stems from two daunting factors. One is the discrepancy between the vast number of exhibitions mounted each year and the small (and dwindling) amount of editorial space that major publications allot to visual arts coverage. The other frustration is the seeming mysteriousness of newspaper and magazine coverage decisions – a process that artists tend to regard as either capricious or conspiratorial and, in either case, beyond their ability to affect.

Of these two obstacles, the first – the sheer math – is worse than you probably imagine, while the second is far less baffling than it seems. In other words, the odds against any one show getting reviewed are dishearteningly high, but there are a few simple, concrete things you can do to improve your editorial chances – especially in the long run.

## The Lay of the Land

First of all, be realistic in your expectations. Every year, art schools and universities churn out thousands of hopeful new studio-art grads, all of them looking for shows and critical coverage. These recruits join a huge standing army of art-world veterans, all struggling for recognition and many hoping to reinvigorate what they regard as a stalled career. Consequently, the gatekeepers – curators, dealers, critics, and collectors – tend to operate (whether they realize it or not) in market terms. Like analysts on the lookout for either hot stocks or blue-chip investments, they are interested primarily in those few young (i.e., under 35) artists who have somehow caught art-conversational fire and, at the other extreme, in stalwarts who have managed to show their work in well-regarded venues over the course of three decades or more.

Meanwhile, newspapers across the country are cutting back their visual arts coverage, while art magazines – though ever more jazzy in design – strive to remain specialty publications whose page counts and formats are delimited by the restricted size of their subscriber "universe." In a given year, something like 27,000 art exhibitions take place in the US. A national art magazine, which must also cover more and more activities abroad, has less than 500 editorial slots for feature articles, reports, and reviews. Consequently, perhaps two percent of the shows with a reasonable claim on critical attention will actually receive coverage – meaning that, on average, 98 times out of 100 it will not be yours.

Yet we all know that certain artists repeatedly beat these numbers, garnering, in effect, more than their mathematical share of reviewer notices. What's different about them? Or, more to the point, what exactly do they do to bring about this seeming miracle?

One essential is that they, or the people behind them (dealer, spouse, friend, etc.), understand the publishing process. They know that newspaper reviewers and art-magazine writers, whether working on staff or freelance, are almost always well-intentioned people in a cruelly difficult situation. In order to do their job properly, these critics have to be well educated and in command of several very different sets of intellectual skills: formal analysis of artwork, easy familiarity with art history, awareness of present-day social and theoretical currents, as well as fluency in structuring precise, evocative language into a compelling aesthetic argument. (If they were lawyers, they would have to be fit to stand before the Supreme Court.) And for all this, art writers are, with a few rare exceptions, paid much less per hour than your local framer, your shoe repairman, or your dry cleaner.

These critics – smart, underpaid, overworked – are assigned their reviews by or propose them to editors, who are themselves continuously overwhelmed with press releases, catalogues, e-mail solicitations, books, and surface mail, and who in turn work for publishers subject to the profit imperative and the importuning of advertisers. In newspapers, this gives rise to a publisher's mantra that goes "Why are we wasting space on something only a very few effete readers will notice?" At art magazines, that question is obviated through niche marketing – no serious art magazine in the United States today has a paid circulation over 90,000; compare this to a *Better Homes & Gardens* tally of 7,700,000.

Major newspapers deign to review art only because the owners want to show editorial range, and because the small number of readers and advertisers who care at all about visual culture tend to care a lot. Art magazines – since their readership consists mostly of people in the field (artists, teachers, students, curators, dealers, collectors) – take serious interest for granted. The best of them base their coverage decisions on that one overriding criterion – what is of compelling interest to our readers? – rather than the parochial, self-motivated appeals of advertisers. And what is it readers in the contemporary art field are interested in? Ask yourself. In all probability, you will find that your responses cluster around news of the tribe – who in this crazy business is doing what – and formal, theoretical, or historical developments that seem to open new possibilities for artistic practice.

In the end, the likelihood of a review comes down to what you do to make your show engaging and discussable.

**Make Good Work**

This one is so obvious, and so essential, that it risks being overlooked. But the fact is nothing will happen until your work catches some practiced eye; and all the diplomacy in the world won't redeem it if it fails to elicit that primal response. Again and again, one hears the same question from hard-nosed editors when a show is proposed for review: "Is it interesting?" If the answer is no, nothing else matters much. The suggestion is dropped, and critical attention moves on.

What makes a body of work "interesting" in our age of rampant cultural and aesthetic pluralism? Broadly speaking, one of two things – an established form or idea executed with supreme conceptual sophistication and technical proficiency (think Richard Serra at

MoMA), or some instance of genuine innovation in subject matter, approach, emotional import, or technique, e.g., Damien Hirst the first time he took a meat saw to an undressed cow carcass. You don't have to go to wild extremes, but you do have to follow through on your conceptual device, or your intuitive impulse, with convincing skill and unflinching confidence.

## Have a Strong Background

Yes, that sounds a little like "choose your parents carefully." In fact, though, you have great control over your vocational preparation. The trick is to recognize that fact early enough and act on it. Choosing an esteemed school for your studio training; working assiduously while you're there; cultivating good relations with instructors, fellow students, visiting artists, and other art-world professionals; showing your work early in student exhibitions or alternative spaces; getting yourself into good residency programs; winning prizes and grants; getting your name into print, even in student publications or group-show catalogues – it all counts.

Remember that an editor's next questions (after "Is the work interesting?") will almost invariably be: "Who is this artist? Where did he or she train? Had any previous shows? Any write-ups?"

## Show Signs of Dedication

Amid such intense competition, no one has much time or sympathy for the half-hearted. Sunday painters or artists who cannot bring themselves to give up their beach house in order to tough it out at a good art school or in a cheap-rent neighborhood with other full-time devotees place themselves at a disadvantage. Everything you put ahead of making good art – be it a lucrative career, family, or a political cause – leaves you one more step behind those who put art first and foremost. After all, given the option, who would you choose to review – a dabbler who dresses well, drives a nice car, and is beloved by his kids, or a quiet fanatic who (whether for good reasons or bad) lives, breathes, thinks, and eats his art as though it were manna from heaven?

One practical way to demonstrate strong dedication is to serve for a while as an assistant to a well-established artist. Besides providing a bit of income without detouring you from your principal pursuit, this gives you practical, hands-on experience in the studio and something intangible that no coursework or hearsay can match: exposure to the everyday reality of conducting an artistic career. What does a successful artist actually do every day? How much time does he or she devote to artmaking and how much to career administration or strategic socializing? How do you conduct yourself with other artists, or with fabricators, shippers, and registrars? What kinds of relationships are cultivated with dealers, critics, curators, and collectors? Do drugs help?

**Hang Out**

The art world operates largely through word of mouth. By this I do not mean the lengthy disquisitions that take place in classrooms and at academic seminars, though all that palaver becomes important for the historical winners.

No, I mean instead the numerous, quick, glancing verbal exchanges that shape a critical life on the run. Certainly nothing is written about that is not talked about first. But the communications that change artists' lives often take the form of sidewalk exchanges between, say, a *New York Times* writer and a Whitney curator that go something like this:

"Hey, did you see So-and-so's show at Jack Tilton?"

"No, how is it?"

"Big red rectangles with worked-up surfaces. Some weirdness going on with these, like, blue false perspective lines or something. Interesting, you should check it out."

"Huh? He used to work for Chuck Close, didn't he?"

"Yeah, studied at Cal Arts with Baldessari, too, I think."

"OK, I'll take a look."

The system produces more art, more artists, more shows, and more publicity than anyone can sanely assimilate. Amid this ceaseless clamor, the key decision-makers (who themselves see an enormous amount of work firsthand) tend to check their own reactions against the candid judgments of a few trusted colleagues. And also – most pointedly – established artists. Many dealers rely heavily on the recommendations made to them by artists already in their stable. Any savvy critic, curator, or collector is bound to snap to attention if Robert Ryman says, "You know, I saw some pretty intriguing work by a new painter the other day . . ."

We all remember people we've met much more easily than people we haven't. You should be on the scene – that is, at the openings, the panel discussions, the parties, the dinners – often enough to be familiar (so that your name comes readily to mind when someone is attempting to fill out a show or develop an article) but less frequently than will render you a nuisance, paradoxically invisible by virtue of your omnipresence.

Connections are made on the turn of a heel. You never know who you may find standing next to you at a Jenny Saville show, who will be your left-hand seatmate at dinner in deepest Bushwick. And when that person turns out to be a key art-world figure, you'd best have something relevant to say – preferably something like, "Oh, I saw the video show you curated last month at DiverseWorks. Really liked the way you brought in references to Nauman's early stuff. Do you happen to know the work of Such-and-such, a young German artist who . . ."

Awareness of other people, of contemporary currents, of the wider world, etc., has rather a better effect than "Hi, I'm a video artist too, here's my DVD, will you come to my studio?"

And speaking of the studio, don't let it become a burial site. It is a place for producing art meant for other people to see, not a place to sequester yourself in remote fastness, away from the challenges of other artists' work, the judgments of critics and curators, or occasional requests to verbalize, succinctly and compellingly, what your project is all about. Your workspace should be a refuge, of course, but one where creative activity is punctuated by contemplation – not a cavern for nursing resentments.

**Be Professional**
We all carry in our minds the image of the recalcitrant genius – the tormented, extravagantly gifted soul who can say little or nothing about his work, who disdains the opinions of experts and the ignorant public alike, who uses and discards his less brilliant fellows. Yeah, well, get real and file that myth with the other fairy tales of your lost childhood. No curator, critic, or editor today has time or patience for such self-indulgence. They all have plans to fulfill and deadlines to meet. Anything you do to make their jobs easier works to your benefit; anytime you make their lives harder, you subvert your own chances for selection and coverage.

Specifically, reviewers need an invitation card announcing your show, a press release orienting them to your new work, and high-quality slides or digital images of the pieces on view. If your gallery doesn't supply these items, prepare them yourself. Also have press packets ready for any writer who requests one. These should include all of the above, along with your CV and photocopies of any significant reviews or essays previously published on your work. Stand ready to discuss your work if asked – be it during a gallery tour, a studio visit, a formal interview, or casual chitchat over a beer. Promptly respond to any subsequent e-mails or calls. Have a well-designed website where people can easily check out your work and your history. Finally, stop worrying about your nonconformist image and get a damned business card.

### Grow Articulate

What is your intent in this work? What are its wellsprings in art history and/or your personal experience? Why did you choose this particular medium for this particular project? How do you see your new output in relation to other work being produced today?

These are the kinds of questions art writers – and their editors and readers – want answered. If you don't supply clear responses, in a concise and thoughtful manner, someone else will have to take their best guess, or else ignore your work altogether.

This does not mean you should dictate critical interpretation. Indeed, a writer may well disagree with your own analytic assessment. Don't worry about it. What the critic wants from you is a point of departure – something to confirm, expand, amend, or even dispute. Through the push-pull of conflicting views, new insights arise. A review is the beginning of a lively discussion, not the final verdict of history.

Some artists are glib to a fault; others are virtually speechless. If you are unable to put your signature concept into words, find someone to compose a statement for you. Keep it factual; leave the-sun-the-moon-and-the-stars for your diary. Then make the document part of your press pack.

## Remember Names

In the mad rush of shows, movements, and people, names are hyper-concentrates of essential information. You should know the names not only of international art-world luminaries but of every good artist, dealer, critic, curator, and collector in your local area. If you don't know their names, how – and why – are they ever going to get to know yours? The main trick to career advancement, after all, is to get your name inside, say, Robert Storr's head. Don't know who Robert Storr is? Perhaps you should consider a future in retail sales.

## Seek Help

No, not psychotherapy – although I wouldn't necessarily rule it out. Rather, I'm referring here to the grim fact that, except for the obvious art stars, virtually all artists need a livelihood from some other income source. For some – in fact for many more than will admit it – that source is family money: checks from mom and dad back home, or dividends from investments made by some wily though embarrassingly bourgeois forebear. ("No trust funds, no art world" is a bohemian verity.) Other artists will find themselves reliant on the largesse of a working spouse or life partner. (Caution: dumping your erstwhile mate and benefactor once you become famous is considered bad form even in hipsterdom.) As a last resort, you need either a patron – a creature now rarer than the albino unicorn – or a real-world job.

The problem with regular employment, of course, is that it steals time and energy from your artmaking schedule, often plunging you into a mentally debilitating milieu. Even the one seemingly non-alien endeavor, teaching art, has its own hazards. Universities tend to be located outside the art-world bubble, thus undermining your "hanging out" strategy and putting you at risk – particularly if you start teaching too early in your career – of slipping from the OK condition of "an artist who teaches" to the near-death status of "a teacher who makes art."

By and large, the people who can sustain themselves in the art world without a side job are also the people who can afford assistants to do prep work in the studio, conduct research, fetch supplies, spy on rivals, and draft the endless letters and grant applications that orchestrating an art career now requires. Get used to that fact. Figure out how to compensate for it. Life, as you may have noted on other occasions, is not fair.

**Cultivate Bemusement**

Never forget that the work is what really matters – and the rest is a game. If you are dedicated to your art, and true to your own deepest experience when making it, you have already gained the greatest reward any profession can offer. Your career trajectory, your financial compensation, your fame or lack of it, your place in the ever-shifting social scene are all secondary considerations, and largely subject to the whims of chance. The more conscious you are of the arbitrary nature of the "success" game, the easier it is to play. Who's up today? What show/artist/movement/idea will become vitally important next week? It's all entertainment compared to the core issues of health, work, and love. Ironically, a Zen-like detachment allows you to think more clearly, maneuver more wisely, react more graciously, and find wry fascination in whatever results.

**Be Nice**

Attitude is for high school. The grownups who populate the art world just want to maximize their own efficiency (time is short and art is endless) and to interact with reasonably cooperative peers. Yes, as an artist, you may have to stand up for the integrity of your work sometimes, if you're being pressured to change it for bad reasons. But this is not the same as stamping your foot and demanding that your latest gestural abstraction get the big gallery wall, where it's the first thing viewers see when they exit the elevator into a group show. Or that it appear next month on the front cover of *Artforum*.

Despite what you may have heard, art writers and curators are basically regular folk with an unusual love of art (they sure ain't doing it for the money) and a genuine openness to meeting artists – so long as the artists are tactful and (corny as this may sound) fundamentally kind. When you meet them, relax and be frank about who you are and what you do. When asked (but not before), proffer your business card or your show announcement. Be willing to receive them in your studio in a gracious and timely fashion (not "as soon as I finish a few more paintings"). Don't harass them. Once a visitor has the information requested, there's nothing to be gained – and considerable goodwill to be lost – by calling and e-mailing obsessively. Above all, don't play the tit-for-tat game: "I gave you dinner, now where's my review?"

## Ten Tips for Getting Reviewed

- Make good work

- Have a strong background

- Show signs of dedication

- Hang out

- Be professional

- Grow articulate

- Remember names

- Seek help

- Cultivate bemusement

- Be nice

Being polite is a virtue in itself, but it can also have pragmatic effects. Never, for example, bully or patronize junior personnel. You'd be amazed how often that silly-looking boy at the front desk has the ear of his elusive, globe-trotting boss. Today's 23-year-old mail sorter may well be tomorrow's 33-year *ARTnews* editor or Guggenheim curator.

I recall that a persistent intern once hauled me off, feet dragging, to see a friend's show in a coffee-shop gallery – an installation by an obscure immigrant artist who, eight years later, was world-renowned. Another former intern is now director of one of the country's premier museums, located in Washington, DC. So it goes.

Basically, people are people everywhere – yes, even in Chelsea. Art workers are trying hard to cope in a brutally Darwinian arena; they hope to survive, to do well, and be treated respectfully. And to have a laugh now and then. So why not oblige? It's hardly an accident that the most successful artists are often the most personable.

**Richard Vine** is the senior editor for Asia (and former managing editor) of *Art in America*. He has taught at such institutions as the School of the Art Institute of Chicago, the American Conservatory of Music, Chicago, and New York University, and has served as editor-in-chief of the *Chicago Review* and of *Dialogue: An Art Journal*. His articles on art, literature, and intellectual history have appeared in numerous journals, including *Salmagundi, Modern Poetry Studies,* and the *New Criterion*. He is author of *Odd Nedrum: Paintings, Sketches, and Drawings,* published by Gyldendal/D.A.P. in 2001.

## Being Written About, Or a Catalogue Essay Is Not a Review, and Vice Versa

By Peter Frank

Despite the burgeoning number of commentary sites on the Internet – which itself may be a symptom of the problem – there is at present a crisis of practice in art criticism. Putting aside questions of critical authority (let's face it, the "golden age" of critical commentary is over, at least on these shores), we can agree that there simply aren't enough outlets for art criticism in America.

Perhaps there never were, and perhaps there is a whole vast understratum of little magazines that you and I never see that serves the same purpose as did the small-circulation journals of yesteryear, the ones that produced the likes of Clement Greenberg.

Actually, there is an understratum of *eensy*-circulation periodicals, apparently put out by enterprising youngsters who have been fortunate enough to squeeze a bit of funding out of their graduate programs. But they don't seem to exercise the same influence as the *Partisan Review* (for example) did a half-century or more ago. (Yes, we still have *The New Republic* and *The Nation* and so forth – oh, and the come-lately but come-on-strong *New Criterion* – but even these respected journals, with their articulate and outspoken critics, are shadows of their former selves.) Blame it on TV, video, blogs, websites, whatever.

More to the point, however, the art magazines themselves, although apparently dwindling in number or number of pages, are covering fewer and fewer artists within their increasing mass of ads. You are less likely to get reviewed in *Art in America* or *Flash Art*, not because there are fewer reviewers, but because there are fewer review pages. Reviews have long been viewed as the broke or renegade relative, a good class system or two below that of articles, analyses, etc. – although if you look closely at many art-mag articles, they are actually just very long reviews of (supposedly) Very Important Shows.

Your last recourse to being reviewed, the local publication – daily, weekly, monthly, citywide, neighborhood, niche – may have a jones for art that you can exploit. But they're not nearly as likely to have a good writer on art, much less a good structure for publishing art commentary. A whole lot of wholesale press-release quoting can go on in these rags, and even those that take visual art seriously don't take it as seriously as they do the entertainment arts.

Yeah, in great part it is a matter of who pays the piper, and you and/or your local gallery are not likely to compete with a movie theater's (or TV network's) daily full-page spread. But it's also most editors' commitment to answering to (rather than edifying) the tastes of their readership that keeps the ratio of movie reviews to art reviews so lopsided.

In other words, you'll have to do more than sleep with everybody to get written about. There are simply not enough places publishing writing about art – or publishing *enough* writing about art – and the competition for their attention is fiercer than ever. Art supplies may be expensive, but ink is downright precious.

Of course, maybe getting reviewed online is enough, and in certain ways more advantageous. (Now someone in Turkey can access what somebody thinks about your art – as well as what *you* think about your art, if you have a website.) If you're under a certain age, you've long since become habituated to online modes and mores, and if you're older than that, well, it's here, it's near, get used to it.

But even early-20-somethings admit to the pleasure and authority of hard copy beautifully produced. And many art folks, of all ages, are doing something about it. We may indeed see a spike in new art mags in the next decade. But can we count on them covering the waterfront? Will they get to your show? Will they want to?

Nobody does what *ARTnews* did in the 1950s: send a writer to *every show in Manhattan*, and give every show at least two lines in the review section. Wouldn't that be cool? But that was then, when New York City featured fewer gallery shows than, say, Houston does now. Could a magazine devoted entirely to reviews be viable on a national level? Quite possibly. (I think local-level review-only publications can work, too, but either as e-zines or as blogs, not as glossies.)

You get where I'm coming from – and going to: if you want to be written about seriously, publish it yourself. And yes, the corollary is, you can't just buy yourself a review, even a bad one. The art world being the global daisy chain that it is, you can indeed get reviewed by a friend, or a friend of a friend, or someone who wants to get into your head or your studio, or your pants or your wallet. But you can't depend on that *protektsia*. (Pardon my Russian. The Soviet-era term means "connections," but in a nebulous, blood-is-thicker-than-water-but-thirsty-people-take-what-they-can-get kind of way.) And having a reviewer bud doesn't get the assignment past his or her editor – nor does having an editor BFF get a reviewer interested in taking the assignment.

And finally, and in many ways most importantly, a review, I repeat, ain't no article. A review is not an in-depth appraisal of your oeuvre to date; it is a relatively superficial response to a display of your work. This is not to dismiss the value of reviews; well beyond their potential function as consumer guides (itself useful), reviews, singly and in the aggregate, constantly take the temperature of the artistic discourse as it filters to the public showcase. Shows, after all, are (or at least can – should – be) significant occurrences, engaging our interest in and of themselves and also as symptoms of broader phenomena.

But in the space of a paragraph or three – 100 to 400 words, maybe? – what gets said? And given that the reviewer is focusing on what's hanging rather than what you've accomplished over the last umpteen months or years, what does the review say about what you're all about?

Admirable is the review (and reviewer) that can convey a vivid sense of that show of yours. Magical is the review that can put that show of yours in the larger context of your career achievement, the breadth of art history, or even both – in the space of 100 to 400 words. It's doable (although obviously not exhaustively), but it isn't likely.

You doubtless believe that your art merits in-depth discussion. Assuming it does, you're very unlikely to get that discussion, even if you can get reviewed. Again, if you want to get written about seriously, publish it yourself. And don't be embarrassed about it. Artists worse than you are doing it. And they're getting writers to write it because those writers are looking not only for income, but for outlets. They – we – are writing catalogues, brochures, mini-monographs, and even website texts, and all these formats are getting before the eyes of people whom you need to have see what you do – curators, gallerists, collectors, commissioners, boards of trustees, interior designers, art department heads, parents, and librarians, among others.

There is a whole new commerce in self-published catalogues and monographs. American artists have gotten over the "vanity" taboo that once shrouded this kind of publication – even though so many of them did it anyway in more roundabout ways, and even though their European counterparts rarely flinch when the opportunity arises. We now view such publications as vital tools in the promulgation of one's work and chiseling of one's artistic profile. Doing your own book is light years from doing your own résumé or press packet or business card, and it's even a status advance over a website (although a website is a decided plus in and of itself). Even having a brochure done enhances the tenor of your achievement in people's eyes; indeed, it puts your achievement in people's eyes.

A publication entirely devoted to your work will obviously be a source of great satisfaction and reassurance (at least if done reasonably well). But it could be a source of great self-awareness as well. Seeing your works displayed in a logical sequence in the book, and then reading what someone with virtually no vested interest in the work has to say about it, can provide you revelations galore about your art and your relationship to it and your relationship to the world.

It is not an ego-stroke. Indeed, you should avoid any writer who gushes and bloviates at the expense of penetrating discussion. This is a chance to get something deep and serious said about the work into which you've invested so much depth and seriousness, something much more profound than a reviewer could muster in a few hundred words.

Sure, whatever is written will favor your art; even if you wanted constructive criticism (or a purifying excoriation – your kink is my command), you don't want it administered in public, and the public doesn't expect or want to read negative stuff in a publication devoted entirely to your work.

A commissioned essay is necessarily an endorsement of your art. It's a highfalutin' advertorial, and as such should not inspire doubt in the mind or eye of the reader. (As they say, there ain't no such thing as an adversarial advertorial.) When you pay for an essay, you pay not for critical distance, but for insight – perhaps born of critical distance, but not (re-)enacting it. It's obvious you're paying the piper in this instance, and what should be most obvious are the noble reasons why: the writer has a special understanding of your work, he or she has an ability to convey that understanding in prose, and he or she is happy to be placed in a position of advocacy.

If the writer is a "name" bound to attract interest simply with the by- or tag-line, so much the better. But if that writer whips up a piece that is insensitive to the work, hurts the eyes and ears to read, and generally sounds as if it were phoned in, then having a "name" writer backfires, because it is obvious you bought the name, you didn't attract it with the art itself.

(Some writers, having philosophical axes to grind, will place you in the context of their ongoing critical argument. If this provides a dynamic context for understanding what you do, you're ahead of the game; but if it shrinks what you do down into one more example of what the critic has been flogging, you lose. The book should be about your work, not about the writer's.)

One more thing: the writer of your catalogue can't review the show for (or simultaneous to) which the catalogue has been produced. Even if he or she were able to land the assignment from the conflict-of-interest-wary editor, his or her critical voice would be publicly compromised – and effectively co-opted by the far more extensive, eloquent, and penetrating commentary you already paid to have published.

There may be an opportunity to reprint the essay itself in an art (or other kind of) journal, and that would be gravy; but in that case, you or the writer must be sure the editor doesn't think the piece is a labor of the writer's love. (If it's a labor of the writer's love for you, rather than the artwork per se, then we have another conflict-of-interest problem altogether – depending on how requited that love is . . .)

At any rate, you may simply be able to buy, and even distribute, better commentary for yourself than you can get from a review. And there is absolutely nothing wrong with that – especially given the above-lamented state of contemporary art reviewing. Never mind "any press is good press." Unless you're going for box office and walk-in sales, the best press on you is the best *writing* on you.

It goes without saying that your publication should have high production values, including good design, good printing, good editing, and the like. It should also provide the reader basic knowledge about what you do and have done as an artist, and should thus have some sort of bio or résumé, and perhaps a statement from you about the art you make. (Don't insist you can't write such a statement. If you can type or hold a pen, you can write – and someone else can edit. And if you're making art, you have a statement to make. Don't sweat spelling, no matter how dyslexic you are; between spell-check and spot check, the merest errors can come right out. And don't worry about length, a paragraph is fine. In fact, do worry about length if your statement is longer than the critic's essay.)

Oh, and if the gallerist or representative or whomever you're working with wants to take responsibility for the publication, don't be a control freak – but don't be a patsy either. Have a good sense of what you think is appropriate to your work, but also a good sense of what your working partner's modus operandi is. Many galleries, for instance, like to publish catalogues or brochures in a standard format readily recognizable as theirs. Appearing in this way (presuming that format suffices to make the reproductions of your work look good) is mutually beneficial. But if it's not your publication, then you shouldn't have to pay for much of anything (except by pre-arrangement, as in the case of a rep or advisor). Maybe you eat the photographer's fee (in which case you maintain control over the digital files – I nearly said "negatives," showing my age), but the gallerist will have to eat the printer's fee. (Mailing and all those other matters are separate points of negotiation.)

There are many other fine, and not so fine, and even gross points to address, and we're nowhere near Detroit. But if I'm cracking jokes like that, it's inarguably time to stanch this admittedly free-flowing commentative efflux. If this were a lecture, we could indulge in a lengthy Q&A, and I'd probably learn as much as you would. I'm not new to this business, but, given that it's all about art, I'll bid the business goodbye the minute it stops being new. I hope we get to meet over this matter, and I hope that until then, the business of being an artist remains perpetually new for you, too – perpetually new, but not perpetually daunting.

**Peter Frank** is senior curator at the Riverside (CA) Art Museum and contributing art critic for *The Huffington Post,* formerly Editor of *The Magazine-Los Angeles,* and art critic for *Angeleno* magazine and the *L.A. Weekly.* In New York City he served as art critic for *The Village Voice* and *The SoHo Weekly News.* Frank has organized and assisted with numerous theme and survey exhibitions for such prestigious institutions and organizations as the Guggenheim Museum, Independent Curators Inc., The Alternative Museum, and Artists Space in New York City; the Museo Reina Sofia in Madrid, Spain; Documenta in Kassel, Germany; and the Los Angeles County Museum of Art, Museum of Contemporary Art, and Otis Art Institute in Los Angeles. He has published numerous books and catalogues, the latest a monograph on the painter Robert De Niro, Sr.

## Forging Your Brand: Standing Out in the Art World

By Steve Rockwell

A talented friend of mine once confessed to me, "I don't think I can be an artist, because I have nothing to say."

The statement hit a nerve, since it came at a time in my own career when I was struggling with that very thing. Wanting to be an artist was never in doubt, I just wasn't sure what my message was. I had always admired the certainty of the career path of Dutch artist Piet Mondrian who had started with landscapes, that over time crystallized into a simple grid of black lines with the colors red, blue, yellow, white. In the end he had arrived at a product so iconic, that since the '60s, it continues to be imitated in design, architecture, and by other artists. Just recently, a friend of mine received Mondrian pajamas as a gift.

Whether Mondrian was aware of it or not, his career demonstrates one of the fundamental principles of marketing – focus. When I looked over my own artistic production at the time, it resembled a hodge-podge of styles and subjects. I couldn't decide whether I wanted to be an abstract painter or a figurative artist. The label semi-abstract painter seemed to fit, which bothered me because it indicated lack of resolve.

Communication itself was a struggle. Even when I had something specific to say, no one seemed to get what that was. In the end, I had to admit that I couldn't stick to a subject. I envied the Renaissance artist whose themes and subjects were handed to him by his patrons and society as a whole. I found justification for my pluralism in the work of Pablo Picasso, who had been the master of many styles. To some critics, that was a weakness.

Nevertheless, Picasso teaches us another marketing principle: line extension, or brand extension. Picasso, in fact, created a dazzling number of "product" lines, from his Blue and Pink periods to Analytical and Synthetic Cubism, Surrealism, Neo-classicism, and the Expressionism of his later work. They were prodigiously explored in drawing, painting, sculpture, ceramics, and printmaking. In a sense, Pablo Picasso became the General Motors of art, and to the French, a whole cultural industry.

However, anyone tempted to follow Picasso's example should consider the keystone to Picasso's imposing artistic edifice – Cubism. From it followed much of modern art. Being the undisputed leader in his field, he could afford to extend his brand. But even then it was seen by some to be a failing. What lent his line extension credibility was that his restlessness was a testament to his creativity.

By the 1940s and '50s our image of Picasso as archetypal genius of the 20th-century art was fixed. Picasso himself became the brand. The image of a short, tanned Spaniard in a striped T-shirt on the beach in Cannes or at a bullfight in Arles was etched into our minds. How many of us know what Piet Mondrian looked like? Picasso produced so many competing products that our focus shifted to him as an artist celebrity.

The Surrealist movement was founded and led by André Breton, but when we think of Surrealism, more often than not, it is Salvador Dali who comes to mind. Whether it is his thin, extravagantly curled moustache, or his painting of a melting watch, there is, perhaps, no other artist who is so synonymous with a single art movement. Dali exemplifies territory and market segmentation. Since 'isms aren't geographical, but exist in the mind, a territory's definition is purely perceptual. Once established, perception is difficult to change. If I perceive you to be the leader, even facts are unlikely to alter what I already seem to know.

Surrealism as a movement had many adherents. Among Dali, Max Ernst, Jóan Miro, René Magritte, and Yves Tanguy, who was the better artist? We all have our opinions. In any event, Dali was successful in claiming the territory of Surrealism in our minds. He set out to conquer the attention of the public, pushing his art well beyond the canvas, to the point of equating the movement with himself.

"Surrealism is me," he declared. Who else was prepared to heave a brick through a store window and be arrested for the sake of publicity? Was it madness or a calculated performance? While it wasn't always possible to manipulate critical response to his work, Dali acted decisively in areas that he could control.

Major shifts in art may be propelled by a singular seminal innovation. Europe defined avant-garde art for the first half of the 20th century, but its art had an Achilles' heel. Here is where the military principle of offensive warfare may be applied to marketing. The strength of European art was its innovations in modern art itself. Its weakness was easel painting, which pre-conditioned a painting's size and its paint application. What was the tipping point?

When Jackson Pollock flung his paint, the easel toppled, and with it the European dominance of art. The wrist movement became an arm movement, and paint poured to the edges. The scale and scope of art shifted. Something as simple as a drip forced the canvas to the floor, allowing the artist to work on it all over, using the whole body in rhythmic actions. We may argue, "Who was the better artist, Pollock or Willem de Kooning?" "Jackson broke the ice," de Kooning admitted. That was the tipping point.

The '60s saw the monolith of Abstract Expressionism break into segments, to use a marketing term, and modern art devolved into Postmodernism. If art until then had been a dry goods store, it now became a supermarket. One of its segments was Pop Art, and the artist most identified with the movement is Andy Warhol.

Already a successful commercial artist when he began to exhibit his art, Warhol had no difficulty reconciling commerce and art. When he set out to construct his artist persona, he was careful to set his brand apart from the rest. Picasso had been without question the genius, Dali the paranoid madman, and Pollock the macho hero. If Dali had been the royalist dandy, then Warhol would work in a factory. If Jackson was a he-man, Andy would be androgynous. If Picasso was brilliant and intense, Warhol would be inarticulate and robotic. Having fashioned a distinct identity, and assumed leadership in his market segment, it was possible for Warhol to extend his brand to film, portraiture, photography, and magazines. Above all, Warhol was the master of turning negatives into positives. With the lemons that life had awarded him, he wasn't content to set up a lemonade stand, it was going to be a whole industry.

His philosophy ran counter to conventional wisdom. The human impulse is to conceal or fix our natural imperfections. Instead he thought that flaws should be exaggerated. His calcimine complexion could be made to look even whiter. Bad hair could be made to look worse with a bad wig. Weakness could be a strength.

Instead of duking it out with Roy Lichtenstein over the comic-book style, he decided instead to cut his losses. When he turned to the then-lowly photograph and married it to the silkscreen, it spawned a lucrative career in portraiture. In his portraits, the very limitation of screening process and its inability to capture detail meant that his sitters would always look perfect. No bags under their eyes, no wrinkles. Warhol might have emphasized his own flaws, but never those of his subjects.

As the contemporary art market continues to fragment, and as ever more artists join the fight over pieces of the global art pie, how will your brand get the notice it deserves? How do we wield the sword of attention to slay the dragon of disinterest?

Courtesy of the computer and web technologies, we are grappling with a surfeit of information in every area of our lives. How many telephone numbers, passwords, and e-mail addresses can anyone keep track of? The truth is that our capacity to hold pieces of data in our minds at any given time is very limited.

The same holds true for the stream of sensory input that we need to manage from day to day. We adapt by instinctively resorting to a technique of information compression. Throughout history the principle has applied to innovations in thought and technology. Cumbersome Roman numerals gave way to the Arabic numbers. An alphabet restricted to a finite number of letters replaced thousands of pictograms. Ironically, it is these very advancements that have propelled the explosion of knowledge.

How does the technique of compression apply to art? It is helpful to define a focal point as the center of interest or activity. At the nexus of attention is the multitude of pieces of information reduced to binary pairings: Picasso and Cubism, Duchamp and ready-made, Pollock and drip, Lichtenstein and comics, Johns and flag, Segal and plaster cast, Rosenquist and billboard, Smithson and *Spiral Jetty*, Judd and box, Ryman and white, and so on. The obstacle to the emerging and practicing artists is that these pairings amount to a kind of ownership in the mind of the public, a brand that stakes out territory and is resistant to encroachment.

Happily for the artist today, the hastened fragmentation of art movements has multiplied opportunities to forge unique, marketable brands. As photography, cartoon and illustrative art, computer-generated work, sculpture, conceptual and performance art collide, unpredictable mutations present ever-new creative possibilities.

A case in point is the 1998 "Pop Surrealism" exhibition at the Aldrich Museum of Contemporary Art. Co-curated by Dominique Nahas, Ingrid Schaffner, and Richard Klein, the show was a graphic demonstration of the fertile collision between the low-brow medium of comic art and the "high" art of the Symbolists and the Surrealists.

The resulting undulations between "shallow" pop and the "deep" genres spawned a string of surprising bedfellows, from Robert Williams and Jim Shaw to Cindy Sherman and

Sue Williams, and from Art Spiegelman and John Waters to Lisa Yuskavage and Inka Essenhigh, to name just a few.

Coincident with the split and fracture of art's 'isms has been the mushroom sprouting of galleries and the number of artists that they represent. With an average stable of perhaps 30 artists and a conservative estimate of 750 galleries (the average listing in *Gallery Guide*) for New York City, we arrive at more than 20,000 artists. Many more artists don't have New York representation at all.

This pattern of gallery representation is repeated throughout cities and art centers across North and South America. Combine this with Europe, Asia, and the Pacific Rim countries, the prospects for being noticed are simply daunting if not impossible altogether. Even for the art specialist, the global information load is just too much to absorb.

What increases your chances of survival? First and foremost, find your focus. Define your public image. Resist spreading yourself too thin. Position your specialty where it will stand apart from your competition. A perceived shortcoming might be the very thing that lends definition to your artist identity. That uniqueness may be your gold mine.

Whether your focus is natural or invented, it will reflect an innate truth or be a response to a genuine situation or need. Forced to stay in a hotel with his family because of a house fire, artist Marcel Dzama began drawing with ink on letterhead paper. The loss of a working studio meant resorting to available resources at hand – pen-and-ink on hotel stationery. Root beer became his watercolor. With this constraint in medium and size, Dzama produced hundreds of portable works of art that quickly garnered him success in the international art market.

My own need to make my message less subjective drove me to make the creative process participatory. A 1988 sculptural work titled *Gallery Space* involved 64 art galleries, and was inspired by an early Sol LeWitt wall drawing. With the involvement of participants, the floor sculpture of open cubes resulted in a randomly generated labyrinth. The galleries themselves became the content, their involvement contributing to the particular shape of the labyrinth. This in turn inspired the bookwork *Meditations on Space*, which was followed by the publication of *d'Art International* magazine in 1998. With editorial contributors and advertisers as my content, I began to discover creative possibilities in the magazine medium itself.

From the start I viewed the tombstone ad as a missed opportunity. Is it possible for a gallery advertisement to be more than an exhibition announcement?

In advertising, a "tombstone" is a newspaper or magazine print advertisement, generally with black text centered on a white background and enclosed in a box. The name derives from its similarity to the text on a grave marker. Since gallery listings, mailed and e-mailed invitations, and word of mouth account for the bulk of gallery attendance, it's possible that the identical message need not be repeated in a print ad. While gallery and museum advertising already seem to be shifting from the tombstone format, why not open up the print ad space to its full communicative potential?

In 2002 I launched an ad campaign in *d'Art* with five artists over four issues. Spanning more that a year, the project exploited the print medium to focus attention on the message of the artist in depth. The approach may be applied equally well to galleries, museums, and institutions.

A strategic harnessing of web, e-mail, and print, with a consistent strategy and message might be our best defense against the rising tide of information.

**Steve Rockwell** is the publisher and editor of *d'Art International* magazine. First released in Los Angeles in 1998, *d'Art* also covers contemporary art in New York City, Toronto, San Antonio, and Richmond, Va. *d'Art* was itself the product of a 1995 narrative performance art piece entitled *Meditations on Space*, which involved 175 art galleries throughout Europe and North America. Rockwell's *Color Match* tournaments have recently become global.

## Eureka: The Creative Brain and Getting Artists to Talk About It

By Robert Mahoney

A gulf separates how art is talked about within the art world, and what people really want to know about artists and their work. All of my experience as an art critic and as a public relations officer at a small museum as well as writing art-critical responses and press materials for artists has made me all too aware of this situation.

I confess to nodding off when I hear artists go on, in well-schooled statements of watered down formalism, talking ad nauseum about form and color, line and composition.

Most published art criticism today also continues to glide along using the lingua franca of tired formalism. In most cases, art critics seem content to skate along on the surface of art, rarely attempting to get down into the art or the artist's mind, to begin to explain what is really going on.

Perhaps contemporary art criticism is rendered ultimately shallow by the restricted access into the interior given by living artists, whom, however much they chat on about technique, are afraid to divulge trade secrets.

Yet works of anthropology-inspired art history get down into the brain of the artist all the time. Lately, my art critical thinking has moved toward a more anthropological approach to art, curious about how art reflects behavior in society at large, less interested in the mechanics of technique. My writing is increasingly being informed by psychology and anthropology.

My inquiry into an artist's motives and ideas is a form of social constructionist-based narrative therapy, which explores the story people create for themselves, and then sees what can be done if a story has become too narrow and constricting, to re-author the story. It happens quite often in art as in life that one gets trapped in a story – due to location, market, age, or lifecourse – and it is necessary for artists to rethink their stories as a first step to finding a way out.

I listen to the stories that artists have to tell about their work, but then I have some questions. My questions are informed by a newer discourse in psychology called "appreciative inquiry," which seeks to find strengths, rather than constantly go on about the negatives.

Appreciative inquiry is based on the idea of the heliotrope, or sunflower, always moving toward nourishing sunlight: the premise is that if you discover a person's strengths, you can then guide a person to always be moving toward their strengths.

All of my questions are intended to find the strengths inside artists, and this requires getting into their heads or minds.

My approach is what anthropologists call "emic," defined by the *Encarta World English Dictionary* as "relating to the organization and interpretation of data that makes use of the categories of people being studied." This is opposed to "etic" or "making use of pre-established categories for organizing and interpreting anthropological data, rather than categories recognized within the culture being studied," according to the same source.

In following the emic approach, I try to get down into the mindset of the "native" (in this case, the artist) to find out what is really going on when they make their art. In doing so, I am aware that I am, in effect, using a flashlight in a dark room, and that in one press release I can only illuminate so much. But the purpose of my questions is to bring out some insights about an artist's work that will be of interest not only to insiders, but also to the general public.

It has always been my experience – and my intuition since the 1970s – that artists or highly creative people of all kinds have different kinds of brains than "normal" people. Brain science now appears to agree. Nancy C. Andreasen, in *The Creative Brain: The Science of Genius*, 2005, argues that the creative brain is, in fact, neurologically different than the normal brain.

She posits that there is an associative cortex underlying all the various locales and pathways of the brain, which is more pronounced in highly creative as opposed to less-creative persons. In that cortex "the brain begins by disorganizing, making links between shadowy forms of objects or symbols or words or remembered experiences that have not previously been linked" (Andreasen, p. 77).

Most artists have trouble describing the state of mind when "associative links run wild, creating new connections, many of which seem strange or implausible" (Andreasen, p. 77).

Many artists often suffer from the congestion that such associative gridlock causes them, and Andreasen conjectures that this may be the reason why in history genius was linked to madness, and artists often struggle with depression and addiction.

In any case, at some point, order emerges. This usually occurs when artists have a sudden, *eureka!* moment, when everything comes together, and is laid out before them, and from that point on the artists are, in fact, chasing after the art, as it pours out.

Andreasen derived her idea of this sudden moment both from new ideas that the brain is a self-organizing system and from testimony from Samuel T. Coleridge, in particular about the creative process that led him to write "Kubla Khan," which she interprets as a description of the creative process.

Coleridge wrote that he had had a (probably opium-soaked) dream, and that in it "all the images rose up before him as *things*, with the parallel production of the correspondent expressions, without any sensation or consciousness of effort" (Andreasen, p. 21).

When he woke up, he hurriedly scribbled everything down, but then was interrupted by a neighbor and it never came back.

In trying to figure out what Coleridge meant by describing the product of his eureka moment as *things*, Andreasen refers to a supporting testimony from the composer Bach.

He also describes a creative process in which his cluttered mind was suddenly cleared up by the appearance of a whole body of finished works, that "I do not hear in my imagination . . . successively, but I hear them, as it were, all at once (*gleich alles zusammen*)" (Andreasen, p. 41).

The suggestion is that the compression of "everything-at-once," suddenly seeing the whole of the work of art before one, transmutes a mere associative idea into some sort of *thing*, which then becomes a work of art.

From this observation, Andreasen builds a model of creation in which an artist 1) enters a state of mind so confused and cluttered it seems to be apart from reality, 2) then has a eureka moment, as everything comes together, and 3) after which everything runs effortlessly, so much so that the artist feels almost invisible and often, as in a dream, can't believe what he or she is doing.

This is a very suggestive image of how the creative brain works, and what fascinates me is that the questions I ask artists in order to help them express their views to the public correspond with this model. The eureka moment, that moment of inspiration that commenced not just the creative life but even any body of work, is always known by artists, the public always likes to hear about it, and I always ask artists about it.

A lot of artists are shy about giving up this specific moment, but it is something that, in my view, adds a great deal of credibility to a body of work, especially if the artist can be very specific about it.

Most of the time, I have found, the eureka moment has little to do with form or color, line or composition: it partakes of the unconscious – is born of a bolt of lightning within the unconscious – and brings with it a lot of interests and passions that unite an artist's routine and creative life. This means that in addition to asking about the eureka moment, then, I also have to ask about the associative cortex from which it emerged.

Of all of the constructs of psychology, the one that has stayed with me as part of my critical arsenal over the years is a belief in the unconscious. I also believe that most great art remains imbued, after its conscious creation, with the ambience of the unconscious. As a result, I am also interested in helping artists articulate what exactly lives in that associative cortex that Andreasen likens to the unconscious. I think it is very helpful, in explaining why people are attracted to art, to outline in some detail the "inner culture" of *things* in the artist's unconscious.

Ernst Cassirer in *An Essay on Man*, 1944, said that humans are symbolic animals, and that unless we "can succeed in finding a clue of Ariadne to lead us out of this labyrinth [of the complexity of modern philosophy], we can have no real insight into the general character of human culture, and we shall remain lost in a mass of disconnected and disintegrated data, which seem to lack all conceptual unity."

Following this maxim (but not, strictly speaking, Cassirer's project), the artist's unconscious can be seen as a distinct "culture," a growth of Ariadne-threads in a Petri dish, shaped by constructs that make that culture distinctly different from mainstream minds, to the point of possibly having developed a sense of reality that is all one's own.

As a result, I try to probe into what Pierre Bourdieu calls the "habitus" of an artist's mind, which consists of all of the internalizations, predispositions, and beliefs that compose (but also constrain) the culture of the artist's mind.

244

Over the years I have been made aware of the fact that lying deep down underneath all the pale descriptions of form and color, line and composition, artists are inspired by and operate by ideas and principles that seem like strange "superstitions" (Andreasen's "strange and implausible" ideas) compared to everyday rational thought. (I recollect one interview, slogging through form-and-color chitchat, until I asked what was *really* going through the artist's mind when she painted some peculiar portraits. The artist then confessed that, while she was out taking a walk one day, she felt the spirits of her ancestors in the wind, and rushed back to start painting: that's how art is made!)

These superstitions or habitus-related cognitions are often piquant and spicy and as such may be the catalyst that helps the creative brain boil over into a eureka moment. (A personal example: I find I write best with a pen I've found lying on the floor.)

In art history and in contemporary art, it is important to acknowledge these thought processes and much work has been done along these lines. Caroline Bynum's study of medieval mindsets (C. W. Bynum, "Bleeding hosts and their contact relics in late medieval northern Germany," *The Medieval History Journal, 7*, 2004, pp. 227-241) has helped me here, but James Hall in *Michelangelo and the Reinvention of the Human Body*, 2005, offers another example: apparently Michelangelo painted barrel-chested men because he had read that the heart is the window of the soul; he wanted to open a physical window into the heart on the body, that's why his chests are so square and broad.

The fact that Coleridge used the word *things* to describe how "Kubla Khan" manifested itself in his mind has always seemed curious to me. I continue to explore why he did so (there is considerable scholarly literature on the topic). By positing things *deep* in the dreaming mind, Coleridge seemed to foreshadow the invention of the unconscious.

Though Freud's architecture of id, ego, and superego has been tossed onto the dustbin of history, others still seek to define what *things* exist in the unconscious. For example, object-relations psychologists have populated the unconscious with what they call *objects*, which are defined as internalizations of relations one has had with significant others.

Like *objects*, Coleridge's *things* may have been created by an intensely symbolic internalization of values or feelings: a classic process by which a *thing* (or *object*) is created in the unconscious is "introjection," for example, by which one comes to treat oneself as significant others have treated one (for better or worse).

An object-relations interpretation of Mary Shelley's *Frankenstein* is that the monster is a *thing* evoking both Shelley's deceased mother and aloof father. Artist's superstitions may be related to such *objects*, meaning that they may communicate more than they seem.

The word *thing* also comes up in narrative therapy when it makes use of a strategy called "externalization," by which the client is guided to "visualize the problem in a concrete form, as a *thing* [my italics] that resides separate from them." (Rockquemore and Laszloffy, "Multiple realities: a relational narrative approach in therapy with black-white mixed-race clients." *Family Relations,* 2003, p. 121).

The point is to help the client "recognize that they are more than their identified problem" and to "begin to develop a relationship with the problem, as an entity over which they can eventually exercise mastery." (Rockquemore and Laszloffy, p. 121).

So a therapist might ask a client, "Can you describe what the fear looks like? What color is the fear? What physical form does the fear resemble?" or "If the fear was standing next to you how big would it be in relation to you?" (Rockquemore and Laszloffy, p. 123).

In order to get down into the unconscious, I also inquire as well into the various ways in which, I believe, the associative cortex is reflected in the work of art subsequently produced by the artist. This entails trying to describe a few different constructs: the *thing*, but also the milieu, the moral and the mask, all frameworks within unconscious-imbued art. Here, I will only discuss the first. The *thing* (which may well relate to Coleridge's *things*) consists of some irrepressible passion that engages artists even when they are not making art, as in, "What's your thing?"

The *thing* is all-giving and ever-resourceful (the opposite, therefore, of an addiction), can always be depended upon to get one's engine revved up, banish a bad mood, break up a writer's block, and put one back in the flow of creative thinking. You know you are in the presence of a *thing* in art, because it's obvious the artist is having a lot of fun with it. (Yes, great art is fun too.)

Once artists are free to admit that they are crazily passionate about some *thing* outside of art, that still nourishes their art, you'd be surprised what you hear. I've learned that one artist gets most of her ideas not in the studio but in her garden, another was replenished with ideas by taking the same walk through town every day, another responds to stoop sales and street finds, another was into obscure horror movies, another horse-racing, another visited candy stores and bakeries, and so on.

Also, while *normal* people may have to travel the world to get inspired, it doesn't take a lot to get a creative brain going. This passionate *thing*, therefore, is usually quite specific, controlled by a careful protocol, often quite secret, hidden, in the manner of Kepler's statement, "I live in a *secret frenzy*" – possibly the best two-word description ever of the creative brain at work (J. W. Connor, *Kepler's Witch*, 2004, p. 329), under the surface of an otherwise nondescript life.

This *thing*, in my view, is a reflection in conscious life and in art of the jumble of images in Andreasen's associative cortex that precedes a eureka moment: it sets the stage, creates a predisposition, for the eureka moment.

Why do I ask artists about their *thing*? Because people love to hear that art emerges not from dry formal exercises in a studio, but from love of life in various quite specific ways. By finding evidence of a *thing* and its impact on a body of work, I get a sense of the fullness of the unconscious at work in an artist's art. If an artist is able to describe some of his or her passions, what *things* fill up the unconscious of their art, and then articulate the eureka moment – the lightning strike – that brought everything together, then I am fairly sure that I am in the presence of an inspired, pulled-together, and mature artist.

One last thing: many artists are shy at revealing these *things*. According to the theoretical construct of metacognition, which consists of the constant stream of reflection and stratagem by which all humans think all the time about what they are doing, artists need not fear. Metacognition happens: brain scientists refer to it as the "*ghost* in the machine." (I sense I encounter this *ghost* whenever I take a nap, and have the distinct impression that I have been awake and talking to myself the whole time.)

Educators also find that the best students are always metacognitively strategizing about their work, while other students do not reflect enough.

Good, great artists reflect a lot about their art. Indeed, Hall argues that the *ignudi* (athletic male nudes) on Michelangelo's Sistine Chapel represent *spiritelli*, or thought balloons, and, in effect, that they are explainable as figural representations of Michelangelo the artist thinking about the work he is doing while he is doing it.

Metacognition is also linked to the fact that once artists set out on a body of work, they may then reflect upon certain aspects of where they are going with it and then head off in another direction, contributing to what I term a *cascade* of concerns nonetheless still part of an expanded body of work.

Metacognition also explains why visual art in particular is so recursive. Artists are always rebooting to the freshness of the new present moment, taking another shot, trying again, setting off as if for the first time (often having forgotten what they did last week) to get it right, even after having done so a hundred times before.

Mastery and maturity in art and all creative effort are marked by the commanding power of metacognition, a willingness to talk about everything without fear that by doing so it may all go poof! It won't, especially if, as Andreasen believes, the creative brain is a distinct neurological endowment that one is both blessed and cursed with.

Anyone with a creative brain knows one thing: it just won't shut up. So, artists should feel free to explore the inner workings of their creative brains – the *things* of the unconscious, the eureka moment – and help me as a writer express the true sources of their strength as artists to a public that really does want to know what it takes to experience the "secret frenzy" of using all of one's brain in being truly alive – and we'll leave form and color and line and composition to the critics.

**Bibliography:**

Andreasen, Nancy C. *The Creative Brain: The Science of Genius.* (London: Penguin Books, A Plume Book, 2005).

Bynum, C.W. "Bleeding hosts and their contact relics in late medieval northern Germany." *The Medieval History Journal, 7,* (2004): 227-241.

Cassirer, Ernst. *An Essay on Man.* (New Haven: Yale University Press, 2004).

Connor, J.W. (2004). *Kepler's Witch.* (San Francisco: Harper, 2004): 329.

*Encarta World English Dictionary.* (New York: St. Martin's Press, 1999).

Hall, James. *Michelangelo and the Reinvention of the Human Body.* (New York: Farrar, Straus and Giroux, 2005).

Rockquemore, K.A. and Laszloffy, T.A. "Multiple realities: a relational narrative approach in therapy with black-white mixed-race clients." *Family Relations,* (2003): 52, 119-128.

**Robert Mahoney** has been an art writer in New York City for over 30 years, writing for such publications as *ARTS, FLASH ART, Contemporanea, Tema Celeste* and *Cover* magazines. He currently writes for *TIME OUT New York,* and *Artnet.com* and contributes to *edificerex.com* and *d'Art International.* Mahoney is also the author of numerous catalog essays on contemporary artists, his writing having been presented in conjunction with exhibitions around the world. Mahoney served as public information officer at the Queens Museum of Art, Queens, New York City, where he brought high-profile coverage to exhibitions of contemporary art.

# Tools

# Making A Statement

By Mary Hrbacek

While the artist's statement has long been a staple of every portfolio, the literary or narrative component of an artist's presentation has risen in significance. It is no longer sufficient for artists to develop their work to a high level; they must also be articulate about it.

To begin with, it is a useful procedure to identify the components of a good artist's statement by reading those found at galleries, especially when the exhibition on view resonates with the concerns of your own work. By examining other artists' statements, you can learn what types of information will illuminate your work and how to develop and structure your own statement. But be sure to use words and phrases of your own choosing when you eventually sit down to write.

Writing a statement can act as an aid in focusing on the ideas embodied in your work, and how this fits in the larger scheme of contemporary art. You must identify what aspects of your art make connections to the wider field. This is the first stage in "branding," which is the defining process that helps you stake out your turf by identifying the unique qualities of your art. You must not only realize where the work fits, but also what distinguishes it from other work that you have positioned yourself with. By exploring how your work is like and how it differs from other, or even similar artwork, you develop a better understanding of your own artistic uniqueness.

To begin to position your own work, ask yourself where it fits on the art historical continuum. You may find yourself gravitating to both current and historical movements; in each instance you may share a common inspiration or aesthetic ancestor. You may need to review styles, techniques, and related ways of working in order to locate yourself in this or that tradition, and you will find it useful to review the various movements of art you want to consider.

The visual arts encompass two-dimensional works, such as drawings and paintings, works on paper, prints, photographs, and collages. Three-dimensional expressions include, of course, sculpture, but today they also may encompass installation and nature-based art and/or earth works. And in multi-media works, artists are combining multiple techniques. Video, performance, and new media are popular forms; there is also conceptual art, sound or light art, computer-based art, and animation.

I have tried to include as many contemporary art forms as possible, but due to the number of innovative artists operating on the contemporary art scene, many hybrid forms and amalgams are being discovered; thus it is impossible to list them all.

Beyond locating your artwork in the broad spectrum of the mediums, you will want to go even further and align it with certain art styles and movements. Is it abstract or realistic? If it is abstract, is it hard-edged or lyrical? If realistic, does it fit within traditional genres, like portraits, figural, still life, or landscape? Is it expressionistic, impressionistic, or minimalistic?

If your work is sculptural, are you working with the more traditional materials such as marble, wood, clay, or plaster? Or are you using less orthodox materials such as found objects, food, or even the earth itself?

If you're a photographer, are you recording what you see, creating your own scene, or documenting an ephemeral arrangement or performance? Is it "straight" photography with no manipulation in the darkroom or on the computer?

Or do you eschew the physical for the cerebral as in conceptual art? Perhaps time and the passage of time is your bottom line. Your work may have a poetic basis that makes a statement about change and transformation.

Once you have found a place to position your art vis-à-vis the larger art world, you might feel a loss of individuality. But as you focus on the specifics that make your work unique, you will discover your individuality within a larger context. Then you will be in a position to establish your own "brand."

At this stage in your process, do not be concerned with labels or categories. Think about what has led to your own special vision, and whether or not you are part of a clearly defined trend. Why is your approach to artmaking so fulfilling? What colors do you favor and how do you feel when you contemplate them? Do you like creating many layers? Does process intrigue you? You may wish to elaborate on your choice of subject, including the factors determining that choice. You may be convinced that a discussion of your processes, including choice of materials, is an important step in illuminating and clarifying your work for a public audience. Your statement might mention sources of artistic inspiration, artists you feel akin to, and why you feel or see a connection.

Ask yourself, from a deeply emotional and analytical standpoint, why you do what you do. Does your art fulfill a special personal need or intellectual requirement? Find a title or phrase that might suggest several interpretations or meanings that attract you. You can refine and redefine it as you gradually become clearer about what you want to say.

The statement should not be too lengthy, preferably less than a typewritten page. If your statement takes more than a few minutes to read, it may be too long or too complicated. Practice making a concise verbal statement that convincingly describes your work, and that expresses your feelings.

Once you complete these exercises, you will be on your way to making a successful statement. And remember that you *cannot* get it wrong.

Do not worry if the statement must be adjusted over time; your art and art practice is subject to flux. The statement needs to be refined and updated to reflect your changing thoughts and shifting perceptions.

Once you have carefully crafted your statement, it can be used to formulate a press release, which, in turn, becomes a major tool for bringing your message to the public.

A brief biographical summary, which is written in narrative form, will tell your story, and complements your artist statement; alternatively you can use a chronological résumé, which simply lists your achievements. Regardless of which format you choose – and cases can be made for selecting one over the other – both chronicle your career and provide the same basic information.

Factual data such as birth date, place of birth, and where you currently live and work are important. Your art education, including the schools you have attended, with whom you have studied with (especially if a respected and recognized name), and the degrees you have earned, provide the public with basic information and valuable insights.

Your professional accomplishments, including exhibitions (with the titles in quote marks, date, and location), commissions (where, what, when, and who commissioned them), grants, residencies, art colonies, professional affiliations, museums and public collections, and special awards are included in your biography.

You can mention professional activities that are worthy of special notice, such as panel discussions or public lectures you have delivered, with the dates and location. Use your judgment in selecting your most significant achievements. In all cases, give the pertinent details so that the reader can position you within the field of art from your involvements and activities.

In a culture where reading fluency is more common than visual literacy, written materials, such as your artist's statement and biography, can provide an entrée into your work for your audience.

**Mary Hrbacek** has been writing about art in New York City since the late 1990s. She has had more than one hundred reviews published in *The M Magazine/The New York Art World*, and has written for *NY Arts Magazine, NY Artbeat.com,* and *d'Art International.* Her commentary spans a broad spectrum of art, from the contemporary cutting-edge to the Old Masters. She has covered exhibitions at the Metropolitan Museum, the Whitney Museum of American Art, and the Museum of Modern Art as well as the Armory Show, the Affordable Art Fair, and two consecutive Venice Biennials.

# Opportunity Calls
By Edward Leffingwell

Hurtling over the challenges of today's increasingly complex and overheated art scene, the prospect of a career in the arts may seem increasingly less viable, or worse yet, an oxymoron.

Each year skeptical parents recoil from the staggering costs associated with training their children to be fine artists. It can cost from $30,000 to in excess of $50,000 a year in tuition and fees to enroll students in an academic studio program. Scholarships provide financial aid to the lucky few while, at the same time, they introduce all students to the competitive nature of the art world.

Still legions of aspiring practitioners of all ages and levels of ability confront competition and seek access to a variety of resources in order to make an art career viable. Grants continue to support an astonishing offering of nonprofit programs; fellowships and residencies welcome candidates in search of an environment suited to their disciplines; artist colonies provide a respite from the demands of daily life; and public art projects and commercial gallery opportunities are available to tenacious artists.

Chronicling the evolution of the art world vis à vis the concept of job creation and the distribution of art in the pre-blog world, Kim Levin a New York City-based art critic, then attached to *The Village Voice*, collaborated several years ago with John Salvest, a curator/artist colleague from Memphis whose work is based on the concept of accumulation. Their collaboration functioned as a model for an understanding of the machinery and distribution of contemporary art.

Admirers of each other's work, the two devised and mounted "Itineraries," a complex exhibition representing the marketplace of art as recorded in the critic's annotated peregrinations through the downtown art precincts of New York City, from SoHo to Chelsea, over a period of decades, as these neighborhoods took form and changed. In the fall of 2003, the Levin/Salvest project, composed of gallery mailers, fliers, and the ephemera fundamental to the promotion of exhibitions, was installed at the nonprofit Delta Axis @ Marshall Arts in Memphis, known nationally as a city engaged in the arts.

Objectifying a chronology that spanned decades, the project maintained the interest it had generated and seemed especially appropriate to its installation at Ronald Feldman Gallery, a sympathetic, politically savvy first-generation SoHo gallery. Sensitively mounted, the exhibition offered a study in the taxonomies of the contemporary art world through the eyes of the show's organizers. The product of this collaborative act, "Itineraries", assumed its form as a selective narrative on the distribution systems of art and commerce. Downtown exhibition announcements dated from 1975 to 1991 documented a period marked by the rise of concept-driven art fed by information, becoming an acceptable medium for the making of art. Annotated gallery maps attached with map pins to gallery walls tracked Levin's route through the warren of galleries that populated SoHo, and then followed the real estate shift in 1992 to Chelsea. Despite the interest in and support of this project in Memphis and New York City, valiant art workers, individual and institutional support, and a solid history of grants including The Andy Warhol Foundation for the Visual Arts and the National Endowment for the Arts (NEA), the programs of Delta Axis folded in the late summer of 2009, its supporters kneecapped by the advancing wave of a worsening economy.

On a more positive note, as a national bellwether, the American Recovery and Reinvestment Act of 2009, distinguished by its investment in the nonprofit arts industry, played a significant part in the future of a recovering economy. Administered under the auspices of the NEA and through its mandate, projects were intended to create and protect jobs in the arts nationwide, or hopefully to present that as a possibility.

To place this in historical context, President Lyndon Johnson established the Endowment in 1965 through the National Foundation on the Arts and the Humanities Act as an independent government agency offering support for projects of "artistic excellence." From the mid-1980s to the mid-1990s, Congress granted the NEA funding that ranged from $160 million to $180 million. In 1996, Congress cut funding to $99.5 million in response to a conservative agenda, a result of the culture war that raged in the country.

In the 1990s, a serious spate of bad press altered the NEA forever. It started with what became known as the NEA Four – performance artists Karen Finley, Tim Miller, John Fleck, and Holly Hughes. After having been awarded grants through the NEA's peer process review, the head of the Endowment, John Frohnmayer, vetoed them on the grounds their work was obscene. This set off a legal battle that ended in district and circuit courts finding in favor of the NEA Four in 1993 and 1996. They had argued that their right to free speech had been violated.

In response to their challenge, the NEA revised its charter to add the criterion of "general standards of decency" in considering applicants. After the 1996 decision, Finley fought against the decency clause. In 1998 in the National Endowment for the Arts v. Finley, the Supreme Court reversed part of the lower courts' rulings and declared the decency clause constitutional.

The conservative culture warriors also vanquished grants to individuals. Although visual artists are no longer the direct focus of Endowment programs, through its investment in the re-granting programs of the nonprofit arts industry, the NEA continues to play a significant part in the future of artists and arts organizations. Its fiscal support of the visual arts is specifically channeled through a diversity of arts organizations and a variety of disciplines intending the creation and protection of jobs in the arts nationwide.

The Endowment's fortunes have been helped by President Barack Obama, who signed a bill in late 2009 increasing the allocations for the National Endowment for the Arts and the National Endowment for the Humanities by $12.5 million each, setting these agency budgets at $167.5 million. Those funds are distributed in the form of more than 2,000 grants in support of Endowment-defined initiatives.

On a case-by-case basis, grants go forward, although the budgets of state arts councils have been cut and state funding represents an ever-shrinking percentage of its total. Faced with this reality, state and local arts councils are pursuing alternative revenue streams. In late 2009, organizations with funding from the state of Missouri carried little of the brunt of state tax cuts to the arts. Although its State Arts Council faced a cut of $10 million, it had access to a fund made up of revenues from an income tax levied on the out-of-state entertainers and professional athletes who perform in Missouri.

In another approach widely followed, the Community Redevelopment Agency in downtown Los Angeles initiated a mitigation program, crafting legislation designed to permit the administration of grants to artists as contracts for services, the wherewithal coming from developers and redevelopment programs.

Today part of the creation of a career hinges on paying attention and asking questions, not the least of which is "How can I get the time, space, and money to develop my art and advance my career?" Opportunities can be accessed by informed artists turning to nonprofit resources specifically designed to support artists with a generous offering of programs of fellowships, grants, and awards; artist-in-residencies and stays at artist colonies; and internships. Professional contacts and even luck may help the persistent candidate to craft a viable application for grants and residencies and to leverage meaningful support. In addition, commercial galleries and public art projects offer other paths to a viable art career.

Research is critical to identify those resources. Artists must place what they don't know in the light of what they do, and proceed from there. Boot up the laptop and try a simple search for grants in the arts. (You can get a head start by consulting the "Information Resources," pp. 297-362 in this book.)

Awards may go to emerging artists or mid-career artists, artists under 30 or mature artists, the unknown or the under-recognized, artists who live within a specified geographical area or open to all regardless of residency, medium specific or wide open. These and other restrictions can apply. Research may reveal one that is tailor-made for you. You must apply to some programs while others find you. The award amounts vary wildly from just a few hundred dollars to the so-called "genius grants" of $500,000 parceled out to well recognized artists by the John D. and Catherine T. MacArthur Foundation (www.macfound.org).

For an overview of opportunities, consult the nonprofit Foundation Center (http://foundationcenter.org). Based in New York City with field offices in Atlanta, Cleveland, San Francisco, and Washington, DC, it is supported by over 500 foundation members. Active in the field of organized philanthropy, the Center remains the fountainhead for information concerning grant resources today. Among much else, nonprofit organizations identified through the Center administer funds in support of individual artists. Simple searches guide users to an organization's programs and help inform artists of the variety of programs that distribute awards in specific disciplines.

Its online subscription database, Foundation Directory Online, covers nearly 100,000 foundations nationwide and tracks corporate donors. While memberships are available through monthly subscription, the Directory can be used free of charge on site at all Center locations.

Among the resources to be found is United States Artists (www.unitedstatesartists.org), which from its headquarters in Los Angeles, supports the work of emerging, mid-career, and established artists. Unrestricted grants in the amount of $50,000 are awarded annually to 50 recipients in a broad spectrum of disciplines. There are no applications. Anonymous critics, scholars, and artists propose candidates.

The Pollock-Krasner Foundation (www.pkf.org/grant.html) awards grants to individuals based on artistic merit and financial need. On a year-round basis, the Foundation considers applications from painters, sculptors, and artists working on paper including printmakers. They are intended to support expenses for professional work and living and are determined by an assessment of need.

Similarly structured, The Adolph and Esther Gottlieb Foundation (www.gottliebfoundation.org) provides 12 Individual Support Grants annually to artists who have demonstrated maturity in their dedication to painting, sculpture, or printmaking rather than by the usual standards of financial success. Eligibility requires financial disclosure.

The New York Foundation for the Arts (NYFA) (www.nyfa.org/afp) offers individual fellowships supporting the work of artists living in the state. Its Artists' Fellowships consist of unrestricted cash awards of $7,000 each year. Grants are awarded in 16 disciplines, with applications accepted in eight categories each year. In 2009, NYFA awarded 131 Fellowships to 134 artists. Since the program's inception in 1985, NYFA has awarded more than $22 million to 3,688 artists.

The Queens Council on the Arts (http://queenscouncilarts.org/index) supports Queens County artists and arts organizations with a variety of programming and events, including Project Diversity Queens, the Individual and Teaching Artist Initiatives, and the Arts in the Schools grant program. As a fully financed consultancy with an established professional development specialist, The Individual Artist Initiative invigorates the careers of artists and is awarded annually to ten emerging Queens artists in any discipline  A grant program for individual artists of color in New York City provides $2,000 fellowships for artistic and professional development. Over the years QCA has awarded more than $2 million in grants.

Artists work together for the benefit of their colleagues. For example, visual artists established the Foundation for Contemporary Arts (www.foundationforcontemporaryarts.org/grant_programs) to encourage innovation and potential by providing works of art for sale in support of grants to artists working in a variety of mediums. The Foundation maintains a fund to help artists with unexpected emergencies, providing modest support for them to respond to opportunities or to defray expenses for projects nearing completion.

Time and space are critical to the development of every artist. Artist-in-residency programs provide both. Duration, amount of financial support (including none), studio facilities, and living situations run the gamut. Many of the same criteria discussed above apply to artist residencies in museums, educational programs, and other nonprofit organizations. As might be expected, there are many in the New York City area.

In Brooklyn, the Marie Walsh Sharpe Art Foundation (http://sharpeartfd.org) offers free studio space supported by underwriters that include prominent artists and well-known foundations. The program is situated in the Dumbo area of Brooklyn, and provides non-residential workspace specifically to visual artists, but no stipend. Studios are available to New York City artists in need of adequate studio space and to those elsewhere who might benefit from time spent in New York City. They are chosen by a changing jury.

An established residency program, the Edward F. Albee Foundation (www.albeefoundation.org) serves writers, visual artists, and composers who work without disturbance not far from the center of Montauk, Long Island, on the Atlantic Ocean. The foundation was established in 1967 by the renowned playwright and during the summer months offers one-month residencies for up to six participants. Writers and composers are offered a room, and visual artists a room and studio space. Residents provide their own meals and transportation.

Located in SoHo, Location One's (www.location1.org/residency) programs include an artist-in-residency of five to ten months. Candidates must be working artists with at least three years of practice and exhibition history and an active interest in new forms of expression in a variety of disciplines. Artists from abroad are selected through a process that includes a short list of candidates from which Location One selects an artist-in-residence. Curators, critics, and staff propose American artists.

A nonprofit organization supporting artists' initiatives, including a highly structured studio program in Chelsea, CUE Art Foundation (www.cueartfoundation.org) provides assistance to under-recognized artists at various career stages. CUE programs are supported by The National Endowment for the Arts, New York Department of Cultural Affairs, New York State Council on the Arts, and New York State Council for the Humanities. Although the State of New York, as of November 2009, is strapped for resources, the CUE residency program includes five artists in each program year, offering time and working space to a diverse group of artists provided with the possibility to produce new work or further work in progress. The artists are chosen for each program year and are offered 10-week residencies in 400-square-foot studios. In addition to the use of the space, CUE facilitates meetings with participants and professionals to foster connections with professionals in the field. Unusual for granting programs, artists receive a $1,200 allocation to defray associated costs.

Based in New York City, Eyebeam Atelier (Fellowships: tinyurl.com/EBF10, Residencies: tinyurl.com/EBRWS10) supports a program of unusual duration and interest providing artists with access to equipment and technicians appropriate to their work. Since 1996, Eyebeam has provided more than 130 residencies and fellowships in programs accessible to the public. Residencies provide a five-month program for production and presentation of projects addressing a range of disciplines that include art, technology, and culture. Eyebeam's current Research Groups include Sustainability, Education, Open Culture,

Project Blackbird (Humor and Code), and Urban Research. Residents receive a $5,000 stipend. Eyebeam Fellowships provide an 11-month opportunity and a $30,000 award to develop new research, lead research-group inquiries, and develop innovative technology with support over a longer period of time.

Skowhegan School of Painting and Sculpture (*www.skowheganart.org*) in Skowhegan, ME, offers a residency program for emerging visual artists. Artists are provided with a private studio, room, board, and weekly private and group critiques by leading professional artists. Sixty-five artists are accepted annually. Admission panels consider those enrolled in academic programs and artists who have been working independently.

The artist-in-residency program of Headlands Center for the Arts (www.headlands.org) in Sausalito, CA, offers generous opportunities for emerging and mid-career artists. They are awarded monthly stipends, room, board, travel expenses, and studios. The program addresses the work of artists in all disciplines from the United States and abroad. Successful candidates are selected for quality of work and an evident interest in residency.

The Lawndale Artist Studio Program (www.lawndaleartcenter.org), Houston, TX, is committed to the work of Gulf Coast artists and is supported by the prestigious Cullen Foundation, the National Endowment for the Arts, the deep pockets of The Brown Foundation, and the Houston Endowment. Studio space is provided for three professionals in the field who enjoy access to Lawndale's studios 24-hours a day for a term of nine months, and receive $500 monthly stipends and $1,500 for materials.

Artist colonies exist to provide material sustenance and a place of retreat. One of the most prestigious is The MacDowell Colony (www.macdowellcolony.org) in Peterborough, NH. It offers residencies for up to eight weeks with suitable studios and stipends for the exceptional artist. It provides participants three meals a day (picnic baskets appear on their doorstep at lunch time "to minimize workday interruptions" per its website). The Colony accepts applications from artists working in a broad variety of disciplines. Acceptance is based on artistic excellence.

The Corporation of Yaddo (http://www.yaddo.org) in Saratoga Springs, NY, helps to provide artists with housing, meals, and studios or workspace. Master artists are identified to collaborate with resident artists in visual, literary, music, and performing arts. Artists qualifying for residency are working at the professional level in their fields. Yaddo accepts approximately 200 participants each year, or roughly 18% of applicants.

Percent-for-art programs offer considerable opportunities for artists. They labor to introduce cultural facilities and art objects to public and private architectural programs. In this program model, architects and landscape designers attempt to work together with artists as they move from the practice of studio art to the collaborative needs of public art, occupying newly created jobs in the field.

In New York City, for example, the Percent for Art Program selects professional fine artists to create permanent public art in city-owned buildings. The Percent for Art Law mandates that 1% of the capital budget for new or reconstructed buildings be allocated for art, with commissions ranging from $50,000 to $400,000. The artist's fee is 20% of the total allocation. A valuable consideration, the word "professional" in this process refers to the nature of the commitment of the artist to an art form as primary vocation rather than the amount of financial remuneration earned from the creative endeavor. The city's Department of Cultural Affairs (www.nyc.gov/culture) requests that artists submit qualifications and letters of interest to be considered for panel review and the opportunity to be considered as finalists for the commission of permanent artwork.

In Los Angeles, the Community Redevelopment Agency (http:/culturela.org) has spearheaded percent-for-art projects in downtown LA. The city's Department of Cultural Affairs has awarded in excess of $3 million in grants annually to more than 300 artists and nonprofit arts organizations. It administers the Artist-in-Residence (A.I.R.) and City of Los Angeles (C.O.L.A.) Individual Artist Fellowships. Each fellow is peer-reviewed in a nonthematic selection process and is granted $10,000.

Founded by artists in 1997, Dumbo Arts Center (DAC) (www.dumboartfestival.org) was the first to locate in this formerly industrial area of Brooklyn with the intention of being a center for the arts. It presents exhibitions, commissions site-specific art, and offers educational programs. Curators are selected by open call, with an emphasis on the experimental. According to its originators, the annual D.U.M.B.O. Art Under the Bridge Festival is the largest urban forum for experimental art in the country, involving some 1,500 artists and transforming Dumbo into a vibrant public art arena.

Similarly constructed, the Public Art Fund (PAF) (http://www.publicartfund.org) presents projects, commissions, installations, and exhibitions in New York City's public spaces. It identifies, coordinates, and realizes major projects by established and emerging artists. In its 25-year history, PAF has responded to changes in the cultural resources of the city.

There are programs in association with museums and other institutions that are intended to introduce artists to the role of such organizations in the workings of the art world. The Whitney Museum of American Art's (www.whitney.org/Research/ISP) one-year Independent Studies Program is composed of art history and studio programs that include Critical Studies, Curatorial Studies, and the Studio Program for Artists. It includes many visiting influential artists, art historians, and critics, and involves the reading of theory.

Internships are another avenue of entrée for younger applicants. They differ in requirements, but often provide access to innovative artists' programs and staff. The intern program at Long Island City's P.S.1 Contemporary Art Center (www.ps1.org), an affiliate of the Museum of Modern Art, is open to college students and the recently graduated with significant communication skills. With a hands-on approach, it "provides the opportunity to learn about the operations of a nonprofit art institution and to work alongside some of the world's most exciting contemporary artists and curators," according to its website. Participants are expected to work two seven-hour days a week.

Many organizations have a number of programs to support artists. For example, Art in General (http://www.artingeneral.org) in New York City assists artists with the production and presentation of new work. It organizes and presents exhibitions, hosts a national and international artist residency program, and, through educational in-school art training, offers regular public programs, and membership events. Exhibition programs focus on the commissioning of new work that Art in General exhibits, presents, and promotes. Successful candidates receive an artist's fee of $3,000 and a project budget of between $3,000-$5,000 for research, production, and installation. The residency program is by invitation only.

Commercial galleries provide no small element in creating a narrative of art that may sustain professional survival. Trained staff and marketable objects produced by artists are needed to secure repeat consumers and a positive cash flow. Galleries may draw on artists already vetted through the exhibition programs of the nonprofit sectors, including the laboratory of the artist's studio and public art, helping to support the new and not yet commercially viable.

Full or part-time jobs working with established artists or exhibition spaces can place artists in the "right place at the right time" to meet the curator, collector, gallerist who can advance their careers.

Carefully conceived, designed, packaged, printed, stuffed, mailed, or otherwise disseminated, an enormous amount of information in the form of exhibition announcements and press releases further the conversation about contemporary art. These documents are the first line of engagement with the viewer, the elements intended to represent or introduce others into that conversation.

As traditional publishing venues for artists and critics to communicate ideas or document exhibitions have diminished, opportunities to "publish" on the web have increased to what may seem to be the endless screed of the blogging art press.

There are dedicated artists who forego these formalized and conventional ways intended to assist in career building. They create their own "development programs."

Just as the art world thrives on originality, so does making the journey to recognition. Take for example, Robert Bergman, a photographer now living in New York City, who in 2009 at the age of 65 presented his first solo shows at the National Gallery of Art in Washington, DC, and in New York City at P.S.1, and in a Chelsea gallery given over to photography.

Turned away in a portfolio review at the Museum of Modern Art, he published a volume of his photographs in 1998, *A Kind of Rapture*, with an introduction by Toni Morrison, the Nobel laureate writer, and afterword by the art historian Meyer Schapiro. Slowly the machinery of recognition and understanding moved forward. He'd stuck to his guns and was interested in little else.

Bergman did it his way. It's up to you to do it your way.

**Edward Leffingwell** is corresponding editor for Brazil to the journal *Art in America*. An independent critic and curator, he has written at length on contemporary art and photography for such journals as *Parkett, Poliester, Americás, American Art*, and *Aperture*. In the last 25 years he has organized exhibitions, programs, and publications for various contemporary arts institutions. From 1985 to 1988 he served as chief curator and program director for P.S.1, Contemporary Art Center, Long Island City. In 1988, he was appointed director of visual arts for the City of Los Angeles and Los Angeles Municipal Art Galleries. There he developed a multi-institutional exhibition and publications program and from 1992 until 1995 served as its executive director. Leffingwell has published hundreds of reviews and many catalogue essays. He is a member of AICA-USA (Association International des Critiques d'Art). Leffingwell lives and works in New York City.

# Anatomy of an Online Campaign

By Iyna Bort Caruso

You've got the talent but do you have the buzz? These days, it takes the one-two punch of marketing and public relations to enhance your brand image. And if you don't think of yourself as a brand, now's the time to start.

The artists who have the edge are media savvy, and for many of them the Internet has become their platform of choice. It's economical yet effective. Just imagine if YouTube and MySpace were around when Salvador Dali, Pablo Picasso, or Jackson Pollock were starting out.

Good online branding generates electricity. It sets you apart from the pack and helps boost your profile – and your sales.

## What's the Story? Defining Goals

Every successful media campaign starts with a set of objectives. It's crucial to have a clear idea of your goals from the outset. Do you want to drive traffic to your website? Increase sales of your work? Improve attendance at your exhibitions?

To rise above marketplace clutter and get noticed, you've got to have a compelling story to tell. Being a talented artist is rarely enough. You have to give people a reason to care. Sometimes, the most successful storylines are not always the most obvious.

Start by brainstorming a list of everything that makes you and your work distinctive. The story that sticks might be about how you find your subjects, about your approach, or your journey as a fine artist. Maybe even about the job or lifestyle you left behind. Is yours a feel-good story? A rags-to-riches tale? Find the drama.

Always try to find a timely angle to your story – an exhibition, an important sale, or a newly conferred award. A news page imparts a sense of urgency.

Another approach to getting your name out is to take advantage of your standing as an art expert. As an authority, you're uniquely qualified to weigh in and offer yourself up to members of the media as a specialist on emerging trends, art-buying tips, or best gallery bets, for instance.

Once you've defined your story angle and refined your message, turn it into a news release. The news release is one of your most important marketing tools. It gives you credibility and visibility – as long as it serves the interests of the media outlet and its readers/viewers and not just your own.

Tread cautiously. Getting your name out without appearing self-serving and self-aggrandizing is a balancing act. Do-it-yourself campaigners can be seen as shameless self-promoters if they're overly aggressive. Avoid exaggerations, misrepresentations, and misleading statements. And always, always remember: sell the story, not yourself.

### Good to Meet You: The Media List

Your job is to meet the media's needs and target audiences. Those viewers and readers vary from outlet to outlet. The release you send to a general interest online magazine, for instance, is not the same version you should be sending to a blogger or special interest website. Alter your pitches and massage the message to meet the editorial needs of each e-zine, website, or blog.

Developing a targeted media list takes some sleuthing. Compile a list of websites and blogs where you'd love to appear. Note the bylines of art reviewers and feature writers associated with your wish-list publications. And don't stop there.

Try to connect with those writers by putting an emphasis on the *relations* in public relations. Get to know local writers in your area who cover the art beat. Read their work, meet them in person when you can and be as accessible as possible if they want to talk. When appropriate, send a personal invitation to your next exhibition to assignment editors, writers, bloggers, or news reporters.

The most effective publicity initiatives are the ones conducted over a sustained period of time. Realize you're competing for time and coverage along with lots of other artists, agents, and publicists. Be brief, be available, and be polite. Make a reporter's job easy. Have high-resolution digital art available, if requested, and always return phone calls or e-mails promptly.

### Staking a Claim: Website

You do have a website, don't you? A strong online presence is probably the most cost-effective investment you can make in your career. It's an opportunity to tell your story, control the message, and showcase your work.

As an artist, your home page should reflect your creative edge. It should instantly communicate who you are and what you're "selling" – even if you're selling reputation.

Make the navigation intuitive. Search websites of both artists and non-artists alike to get ideas on style, navigation, and features. Think about the elements that make you stop and spend time on a particular site. At a minimum, your site should include your artist statement, images of your work, and a contact page. Build a press section, which can include recent media clips, an exhibition schedule, an archive of your press releases, and a list of suggested story ideas.

Beyond the basics, create a field to capture e-mail addresses with an eye to developing a mailing list, even if you don't act on this list right away. Also think about creating a viral element such as a digital postcard of your artwork that site visitors can forward to friends. Once your site is up and running, add your Web address to your signature file so it appears on every e-mail message you send out.

A website is the basis of your online efforts. Build on it from there.

### Hear All About It: Electronic Newsletters

Have ongoing news or inside information that can benefit readers. Consider developing an e-newsletter if you have enough fresh ideas to make it worthwhile. Sure you can promote your own exhibitions and news, but a newsletter should give readers other takeaways. Develop a distribution list that includes members of the media, past and potential buyers, friends, and friends of friends.

### You'll Say Anything to Get Attention: Blogs

Got a lot to say and a lot of time to say it? A blog is a cheap and easy vehicle to create a dialogue and build a relationship with your audience. As always, crafting your message is key. You have to hook your readers with compelling copy, and give them a reason to come back time and again.

## Explosive: E-mail Blasts

An e-mail blast is a way to update a targeted list of "friendlies" of your important news – exhibitions, awards, media appearances – on an as-needed basis. The e-mail message should be timely, relevant, and trustworthy. An effective message can turn into a viral marketing campaign that gets passed along from one recipient to another. A bad message goes into the spam folder.

## On the Tube: Video Marketing

Artists are using video marketing outlets like YouTube more than ever to create viral marketing campaigns. How can you transform your expertise into compelling TV? Do you have an original technique to demonstrate? What about a tour of your studio? Visit YouTube to check out some of the clever ways artists are using the medium to attract a worldwide following (see "Lights, Camera, Action!," p. 281).

## Just Friends: Social Networking Sites

Free online networking sites like MySpace give you an opportunity to create a profile, upload images of your works, and participate in forums. MySpace is one of the most popular sites on the Web, but there are dozens of other social networking sites all providing prime real estate to showcase your art to millions of people free of charge.

The most important element of any branding campaign, something upon which all marketing and public relations specialists agree, is that once you build your online image, you have to live up to it. People are much more likely to be attracted to your work if they sense you're passionate and love what you do.

**Iyna Bort Caruso** is a widely published feature writer, author, and copywriter whose work appears regularly in print, online, and on air. Her articles have appeared in *The New York Times*, *The Wall Street Journal*, *CountryLiving.com*, *Newsday*, and *The Washington Post*. She has also written New York Emmy Award-winning promotional scripts, web content, online sweepstakes, brochures, signage, and ads for corporations, agencies, and nonprofits.

# Do You Need a Website?

By Alison Slon

Yes, you need a website if you want to be taken seriously as a professional artist.

Even if it's a one-page site, you are at least staking out your presence on the Web. A one page website with your name, contact information, and an image of your work would be something like having a postcard made for an exhibition. You are letting people know that you are actively showing, giving an example of your work, and getting your name out there.

The difference between the postcard and the one-page site is that the postcard is addressed and stamped and sent to a finite list, usually to announce a show that will be on for a limited time. It has a brief shelf life, the duration of your show, and then it is tossed in the garbage and the extra cards (you probably got a better deal on printing by ordering 500 or more) end up in a box in your studio taking up space.

Your website stays live as long as you are paying for hosting, which is relatively inexpensive (one year of web hosting is equal to about a month and a half of an average cell phone bill) and, most importantly, everyone can find you.

Most artists need more than a one-page site. You may want to feature a recent body of work, much like a solo exhibition in a gallery or an exhibition catalogue, or you may want to archive many different periods of your career in different sections. There is no one way to organize things and only you, the artist, can decide how you want your work arranged. You can seek advice from a professional artist advisor for help in organizing your work, but you must spend some time thinking about it before you begin the design process. The structure of your site is extremely important to the design and programming of it.

Web design is flexible, and there are endless possibilities including animation, video, sound effects, etc. But before you start thinking about all the "what if's" like, "what if we have sharks swimming across the page and when you click on them bubbles come out of their jaws and then they turn into dolphins," or whatever fabulous idea you have, you must establish a structure or what is called a "navigation." If you've ever been to a website you know what that is.

Similar to a table of contents, the main navigation (nav) is the outline of your site, and because it is interactive each word or button is a link to a section or page. I've designed and built websites for artists who do not even own computers. They are aware that everyone else does and realize that it is important to have a good website.

Being tech-savvy is by no means a prerequisite, and if you feel as though you have to drop everything and go back to school, or go out and buy a new computer with all the latest upgrades just to understand what your web designer is talking about, you should fire your designer and get someone else.

One artist I work with can tell me exactly how he wants his site organized; where he needs to add new work, or rearrange existing pieces; and what exactly the biographical section should say and yet he's never used a computer in his life. He will look at his site on my computer and make comments, even direct me with color corrections on his paintings, but when it comes to how it works, he's just not interested. He's got better things to do in the studio.

Chances are you do know something about websites, have figured out what you want your site to look like and how it should work before you begin talking to web designers. You can also make your site yourself, of course. There is no license required. There are artists, animators mostly, whose websites are their primary art form. There aren't any rules here, but unless you have a passion for code you may be better off working with a web designer.

First things first: navigation. I can't stress this enough. Before anything is coded for your site, you must establish a clear navigation structure. The nav should always appear in the same location on the page and should be consistent throughout the entire site.

You are not making a website to confuse people and get them lost. You are making a site to store examples of your work, and other relevant information. You want people to stay to look at everything and read the reviews that have been published about you. As soon as a user has to stop thinking about your work to figure out how to get to the next painting or next section, you've lost them. A well-designed navigation should mean that this won't happen and is essential to creating a good user experience.

When I first start working on a new artist site, I suggest that the client look around at other sites and tell me what they like and don't like about them. This does not mean copying someone else's design. It simply helps to establish a dialogue with the client and begins the process of honing down what needs to be in the nav.

Maybe you like that a site has an intro in Flash that previews the work. This is called a splash page and need not be designed initially as it has no bearing on the site's structure and can be added on later.

Perhaps you prefer going right to a main content page as soon as you type in the url. What's a url? Your url is your address on the World Wide Web – www. It is typed into the browser window and points the browser to a specific location. There are certain protocols, which must be followed, but anything that has not already been taken as a name can be used. For example: http://www.artistname.com.

For artist sites, it's generally a good idea to use the same name that you use professionally so that people who google you will find your site.

Think of the navigation structure as tiers or levels. You can draw it on paper something like a family tree. The top level, often called the home page or index, is the first thing you see when you enter a site. The content of this page can be introductory text with an image or two, or be a section of the site that you want to feature such as recent work. Your name or the title of the site should be prominent, commonly at the top left of the page, but not always.

The navigation bar with links to the second tier or level should appear either on the left side of the page stacked vertically, or across the top horizontally. This nav bar is a concise general list of the contents of the site. It should be limited to five or six links to the content. The nav bar will appear on every page and should be clear and simple. I suggest that you include the following, but this is very subjective and depends on the nature of your work: Images, Biographical Statement or Chronological Résumé, Press Coverage or Reviews, Links, and Contact Information.

I designed a site a few years ago for an artist whose body of work includes both sculpture and drawings. She wanted each to have equal importance on the nav bar so we kept the navigation simple and have the following headers: Sculpture, Drawings, Biography, and Contact Information. Her extensive archive of essays and articles written about her work is within Biography and has two sections: Résumé and Press.

Another artist wanted to have her paintings organized chronologically by exhibitions or two-year periods (2003-2005, 2001-2003, etc.). On her nav bar the word "Images," takes you to all of her selected works beginning with the most recent group and with a sub navigation allowing the viewer to move easily between the sub groups. Her main nav bar reads like this: Images, Bio, Press, Galleries, and Contact.

## How to Get Googled

At some point during the design process, artists will ask me how to get their site into the search engines, which means when you type your name into Google, a link to your site shows up in the search results.

How Google works is beyond the scope of this book. The algorithms used to make this vast search engine work are constantly being revised and a technical explanation would probably be obsolete by the time this goes to press.

The beauty of it is that it works and we don't have to know how, but it helps to grasp the concept and know a few key elements so that when your site is live, Google's "spiders" will find it. Hidden in the source code of a website are two important sections, "Meta Tags" and "Meta Words." Here you can list a series of words that can be searched and a brief description of the content. When a web surfer types them in, there will be links to your site. A click translates to a hit for you.

In designing this one, we had several discussions over whether "Galleries" should be called "Links." She finally chose "Galleries" because, in her case, she is represented by more than one gallery both in the United States and in Europe and felt it important to give each a clear placement on her site.

Links is a more general term for a section that can include anything you like and links to other websites, for example exhibition spaces where you have exhibited, other online archives of your work, the press where you have your printing done if you make print editions, and even other artist sites with whom you are affiliated.

Another example is a site I designed recently for an artist who does both large installations and print editions. On her nav bar, she decided on the following: "Selected Work", "CV", "Bibliography", "Links", "Contact". Within "Selected Work" she has two sections: "Floor Works" and "Wall Works". Within "Wall Works" she decided to include only a few examples of her print editions with a link to the press where she makes them. The press has a good site with her editions clearly arranged, and she did not feel the need to duplicate this on her own site. We could link directly to her section on its site.

So there's no one way to do it. Just keep it simple. It's not really simple, but the viewer, your audience, should not know that, and should never find that your site is cumbersome or difficult to figure out. Remember that when it comes to interactive design, everything should link to everything else; and you never want to lose your audience. Like in a good performance, the experience of the audience should be a pleasant one, you are trying to communicate not confuse.

**Alison Slon** is an art director for interactive media and web design. She has designed and produced sites for both artists and corporate clients and has recently completed the redesign of KTCassoc.com. She was an assistant professor at Pratt Institute in Brooklyn, NY, in the department of Computer Graphics and Interactive Media and has an MA from New York Institute of Technology in Communications and Computer Graphics. Her clients include: The Lego Company, Citigroup Smith Barney, JWT, C2 Creative, HBO.com, CBS.com, Time Warner, Condé Nast Publications and Scholastic. For more information go to: www.alisonslon.com.

# Your Presence on the Internet

By Henry Auvil

One of the absolute essentials for achieving success as an artist today is a cogent, powerful and well-conceived presence on the Web. Your website is more than just your online portfolio or a handy marketing tool – it is an expression of who you are as an artist and the answer to the question, "How have I chosen to present myself and my work to a potentially global audience?"

As an administrator for Katharine T. Carter & Associates, I view literally hundreds of artist's websites per year, and can assure you that the experience runs the gamut from the exhilaration of stumbling upon fresh, unbridled talent to frustration and stupefaction at the lengths some artists will go to shoot themselves in the foot. I will outline here what you should strive for and what to avoid in crafting your online presence, detailing the positive strengths that will maximize the attention art world professionals will extend to your website.

When conceiving an artist website, certain words should be brought to mind and remain there as markers and goals. Chief among them I would choose Simplicity, Cohesion, Elegance, and Brevity.

## Simplicity

At one point in the brief history of website design, it was fashionable to employ clever Flash animation intro pages with bouncing flourishes and words that went darting off when touched by a cursor. This fashion, like really big shoulder pads, has thankfully passed. I assure you that when confronted with a fanciful animated opening webpage, 99% of viewers scramble for the "Skip Intro" button.

Never force your viewer to stare at a little clock or counter telling them the percentage of the page that has opened so far. Instead, be sure the home page opens instantly. Site navigation should be apparent to the viewer with minimal study, essentially letting them know where they can see your images, read your written materials, view your vitae and contact you. Don't offer more choices than that. Wherever the viewer goes on the site, the navigation controls should remain visible so that no one ever feels "lost."

Do not employ any graphic elements that would detract from your work, and avoid overly stylized fonts or (heaven forbid) your own signature. Use a font that is easy on the eyes and classic. Choose a neutral color scheme that complements your work. As a rule, black backgrounds suck the life out of most artwork; there is an obvious reason most galleries are painted white.

Some web designers have a penchant for introducing gimmicks, such as having an image expand and do something kinetic when the thumbnail is clicked. Avoid this like the plague. Any sort of bells and whistles gimmickry is detracting from the main purpose of presenting your work in its purest essence. Pages containing your personal musings and studio photos have no place here. NEVER include background music, poetry, or a photo of yourself.

**Cohesion**

To present yourself and your work in the best light, everything you include must coalesce to form a logical and complete picture. For many years, I worked as a photo producer for editorial and advertising clients. I was always struck by the way the art directors/editors and creative team were intuitively in sync about how they presented a dress or shoe or food product by constructing a complete world around it to reinforce its centrality and specialness. In other words, they were "telling a story" in which the product was the hero, and anything that deflected from the narrative was immediately recognized as superfluous, and deleted.

You might say, "OK, but those are marketers and stylists. I am an artist." I don't think it is a stretch to think of your website as a big multi-page ad campaign in a glossy magazine. When you invite an art professional to visit your site, a very visually attuned person will be assessing your work in the context of not only your talents and accomplishments but also your taste, and believe me, they know what all the signs and signifiers mean. A poorly chosen inclusion or dissonant design element will impact on their impression of the complete message.

The only essential elements to include on an artist website are:

• A gallery of works, which should be heavily weighted to very recent output. The jpegs should open instantly and be clearly labeled with title, dimensions, medium and date. If you are including various groups of work, separate them into different galleries such as "Paintings," "Drawings," "Prints." Don't include too many bodies of work, or any explorations that are not central to your current and most critical creative involvements. Early work should also be separated into its own gallery and kept to a minimum. Do not include more that eight to ten works in any gallery, unless you are only showing one body of work, in which case 20 to 25 images is appropriate.

• Written support pieces, concise and well chosen. This would include a brief artist's statement, a critic's essay, a résumé, and bibliography. Do not include reviews and other press here – that can be sent in hard copy when interest is expressed.

• If you have extensive gallery affiliation, it is appropriate to list where you are represented as collectors will be among your target website visitors.

• A contact page with all your information and/or an e-mail link.

**Elegance**

When asked to define true style, the late, great fashion editor Diana Vreeland said, "Elegance is refusal." I take this to mean that an innate sense of elegance does not bow to the temptation to dress something up when it is already perfectly suitable in and of itself. To reflect this sentiment in your website does not mean conforming to a set look or proscribed layout; rather, it means all the elements included contribute seamlessly to the whole. Nothing cries out for attention on its own. Simplicity does not necessarily have to be austere, but no truly refined style, be it Minimalism or the Baroque, ever tolerates anything superfluous.

Here is a brief catalogue of egregious choices I have seen on artist websites. Mind you, these artists were all submitting for consideration, and presumably felt they were being shown at their very best by their websites:

• I have seen numerous variations on a homepage adorned with a lovely sunset or floral motif, and an artist-written statement about how art has been a major part of her life since early childhood. Finished before we even got started.

• An image gallery where a row of thumbnails is moving rapidly to the right and another row below it is moving to the left. Apparently the viewer is supposed to chase the image they would like to see with the cursor and hopefully zap it to enlarge before it disappears. This is supposed to be a means of presenting your work, not a game of Pacman.

• Some sites are designed with such impenetrable navigation that the viewer is lost after the first click. Links open new pages. Cryptic menus lead to yet further menus. Links that go nowhere. Mysterious web pages popping up in new windows. Within minutes the viewer feels he is lost in a labyrinth and bails out without ever seeing the first work of art.

• The artist invites you to view his gallery of fine art, but first you learn about the prints for sale in his online shop, his T-shirt line, and the custom airbrushed skateboard business he is running on the side. You somehow forget to view the art.

• You open a very poorly executed homemade site, where the artist has posted an "Under Construction" sign and an apology for the fact that his newer, better website is not finished yet.

We may not be able to define elegance as deftly as Mrs. Vreeland, but we certainly know its lack when we see it.

**Brevity**

This can't be stressed too strongly. The most frequent advice we give to artists when asked to critique their website is to pare it down. I honestly feel that a great artist website will allow professionals to feel completely familiarized with the artist and work after about five minutes on the site, without feeling they have missed anything. This is not to say that he or she might not linger for more time if they care to read all the written pieces and carefully scrutinize each work, but a well-designed site will give these very time-challenged individuals a clear sense of the work and indeed the entire "bigger picture" in a very short amount of time. And believe me, having spared them any wasted time will be a big point in your favor.

To summarize, creating a successful artist website is as much a process of reduction as it is inclusion, and this takes a highly refined ability to edit. It would likely be advantageous to enlist the assistance of another person – perhaps a critic, art historian, or curator – to help you make the final choices for inclusion once you have determined the exact number of images you will allow. The choice of a web designer who is experienced in art-related marketing rather than only building corporate commerce sites is another savvy move.

Be wise in your choices, work out all the kinks, get the site online, and say "hello" to the entire world.

**Henry Auvil** was formerly an advertising and editorial photo producer, prop stylist, and art director, editor of the Miami Beach-based culture magazine *Antenna*, and freelance writer for *South Florida* magazine and *Details*.

# Lights, Camera, Action!
By Anne Leith

Over the past decade, video became increasingly accessible to the general public through the development of digital technologies, not only on the Internet but also at home and at work. The visual arts sector has embraced this medium, not only creatively but also as a marketing and communications tool.

Video can provide a unique and dynamic window into the world of the artist. A documentary accompanying an exhibition can really add to the interest – both from the public and the press – of the show. Your back-story enriches the experience of the work itself. The opportunity to hear first hand about the process of making art and to see your work in your studio offers an intimate perspective on the creative experience.

If the educational component of the artist's work is particularly compelling, the video can easily be shown independent of the exhibition in schools or other institutional settings. This is an effective and inexpensive way to disseminate information and ideas as expressed through the creative process, as well as expanding your audience.

As a marketing tool, video is extremely effective. Most artists remember the frustration of sending slide sheets to galleries and other venues. A short video can not only show the work, but can get the message across in a way that the traditional written artist's statement often fails to do. Reproduction of a master DVD is also relatively inexpensive and can save money on mailings.

A video profile of an artist can also be used on a website and/or formatted to send as an e-mail attachment, providing it is not too long. All these applications can come from the same footage. There is also the possibility to edit the raw footage into different "products" destined for different usages (marketing, education, archival, grant proposals, insurance documentation, etc.). The value of having an interview at a particular moment in your career in the archives should not be overlooked.

## Not One for All: Preparing a Successful Multiple-Use Video
Defining the project's objectives is the first step. What are the key points that are to be made? Who is the audience? What materials are available? What interview style (if an interview is appropriate) is to be used?

The shoot typically will involve two to four people in the crew/supervisory team. People that are not essential participants in the interview should not be present at the shoot. Pets should be excluded from the location when possible. Set-up of cameras, lights, and microphones should take about 20 minutes. Breakdown also takes about 20 minutes.

Be aware of the time needed for the shoot/interview. For a three to four minute video, an interview of approximately 30 to 40 minutes should suffice. For an edited interview of 10 minutes, 1.5 hours of interview are necessary.

You need to determine the interview format. A simple "talking-head" interview format with the interviewer off camera is an effective format for an artist profile. You can be seen speaking about the work, and parts of the interview can be used as a voice-over while the artwork is on screen. The interviewer is completely edited out. The video crew may be able to provide a professional interviewer upon request.

Another format is the "conversation-style" interview, where the interviewer and you are both on camera and speak together in a question/answer discussion. This can be effective in cases where the interviewer is a high-profile art professional such as a curator or museum director, whose participation in the video validates the importance of your work.

Multiple interviews interspersed with footage and still photos and the studio/artwork can also be effective, but would typically be used only in a longer documentary style video.

The selected interviewer should research the subject and prepare an outline of subjects that will be covered. These should then be shared and discussed with you several days prior to the shoot so that you can freshen your memories on dates, names, or other details important to the story line.

The duration of the piece can vary for different usages. Generally a three to four minute piece should be considered the maximum length for a marketing campaign that includes website or e-mail use. This keeps the download time to an acceptable length for the viewer. While this sounds short, it is quite remarkable the amount of information that can be presented. A judicious blend of interview and image keeps the pace up and retains the interest of the viewer. In cases where a longer documentary video is appropriate, a shorter version can always be created through editing.

High-quality still images are *essential* for a successful video product. Good images of the artwork should be digitized in either PICT or TIF format for the video producers. These are uncompressed formats and of a higher resolution and quality than a compressed jpegs designed for e-mail attachments. Video is a horizontal format based on a proportion of 720 pixels (horizontal) x 460 pixels (vertical). This is something to keep in mind while selecting images for video – vertical images don't look as good on the screen (think wide-screen or movie theaters). Ideally for video the digitized image should be a minimum of 300 dpi. This allows the post-production crew to add movement to the images, such as panning or zooming, without a loss in image quality. These images should be provided to the videographer prior to the interview shoot on a CD or DVD.

The shoot location is important. That it is quiet without excessive construction or traffic noise is, obviously, preferable. All telephones and other sound makers, such as air conditioning or forced-air heating systems, should be turned off for the duration of the interview. Ideally the location of the shoot will reflect in some way your interests and/or personal space and style.

Natural lighting is not a plus. The professional video crew provides the necessary lighting. Existing indoor lighting may be used at the crew's discretion. A minimum of two three-prong electrical outlets is necessary.

Attire and makeup should be simple. Obviously you want to look good, but don't overdo it. A simple matte powder is recommended to avoid facial shine under the hot lights. Artists should bring their own face powder matched to their skin tones for any retouches. Avoid wearing white or black around the face (shirts, scarves, ties) since that can throw off the color balance on the video camera in respect to the face. While jewelry can look very good on camera, avoid any pieces that jangle such as charm bracelets, since the microphones will pick up the sound.

Post-production editing can make or break the effectiveness of the video. You should work closely with the video team (interviewer/videographer/editor) to be sure that the goals for the video are clearly communicated and agreed upon in advance. Typically there is a designated point-person on the video team to work with the client.

There should be a minimum of two review sessions. The first is after the initial edit of the footage. The client should review the product and work with the editor to refine the message. At this time any corrections, such as the identifications of dates/titles/year of artwork, or people/places in images, should be made, and credit lines and/or logos reviewed. All still images should have already been provided to the videographer prior to filming. Then after revisions are made, a final review session should take place prior to the creation of the master DVD.

A musical soundtrack can be added. This is especially effective in videos where there are long stretches of images without any voice-over. Slide shows of this style can work very well as backgrounds to presentations. Music in an interview/personal profile piece should be used primarily at the beginning and end of the video, and sometimes to smooth transitions from subject to subject. However, for the interview format, music is not essential.

Be aware that the unauthorized use of music on such a video is illegal unless the videographer obtains permission and pays for the right to use the song from the music publisher. To purchase the "one-time use" of a song can be very expensive. Some videography teams create original music for each client to provide the appropriate ambiance while avoiding copyright fees.

**What Can You Expect? The Finished Product**

A professional videography company should be able to provide you with edited footage. This is what you need for marketing. A well-edited story with appropriately placed images can be very effective.

This should be delivered on a master DVD, which is easily copied on a home computer in small quantities (up to 30 copies), or by a professional company in large quantities for about $5 per piece. The copying of the DVD could be done through the videographer, upon prior agreement on cost.

Be aware that the videographer retains the copyright on all the footage unless previously negotiated with the client.

The videographer/editor could work with you to select or edit together a clip that would be effective for your website. The duration should be 30-seconds to three-minutes maximum. The selected clip would then be formatted for the Web designer for insertion into the website. This clip could also be formatted for e-mail.

A reasonable budget for video projects that include one interview and related images is around $3,500, or approximately $1,000 per minute. Prices vary depending on travel for the crew and number of filming sites and interviews. There could also be an additional fee for web clips depending on whether the content required re-editing or other changes.

Preparation is the key to a successful and cost-effective video. Knowing your goals, preparing the digitized image CDs in advance in the proper format for the video team, and working closely with the interviewer/editor ensures that the video will be an effective communication tool. Good preparation can also keep down the costs.

Video communicates in a dynamic way that is appropriate for the culture of today, and is a perfect fit for the promotion and dissemination of the arts.

**Anne Leith** is the principal of AllartStudio, a video production firm based in New York City and Weston, VT. Leith is a proficient video editor and interviewer, as well as an art historian and published art critic. She has worked for the Solomon R. Guggenheim Museum in New York City and the Peggy Guggenheim Collection in Venice, Italy, and was instrumental in the development of the Deutsche Guggenheim Museum in Berlin. (www.allartstudio.com)

### Multi-Tasking

- Define the project's objectives.
- Determine interview format.
- Gear the duration of the tape to the use.
- High-quality images are essential.
- Choose the shoot location carefully.
- Attire and makeup should be simple.

# Making It to Print

By Bill Mutter

Once you've gotten an exhibition scheduled, the more support and marketing of your work the better. Anything in print, from a simple announcement card to a catalogue of the exhibition itself, lends credibility to the work.

A catalogue of the exhibition is a wonderful adjunct, if one can afford one. It serves many purposes. It is permanent documentation of the show, people take it home, show it to friends, collectors, critics, gallery owners, museum curators, and so on.

Though the catalogue is most effective at the time of the show, it is also an historical document of the artist's development at that point and will be of value long after the announcements have been thrown away and the reviews read and forgotten.

## How Big? How Good? Catalogue Size and Quality

The ideal catalogue would contain images of all the works in the exhibition. But that may be too costly, so selecting how many photos go into the catalogue and if any will be in color becomes very important.

Catalogues can be printed with a "separate cover" (the cover is heavier than the text) or with a "self-cover" (the cover is the same weight as the text). If you decide on a self-cover, you will want a cover weight stock throughout, not a text weight. Text weight is too light. The catalogue must also feel good when held in the hand.

The overall size must be considered because catalogues are often included in mailings. You don't want some odd-sized catalogue that requires custom-made envelopes. If you plan to do a mailing of the catalogue alone, your printer can give you standard envelope sizes to choose from. Decide on the envelope size and design the catalogue to fit.

## What's It Look Like?: Catalogue Design

Here's a tip for those non-graphic designers who want to design their own catalogue: Don't.

With the advent of desktop publishing, many people decided that they could design whatever they needed. The results almost always look awful. I've noticed that people who have designed their own catalogues are pleased anyway, because they saved money and, after all, they designed it themselves.

Organizing visual elements from the size of the catalogue to how the images fit on the page and how they relate to the text is a difficult task. It requires years of experience as well as looking at excellent graphic design, in general. It isn't at all slapping pictures on a page.

Though the catalogue is second in importance to the art itself, art can be diminished if presented badly. A poorly designed catalogue is like an awkwardly installed exhibition. Everyone will notice and it detracts from the art.

### What's the Relationship? Working with a Graphic Designer

As a fine artist myself, I enjoy designing artists' catalogs. My first step is to understand the work by discussing it with the artist. Some artists are quite articulate about their work and have a clear sense of what they think their art is about. Some don't feel that they have any particular insights into their work at all.

This discussion helps the artist and me to feel comfortable working together, and it helps me in designing the printed piece. I respond to the person as well as to the art.

### How Much? The Budget

You must know what your budget will get you before the design and production process can begin.

There are many line items to be considered in creating a budget for your catalogue. How big, meaning both overall dimensions and number of pages? How many images? In color or black-and-white? What's the photographer's fee for shooting the work? Is there an essay and who's writing it? How many words, and how much is the writer's fee? And who's writing all those other bits of text? Someone has to compose those captions, lists of works in the exhibition, even the résumé. A good editor helps it all "read well." And it all must be proofread many times, by as many eyes as you can muster.

All this needs to be discussed with your designer, and he or she will get a rough estimate from a printer as to production costs. If many adjustments are made after the original estimate, the designer will get the job re-estimated.

Make sure, too, that you manage the deadline. If the catalogues must be ready for the opening, you don't want to go to the last minute. Shipping overnight, even a small number of catalogues, can still get very expensive.

### How's It Done? The Design Process

After these considerations are worked out, the designer can begin the design process. When the designer is satisfied with a design, the artist gets a color "comprehensive" or "comp" for consideration. This is a "dummy" of what the printed piece will look like. It is useful because you and the designer can see the actual size and pacing of images, styling of type, etc. You also use the comp for proofreading the essay and the captions. Again have people you trust proofread, too. *Do not rely entirely on spellcheck.* (There's always something hiding, whether it's a typo that is a real work – I mean *word* – or a sentence that isn't quite clear.)

The designer will also get a dummy on the suggested paper stock, trimmed to size, and the correct number of pages. This is important because it gives the artist and designer a real sense of how the printed piece will feel when held in the hands.

### How Faithful Are the Pix? Photographing the Work

Once the works are selected for the exhibition, they need to be photographed. And here's another tip for those of you non-professional photographers who want to shoot your own work: Don't.

Traditionally, color work for reproduction was shot as 4" x 5" (or larger) transparencies. But today most photographers have switched over to digital photography, which, in my opinion, is as good as – if not better – than film.

If you get work shot digitally, get good color prints from an output service (yet another expense) to match color. Computer screens, unless carefully calibrated, do not provide accurate color. With 4" x 5" transparencies, make sure that what you get is accurate to your art. The printer's job is to match as closely as possible the digital files or the transparencies.

### How Close? Working with the Printer

Designers usually have relationships with a variety of printers and can recommend a printer who is right for the project.

After the artist signs off on the design, the designer prepares and sends the digital files to the printer along with the digital photography or the 4" x 5" transparencies, a black-and-white dummy of the catalogue itself as well as the estimate, and all other details relating to the job.

## How Accurate? Approving Color

Your responsibility is to sign off on the final color proofs supplied by the printer. If you approve all color work, the back of each proof includes your signature with "OK" and the date. Occasionally, a color proof will not be accurate. If so, keep your directions simple. Say "too red" or "too dark," for example. They will figure it out. Your designer can help here, too, if need be.

Mark those comments on the back of the proof returned to the printer. Sometimes printers say that this is as close as their technology can come to matching the original photography. Any change will then be billable. The second color proof will be different from the first, but not necessarily better. Before these costs are incurred, the designer should pass this information on to you.

Once you have approved the color work, your responsibilities are over, but the designer's responsibility continues. Once the color is signed off on, the printer supplies the designer with a blueprint of the job as well as composed sheets, which look exactly like a printed piece. This is the designer's final check before the job goes to press. Here is the last chance to check for typos, size and cropping of images, and making sure they are right side-up and not flopped, checking accuracy of color, etc.

If possible, the designer goes "on press" to insure that the finished catalogue is true to the original design, and the color is correct. Once printed, the catalogue goes to the bindery for finishing, is boxed up, and shipped.

Once finished, the catalogue becomes a permanent record of a temporary exhibition.

**Bill Mutter** is a graphic designer and was for more than 20 years a partner in the award-winning New York City-based design group, James Orlandi and Associates, Inc. Clients included MasterCard International, Texaco, Inc., Coopers & Lybrand, IBM, Hilton International, and The Queens Museum of Art. He is also a ceramic sculptor currently teaching at Drew University in Madison, NJ and at LaGuardia Community College in Queens.

## Art Attack

By Karen S. Chambers

A number of years ago, I lectured to a graduate-level "Professional Practices" class at the Rhode Island School of Design. The students were ready to set out on their careers, to leave the ivory tower of academia where art is a pure and noble pursuit. For them, art was a vocation in the religious sense.

I blasphemed when I told them that the most important piece of paper they would ever acquire wasn't that MFA, but a mailing list.

The students immediately pegged me as an infidel. They were on a crusade to conquer the art world, armed with only their talent. The mere sight of their work would cause the art world to surrender to their artistic visions.

They believed that talent was the only armament needed for success, which can be measured by being shown, written about, and collected. (For each artist, winning the war – succeeding in the art world – means something different. It may be having a one-person show at the local art center or a retrospective at the Museum of Modern Art.)

Although talent certainly helps, success generally comes to those artists who enlist for the duration and understand the rules of engagement. To succeed in their quest to win over an army of curators, gallerists, critics, and collectors – the "enemy"– means first engaging them. They need to gather intelligence about the enemy, and learn how to avoid the minefields of the art world.

The "Information Resources" (pp. 295-362) should be seen as the arsenal of weapons (where to find art supplies, reproduce photographs, frame the work, etc.) and strategies that artist-warriors need to win the war for recognition.

Winning the art war, like any other war, also takes a lot of grunt work. The "Information Resources" provides practical advice to take care of those chores that take you out of the studio, but which are vital to success. For example, there are books to be kept, contracts to be written, works to be shipped, and so forth.

If you can hire experts to take care of those chores, congratulations. But even if you have a support team covering everything that has to be done to advance your career, with the exception of actually making the art – although there are exceptions there, e.g., Donald Judd, Red Grooms, Jeff Koons – there will come a time when their expertise does not address exactly what you need to know. Having a CPA may relieve you of the burden of preparing your own taxes, but knowing that there's the *Do-It-Yourself QUICK-FIX TaxKit*, published annually, is not a bad thing.

But even if you can afford to keep those professionals on payroll, retainer, or even just open to your call, you still need to identify those experts. You can query your friends, colleagues, and acquaintances for their recommendations. But the "Information Resources" includes many more sources to identify someone who can perform the service or to learn where you can acquire the knowledge and skills yourself.

The individual categories were devised to address specific areas. For example, there are enough legal issues to warrant the "Legal Resources" section. And if *DuBoff's Art Law in a Nutshell* doesn't help, there is always the Volunteer Lawyers for the Arts to turn to. Both are listed in this section.

The individual categories are intended to be as comprehensive as possible. Thus, the "Travel" section lists hotels, booking services, and room-exchange sites. There are also travel guidebooks, highlighting the arts of the destination. The official website of the Art Museum Network (www.amn.org) links to member museums' sites and is another resource to help travelers plan their itineraries to get their art fix.

With nearly a thousand entries, how can you find what you need? Many are annotated, or the name of the resource tells the story, i.e., *How to Profit from the Art Print Market*, which logically enough appears in the "Fine Art Prints" section. But since the book also offers marketing tips, it is also found in "Mailing Lists/Marketing" and "Tool Kit" (practical advice about how to navigate the art world) sections. Thus, many entries are in multiple categories because they are germane to more than one topic.

## Research, Research, Research

Maintaining a mailing list is a never-ending task as collectors move, curators change jobs, galleries open and close, and new critics come on the scene.

Some of the names on your mailing list represent personal contacts. (Don't forget people like your doctor, dentist, and yoga teacher.) And there's a reason for guest books at exhibitions. These names definitely need to be added to your master mailing list. Even if it was a group show, someone who came to see another artist's work also saw yours.

But there is also a need for more specialized lists for more targeted communications. For example, critics may receive a press release and photos along with an invitation to the opening of your exhibition, unveiling of a commission, or some other event. Collectors – or potential collectors – might get only the announcement.

There can even be a list of recipients that rate a personal and handwritten note – or a good facsimile. The internationally known glass artist Dale Chihuly is a master of promotion. When sending out a mailing, he often includes a scrawled note that looks handwritten, but is actually photocopied. Why not make color copy of a note written in blue ink, for an even more personal look?

But what about those other people who you don't know personally? How do you reach the critics and curators you'd like to visit your studio or, at least, look at photographs of your works?

Compiling that information takes time, but "Information Resources" gives you a starting point with the "Critics/Media" section. There are entries for media directories, such as those from R.R. Bowker, as well as the Association of

Quite a number of entries are books, but there's no need to judge them by their covers. You don't even have to thumb through the book itself. Both Barnes and Noble's (barnesandnoble.com) and Amazon.com's websites offer the publisher's description.

More importantly reader reviews on both sites offer extremely candid and opinionated takes on the book. It is not so unusual for one reader to praise while another pans the same book. Reading the conflicting reviews allows to you to judge for yourself.

Both sites offer a selection of volumes that readers who bought the tome in question also purchased. Amazon recommends other books that are Best Together, and its Listmania offers customers' own suggestions.

In addition to offering all of this information to evaluate the book in question, it just takes a click – or two – to acquire the book either new or used.

In the "Information Resources," contact information is provided in as many formats as possible – physical location, mailing address, phone and fax numbers, e-mail addresses, and website.

Naturally we've tried to make our entries as correct and current as possible, but things change quickly. If a url address leads you to a dead end, don't give up. A search on the Internet will yield similar sites.

Although Google dominates the search-engine business, having even become the verb to describe the activity of searching the Web, I prefer MetaCrawler. It scours several search engines, including Google, to come up with a conveniently edited list of matches or near matches.

For example, a search for *American Art Directory* on MetaCrawler produced 78 sites gathered from Google, Yahoo! Search, and Windows Live. Google produced 41,000, and Yahoo!Search came up with 60,200. I'd call that "TMI" – too much information.

But MetaCrawler's more manageable 78 hits included www.art-search.us, which links to sites like Café Art Galleries, Art Transportation, and Magazines. The AskArt.com site has an extensive Art Glossary as well as a Dealer/Gallery Directory.

So arm yourself with the best weapons and use the "Information Resources" guide to plan your attack on the art world.

**Karen S. Chambers** has been a free-lance curator, editor, and writer for an international array of publications including *Aeqai, Art in America, American Style, Ceramics Art & Perception* (Australia), and *Neues Glas* (Germany). Chambers has served as the editor of *New Work*, now *Glass Quarterly*, and *Craft International.* In adition to staff positions at The Dayton Art Institute and The Contemporary Arts Center, Cincinnati, she has worked for leading New York City commercial art galleries, including Seprone Westwater Fischer and Droll/Kolbert. As an independent curator, she has organized exhibitions for the Tampa Museum of Art and the United States Information Agency.

College and University Museums and Galleries, which lists 1,200 college and university professionals on its website. And in keeping with including resources that are also pertinent to the category, Susan Abbott's *Fine Art Publicity: The Complete Guide for Galleries and Artists* gives practical tools for attracting media attention, and Ariane Goodwin's *Writing the Artist Statement* helps you craft your message.

Also found in the Critics/Media section is The *American Art Directory* (p. 309) with listings of National and Regional Art Organizations; Museums; Libraries; Associations in the US and Canada; Art Schools with contact data, degree programs, scholarship programs, entrance requirements, and tuition information; Museums Abroad; Schools Abroad; State Directors and Supervisors of Art Education; State Arts Councils; Art Magazines, Editors, and Critics; Scholarships and Fellowships; Open Exhibitions; and Traveling Exhibition Booking Agencies.

And they're all indexed by subject, personnel, and organization.

You may not want to shell out the $400 for the newest edition, when your local library probably already has.

You do not have to do all of the work of compiling these lists yourself. There are shortcuts to get to your target audience. Mailing lists of associations and individuals are available directly from the organizations or from companies devoted to this business, such as InFocus Marketing and InfocusUSA. Cost varies from minimal to hundreds of dollars.

But to borrow from that MasterCard ad campaign — the mailing list is "priceless."

# Information Resources
*by Katharine T. Carter and Karen S. Chambers*

## Art Consultants/Corporate Collections

*Art in America Annual Guide to Museums/ Galleries/Artists.* Published in August. *Art in America*, 575 Broadway, New York, NY 10012. (212) 941-2800. (www.artinamericamagazine.com).

*ArtNetwork*, PO Box 1360, Nevada City, CA 95959. (800) 383-0677, (530) 470-0862, e-mail: info@artmarketing.com. (www.artmarketing.com). Resource for books, mailing lists, art and travel, marketing software, living artists, and an online gallery.

Caroll Michels, Career Advisory Service for Emerging and Established Artists, 1724 Burgos Drive, Sarasota, FL 34238. (941) 927-5277, fax: (941) 927-5278, e-mail: carollmichels@gmail.com (www.carollmichels.com). Annotated mailing lists for Curators; Art Consultants; Curators and Art Consultants; Critics; Interior Design & Architecture Press Contacts; International, National, and Regional Press Contacts; and New York Area Press Contacts, available in printout (formatted for reproduction on labels), floppy disk (PC and Mac), CD-Rom (PC and Mac) formats. *The Newsletter*, published nine times/year with names addresses of art consultants, resources, news, and opportunities. (www.carollmichels.com/resources).

*Corporate Art Consulting*, Susan Abbott. 2nd ed., 1994. Allworth Press, 10 E. 23rd St., New York, NY 10010. (800) 491-2808. (www.allworth.com).

*Corporate Art*, Rosanne Martorella, Rutgers University Press. Available on Amazon.com.

"The Corporate Art Brief," The Humanities Exchange, PO Box 1608, Largo, FL 33779. (514) 935-1228, fax: (514) 935-1299. (www.humanities-exchange.org/artbrief). Nonprofit serves as clearing house for information on exhibition exchange and other art world news. On-line news site about the corporate art world.

*Corporate Museums, Galleries, and Visitor's Centers: A Directory*, Victor J. Danilov. 1991. Greenwood Press, 88 Post Rd. W, Westport, CT 06881. (203) 226-3571. (www.greenwood.com).

*Fine Art Representatives & Corporations Collecting Art*, edited by Constance Franklin, 2nd ed., 1990. Art Network Press, PO Box 1360, Nevada City, CA 95959. (800) 383-0677. (www.artmarketing.com).

*International Directory of Corporate Art Collections*, The Humanities Exchange, PO Box 1608, Largo, FL 33779. (514) 935-1228, fax: (514) 935-1299, e-mail: internationaldirectory@earthlink.net. (www.humanities-exchange.org). Nonprofit serves as clearing house for information on exhibition exchange and other art world news. Artist's, Museum, and Gallery/Art Advisor editions available on CD in three different formats (MS Word, Adobe PDF, and Asksam for PC) or spiral-bound printout.

www.humanities-exchange.org/artbrief. The Humanities Exchange, PO Box 1608, Largo, FL 33779. (514) 935-1228, fax: (514) 935-1299, e-mail: corporate.directory@earthlink.net. News and current events from the corporate art world, compiled by the editors of the *International Directory of Corporate Art Collections and International Art Alliance.*

## Art Fairs/Festivals

American Craft Council, Retail Shows, 72 Spring St., New York, NY 10012. (800) 836-3470. (www.craftcouncil.org).  Held in Baltimore, MD; Atlanta, GA; St. Paul, MN; San Francisco, CA; Charlotte, NC; and Sarasota, FL.

Art 20, Sanford L. Smith & Associates, 447 W. 24th St., New York, NY  10011. (212) 777-5218, e-mail: info@sanfordsmith.com. (www.sanfordsmith.com).

Art Basel Miami, MCH Swiss Exhibition (Basel) Ltd., Art Basel, CH-4005 Basel, Switzerland. (41) 58-200-20-20, fax: (41) 58-206-26-86, e-mail: miamibeach@artbasel.com. (www.artbasel.com).  Florida representative: Robert Goodman, Garber & Goodman, Inc., 300 41st St., ste. 214, Miami Beach, FL  33140. (305) 674-1292, fax: (305) 673-1242, e-mail: flordiaoffice@artbasel.com. (www.artbasel.com).

Art Basel, MCH Swiss Exhibition (Basel) Ltd., Art Basel, CH-4005 Basel, Switzerland. (41) 58-200-20-20, fax: (41) 58-206-26-86, e-mail: info@artbasel.com. (www.artbasel.com).

Art Chicago, Merchandise Mart Properties, ste. 470, The Merchandise Mart, Chicago, IL 60654. (800) 677-6278, (312) 527-4141. (www.mmart.com/artchicago/show).

Art Fairs International, *NY Arts Magazine*, 473 Broadway, 7th flr., New York, NY  10013. (212) 274-8993, fax: (212) 226-3400, e-mail: info@nyartsmagazine.com. (www.artfairsinternational.com).

Art Miami, The Moore Bldg., 4040 NE Second Ave., ste. 304, Miami, FL  33137. (866) 727-7953, (305) 573-1388 (International), fax: (305) 573-1561, e-mail: info@art-miami.com. (www.art-miami.com).  Produced by Summit Business Media.

Art Santa Fe, London International, 200 W. Marcy St., ste. 101, Santa Fe, NM  87501. E-mail: artfair@artsantafe.com. (www.artsantafe.com).

Artexpo Las Vegas, The Art Group, Summit Business Media, 6000 Lombardo Ctr. Dr., ste. 420, Seven Hills, OH  44131. (888) 322-5226, (216) 328-8926, fax: (216) 328-9452. (www.artexpos.com).  SOLO, devoted to showcasing the work of the world's emerging, independent artists.

Artexpo New York, The Art Group, Summit Business Media, 6000 Lombardo Ctr. Dr., ste. 420, Seven Hills, OH  44131. (888) 608-5300, (216) 328-8926, fax: (216) 328-9452. (www.artexpos.com).  Includes SOLO, devoted to showcasing the work of the world's emerging, independent artists.

Artrider Craft Shows in New York, NY; Morristown, NJ; Lyndhurst, NY; and Guilford, CT. Artrider Productions, PO Box 29, Woodstock, NY  12498. (845) 331-7900, fax: (845) 331-7484, e-mail: crafts@artrider.com. (www.artrider.com).

*Arts Festival Work Kit*, Pam Korza and Dian Magie. 1989. AES Publications, Arts Extension Service, University of Massachusetts Amherst, Division of Outreach, 100 Venture Way, ste. 201, Amherst, MA 01003. (413) 545-2360, fax: (413) 577-3838, e-mail: aes@outreach.umass.edu. (www.umass.edu).

*Fairs and Festivals.* AES Publications, Arts Extension Service, University of Massachusetts Amherst, Division of Outreach, 100 Venture Way, ste. 201, Amherst, MA 01003. (413) 545-2360, fax: (413) 577-3838, e-mail: aes@outreach.umass.edu. (www.umass.edu).

Fine Art + Design (formerly Art Scottsdale and Scottsdale Antiques & Fine Art Show), K.R. Martindale Show Management, 1154 Grant Ave., Venice, CA 90291. (310) 822-9145, fax: (310) 822-9179. (www.krmartindaleshowmanagement.com).

*Greg Lawler's Art Fair SourceBook*, 2003 NE 11th Ave., Portland, OR 97212. (800) 358-2045, fax: (503) 331-0876. (www.artfairsourcebook.com). Guide to national juried art and craft shows. Published in fall (main ed.) and summer (preview).

LA Art Show, Fine Art Dealers Association, K. R. Martindale Show Management, 1154 Grant Ave., Venice, CA 90291. (310) 822-9145, fax: (310) 822-9179, e-mail: info@lasartshow.com. (www.laartshow.com, www.fada.com, www.kmartindale.com).

Latin American Art Show, K.R. Martindale Show Management, 1154 Grant Ave., Venice, CA 90291. (310) 822-9145, fax: (310) 822-9179. (www.krmartindaleshowmanagement.com).

Marin Show, K.R. Martindale Show Management, 1154 Grant Ave., Venice, CA 90291. (310) 822-9145, fax: (310) 822-9179. (www.krmartindaleshowmanagement.com).

Minneapolis Print and Drawing Fair, Minneapolis Institute of Arts, 2400 3rd Ave. S., Minneapolis, MN 55404. (888) 642-2787, (612) 870-30000, fax: (612) 870-3004. (www.artsmia.org).

Modernism, Sanford L. Smith & Associates, 447 W. 24th St., New York, NY 10011. (212) 777-5218, e-mail: info@sanfordsmith.com. (www.sanfordsmith.com).

NY Antiquarian Book Fair, Sanford L. Smith & Associates, 447 W. 24th St., New York, NY 10011. (212) 777-5218, e-mail: info@sanfordsmith.com. (www.sanfordsmith.com).

Outsider Art Fair, Sanford L. Smith & Associates, 447 W. 24th St., New York, NY 10011. (212) 777-5218, e-mail: info@sanfordsmith.com. (www.sanfordsmith.com).

Palm Beach Fair, IFAE (International Fine Art Expositions), 1555 Palm Beach Lakes Blvd., ste. 200, West Palm Beach, FL 33401. (561) 209-1300. (www.palmbeachfair.com. Includes palmbeach3 CONTEMPORARY. Established and emerging international art dealers present a mix of post-1950 paintings, sculpture, works on paper, video, and installation art. (www. palmbeach3.com). palmbeach3 ART + DESIGN (Classic and contemporary works from galleries worldwide).

Sanford L. Smith & Associates, 447 W. 24th St., New York, NY 10011. (212) 777-5218, e-mail: info@sanfordsmith.com. (www.sanfordsmith.com). Producer of Art 20, Modernism, Outsider Art Fair, Works on Paper, NY Antiquarian Book Fair.

Scope, 355 W. 36th St., 3rd flr., New York, NY 10018. (212) 268-1522, fax: (212) 268-1523, e-mail: info@scope-art.com (www.scope-art.com). Art fairs in New York, Basel, Hamptons, London, Miami.

SOFA (Sculpture Objects Functional Art), Expressions of Culture, a DMG World Media company, 4401 N. Ravenswood, ste. 301, Chicago, IL 60640. (800) 563-7632, (773) 506-8860, fax: (773) 506-8892, e-mail: info@sofaexpo.com. (www.sofaexpo.com). Art-in-craft-media fairs held annually in Chicago, New York, and Santa Fe.

Southeastern Wildlife Exposition, 211 Meeting St., Charleston, SC, 29401. (843) 723-1748, fax: (843) 723-4729, e-mail: sewe@sewe.com. (www.sewe.com). Largest wildlife art exposition in the country.

*Sunshine Artist*, Palm House Publishing, 4075 LB, McLeod Rd., ste. E, Orlando, FL 32811. (800) 597-2573. "America's Premier Show and Festival Magazine." (sunshineartist.com).

The ADAA Art Show, Art Dealers Association of America, 575 Madison Ave., New York, NY 10022. (212) 940-8590, fax: (212) 940-6484, e-mail: adaa@artdealers.org. (www.artdealers.org).

The Affordable Art Fair, 20 W. 22nd St., ste. 1512, New York, NY 10010. (212) 255-2003, fax: (212) 255-2024, e-mail: info@aafny.com. (www.aafny.com).

The Armory Show, The International Fair of New Art, 530 W. 25th St., 3rd flr., New York, NY 10001. (212) 645-6440, fax: (212) 645-0655, e-mail: info@thearmoryshow.com. (www.thearmoryshow.com).

The Photography Show, Association of International Photography Art Dealers, 1767 P St., NW, ste. 200, Washington, DC 20036. (202) 986-0105, fax: (202) 986-0448, e-mail: info@aipd.com. (www.aipd.com).

Vision, Chicago Art Dealers Association (CADA), 730 N. Franklin, St., Chicago, IL 60610. (312) 649-0065, e-mail: CADAChicago@aol.com. Two-week event showcasing outstanding artwork in the city's premier galleries with lectures and discussions.

Works on Paper, Sanford L. Smith & Associates, 447 W. 24th St., New York, NY 10011. (212) 777-5218, e-mail: info@sanfordsmith.com. (www.sanfordsmith.com).

www.ArtsOpportunities.org. Southern Arts Federation, 1800 Peachtree St. NW, ste. 808, Atlanta, GA 30309. (404) 874-7244, fax: (404) 873-2148.

www.southarts.org. Online classifieds for arts community, including submission calls.


**Art Materials/Equipment**

Ampersand Art Supply, 1500 E. Fourth St., Austin, TX 78702. (800) 822-1939, fax: (512) 322-9928, e-mail: bords@ampersandart.com. (www.ampersandart.com). Premium art panels and accessories.

B&H Photo, 420 Ninth Ave., New York, NY 10001. (800) 606-6969, (212) 444-6615. (www.bhphotovideo.com). Source for camera equipment and accessories. Closed Saturdays and Jewish holidays.

Barronarts, 302 Butler St., Brooklyn, NY 11217. (800) 286-9179, e-mail: info@barronarts.com. (www.barronarts.com). Frames and stretchers.

Cheap Joe's Art Stuff, (800) 227-2788, e-mail: info@cheapjoes.com. (www.cheapjoes.com). Retail store: 4420 Monroe Rd., Charlotte, NC 28205. (704) 333-2527. Outlet store: 374 Industrial Pk. Dr., Boone, NC 28607. (828) 262-5459.

David Davis Artist Materials & Services, 17 Bleecker St., New York, NY 10012 ; 68 Jay St., Brooklyn, NY, 11201. (800) 965-6554, (212) 260-9544. (www.daviddavisart.com).

Dick Blick Art Materials, PO Box 1267, Galesburg, IL 61402. (800) 828-4548, fax: (800) 621-8293, (309) 343-5785, e-mail: info@dickblick.com. (www.dickblick.com).

Downtown Stretcher Service, 50 Washington St., ste. 535, Brooklyn, NY 11201. (718) 222-2909. Museum quality stretchers. Contact: David Allen Headley.

Flax Art & Design, 140 Valley Dr., Brisbane, CA 94005. (888) 352-9278. (www.flaxart.com).

Jerry's Artarama, 5325 Departure Dr., Raleigh, NC 27616. (800) U-ARTIST, (919 878-6782. (www.jerrysartarama.com).

Mosaic Mercantile, P O Box 78206, San Francisco, CA 94107. (877) 9-MOSAIC, (415) 282-5410, fax: (415) 282-5410, e-mail: info@mosaicmercantile.com. (www.mosaicmercantile.com). Mosaic supplies.

The Art Store, 801 73rd St., Windsor Heights, IA 50312. (877) 550-5503, (515) 244-7000, fax: (515) 244-7056. (www.shoptheartstore.com). Fine art supplies.

Utrecht Art. (800) 223-9132, e-mail: customerservice@utrecht.com. (www.utrecht.com). Fine art supplies. Links to local stores.

www.COE90.com. PO Box 13, Cropseyville, NY 12052. (888) 213-8588, (518) 618-0812, e-mail: customerservice@coe90.com. Glass art supplies.

www.misterart.com. MisterArt, 913 Willard St., Houston, TX 77006. (800) 721-3015, e-mail: customerservice@misterart. Online resource for art and craft supplies, books, and videos.


**Artist Advisors**

Bamberger, Alan. E-mail: artbusiness@artbusiness.com. (www.artbusiness.com). Art consultant, advisor, author, and appraiser.

*Coaching the Artist Within: Advice for Writers, Actors, Visual Artists, and Musicians from America's Foremost Creativity Coach*, Eric Maisel. 2005. New World Library, 14 Pamaron Way, Novato, CA 94949. (800) 972-6657, e-mail: ami@newworldlibrary.com. (www.newworldlibrary.com).

Creativity Coaching Association. (www.creativitycoachingassociation.com). Founded in 2005 to introduce artists to professional creativity coaches to enhance and support their work. Website lists profiles of member coaches, CCA Press, and workshops and retreats.

Davey, Barney. President, Bold Star Communications, PO Box 25386, Scottsdale, AZ 85255. (609) 499-7500, e-mail: barney@barneydavey.com. (www.barneydavey.com), (www.artprintissues.com). "Art Biz Coach" and editor and publisher of *Art Print Issues*, a free-subscription e-zine.

Franklin Covey Corporation, 2200 W. Parkway Blvd., Salt Lake City, UT 84119. (800) 819-1812 (products), (800) 360-5326 (public workshops). (www.franklincovey.com). Time management and goal planning products and seminars.

Gulrich, Kathy. smART Business Coaching, New York, NY. (212) 689-2215. (www.smARTLearningCenter.com). Individual sessions and free e-newsletter.

Harrison, Dick. (www.salestipsforartists.com, www.talkshoe.com). Podcasts about how to promote and sell prints, topics include "Practical Promotion – Give A Little to Get A Lot" and "The Art Biz – Who Gets How Much And Why?"

Katharine T. Carter & Associates, PO Box 609, Kinderhook, NY 12106. (518) 758-8130, fax: (518) 758-8133, (212) 533-9530, fax: (212) 874-7843, e-mail: ktc@ktcassoc.com. (www.ktcassoc.com). Provides museum placement services and promotional support for mid-career artists.

Lang, Cay. *Taking the Leap*, 1506 62nd St, Emeryville, CA 94608. (510) 653-1655. (www.takingtheleap.com). Teaches business skills to artists looking to promote their work.

Michels, Caroll. Career Advisory Service for Emerging and Established Artists, 1724 Burgos Dr., Sarasota, FL 34238. (941) 927-5277, fax: (941) 927-5278, e-mail: carollmichels@gmail.com. (www.carollmichels.com).

Phillips, Renée. Private Career Consultant & Speaker, 200 E. 72nd St., ste. 26L, New York, NY 10021. (212) 472-1660, e-mail: info@manhattanarts.com. (www.manhattanarts.com). Publishes *Presentation Power Tools for Fine Artists* and *$uccess Now! For Artists: A Motivational Guide for the Artrepreneur*.

Prestige Art, 3909 W. Howard St., Skokie, IL 60076. (847) 679-2555, fax: (847) 679-2559, e-mail: prestige@prestigeart.com. (www.prestigeart.com). Company President Louis Shutz consults with artists on publishing and licensing of their work.

Pritzker, Elisa. Casa del Arte, 257 S. Riverside Rd., Highland, NY 12528. (845) 691-5506. (www.pritzkerstudio.com). Two-hour session to determine art goals and simplify planning.

Stamps, Laura. Art Marketing Consultant, PO Box 212534, Columbia, SC 29221. (803) 749-8579, e-mail: laurastamps@mindspring.com. Consultant for billion dollar market of specialized wholesale: print, poster, notecard, and trade show market.

Stanfield, Alyson B. Stanfield Art Associates, PO Box 988, Golden, CO 80402. (303) 273-5904, e-mail: alyson@artbizcoach.com. (www.artbizcoach.com).

Sylvia White/Contemporary Artists' Services, 5737 Kanan Rd., ste. 592, Agoura Hills, CA 91301. Fax: (866) 207-2506. (www.artadvice.com). Management consulting firm specializing in career development of visual artists.

The Tony Robbins Companies, 9888 Carroll Centre Rd., San Diego, CA 92126. (800) 445-8183, (800) 488-6040 (customer service). (www.tonyrobbins.com). Motivational tapes, lectures, and workshops.

Viders, Sue. Art Marketing Consultant, 9739 Tallgrass Circle, Lone Tree, CO 80124. (800) 999-8918, e-mail: viders@worldnet.att.net. (www.sueviders.com). Print marketing advisor and author of *Producing and Marketing Prints*.

## Colonies/Retreats/Residencies

Alliance of Artists Communities, 255 S. Main St., Providence, RI 02903. (401) 351-4320, fax: (401) 351-4507. (www.artistcommunities.org). Web site lists residencies available to artists alphabetically, by discipline, and by region.

ART/OMI, 59 Letter S Rd., Ghent, NY 12075. (518) 392-2181. Office: 55 Fifth Ave., 15th flr., New York, NY 10003. (212) 206-6060, fax: (212) 206-5660. (www.artomi.org).

*Artists and Writers Colonies: Retreats, Residencies, and Respites for the Creative Mind,* Robyn Middleton, Stacey Loomis, Martha Ruttle, and Emily Stephens. Rev. 2000. Available on Amazon.com.

*Artists Communities: A Directory of Residencies that Offer Time and Space for Creativity,* Robert MacNeil and Alliance of Artists' Communities. 3rd ed., 2005. Alliance of Artists Communities, 255 S. Main St., Providence, RI 02903. (401) 351-4320, fax: (401) 351-4507. (www.artistcommunities.org). Allworth Press, 10 E. 23rd St., New York, NY 10010. (800) 491-2808. (www.allworth.com).

Arts International, Lila Wallace Reader's Digest Artists at Giverny Fellowship, 809 United Nations Plaza, New York, NY 10017. (212) 984-5370. (www.wallacefoundation.org).

Bemis Center of Contemporary Arts, 724 S. 12th St., Omaha, NE 68102. (402) 341-7130, (402) 341-9791. (www.bemiscenter.org).

Brandywine Graphics Workshop, 730 S. Broad, Philadelphia, PA 19146. (877) ART.PRINT, (215) 546-3675, fax: (215) 546-2825, e-mail: prints@brandywineworkshop.com. (www.brandywineworkshop.com). Fellowships for regional and nationwide artists and Philadelphia artists under 35.

Dieu Donné Papermill, 315 W. 36th St., New York, NY 10018 (212) 226-0573, fax: (212) 226-6088. (www.dieudonne.org). Nonprofit papermaking studio offering residencies, studio rental, Collector's Series of limited edition prints.

*Getting Your Act Together, Artists Resource: The Watson-Guptill Guide to Academic Programs, Artist Colonies and Artist-in-Residence Programs, Conferences, Workshops,* Karen Chambers. 1999. Watson-Guptill Publications, 770 Broadway, New York, NY 10003. (646) 654-5500, e-mail: info@watsonguptill.com. (www.watsonguptill.com).

iscp International Studio & Curatorial Program. 1040 Metropolitan Ave., 3rd flr., Brooklyn, NY 11211. (718) 387-2900, fax: (718) 387-2966, e-mail: info@iscp-nyc.org. (www.iscp-nyc.org).

Light Work, 316 Waverly Ave., Syracuse, NY 13244. (315) 443-1300, e-mail: info@lightwork.org. (www.lightwork.org).

Lower East Side Printshop, 306 W. 37th St., 6th flr., New York, NY 10018. (212) 673-5390, fax: (212) 979-6493, e-mail: info@printshop.org. (www.printshop.org). Classes, studio rental, editioning, contract printing, and residencies.

Printmaking Council of NJ, 440 River Rd., Somerville, NJ 08876 (908) 725-2110, fax: (908) 725-2484, e-mail: pcnj@printNJ.org. (www.printNJ.org). Specializes in the fine art of printing with classes, residencies, gallery, etc.

Pyramid Atlantic, 8230 Georgia Ave., Silver Spring, MD 20910. (301) 608-9101, fax: (301) 608-9102, e-mail: info@pyramid-atlantic.org. (www.pyramidatlanticartcenter.org). Classes, workshops, studio rental, and residencies in bookmaking, papermaking, and printmaking.

Res Artis: International Association of Residential Art Centres, c/o Marijke Jansen, secretary, Arie Biemondstraat 105, PD Amsterdam, The Netherlands. (31) 20-612-6600, fax: (31) 20-6126600, e-mail: office@resartis.org. (www.resartis.org).

Sculpture Space, 12 Gates St., Utica, NY 13502. (315) 724-8381, fax: (315) 797-6639, e-mail: info@sculpturespace.org. (www.sculpturespace.org).

South Florida Culture Consortium comprised of Broward County Cultural Division, 100 S. Andrew Ave., Ft. Lauderdale, FL 33301. (954) 357-7457, fax: (954) 357-5769, e-mail: culturaldiv@broward.org. (www.broward.org/arts); Miami-Dade County Dept. of Cultural Affairs, 111 NW First St., ste. 625, Miami, FL 33128, (305) 375-6434, fax: (305) 375-3068, e-mail: culture@miamidade.gov. (www.miamidadearts.org); Arts Council of Stuart and Martin County, 80 E. Ocean Blvd., Stuart, FL 34994. (772) 287-6676, fax: (722 288-5301, e-mail: mcca@artinarts.org. (www.martinarts.org); Florida Keys Council of the Arts, 1100 Simonton St., Key West, FL 33040. (305) 295-4369, fax: (305) 295-4372, e-mail: info@keysarts.com. (www.keysarts.com). Palm Beach County Cultural Council, 1555 Palm Beach Lakes Blvd., ste. 300, West Palm Beach, FL 33401. (561) 471-2901, fax: (561) 687-9484, e-mail: marketinginfo@pbcc.org. (www.palmbeachculture.com). Fellowships.

The Bellagio Study and Conference Center, The Rockefeller Foundation, 420 Fifth Ave., New York, NY 10018. (212) 869-8500, fax: (2121) 764-3468. Bellagio Study and Conference Center, Villa Serbelloni, Bellagio (Lago di Como) 22021, Italy. (39) 31-0551, fax: (39) 31-955259. (www.rockfound.org/bellagio). Residencies for artists, composers, and writers.

The Space Program, administered by Marie Walsh Sharpe Foundation, 830 N. Tejon St., ste. 120, Colorado Springs, CO 80903. (800) 776-9815,(719) 635-3220, e-mail: sharpeartfdn@qwest.net. (www.sharpeartfdn.org) Free studio space in DUMBO, Brooklyn, NY.

Vermont Studio Center, PO Box 613, Johnson, VT 05656. (802) 635-2727, e-mail: gary@vermontstudiocenter.org. (www.vermontstudiocenter.org).

Visual Arts Information Hotline, New York Foundation for the Arts (NYFA), 155 Ave. of the Americas, 6th flr., New York, NY 10013. (800) 232-2789, (212) 366-6900. (www.nyfa.org). Referral service for artists, providing information on a wide variety of programs and services available to them.

Women's Studio Workshop, PO Box 489, Rosendale, NY 12472. (845) 658-9133, fax: (845) 658-9031, e-mail: info@wsworkshop.org. (www.wsworkshop.org). Facilities for printmaking letterpress printing, hand papermaking, photography, and ceramics. Fellowships, residencies, and internships offered.

www.washingtonart.com/beltway/resid1.html. Online listing of hundreds of colonies and retreats, organized by region.

## Commercial Galleries

Art Dealers Assn. of America, 575 Madison Ave., New York, NY 10022. (212) 940-8590, fax: (212) 940-6484, e-mail: adaa@artdealers.org. (www.artdealers.org).

*Art Diary International: The World Art Directory*, Giancarlo Politi Editore, edited by *Flash Art Magazine*. Distributed by D.A.P./Distributed Art Publishers, Inc., 155 Ave. of the Americas, New York, NY 10013. (800) 338-2665, fax: (212) 627-9484, e-mail: dap@dapinc.com. (www.artbook.com).

*Art in America Annual Guide to Museums/Galleries/Artists*. Published in August. *Art in America*, 575 Broadway, New York, NY 10012. (212) 941-2800. (www.artinamericamagazine.com).

*Artists' Gallery Guide*, Chicago and Surrounding Area, Chicago Artists' Coalition, 70 E. Lake St., ste. 230, Chicago, IL 60601. (312) 781-0040, fax: (312) 781-0042, e-mail: info@caconline.org. (www.caconline.org).

*Artnow International*, 1000 5th St., Miami, FL 33139. E-mail: info@artnowonline.com. (www.artnowonline.com). Promotes the international art world featuring news about galleries, artists, and events.

*Greg Lawler's Art Fair SourceBook*, 2003 NE 11th Ave., Portland, OR 97212. (800) 358-2045, fax: (503) 331-0876. (www.artfairsourcebook.com). Guide to national juried art and craft shows. Published in fall (main ed.) and summer (preview).

*Philly Gallery Guide*. (www.phillygalleryguide.com). Listing of area art galleries and exhibitions.

Private Art Dealers Association of America, PO Box 872, Lenox Hill Sta., New York, NY 10021. (212) 572-0772, e-mail: pada99@msn.com. (www.pada.net).

*The Collector's Guide*, Wingspread Guides of New Mexico, Inc., 116 Central Ave. SW, ste. 201, Albuquerque, NM 87102. (800) USE-4-ART, e-mail: inquiry@collectorsguide.com. (www.collectorsguide.com).

www.ArtCal.net. New York-area museum and gallery openings, "focusing on underknown galleries and artists at the whim of Editors Barry Hoggard and James Wagner and assistant editor Paddy Johnson."

## Commercial Printing

Avanti Printing, 17962 Sky Park Circle, ste. C, Irvine, CA 92614. (949) 510-1776, e-mail: info@avantiprinting.com. (www.avantiprinting.com).

Futura Printing, 1100 Rte. 34, Oswego, IL 60543. (866) 632-7768. (www.futuraprinting.net). High-speed copying, digital color printing, mailing, creative services, four-color printing, spot color, and binding.

iPrinTeam. (800) 289-5144. (www.iprinteam.com). Offset printing, digital copying, CD and DVD manufacturing, posters and banners, mailing and fulfillment.

PrintPelican.com. (800) 474-0461, e-mail: 4colorprinting@PrintPelican.com. (www.printpelican.com). Links to local offices.

PrintPlace.com, 1130 Ave. H E., Arlington, TX 76011. (877) 405-3949, (817) 701-3555, fax: (817) 701-3565. (www.printplace.com). Full-color printing.

Shutterfly, 2800 Bridge Pkwy., ste. 101, Redwood City, CA 94065. (800) 416-1465, e-mail: progallery@shutterfly.com. (www.shutterfly.com). Prints, cards, photo books, calendars, etc.

Smart Art Press, 2525 Michigan Ave., bldg. C1, Santa Monica, CA 90404. (310) 264-4678, fax: (310) 264-4682. (www.smartartpress.com). Publishes artists' books, monographs, catalogues, and other art emphemera.


## Competitions/Juried Exhibitions

Contact your state/county/local arts council/visual arts coordinator for exhibition opportunities.

*American Art Directory 2010*, National Register Publishing, 890 Mountain Ave., 3rd flr., New Providence, NJ 07974. Editorial: (800) 473-7020, e-mail: NRPeditorial@marquiswhoswho.com; sales: (800) 473-7020, e-mail: NRPsales@marquiswhoswho.com. (www.americanartdir.com). Listings of national and regional art organizations; museums; libraries; associations in the US and Canada; art schools with contact data, degree programs, scholarship programs, entrance requirements, and tuition information; museums abroad; schools abroad; state directors and supervisors of art education; state arts councils; art magazines, editors, and critics; scholarships and fellowships; open exhibitions; and traveling exhibition booking agencies. Indexed by subject, personnel, and organization.

*Art Calendar*, 1500 Park Ctr. Dr., Orlando, FL 32835. (877) 415-3055, fax: (407) 563-7099. (www.ArtCalendar.com). Business magazine for the visual arts. Mission to connect artists with income and exhibition possibilities. Mailing lists available for purchase.

*Artist Deadline List*, PO Box 381067, Harvard Sq. Sta., Cambridge, MA 02238, (617) 576-1214.

*ARTnews*, 48 W. 38th St., 9th flr., New York, NY 10018. (212) 398-1690, e-mail: info@artnewsonline.com. (www.artnewsonline.com). Lists exhibitions and competitions.

*Awards, Honors, and Prizes, Gale Group*, 27500 Drake Rd., Farmington Hills, MI 48331. (800) 877-4253. (www.gale.cengage.com). Extensive directory organized by subject matter.

"Bulletin Board." American Artist, 770 Broadway, New York, NY 10003. (646) 654-5506, e-mail: mail@myamericanartist.com. (www.myamericanartist.com).

Competitions Hotline. PO Box 20445, Louisville, KY 40250. (502) 451-3623, e-mail: hotline@competitions.org. (www.competitions.org).

*International Artist Magazine's Art Competitions*, International Artist Publishing, PO Box 8629, Scottsdale, AZ 85252. (877) 947-0792, fax: (480) 425-0724, e-mail: service@international-artist.com. (www.international-artist.com).

Small Works Competition, New York University, 80 Washington Square East Galleries, New York, NY 10003. (212) 998-5747, fax: (212) 998-5752, e-mail: 80wse@nyu.edu. (www.nyu.edu/pages/galleries). Early January juried exhibition of works no larger than 12" square.

www.southarts.org. Online classifieds for arts community, including submission calls.

## Craft

*American Craft*, American Craft Council, 1224 Marshall St. NE, ste. 200, Minneapolis, MN 54413. (www.americancraftmag.org). Bimonthly.

Art Glass Association of Southern California, 1770 Village Pl., Studio 25, San Diego, CA 92101. (619) 702-8006, membership: (619) 469-1676. (www.agasc.org).

Artisans Center of Virginia, Willow Oak Plaza, Rte. 340 N., 801 W. Broad St., Waynesboro, VA 22980. (877) 508-6069, (540) 946-3294, fax: (540) 946-3296, e-mail: acv@netlos.net. (www.artisanscenterofvirginia.org).

Artrider Craft Shows in New York, NY; Morristown, NJ; Lyndhurst, NY; and Guilford, CT. Artrider, PO Box 29, Woodstock, NY 12498. (845) 331-7900, fax: (845) 331-7484, e-mail: crafts@artrider.com. (www.artrider.com).

Association of Clay and Glass Artists of California (ACGA), 1045 Center St., San Carlos, CA 94070. (925) 254-8457. (www.acga.net).

*Ceramics Monthly*, 735 Ceramic Pl., ste. 100, Westerville, OH 43081. (800) 342-3594. (www.ceramicsmonthly.org).

*Common Ground Glass*, International Guild of Glass Artists, 27829 365th Ave., Platte, SC 57369. (458) 565-4552. (www.igga.org). Quarterly newsletter.

*Craft Arts*, Craft Arts International, PO Box 363, Neutral Bay, Sydney, NSW 2089, Australia. (61) 2-9953-8825, e-mail: subs@craftarts.com.au. (www.craftarts.com.au).

*Creating a Successful Craft Business*, Rogene Robbins and Robert Robbins. 2003. Allworth Press, 10 E. 23rd St., New York, NY 10010. (800) 491-2808. (www.allworth.com).

*Fiberarts*, 201 E. Fourth St., Loveland, CO 80537. Editorial: (970) 613-4679, fax: (970) 669-6117, e-mail: info@fiberarts.com, subscriptions: (800) 875-6208, (760) 291-1531, fax: (760) 738-4805, e-mail: fiberarts@pcspublink.com. (www.fiberartsmagazine.com). Covers contemporary textile art and craft.

Glass Art Society (GAS), 3131 Western Ave., ste. 414, Seattle, WA 98121. (206) 382-1305, fax: (206 382-2630, e-mail: info@glassart.org. (www.glassart.org). National membership organization to promote the glass arts. Publishes *Glass Art Society Journal*, proceedings of annual meeting.

Handmade in America, 125 S. Lexington Ave., Asheville, NC 28801. (828) 252-0121. (www.handmadeinamerica.org). To nurture traditional and contemporary craft in Western North Carolina.

International Guild of Glass Artists, 27829 365th Ave., Platte, SC 57369. (458) 565-4552. (www.igga.org).

Kentucky Craft Marketing Program, Old Capital Annex, 300 W. Broadway, Frankfort, KY 40601, (888) KYCRAFT, (502) 564-8076, e-mail: kyarts@ky.gov. (www.ky.gov).

NCECA (National Council on Education for the Ceramic Arts), 77 Erie Village Sq., ste. 280, Erie, CO 80516. (866) 266-2322, (303) 828-2811, fax: (303) 828-0911, e-mail: office@nceca.net. (www.nceca.net). National membership organization to promote the ceramic arts. Publishes *Journal*, proceedings of annual meeting.

*Opportunities in Arts & Crafts Careers*, Elizabeth Gardner. 2nd ed., 2005. Available on Amazon.com.

*Selling Your Crafts*, Susan Sager. Rev. ed., 2003. Allworth Press, 10 E. 23rd St., New York, NY 10010. (800) 491-2808. (www.allworth.com).

*Shuttle Spindle & Dyepot*, Handweavers Guild of America, 1255 Buford Hwy., ste. 211, Suwanee, GA 30024, (678) 730-0010, fax: (678) 730-0836, e-mail: hga@weavespindye.org. (www.weavespindye.org).

Society of American Mosaic Artists (SAMA), PO Box 428, Orangeburg, SC 29116. E-mail: info@americanmosaics.org, (www.americanmosaics.org).

*The Basic Guide to Selling Crafts on the Internet*, James Dillehay. 2000. Warm Snow Publishers, PO Box 75, Torreon, NM 87061. (505) 384-1195, e-mail: jamesd@craftmarketer.com. (www.craftmarketer.com).

*The Blacksmith's Journal*, Hoffman Publications, PO Box 1699, Washington, MO 63090. (800) 944-6134, e-mail: hpi@blacksmithsjournal.com. (www.blacksmithsjournal.com). Monthly.

The Center for Craft, Creativity & Design, University of North Carolina, Kellogg Ctr., PO Box 1127, 1181 Broyles Rd., Hendersonville, NC 28793, e-mail: info@craftcreativitydesign.org. (www.craftcreativitydesign.org). Regional center to support and advance craft, creativity, and design in education and research, and through community collaborations to demonstrate ways craft and design provide creative solutions for community issues.

The Contemporary Glass Society, c/o Broadfield House Glass Museum, Compton Dr., Kingswinford, West Midlands DY6 9NS, UK (44) 1603-507-737, fax: (44) 1603-507-737. (www.cgs.org.uk).

UrbanGlass, 647 Fulton St., Brooklyn, NY 11217. (718) 625-3685, e-mail: info@urbanglass.org. (www.urbanglass.org). Publishes *Glass Quarterly*.

(www.guild.com). The Guild, 931 E. Main Street, ste. 9, Madison, WI 53703 (877) 223-4600, artists: (608) 616-2002, International: (608) 257-2590, fax: (608) 257-2690, e-mail: art-info@guild.com.  Source book and Website for art glass, objects and accents, art for the wall, furniture and lighting, jewelry, and accessories. Fee for inclusion.

www.WorldArtGlass.com.  Guide to art glass worldwide with more than 1,000 links to art-glass-related sites.


## Critics/Media

*American Art Directory 2010*, National Register Publishing, 890 Mountain Ave., 3rd flr., New Providence, NJ  07974. Editorial: (800) 473-7020, e-mail: NRPeditorial@marquiswhoswho.com; sales: (800) 473-7020, e-mail: NRPsales@marquiswhoswho.com. (www.americanartdir.com)  Listings of national and regional art organizations; museums; libraries; associations in the US and Canada; art schools with contact data, degree programs, scholarship programs, entrance requirements, and tuition information; museums abroad; schools abroad; state directors and supervisors of art education; state arts councils; art magazines, editors, and critics; scholarships and fellowships; open exhibitions; and traveling exhibition booking agencies. Indexed by subject, personnel, and organization.

*Art Diary International: The World Art Directory*, Giancarlo Politi Editore, edited  by *Flash Art Magazine.* Distributed by D.A.P./Distributed Art Publishers, Inc., 155 Ave. of the Americas, New York, NY 10013. (800) 338-2665, fax: (212) 627-9484, e-mail: dap@dapinc.com. (www.artbook.com).

*artUS*, Foundation for International Art Criticism, 530 Molino St., ste. 212, PO Box 86187, Los Angeles, CA 90086. (213) 625-2010, fax: (213) 625-2017, e-mail: artus@artext.org. (www.artext.org).

Bacon's Information, Inc., 332 S. Michigan Ave., Chicago, IL  60604. (312) 992-2400. (www.bacons.com). Nation's largest media database company. Publishes directories for newspaper/magazine, radio/TV/cable, and Internet media.

Burrelle's News Media Directories, Burrelle's Business Research Center, 75 E. Northfield Road, Livingston, NJ  07039-9812. (800) 368-8070, (800) 631-1160, (973) 992-6600, fax: (973) 992-7675. (www.burrelles.com).

Caroll Michels, Career Advisory Service for Emerging and Established Artists, 1724 Burgos Dr., Sarasota, FL 34238. (941) 927-5277, fax: (941) 927-5278, e-mail: carollmichels@gmail.com. (www.carollmichels.com).

*Creative Vision* (15 Minutes of Fame),Television for the Arts, Production of Second St. Studio, Arlington 3115 2nd St. N., Arlington, VA 22201. E-mail: januszkb@erols. (www.users.erols.com/januszkb/vvtv2.html).  Half-hour public access television programs about artists who live in the Greater Washington, DC, metropolitan area. Copies available at The Art League Gallery, 105 N. Union St., Alexandria, VA  22314. (703) 683-1780, fax: (703) 683-5786, e-mail: info@theartleague.org. (www.theartleague.org).

eNR Grassroots PR Program, eNR Services, 20 Glover Ave., 2nd flr., Norwalk, CT 06850. (888) 607-9655, (203) 846-2811, fax: (203) 846-2824, e-mail: mediaq@enr-corp.com. (www.enr-corp.com). Local news for local media.

*Fine Art Publicity: The Complete Guide for Galleries and Artists*, Susan Abbott. 2nd ed., 2005. Allworth Press, 10 E. 23rd St., New York, NY 10010. (800) 491-2808. (www.allworth.com).

International Association of Art Critics (AICA), American Section, an affiliate of Association International des Critiques d'Art 15, rue Martel, F-75010 Paris. e-mail: board@aicausa.org. (www.aica.org).

*Magazine and Newsletter Directory, Vol. 2, Bowker's News Media Directory 2009*. R.R. Bowker, 63 Central Ave., New Providence, NJ 07974. (888) 269-5372, (908) 285-1090. (www.bowker.com).

MediaQ, eNR Services, 20 Glover Ave., 2nd flr., Norwalk, CT 06850. Sales: (888) 607-9101, (203) 846-2811, fax: (203) 846-2824, e-mail: mediaq@enr-corp.com. (www.enr-corp.com). News research application giving users access to print, broadcast, and online content.

MediaSource Monitoring, Cision US (Parent company of Bacon's Information), 332 S. Michigan Ave., Chicago, IL 60604. (866) 639-5087. (www.cision.com). Provides 24/7 online access of all your newspaper, magazine, broadcast, Internet, and blog covering in one location.

*New York Times*, 620 Eighth Ave., New York, NY 10018. (866) 586-7020, (212) 556-1234. (www.nytimes.com). Advertising rates for "arts and entertainment" placement.

*News Media Directories*, PO Box 316, Mount Dora, FL 32757 (800) 749-6399, (904) 383-3023. (www.newsmediadirectories). For Alabama, Florida, Georgia, Ohio, and Tennessee.

*Newspaper Directory, Vol. 1, Bowker's News Media Directory 2009*. R.R. Bowker, 63 Central Ave., Providence, NJ 07974. (888) 269-5372, (908) 285-1090. (www.bowker.com).

NewsWire One, eNR Services, 20 Glover Ave., 2nd flr., Norwalk, CT 06850. (800) 883-0827, e-mail: helpdesk@enr-corp.com. (www.enr-corp.com). Targeted media list creation and press release distribution.

PR Manager, eNR Services, 20 Glover Ave., 2nd flr., Norwalk, CT 06850. (203) 846-2811, sales: (888) 607-9101, fax: (203) 846-2824, e-mail: helpdesk@enr-corp.com. www.enr-corp.com). Provides promotions services, press releases, clipping service, etc. for monthly fee.

*TV and Radio Directory, Vol. 3, Bowker's News Media Directory 2009*. R.R. Bowker, 63 Central Ave., New Providence, NJ 07974. (888) 269-5372, (908) 285-1090. (www.bowker.com).

*Who's Who in American Art*, National Register Publishing, 890 Mountain Ave., 3rd flr., New Providence, NJ 07974. Editorial: (800) 473-7020, e-mail: NRPeditorial@marquiswhoswho.com; sales: (800) 473-7020, e-mail: NRPsales@marquiswhoswho.com. (www.americanartdir.com). Biographical and professional information for notable collectors, consultants, curators, editors, educators, historians, lecturers, and publishers.

www.Washingtonart.com. Broad and in-depth coverage of Washington area art world. E-mail: kkeler@earthlink.net.


## Directories

*2010 Artists & Graphic Designers Market*, edited by Mary Cox and Michael Schweer. 2006. Writer's Digest Books, F & W Publications, 4700 E. Galbraith Rd., Cincinnati, OH 45236. (513) 531-2690. (www.WritersMarket.com), (www.fwpublications.com).

*2010 Photographer's Market*, 33rd annual ed. Writer's Digest Books, F & W Publications, 4700 E. Galbraith Rd., Cincinnati, OH 45236. (800) 258-0929, (513) 531-2690. (www.fwpublications.com).

Access Arts Network, Art World's News Service, PO Box 381067, Harvard Sq. Sta., Cambridge, MA 02238. (617) 576-1214, e-mail: support @artdeadline.com. (www.worldartviews.com). The art world's most comprehensive resource for income and exhibition opportunities, including juried exhibitions and competitions. Directories for galleries, art museums, art centers, etc.

American Architecture. (www.americanarchitecture). Online listing of architects, consulting engineers, developers, realtors, contractors, interior designers, landscape architects, specifications writers, trade consultants, and authorities in building materials with links to professional organizations and governmental bodies.

*American Art Directory 2010*, National Register Publishing, 890 Mountain Ave., 3rd flr., New Providence, NJ 07974. Editorial: (800) 473-7020, e-mail: NRPeditorial@marquiswhoswho.com, sales: (800) 473-7020, e-mail: NRPsales@marquiswhoswho.com. (www.americanartdir.com). Listings of national and regional art organizations; museums; libraries; associations in the US and Canada; art schools with contact data, degree programs, scholarship programs, entrance requirements, and tuition information; museums abroad; schools abroad; state directors and supervisors of art education; state arts councils; art magazines, editors, and critics; scholarships and fellowships; open exhibitions; and traveling exhibition booking agencies. Indexed by subject, personnel, and organization.

American Society of Interior Designers (ASID), 608 Massachusetts Ave. NE, Washington, DC 20002. (202) 546-3480, e-mail: asid@asid.org. (www.asid.org).

American Society of Landscape Architects (ASLA), 636 Eye St. NW, Washington, DC 20001. (888) 999-ASLA, (202) 898-2444. (www.asla.org). Publishes *Landscape Architecture* magazine; online resources include "Firm Finder" (directory of landscape architects), *Sweets Landscape Architecture Directory* (official product guide of ASLA), LATIS (Landscape Architects Technical Information Series), etc.

ArchitectsUSA, 9182 Hemlock Ln., Bridgman, MI 49106. Fax: (312) 416-7981, e-mail: ArchUSAemail-help@yahoo.com. (www.architectsusa.com). Directory of more than 20,000 architectural firms compiled from Yellow Pages listings and architects.

*Architectural Digest*, 6300 Wilshire Blvd., Los Angeles, CA 90048. (323) 965-3700, fax: (323) 965-4975. (www.architecturaldigest.com). "Reader's Directory" listing of designers, architects, and galleries featured in each issue.

Art Dealers Association of America, 575 Madison Ave., New York, NY 10022. (212) 940-8590, fax: (212) 940-6484, e-mail: adaa@artdealers.org. (www.artdealers.org).

*Art Diary International: The World Art Directory*, Giancarlo Politi Editore, edited by *Flash Art Magazine*. Distributed by D.A.P./Distributed Art Publishers, Inc., 155 Ave. of the Americas, New York, NY 10013. (800) 338-2665, fax: (212) 627-9484, e-mail: dap@dapinc.com. (www.artbook.com).

*Art in America Annual Guide to Museums/Galleries/Artists*. Published in August. *Art in America*, 575 Broadway, New York, NY 10012. (212) 941-2800. (www.artinamericamagazine.com).

*Artist's Communities: A Directory of Residencies that Offer Time and Space for Creativity*, Robert MacNeil and Alliance of Artist's Communities. 3rd ed., 2005. Alliance of Artists Communities, 255 S. Main St., Providence, RI 02903. (401) 351-4320, fax: (401) 351-4507. (www.artistcommunities.org). Allworth Press, 10 E. 23rd St., New York, NY 10010. (800) 491-2808. (www.allworth.com).

*Awards, Honors, and Prizes*, Gale Group, 27500 Drake Rd., Farmington Hills, MI 48331. (800) 877-4253, (www.galegroup.com). Extensive directory organized by subject matter.

*Directories of Graduate Programs in the Arts*. College Art Association, 275 Seventh Ave., New York, NY 10001. (212) 691-1051, fax: (212) 627-2381, e-mail: nyoffice@collegeart.org. (www.collegeart.org).

*Encyclopedia of Associations*, Thomson Gale, Electronic Search Assistance, 27500 Drake Rd., Farmington Hills, MI 48331. (800) 877-4253, press 5. (www.gale.cengage.com). Comprehensive source of detailed information on more than 135,000 nonprofit organizations worldwide.

Foundation Directory Online. (800) 424-9836, e-mail: fdonline@foundationcenter.org. (www.fconline.fdncenter.org). Subscription service to database of thousands of grantmaking organizations.

*Getting Your Act Together, Artists Resource: The Watson-Guptill Guide to Academic Programs, Artists' Colonies and Artist-in-Residence Programs, Conferences, Workshops*, Karen Chambers. Watson-Guptill Publications, 770 Broadway, New York, NY 10003. (646) 654-5500, e-mail: info@watsonguptill.com. (www.watsonguptill.com).

*International Auction House Directory*, LTB Gordonsart, 13201 N. 35th Ave., ste. B-20, Phoenix, AZ 85029. (800) 892-4622, (602) 253-6948, fax: (602) 253-2104, e-mail: office@gordonsart.com. (www.gordonsart.com).

*International Directory of Corporate Art Collections*, The Humanities Exchange, PO Box 1608, Largo, FL 33779. (514) 935-1228, fax: (514) 935-1299, e-mail: internationaldirectory@earthlink.net. (www.humanities-exchange.org). Artist's, Museum, and Gallery/Art Advisor editions available on CD in three different formats (MS Word, Adobe PDF, and Asksam for PC) or spiral-bound printout.

*International Directory of Sculpture Parks*, Benbow Bullock. 12 Sandy Beach, Vallejo, CA 94590. (510) 245-2242, fax: (510) 245-2252, e-mail: artnut@artnut.com. (www.artnut.com/intl.html).

International Fine Print Dealers Association (IFPDA), 250 W. 26th St., ste. 405, New York, NY 10001. (212) 674-6095, fax: (212) 674-6783, e-mail: ifpda@ifpda.org. (www.printdealers.com, www.ifpda.org). Produces IFPDA Print Fair. Membership directory available for nominal fee, write: 15 Gramercy Pk. S., ste. 7A, New York, NY 10003.

*Magazine and Newsletter Directory, Vol. 2, Bowker's News Media Directory 2009.* R.R. Bowker, 63 Central Ave., New Providence, NJ 07974. (888) 269-5372, (908) 285-1090. (www.bowker.com).

*Marquis Who's Who in American Art*, National Register Publishing, 890 Mountain Ave, 3rd flr., New Providence, NJ 07974. Editorial: (800) 473-7020, (908) 673-1000, fax: (908) 673-1179, e-mail: america@marquiswhoswho.com, sales: (800) 473-7020, fax: (908) 673-1189, e-mail: sales@marquiswhoswho.com. (www.marquiswhoswho.com).

Michigan State University Main Library, 100 Library, East Lansing, MI 48824. (517) 353-8700. (www.lib.msu.edu/harris23/grants/3arts.htm). Online listing of grant-making organizations provided and regularly updated.

*News Media Directories*, PO Box 316, Mount Dora, FL 32757 (800) 749-6399, (904) 383-3023. (www.newsmediadirectories.com). For Alabama, Florida, Georgia, Ohio, and Tennessee.

*Newspaper Directory, Vol. 1, Bowker's New Media Directory 2009.* R.R. Bowker, 63 Central Ave., New Providence, NJ 07974. (888) 269-5372, (908) 285-1090. (www.bowker.com).

*Photo Arts Santa Fe*, 7358 Beverly Blvd., Los Angeles, CA 90036. (www.photoartssantafe.com). Resource guide to auctions, bookstores, galleries, organizations, photographers, private dealers, schools/universities, services, and workshops for photographers in the Santa Fe area.

*Printworld Directory: Contemporary Prints and Prices*, edited by Selma Smith. 13th ed., 2010. Printworld International, PO Box 1957, West Chester, PA 19380. (800) 788-9101, (610) 431-6654, fax: (610) 431-6653, e-mail: editor@printworlddirectory.com. (www.printworlddirectory.com).

*The Official Museum Directory*, National Register Publishing, 890 Mountain Ave., 3rd flr., New Providence, NJ 07974. (800) 473-7020, fax: (908) 673-1189. (www.officialmuseumdir.com). Published annually. Listings of museums, historic sites, planetariums, technology centers, zoos, etc.

*TV and Radio Direcctory, Vol. 3, Bowker's News Media Directory 2009.* R.R. Bowker, 63 Central Ave., New Providence, NJ 07974. (888) 269-5372, (908) 285-1090. (www.bowker.com).

*Who's Who in American Art*, National Register Publishing, 890 Mountain Ave., 3rd flr., New Providence, NJ 07974. Editorial: (800) 473-7020, e-mail: NRPeditorial@marquiswhoswho.com, sales: (800) 473-7020, e-mail: NRPsales@marquiswhoswho.com. (www.americanartdir.com). Biographical and professional information for notable collectors, consultants, curators, editors, educators, historians, lecturers, and publishers.

*Worldwide Licensing Directory*, A4 Publications, Thornleigh, 35 Hagley Rd., Stourbridge, West Midlands, DY8 1QR, UK.

www.americanarchitects.com. Fee-based directory of architects with links to associations and government, architects, interior designers, and landscape architects.

www.architectsusa.com. ArchitectsUSA, 9182 Hemlock Ln., Bridgman, MI 49106. Fax: (312) 416-7981, e-mail: ArchUSAemail-help@yahoo.com. Directory of more than 20,000 architectural firms compiled from Yellow Pages listings and architects.

www.thenewyorkartworld.com. E-zine with news, reviews, exhibitions, commentary, openings, directory, maps, and archive sections.

www.washingtonart.com/beltway/resid1.html. Online listing of hundreds of colonies and retreats, organized by region.

www.WorldArtGlass.com. Guide to art glass worldwide with more than 1,000 links to art-glass-related sites.


## Education Opportunities

*American Art Directory 2010*, National Register Publishing, 890 Mountain Ave., 3rd flr., New Providence, NJ 07974. Editorial: (800) 473-7020, e-mail: NRPeditorial@marquiswhoswho.com, sales: (800) 473-7020, e-mail: NRPsales@marquiswhoswho.com. (www.americanartdir.com). Listings of national and regional art organizations; museums; libraries; associations in the US and Canada; art schools with contact data, degree programs, scholarship programs, entrance requirements, and tuition information; museums abroad; schools abroad; state directors and supervisors of art education; state arts councils; art magazines, editors, and critics; scholarships and fellowships; open exhibitions; and traveling exhibition booking agencies. Indexed by subject, personnel, and organization.

*Directories of Graduate Programs in the Arts.* College Art Association, 275 Seventh Ave., New York, NY 10001. (212) 691-1051, fax: (212) 627-2381, e-mail: nyoffice@collegeart.org. (www.collegeart.org).

Brandywine Graphics Workshop, 730 S. Broad St., Philadelphia, PA 19146. (877) ART-PRINT, (215) 546-3675 fax: (215) 546-2825, e-mail: prints@brandywineworkshop.com. (www.brandywineworkshop.com).

Dieu Donné Papermill, 315 W. 36th St., New York, NY 10018 (212) 226-0573, fax: (212) 226-6088. (www.dieudonne.org). Nonprofit papermaking studio offering residencies, studio rental, Collector's Series of limited edition prints.

*Getting Your Act Together, Artists Resource: The Watson-Guptill Guide to Academic Programs, Artists' Colonies and Artist-in-Residence Programs, Conferences, Workshops,* Karen Chambers. Watson-Guptill Publications, Incorporated, 770 Broadway, New York, NY 10003. (646) 654-5500, e-mail: info@watsonguptill.com. (www.watsonguptill.com).

## Fine Art Photography

*2010 Photographer's Market,* 33rd annual ed. Writer's Digest, F & W Publications, 4700 E. Galbraith Rd., Cincinnati, OH 45236. (800) 258-0929, (513) 531-2690, e-mail: photomarket@fwpubs.com. (www.fwpublications.com, www.writersdigest.com).

*301 Inkjet Tips and Techniques,* Andrew Darlow. 2007. Thomson Course Technology PTR, 25 Thomson Pl., Boston, MA 02210. (800) 648-7450, e-mail: eSales@thomsonlearning.com. (www.courseptr.com).

Aperture Foundation, 547 W. 27th St., 4th flr., New York, NY 10001. (212) 505-5555, fax: (212) 598-4015. (www.aperture.org).

*Aperture Magazine,* 547 W. 27th St., 4th flr., New York, NY 10001. (212) 505-5555, fax: (212) 598-4015. Subscription Services, PO Box 3000, Denville, NJ 07834. (866) 457-4603, e-mail: custsvc_aperture@fulcoinc.com. (www.aperture.org).

*Camera Arts,* PO Box 2328, Corrales, NM 87048. (800) 894-8439. (www.cameraarts.com).

Custom Color, 2650 North Burlington Ave., Kansas City, MO 64116. (888) 605-4050. (www.customcolor.com). Slide reproductions.

Custom Colour Imaging, 4455 Chesswood Drive, Toronto, Ontario, Canada M3J 2C2. (416) 630-2020, (800) 268-3628 (www.ccimaging.com). Professional Imaging Laboratory.

*Digital Art Studio: Techniques for Combining Inkjet Printing with Traditional Art Materials,* Karin Schminke, Dorothy Simpson Krause, and Bonny Pierce Lhotka. 2004. Watson-Guptill Publications, 770 Broadway, New York, NY 10003. (646) 654-5500, e-mail: info@watsonguptill.com. (www.watsonguptill.com).

*Fine Art Printing for Photographers: Exhibition Quality Prints with Inkjet Printers,* Uwe Steinmueller and Juergen Gulbins. 2008. Rocky Nook, 26 W. Mission St., ste. 3, Santa Barbara, CA 93101. (866) 687-1118, (805) 687-8727, fax: (805) 687-2204. (www.rockynook.com).

George Eastman House, 900 East Ave., Rochester, NY 14607-2298. (585) 271-3361. (www.eastman.org). Traveling exhibitions program.

*International Auction House Directory,* LTB Gordonsart, 13201 N. 35th Ave., ste. B-20, Phoenix, AZ 85029. (800) 892-4622, (602) 253-6948, fax: (602) 253-2104, e-mail: office@gordonsart.com. (www.gordonsart.com).

International Center for Photography (ICP) (Museum), 1133 Ave. of the Americas @ 43rd St., New York, NY 10036. (212) 857-0000, e-mail: info@icp.org. (www.icp.org).

International Center for Photography (ICP) (School), 1114 Ave. of the Americas @ 43rd St., New York, NY 10036. (212) 857-0091, e-mail: info@icp.org. (www.icp.org).

*Licensing Photography*, Richard Weisgrau and Victor S. Perlman. 2006. Allworth Press, 10 E. 23rd St., New York, NY 10010. (800) 491-2808. (www.allworth.com).

Light Work, 316 Waverly Ave., Syracuse, NY 13244. (315) 443-1300, e-mail: info@lightwork.org. (www.lightwork.org).

Maine Photographic Workshops, PO Box 200, 70 Camden St., Rockport, ME 04856. (207) 236-8581, fax: (207) 236-2558, e-mail: info@theworkshops.com. (www.theworkshops.com).

New Mexico Council on Photography, PO Box 162, Santa Fe, NM 87504. (505) 660-4085, e-mail: mickeybond505@aol.com.

Paint Outside the Frame, Marilyn Sholin's Digital Painting Forum for Photographers and Artists. Membership online community for art professionals to discuss their art, sales, marketing, business, and promotional techniques. (www.digitalpaintingforum.com).

Photo Arts Santa Fe, 7358 Beverly Blvd., Los Angeles, CA 90036. (www.photoartssantafe.com). Resource guide to auctions, bookstores, galleries, organizations, photographers, private dealers, schools/universities, services, and workshops for photographers in the Santa Fe area.

*Photograph*, 64 W. 89th St., New York, NY 10024. (212) 787-0401, fax: (212) 799-3054, e-mail: info@photographmag.com. (www.photographmag.com). Bimonthly guide to photography exhibitions, private dealers, resources, and calendar of events in the US Publisher and Editor Bill Mindlin.

Santa Fe Center for Photography, PO Box 2483, Santa Fe, NM 87504. (505) 984-8353. (www.santafecenterforphotography.org).

The AIPAD (Association of International Photography Art Dealers) Photography Show, 1767 P St. NW, ste. 200, Washington, DC 20036. (202) 986-0105, fax: (202) 986-0448, e-mail: info@aipad.com. (www.aipad.com).

The Bridgeman Art Library International, 65 E. 93rd St., New York, NY 10128. (212) 828-1238, e-mail: info@bridgemanart.com. (www.bridgemanart.com). Fine art photographic archive.

*The Gordon's Photography Price Annual 2010*, LTB Gordonsart, 13201 N. 35th Ave., ste. B-20, Phoenix, AZ 85029. (800) 892-4622, (602) 253-6948, fax: (602) 253-2104, e-mail: office@gordonsart.com. (www.gordonsart.com).

*View Camera Magazine*, PO Box 2328, Corrales, NM 87048. (800) 894-8439, (505) 899-8054, fax: (505) 899-7977, e-mail: amiles@viewcamera.com. (www.viewcamera.com). Publication devoted to traditional large format photography.

Visual Studies Workshop, 31 Prince St., Rochester, NY, 14607. (585) 442-8676, e-mail: info@vsw.org. (www.vsw.org).

Women's Studio Workshop, PO Box 489, Rosendale, NY 12472. (845) 658-9133, fax: (845) 658-9031, e-mail: info@wsworkshop.org. (www.wsworkshop.org). Facilities for printmaking, letterpress printing, hand papermaking, photography, and ceramics. Fellowships, residencies, and internships offered.

**Fine Art Prints**

Artcraft Digital Print, 443 Park Ave. S., New York, NY 10016. (212) 213-5339, fax: (212) 213-6511. (www.artcraftdigital.com) Giclée prints. Contact: Anthony Ferrezza.

Black Point Editions, 1739 S. Halsted St., ste. 2F, Chicago, IL 60608. (312) 486-3298, e-mail: nbaker@blackpointeditions.com. (www.blackpointeditions.com). Specializing in black-and-white digital quadtone printing. Contact: Nathan Baker.

Brandywine Graphics Workshop, 730 S. Broad St., Philadelphia, PA 19146. (215) 546-3675, fax: (215) 546-2825, e-mail: prints@brandywineworkshop.com. (www.brandywineworkshop.com).

Dieu Donné Papermill, 315 W. 36th St., New York, NY 10018 (212) 226-0573, fax: (212) 226-6088. (www.dieudonne.org).

Digital Arts Studio, 1082-B Huff Rd., Atlanta, GA 30318. (866) 352-9779, (404) 352-9779, fax: (404) 352-9655, e-mail: info@digitalartsstudio.net. (www.digitalartsstudio.net). Giclée printing.

*Editions Report*, Spring Press, 524 Broadway, New York, NY 10012. (212) 226-7430.

*How to Profit from the Art Print Market*, Barney Davey. 2005. Bold Star Communications, PO Box 25386, Scottsdale, AZ 85255. (602) 499-7500, e-mail: barney@barneydavey.com. (www.Artprintissues.com, www.barneydavey.com).

International Fine Print Dealers Association (IFPDA) Print Fair, 250 W. 26th St., ste. 405, New York, NY 10001. (212) 674-6095, fax: (212) 675-6783, e-mail: ifpda@ifpda.org. (www.ifpda.org, www.printfair.com).

International Fine Print Dealers Association (IFPDA), 250 W. 26th St., ste. 405, New York, NY 10001. (212) 674-6095, fax: (212) 674-6783, e-mail: ifpda@ifpda.org. (www.printdealers.com, www.ifpda.org). Produces IFPDA Print Fair. Membership directory available for nominal fee, write: 15 Gramercy Pk. S., ste. 7A, New York, NY 10003.

Lower East Side Printshop, 306 W. 37th St., 6th flr., New York, NY 10018. (212) 673-5390, fax: (212) 979-6493, e-mail: info@printshop.org. (www.printshop.org). Classes, studio rental, editioning, contract printing, and residencies.

*Marketing Plans for Print Artists*, Sue Viders. 1999. Sue Viders, Art Marketing Consultant, 9739 Tallgrass Circle, Lone Tree, CO 80124. (800)999-7013, e-mail: viders@worldnet.att.net. (www.sueviders.com).

Prestige Art, 3909 W. Howard St., Skokie, IL 60076. (847) 679-2555, fax: (847) 679-2559, e-mail: prestige@prestigeart.com. (www.prestigeart.com). Company President Louis Shutz consults with artists on publishing and licensing of their work.

Printmaking Council of NJ, 440 River Rd., Somerville, NJ 08876 (908) 725-2110, fax: (908) 725-2484, e-mail: pcnj@printNJ.org. (www.printNJ.org). Specializes in the fine art of printing with classes, residencies, gallery, etc.

*Printmaking Today*, Cello Press, 99-101 Kingsland Rd., London E2 8AG, U.K. (44) 20-7739-8645, e-mail: mikesims@pt.cellopress.co.uk, annedesmet@pt.cellopress.co.uk. (www.cellopress.co.uk). Quarterly international coverage.

*Printworld Directory: Contemporary Prints and Prices*, edited by Selma Smith. 13th ed., 2010. Printworld International, PO Box 1957, West Chester, PA 19380. (800) 788-9101, (610) 431-6654, fax: (610) 431-6653, e-mail: editor@printworlddirectory.com. (www.printworlddirectory.com). The Complete International Print Price Source Book.

*Producing and Marketing Prints: The Artist's Complete Guide to Publishing and Selling Reproductions*, Sue Viders, 2nd ed. Sue Viders, Art Marketing Consultant, 9739 Tallgrass Cir., Lone Tree, CO 80124. (800)999-7013, e-mail: viders@worldnet.att.net. (www.sueviders.com).

Pyramid Atlantic, 8230 Georgia Ave., Silver Spring, MD 20910. (301) 608-9101, fax: (301) 608-9102, e-mail: info@pyramid-atlantic.org. (www.pyramidatlanticartcenter.org). Classes, workshops, studio rental, and residencies in bookmaking, papermaking, and printmaking.

RPI Graphic Data Solutions, 1950 Radcliff Dr., Cincinnati, OH 45204. (800) 582-1414, (513) 471-4040, fax: (513) 244-5387, e-mail: bachde@rpigraphic.com. (www.rpigraphic.com). Giclée printing, waterless offset printing.

Sarazen Editions, 51 Morningside Dr., Ossining, NY 10562. (914) 945-0101. (www.sarazeneditions.com). Fine-art digital reproduction service.

*The Gordon's Print Price Annual 2010*. LTB Gordonsart, 13201 N. 35th Ave., ste. B-20, Phoenix, AZ 85029. (800) 892-4622, (602) 253-6948, fax: (602) 253-2104, e-mail: office@gordonsart.com. (www.gordonsart.com).

Women's Studio Workshop, PO Box 489, Rosendale, NY 12472. (845) 658-9133, fax: (845) 658-9031, e-mail: info@wsworkshop.org. (www.wsworkshop.org). Facilities for printmaking, letterpress printing, hand papermaking, photography, and ceramics. Fellowships, residencies, and internships offered.

www.artprintissues.com Barney Davey. 2005. Bold Star Communications, PO Box 25386, Scottsdale, AZ 85255. (609) 499-7500, e-mail: barney@barneydavey.com. (www.barneydavey.com, www.artprintissues.com). E-zine with news, articles, and links to related sites.

## Grants/Fellowships

*American Art Directory 2010*, National Register Publishing, 890 Mountain Ave., 3rd flr., New Providence, NJ  07974. Editorial: (800) 473-7020, e-mail: NRPeditorial@marquiswhoswho.com; sales: (800) 473-7020, e-mail: NRPsales@marquiswhoswho.com. (www.americanartdir.com).  Listings of national and regional art organizations; museums; libraries; associations in the US and Canada; art schools with contact data, degree programs, scholarship programs, entrance requirements, and tuition information; museums abroad; schools abroad; state directors and supervisors of art education; state arts councils; art magazines, editors, and critics; scholarships and fellowships; open exhibitions; and traveling exhibition booking agencies. Indexed by subject, personnel, and organization.

Artist Trust, 1835 12th Ave., Seattle, WA  98122. E-mail: info@artisttrust.org. (www.artisttrust.org).

Brandywine Graphics Workshop, 730 S. Broad, Philadelphia, PA  19146. (877) ART.PRINT, (215) 546-3675, fax: (215) 546-2825, e-mail: prints@brandywineworkshop.com. (www.brandywineworkshop.com).  Fellowships for regional and nationwide artists and Philadelphia artists under 35.

Creative Capital Foundation, 65 Bleecker St., 7th flr., New York, NY  10012. (212) 598-9900. (www.creative-capital.org).  Grants and artist services programs.

*Demystifying Grant Seeking: What You REALLY Need to Do to Get Grants.* Larissa Golden Brown and Martin John. 2001. Jossey-Bass, Imprint of John Wiley & Sons, 111 River St., Hoboken, NJ  07030. (800) 762-2974, fax: (800) 597-3299. (www.josseybass.com).

Foundation Directory Online. (800) 424-9836, e-mail: fdonline@foundationcenter.org. (www.fconline.fdncenter.org).  Subscription service to database of thousands of grantmaking organizations.

*Foundation Grants to Individuals*, The Foundation Center, 79 Fifth Ave., New York, NY 10003. (212) 620-4230. (www.foundationcenter.org/newyork).  Also offices in Atlanta 50 Hurt Plaza, ste. 150, Atlanta, GA  30303. (404) 880-0094. (www.foundationcenter.org/atlanta); Cleveland: 1422 Euclid Ave., ste. 1600, Cleveland, OH 44115. (216) 861-1934. (www.foundationcenter.org/cleveland); San Francisco: 312 Sutter St., Ste. 606, San Francisco, CA  94108. (415) 297-0902. (www.foundationcenter.org/sanfrancisco), Washington: 1627 K St., NW, 3rd flr., Washington, DC 20006. (202) 331-1400. (www.foundationcenter.org/washington).  Most comprehensive database on US grantmakers and their grants. In addition to the Foundation's own offices, Cooperating Collections are free information centers in libraries, community foundations, and other nonprofit resource centers that provide a core collection of Foundation Center publications and services in areas useful to grantseekers.

*Grant Writing For Dummies*, Beverly A. Browning. 3rd ed., 2008. For Dummies, John Wiley & Sons, Inc., 111 River St., Hoboken, NJ  07030. (877) 762-2974, fax: (800) 597-3299. (www.dummies.com).

*Grant Writing*, Patrick W. Miller. 3rd ed., 2009. W. Miller and Associates, 9235 Greenwood Ave., Munster, IN 46321. (219) 838-8333, e-mail: patrickwmiller@sbcglobal.net. (www.pwmilleronline.com).

Marie Walsh Sharpe Foundation, 830 N. Tejon St., ste. 120, Colorado Springs, CO 80903. (719) 635-3220, e-mail: sharpeartfdn@quest.net. (www.sharpeartfdn.org). Offers financial assistance and free space for artists.

Michigan State University Main Library, 100 Library, East Lansing, MI 48824. (517) 353-8700. (www.lib.msu.edu/harris23/grants/3arts.htm). Online listing of grant-making organizations provided and regularly updated.

*Money for Artists, A Guide to Grants and Awards in the Visual Arts.* Chicago Review Press. Available on Amazon.com.

*Money to Work II: Funding for Visual Artists*, Edited by Helen M. Brunner and Donald H. Russell with Grant E. Samuelsen. 1992. Available on Amazon.com.

*Storytelling for Grantseekers: The Guide to Creative Nonprofit Fundraising*, Cheryl A. Clarke. 2nd ed., 2009. Jossey-Bass, Imprint of John Wiley & Sons, 111 River St., Hoboken, NJ 07030. (800) 762-2974, fax: (800) 597-3299. (www.josseybass.com).

*The Everything Grant Writing Book: Create the Perfect Proposal to Raise the Funds You Need (Everything Series)*, Judy Tremore and Nancy Burke Smith. 2003. Available on Amazon.com.

*The First-Time Grantwriters Guide to Success*, Cynthia R. Knowles. 2002. Available on Amazon.com.

The Judith Rothschild Foundation, 1110 Park Ave., New York, NY 10128. (212) 831-4114 (www.judithrothschildfdn.org). Mission to encourage interest in deceased artists.

*The Only Grant-Writing Book You'll Ever Need: Top Grant Writers and Grant Givers Share Their Secrets*, Ellen Karsh and Arlen Sue Fox. 2006. Carroll & Graf, Imprint of Avalon Publishing Group, 245 W. 17th St., 11th flr., New York, NY 10011. (800) 788-3123, fax: (646) 375-2571. (www.carrollandgraf.com).

The Pollock-Krasner Foundation, 863 Park Ave., New York, NY 10021. (212) 527-5400, email: grants@pkf.org. (www.pkf.org).

*Winning Grants: Step by Step*, Mim Carlson (The Alliance for Nonprofit Management). 3rd ed., 2008. Jossey-Bass, Imprint of John Wiley & Sons, 111 River St., Hoboken, NJ 07030. (800) 762-2974, fax: (800) 597-3299. (www.josseybass.com).


## Housing/Studio Space/Real Estate

ArtHouse Oakland, 1212 Broadway, ste. 834, Oakland, CA 94612. (415) 552-2183, e-mail: assistant@arthouseca.org. (www.arthouseca.org).

ArtHouse, 1360 Mission St., ste. 200, San Francisco, CA 94103. (415) 552-2183, e-mail: assistant@arthouseca.org. (www.arthouseca.org).

Artist Relocation Program, City Hall, 300 S. 5th St., PO Box 2267, Paducah, KY 42002. (270) 444-8690, e-mail: artinfo@ci.paduca.ky.us. (www.paducaharts.com).

Artist's Assets. Artist Trust, 1835 12th Ave., Seattle, WA 98122. E-mail: info@artisttrust.org. (www.artisttrust.org). Published annually and available on website as PDF or print version.

Artscape, 171 E. Liberty St., ste. 224, Toronto, Ontario, M6K 3P6, Canada. (419) 392-1038, fax: (416) 535-6260, e-mail: info@torontoartscape.on.ca. (www.torontoartscape.on.ca).

Artspace Projects, Inc., 250 Third Ave. N., ste. 500, Minneapolis, MN 55401. (612) 333-9012, e-mail: info@artspaceusa.org. (www. artspaceusa.org).

Artspace, 230 S. 500 West, ste. 235, Salt Lake City, UT 84101. (801) 333-9012, e-mail: jessica@artspaceutah.org. (www.artspaceutah.org).

Artspacefinder, Artistlink with The Artists Foundation. Massachusetts Cultural Council, 10 St. James Ave., 3rd flr., Boston, MA 02116. (716) 727-3668. (www.artistlink.org). Broker of information about artist housing and studio space in Massachusetts and artist advocate.

City of Seattle Office of Housing, PO Box 94725, Seattle, WA 98124. (206) 684-0721, e-mail: seattle.housing@seattle.gov. (www.ci.seattle.wa.us/housing).

Chicago Artists Resource (CAR), Chicago Dept. of Cultural Affairs, Chicago Cultural Center, 78 E. Washington St., Chicago, IL 60602. (312) 744-6630, fax: (312) 744-2089, e-mail: culture@cityofchicago.org. (www.cityofchicago.org). Online resource for Chicago-area artists with listings for housing/studio space (Square Feet Chicago), calls for entries to juried exhibitions, jobs, etc.

*Conversion Frontiers: Military Bases and Other Opportunities for the Arts*, 1996. ArtHouse, 1360 Mission St., ste. 200, San Francisco, CA 94103. (415) 552-2183, e-mail: assistant@arthouseca.org. (www.arthouseca.org).

Elizabeth Foundation for the Arts Studio Center, PO Box 2670, 323 W. 39th St., New York, NY 10108. (212) 695-0535, e-mail: studio@efal.org. (www.efanyc.org).

Ft. Point Arts Community, Inc., 300 Summer St., Boston, MA 02210. (617) 423-4299, e-mail: info@fortpointarts.org. (www.fortpointarts.org).

*Housing the Arts Collective.* 2000. ArtHouse, 1360 Mission St., ste. 200, San Francisco, CA 94103. (415) 552-2183, e-mail: assistant@arthouseca.org. (www.arthouseca.org).

Live/Work Institute, Thomas Dolan Architecture, Embarcadero West, 173 Filbert St., Oakland, CA 94607. (510) 839-7200, fax: (510) 839-7208, e-mail: td.arch@live-work.com. (www.live-work.com). Nonprofit organization advocates, encourages, and assists development of Live/Work and Zero Commute housing.

*Live-Work Forum Handbook*, Jennifer Spangler. 1999. ArtHouse, 1360 Mission St., ste. 200, San Francisco, CA 94103. (415) 552-2183, e-mail: assistant@arthouseca.org. (www. arthouseca.org).

Lowertown Lofts Cooperative (live/work studios), 255 E. Kellogg Blvd., ste. 505, St. Paul, MN 55101. (651) 227-5473. (www.lowertownlofts.org).

Marie Walsh Sharpe Art Foundation, 830 N. Tejon St., ste. 120, Colorado Springs, CO 80903. (719) 635-3220, e-mail: sharpeartfdn@quest.net. (www.sharpeartfdn.org).

Susan B. Anthony Inc., 456 Broome St., ste. 5A, New York, NY 10013. (212) 941-6266, e-mail: sbargg@aol.com. (www.susanbanthonyrealestate.com). New York City real estate. Art Gallery Real Estate Newsletter on line.

*The Art Studio/Loft Manual: For Ambitious Artists and Creators,* Eric Rudd. 2001. Available on Amazon.com.

Women's Studio Ctr., 2125 44th Ave., Long Island City, NY 11101. (718) 361-5649, e-mail: wsc586@aol.com. (www.womenstudiocenter.org).


## Industry (Trade) Publications

*Art Business News,* Summit Business Media, 6000 Lombardo Ctr. Dr., ste. 420, Cleveland, OH 44131. (216) 328-8926, fax: (216) 328-9352, e-mail: info@SBMediaLLC.com. (www.artbusinessnews.com). Trade publication for gallery and interior-design retail markets.

*Art World News,* 143 Rowayton Ave., Norwalk, CT 06853. (203) 854-8566. (www.artworldnews.com). Monthly trade magazine for art and framing industry.

*Bottom Line,* Licensing Industry Merchandising Association, 350 Fifth Ave. New York, NY 10118. (212) 244-1944. (www.licensing.org). Quarterly licensing newsletter.

*Davenport's Art Reference and Price Guide 2009-2010.* LTB Gordonsart, 13201 N. 35th Ave., ste. B-20, Phoenix, AZ 85029. (800) 892-4622, (602) 253-6948, fax: (602) 253-2104, e-mail: office@gordonsart.com. (www.gordonsart.com). Biographical and pricing information for more than 300,000 artists.

*Décor The Art & Framing Business Resource.* (www.decormagazine.com). Monthly trade magazine for art and the framing business.

*Giftware News,* Talcott Publishing, 20 W. Kinzie, ste. 1200, Chicago, IL 60610. (800) 229-1967, (312) 849-2220, fax: (312) 849-2174. (www.giftwarenews.com).

*IDH: Interior Decorator's Handbook,* E.W. Williams Publications, 370 Lexington Ave., ste. 1409, New York, NY 10017. (212) 661-1516, fax: (212) 661-1713. (www.idhonline.com).

*Interior Design Buyers Guide,* Reed Business Information, 360 Park Ave. S., 17th flr., New York, NY 10010. (646) 746-7275, (646) 746-6400, subscriptions: (800) 900-0804, fax: (646) 746-7428, e-mail: IDBG@reedbusiness.com. (www.resourceguide.interiordesign.net). Online free listing for sculpture, mixed media, mobiles, paintings and prints, photography, etc.

*The Licensing Book* (monthly) and *The Licensing Report* (weekly), Adventure Publishing Group, 286 5th Ave., 3rd flr., New York, NY 10001. (212) 575-4510, fax: (212) 575-4521. (www.licensingbook.com, www.adventurepublishinggroup.com, www.adventurepub.com). Updates on new products, agreements, and properties with special section on art licensing.

## Interior Designers/Architects/Landscape Architects

American Architecture.(www.americanarchitecture.com) Online listing of architects, consulting engineers, developers, realtors, contractors, interior designers, landscape architects, specifications writers, trade consultants, and authorities in building materials with links to professional organizations and governmental bodies.

American Institute of Architects (AIA), 1735 New York Ave., NW, Washington, DC 20006. (202) 626-7300. (www.aia.org). Links to local chapters.

American Public Gardens Association (formerly American Association of Botanical Gardens & Arboreta), 100 West 10th St., ste. 614, Wilmington, DE 19801, (302) 655-7100, fax (302) 655-8100. (www.publicgardens.org).

American Society of Interior Designers (ASID), 608 Massachusetts Ave. NE, Washington, DC 20002. (202) 546-3480, e-mail: asid@asid.org. (www.asid.org).

American Society of Landscape Architects (ASLA), 636 Eye St. NW, Washington, DC 20001. (888) 999-ASLA, (202) 898-2444. (www.asla.org). Publishes *Landscape Architecture* magazine; on-line resources include "Firm Finder" (directory of landscape architects), *Sweets Landscape Architecture Directory* (official product guide of ASLA), LATIS (Landscape Architects Technical Information Series), etc.

ArchitectsUSA, 9182 Hemlock Ln., Bridgman, MI 49106. Fax: (312) 416-7981, e-mail: ArchUSAemail-help@yahoo.com. (www.architectsusa.com). Directory of more than 20,000 architectural firms compiled from Yellow Pages listings and architects.

*Architectural Digest*, 6300 Wilshire Blvd., Los Angeles, CA 90048. (323) 965-3700, fax (323) 965-4975. (www.architecturaldigest.com). "Reader's Directory" listing of designers, architects, and galleries featured in each issue.

Competitions Hotline. PO Box 20445, Louisville, KY 40250. (502) 451-3623, e-mail: hotline@competitions.org. (www.competitions.org).

*Florida Design*, The Magazine for Fine Interior Design & Furnishings, 621 NW 53rd St., Boca Raton, FL 33487. (561) 997-1660. (www.floridadesign.com). Publishes annual "Focus on Art" issue.

General Services Administration (GSA), Art In Architecture Program, 1800 F St., ste. 3300 PMB, Washington, DC 20405. Office of chief architect: (202) 501-1888. (www.gsa.gov). One half of 1 percent of estimated construction cost of federal buildings reserved for public art. Maintains large registry of artists interested in federal commissions.

*IDH: Interior Decorator's Handbook*, E.W. Williams Publications, 370 Lexington Ave., ste. 1409, New York, NY 10017. (212) 661-1516, fax: (212) 661-1713. (www.idhonline.com).

Info USA. Business Lists. e-mail: lists@infousa.com. (www.infousa.com).

International Interior Design Association (IIDA), 341 Merchandise Mart, Chicago, IL 60654. (888) 799-IIDA, (312) 467-1950, e-mail: iidahq@iida.org. (www.iida.org).

*Interior Design Buyers Guide*, Reed Business Information, 360 Park Ave. S., 17th flr., New York, NY 10010. (646) 746-7275, (646) 746-6400, subscriptions: (800) 900-0804, fax: (646) 746-7428, e-mail: IDBG@reedbusiness.com. (www.resourceguide.interiordesign.net). Online free listing for sculpture, mixed media, mobiles, paintings and prints, photography, etc.

The Society of American Registered Architects (SARA), 14 E. 38th St., 11th flr., New York, NY 10016. E-mail: president@sara-national.org. (www.sara-national.org).

*The Sourcebook of Architectural & Interior Art*. Published annually in fall. The Guild, 931 E. Main St., ste. 9, Madison, WI 53703. (877) 223-4600, artists: (877) 616-2002, international: (608) 256-1990, fax: (608) 257-2690, e-mail: sourcebookinfo@guild.com. (www.guild.com). Sourcebook for site-specific architectural and interior artworks for public, corporate, liturgical, and hospitality spaces, distributed gratis to 10,000 architects, interior designers, public art specialists, landscape architects, liturgical consultants, art consultants, and other professionals. Artists pay for page in print ed. and also appear on the website in the Custom Design Ctr.

*The Sourcebook of Residential Art*. Published annually in spring. The Guild, 931 E. Main St., ste. 9, Madison, WI 53703. (877) 223-4600, artists: (877) 616-2002, International: (608) 256-1990, fax: (608) 257-2690, e-mail: sourcebookinfo@guild.com. (www.guild.com). Source book for custom-designed, limited ed., and one-of-a-kind works for the home distributed gratis to 7,000 art consultants, high-end consumers, residential design firms, architectural design firms, and galleries. Artists pay for page in print ed. and also appear on the website in the Custom Design Ctr.

## Internet Resources

*Art Information and the Internet*, Lois Swan Jones. 1998. Greenwood Publishing Group, 88 Post Rd. W., Westport, CT 06881. (213) 226-3571.

Design Latitudes (formerly David Curry Design), 400 Central Park W., ste. 7Y, New York, NY 10025. (212) 222-6630. (www.designlatitudes.com). Website designer.

*Marketing and Buying Fine Art Online: A Guide for Artists and Collectors*, Marques Vickers. 2005. Available on Amazon.com.

*Sell Your Crafts Online*, James Dillehay. 2005. Warm Snow Publishers, PO Box 75, Torreon, NM 87061. (505) 384-1195, e-mail: jamesd@craftmarketer.com. (www.craftmarketer.com).

www.absolutearts.com. World Wide Arts Resources, absolutearts.com, 3678 Loudon St., Granville, OH 43023. (740) 587-3326, fax: (740) 587-4103, e-mail: help@wwar.com and help@absolutearts.com. Contemporary art news and online gallery.

www.americanarchitecture.com. American Architecture. Online listing of architects, consulting engineers, developers, realtors, contractors, interior designers, landscape architects, specifications writers, trade consultants, and authorities in building materials with links to professional organizations and governmental bodies.

www.amn.org. Official website of the world's leading art museums (membership by invitation only) providing information about their collections, exhibitions, and news.

www.architectsusa.com. ArchitectsUSA, 9182 Hemlock Ln., Bridgman, MI 49106. fax: (312) 416-7981, e-mail: ArchUSAemail-help@yahoo.com. Directory of more than 20,000 architectural firms compiled from Yellow Pages listings and architects.

www.artbusinessacademy.com. Links to art schools, artist careers, fine art, frames, oil painting, art supplies, art galleries, and prints.

www.artcat.com. New York-area museum and gallery openings, "focusing on underknown galleries and artists at the whim of Editors Barry Hoggard and James Wagner and assistant editor Paddy Johnson."

www.artcircuits.com, 1172 S. Dixie Hwy., ste. 541, Coral Gables, FL 33146. (305) 661-0511, fax: (305) 669-1455. Art-related information for Greater Miami.

www.artdeadline.com. E-mail: support @artdeadline.com. "The art world's most comprehensive resource for income and exhibition opportunities."

www.art-exchange.com. (800) 647-6336, (501) 624-1044, fax: (501) 624-2859, e-mail: artistsupport@art-exchange.com. Business-to-business exchange to serve the needs of the supply side of the fine art market (artists, publishers, and other sellers) and the buy side (designers and dealers).

www.artfairsourcebook.com. Greg Lawler's Art Fair SourceBook, 2003 NE 11th Ave., Portland, OR 97212. (800) 358-2045, fax: (503) 331-0876. Guide to national juried art and craft shows. Published in fall (main ed.) and summer (preview).

www.artguidenw.com. Art Guide Northwest, 13205 Ninth Ave. NW, Seattle, WA 98177. (206) 367-6831, fax: (206) 365-0476, e-mail: btipton@artguidenw.com. Guide to galleries, museums, and antiques in the Pacific Northwest.

www.artheals.org. The Art and Healing Network.

www.artinfo.com. LTB Holding, LTB USA Inc., 111 Eighth Ave., ste. 302, New York, NY 10011. (212) 447-9555. Daily news about international art world with weekly e-mail newsletter.

www.artiq.com. Art Resources International Ltd., Bonart & Artique Fine Art Publishers, Fields Ln., Brewster, NY 10509. (845) 277-8888, fax: (845) 277-8602, e-mail: sales@fineartpublishers.com. Online gallery for unlimited reproductions of original art. Accepting artist's submissions. Contact: Robin Bonnist.

www.artistbiography.com. Artprice.com, Domaine de la Source BP69, F-69270 St. Romain au Mont D'or, France. (866) 732-0826, e-mail: info@artistbiography.com. Database of contemporary artist's biographies. Free listing.

www.artisthelpnetwork.com. Extensive lists of resources in many categories.

www.artistsnetwork.com. F & W Publications, 4700 E. Galbraith Rd., Cincinnati, OH 45236. (800) 258-0929, (513) 531-2690. (www.fwpublications.com). Interactive artists' community with forums for subjects such as "Tech Talk," "Creativity Corner," "Events & Competitions," etc., and by gallery or medium.

www.ArtistsRegister.com. WESTAF (Western States Arts Federation), 1743 Wazee St., ste. 300, Denver, CO 80202. (303) 629-1166. Nonprofit regional arts service organization dedicated to the arts in the West.

www.artmarketing.com. ArtNetwork, PO Box 1360, Nevada City, CA 95959. (800) 383-0677, (530) 470-0862, e-mail: info@artmarketing.com. Art world hotline – semi-monthly contacts to advance your career. Extensive mailing lists.

www.artnet.com. artnet Worldwide, 61 Broadway, 23rd flr., New York, NY 10006. (800) 4-ARTNET, (212) 497-9700, fax: (212) 497-9707. Information about artists, galleries, auctions, price database, market trends, and events.

www.artnexus.com. ArtNexus, 12955 Biscayne Blvd., ste. 410, Miami, FL 33181. (305) 891-7270, fax: (305) 891-6408, e-mail: info@artnexus.com. Focuses on Latin American art.

www.artnowonline.com. Artnow International, 1550 Bricknell Ave., ste. 205A, Miami, FL 33129. E-mail: themag@artnowonline.com. International news about galleries, artists, and events.

www.artprice.com. Domaine de la Source BP69, F-69270 St. Romain au Mont D'or, France. (866) 732-0826, e-mail: info@artprice.com. 3.7 million auction records and information on 306,000 artists from 4th century to present.

www.artprintissues.com. Barney Davey, Bold Star Communications, PO Box 25386, Scottsdale, AZ 85255. (609) 499-7500, e-mail: barney@barneydavey.com. (www.barneydavey.com, www.artprintissues.com). E-zine with news, articles, and links to related sites.

www.artsmarketing.org. ArtsMarketing.org. (212) 223-2787, e-mail: info@artsmarketing.org.

www.ArtsOpportunities.org. Southern Arts Federation, 1800 Peachtree St., NW, ste. 808, Atlanta, GA 30309. (404) 874-7244, fax: (404) 873-2148.

www.artspan.com. 26 Bridge St., Lambertville, NJ 08530. (866) ARTSPAN, (609) 397-0888. On-line gallery and assistance for setting up Websites.

www.artyear.net. International exhibition guide. Membership Website.

www.asci.org. Art and Science Collaborations, Inc.

www.asianartnow.com. Pacific Bridge Contemporary Southeast Asian Art, 4136 NW 24th Ave., Portland, OR 97211. Online gallery.

www.carollmichels.com. Caroll Michels, Career Advisory Service for Emerging and Established Artists, 1724 Burgos Dr., Sarasota, FL 34238. (941) 927-5277, fax: (941) 927-5278, e-mail: carollmich@aol.com. (www.carollmichels.com). Links to sites for art marketing and art business.

www.chicagoartistsresource.org. Chicago Dept. of Cultural Affairs, Chicago Cultural Center, 78 E. Washington St., Chicago, IL 60602. (312) 744-6630, fax: (312) 744-2089, e-mail: culture@cityofchicago.org. (www.cityofchicago.org). Online resource for Chicago-area artists with listings for housing/studio space (Square Feet Chicago), calls for entries to juried exhibitions, jobs, etc. (312) 742-8811.

www.COE90.com. PO Box 13, Cropseyville, NY 12052. (888) 213-8588, (518) 618-0812, e-mail: customerservice@coe90.com. (www.coe90.com). Glass art supplies.

www.digitalpaintingforum.com Paint Outside the Frame Marilyn Sholin's Digital Painting Forum for Photographers and Artists. Online membership community for art professionals to discuss their art, sales, marketing, business, and promotional techniques.

www.egallery.com. The Electric Art Gallery, The Electric Company, 557 Osprey Point Rd., Crownsville, MD 21032. (410) 923-2446. No charge to artists for exhibiting on a consignment basis.

www.eppraisals.com. WhatsItWorthToYou.com, 40 Sunset Blvd., Perth ON K7H 2Y4, Canada. (888) 205-8550, (613) 264-9032, fax: (720) 294-8179. On-line appraisals.

www.museumsusa.org. The Humanities Exchange, PO Box 1608, Largo, FL 33779. (514) 935-1228, fax: (514) 935-1299. Searchable database of over 1,300 traveling exhibitions. Fee to list.

www.fconline.fdncenter.org. Foundation Directory Online. (800) 424-9836, e-mail: fdonline@foundationcenter.org. Subscription service with database of thousands of grantmaking organizations.

www.fine-art.com. d'Art, Internet for the Fine Arts, Inc., 27711 Brayden Ct., Houston, TX 77386. (866) Fine-Art. Website with listing service, web directory, and artist research forums sections.

www.fwdodgereports. Dodge Reports, McGraw Hill, 1221 Ave. of the Americas, New York, NY 10020. (212) 512-4100. Online resource for construction projects nationwide.

www.GlassArtists.org. Glass-art photo gallery and community, part of BigReef Community Network, formerly known as The Online Photo Sharing Network.

www.gordonsart.com. Auction sales results with more than 155,000 listings by almost 40,000 artists.

www.guild.com. The Guild, 931 E. Main St., ste. 9, Madison, WI 53703. (877) 223-4600, artists: (608) 616-2002, international: (608) 257-2590, fax: (608) 257-2690, e-mail: art-info@guild.com. Source book and website for art glass, objects and accents, art for the wall, furniture and lighting, jewelry, and accessories.

www.humanities-exchange.org. The Humanities Exchange, PO Box 1608, Largo, FL 33779. (514) 935-1228, fax: (514) 935-1299, e-mail: corporate.directory@earthlink.net. News and current events from the corporate art world, compiled by the editors of the *International Directory of Corporate Art* and International Art Alliance.

www.museumnetwork.com. Information about museums and other cultural institutions internationally, including virtual tours, e-commerce with museum shops, etc. Committed to providing information, assistance, and online infrastructure to the professional museum community.

www.nyartsmagazine.com. *NY Arts Magazine*, 473 Broadway, 7th flr., New York, NY 10013. (212) 274-8993, fax: (212) 226-3400, e-mail: info@nyartsmagazine.com. Links to affiliate sites: NY Arts Beijing Space, Art Fairs International, Broadway Gallery, World Art Media, e-World Art Media, Art Erotica Review, and Hackers International.

www.phillygalleryguide.com. *Philly Gallery Guide.* Listing of area art galleries and exhibitions.

www.photographyart.com Bruce Burgin, 107 Myers Ave., Beckley, WV 25801.
(304) 252-4060, (304) 575-6491, e-mail: bruceburgin@photographyart.com.
Online gallery for photographers and galleries.

www.portraitartist.com. *The Portrait Artist: A Stroke of Genius*, listing of portrait painters and sculptors.

www.resourceguide.interiordesign.net. *Interior Design Buyers Guide*, Reed Business Information, 360 Park Ave. S., 17th flr., New York, NY 10010. (646) 746-7275, (646) 746-6400, subscriptions: (800) 900-0804, fax: (646) 746-7428, e-mail: IDBG@reedbusiness.com.

www.saatchi-gallery.co/uk. Interactive forum for contemporary art with information about art fairs, grants, museum and gallery exhibitions, etc. Bills itself as "The World's Interactive Art Gallery."

www.salestipsforartists, www.talkshoe.com. Podcasts about how to promote and sell prints. Topics include "Practical Promotion – Give A Little to Get A Lot" and "The Art Biz – Who Gets How Much And Why?" by Dick Harrison, artist advisor and retired art print representative.

www.southarts.org. Southern Visual Arts Network (SEVAN), Southern Arts Federation, 1800 Peachtree St. NW, ste. 808, Atlanta, GA 30309. (404) 874-7244, fax: (404) 873-2148. Listserv to connect members of the Southeast's visual arts community; visit SEVAN Yahoo Group for more information.

www.springboardforthearts.org. Online resource for Minnesota artists with listings for jobs, real estate, studio insurance, and other artist concerns.

www.thenewyorkartworld.com. E-zine with news, reviews, exhibitions, commentary, openings, directory, maps, and archive sections.

www.three.org/openart. The Open Art Network. Devises and promotes standards that encourage an open architecture for the Internet and digital media.

www.urbanartnetwork.com. Urban Art Network, Portland, OR. No office location. Dedicated to the empowerment of independent artists in the Portland, OR, area. Sponsors Street Gallery in the Pearl District on First Thursday.

www.vlany.org. Volunteer Lawyers for the Arts (VLA), The Paley Bldg., 1 E. 53rd St., 6th flr., New York, NY 10022. (212) 319-ARTS, ext. 1, fax: (212) 752-6575. Website Resources has information on topics such as intellectual property, copyright, contracts, etc.

www.voicesandvenues.com. South Florida Culture Consortium comprised of Broward County Cultural Division, 100 S. Andrew Ave., Ft. Lauderdale, FL 33301. (954) 357-7457, fax: (954) 357-5769, e-mail: culturaldiv@broward.org. (www.broward.org/arts); Miami-Dade County Dept. of Cultural Affairs, 111 NW First St., ste. 625, Miami, FL 33128. (305) 375-6434, fax: (305) 375-3068, e-mail: culture@miamidade.gov. (www.miamidadearts.org); Arts Council of Stuart and Martin County, 80 E. Ocean Blvd., Stuart, FL 34994. (772) 287-6676, fax: (722) 288-5301, e-mail: mcca@artinarts.org. (www.martinarts.org); Florida Keys Council of the Arts, 1100 Simonton St., Key West, FL 33040. (305) 295-4369, fax: (305) 295-4372, e-mail: info@keysarts.com. (www.keysarts.com). Palm Beach County Cultural Council, 1555 Palm Beach Lakes Blvd., ste. 300, West Palm Beach, FL 33401. (561) 471-2901, fax: (561) 687-9484, e-mail: marketinginfo@pbcc.org. (www.palmbeachculture.com).

www.Washingtonart.com. Broad and in-depth coverage of Washington-area art world. E-mail: kkeler@earthlink.net.

www.washingtonart.com/beltway/resid1.html. On-line listing of colonies and retreats, organized by region.

www.Washingtonart.net. Broad and in-depth coverage of Washington-area art world.

www.WebRing.com. Online network of personal and business communities spanning many categories, including art.

www.wordpress.com. Web host for bloggers.

www.WorldArtGlass.com. Guide to art glass worldwide with more than 1,000 links to art-glass-related sites.

www.worldpress.org/culture.htm. Daily news about visual arts, books, film, music, and film.

www.wwar.com and www.absolutearts.com World Wide Arts Resources, 3678 Loudon St., Granville, OH 43023. (740) 587-3326, fax: (740) 587-4103, e-mail: help@wwar.com, help@absolutearts.com. Contemporary art news. Online gallery.

www.zpub.com/public. Public art on the Internet.


## Legal Resources

*Art Law Handbook: 2003 Cumulative Supplement*, Roy S. Kaufman. 2004. Aspen Publishers, 76 Ninth Ave., 7th flr., New York, NY 10011. (800) 638-8437, (212) 771-0600, fax: (212) 771-0885. (aspenpublishers.com).

*Art Law: The Guide for Collectors, Investors, Dealers, and Artists*, Ralph E. Lerner and Judith Bresler. 2005. Available on Amazon.com.

*Art, the Art Community, and the Law: A Legal and Business Guide for Artists, Collectors, Gallery Owners, and Curators.* 1994. Self-Counsel Press, 1704 N. State St., Bellingham, WA 98225. (360) 676-4530, (877) 877-6490, fax: 360-676-4549. (www.self-counsel.com).

www.artisthelpnetwork.com. Website for fine artists organized into seven general categories: Career; Exhibitions, Commissions, and Sales; Money; Presentation Tools; Legal; Creature Comforts; and other Resources. Produced by Caroll Michels, Career Advisory Service for Emerging and Established Artists, 1724 Burgos Dr., Sarasota, FL 34238. (941) 927-5277, fax: (941) 927-5278, e-mail: carollmich@aol.com. (www.carollmichels.com).

*Business and Legal Forms for Fine Artists,* Tad Crawford. 3rd ed., 2005 Allworth Press, 10 E. 23rd St., New York, NY 10010. (800) 491-2808. (www.allworth.com).

*DuBoff's Art Law in a Nutshell,* Leonard D. DuBoff. 4th ed., 2006. Thomson West, 610 Opperman Dr., Eagan, MN 55123. (800) 344-5008, (651) 687-4919. (www.west.thomson.com).

*Law Ethics and the Visual Arts,* John Henry Merryman, Albert Edward Elsen, and Stephen K. Urice. 2007. Aspen Law & Business, 76 Ninth Ave., 7th flr., New York, NY 10011. (800) 638-8437, (212) 771-0600, fax: (212) 771-0885. (aspenpublishers.com).

*Legal Guide for the Visual Artist,* Tad Crawford. 4th ed., 1999. Allworth Press, 10 E. 23rd St., New York, NY 10010. (800) 491-2808. (www.allworth.com).

*The Artist-Gallery Partnership: A Practical Guide to Consigning Art,* Tad Crawford and Susan Mellon. 2nd ed., 1998. Allworth Press, 10 E. 23rd St., New York, NY 10010. (800) 491-2808. (www.allworth.com).

*The Artist's Tax Workbook,* Americans for the Arts, 1000 Vermont Ave. NW, 6th flr., Washington, DC 20005 (202) 371-2830, fax: (202) 371-0424; One E. 53rd St., 2nd flr., New York, NY 10022. (212) 223-2787, fax: (212) 980-4857. (www.americansforthearts.org).

*The Copyright Guide: A Friendly Handbook to Protecting and Profiting from Copyrights,* Lee Wilson. 3rd ed., 2003. Allworth Press, 10 E. 23rd St., New York, NY 10010. (800) 491-2808. (www.allworth.com).

*The Law (in Plain English) for Galleries,* Leonard Duboff. 2nd edition, 1999. Allworth Press, 10 E. 23rd St., New York, NY 10010. (800) 491-2808. (www.allworth.com).

Volunteer Lawyers for the Arts (VLA), The Paley Bldg., 1 E. 53rd St., 6th flr., New York, NY 10022. (212) 319-ARTS, ext. 1, fax: (212) 752-6575. (www.vlany.org). Website "Resources" has information on topics such as intellectual property, copyright, contracts, etc.


**Mailing Lists/Marketing**

*10 Factors for Creating Marketable Artwork,* edited by Sue Viders. Nd. The National Network for Artist Placement (NNAP), 935 West Ave. 37, Los Angeles, CA 90065. (800) 354-5348, (323) 222-4035, e-mail: NNAPnow@aol.com. (www.artistsplacement.com).

*10 Steps to Marketing Artwork,* Sue Viders. 3rd ed. The National Network for Artist Placement (NNAP), 935 West Ave. 37, Los Angeles, CA 90065. (800) 354-5348, (323) 222-4035, e-mail: NNAPnow@aol.com. (www.artistsplacement.com).

*Art Sales Index*, LTB Gordonsart, 13201 N. 35th Ave., ste. B-20, Phoenix, AZ 85029.
(800) 892-4622, (602) 253-6948, fax: (602) 253-2104, e-mail: office@gordonsart.com.
(www.gordonsart.com). Auction sales results from the previous year with more than 155,000
listings by almost 40,000 artists.

*2010 Artists & Graphic Designers Market*, edited by Mary Cox and Michael Schweer.
Writer's Digest Books, F & W Publications, 4700 E. Galbraith Rd., Cincinnati, OH 45236.
(513) 531-2690. (www.WritersMarket.com, www.fwpublications.com).

*2010 Photographer's Market*, 33rd annual ed. Writer's Digest, F & W Publications,
4700 E. Galbraith Rd., Cincinnati, OH 45236. (800) 258-0929, (513) 531-2690,
e-mail: photomarket@fwpubs.com.

AAMG (Association of Academic Museums & Galleries), Philip and Muriel Berman Museum
of Art at Ursinus College, 601 E. Main St., Collegeville, PA 19426. (www.aamg-us.org).
400 member organization to promote welfare of museums and galleries associated with
institutions of higher education and welfare of their staffs. General research in categorical areas.

ADBASE, 298 Markham St., ste. 5, Toronto, ON M6J 2G6, Canada. (877) 500-0057,
(416) 960-4240, fax: (416) 960-4260, e-mail: sales@adbase.com, support@adbase.com.
(www.adbase.com). Online mailing lists of "creative service buyers."

*An Artist's Guide – Making It in New York City*, Daniel Grant. 2001. Allworth Press,
10 E. 23rd St., New York, NY 10010. (800) 491-2808. (www.allworth.com).

*Art Calendar*, 1500 Park Ctr. Dr., Orlando, FL 32835. (407) 563-7000, fax: (407) 563-7099.
(www.ArtCalendar.com). Business magazine for the visual arts. Connects artists with income
and exhibition possibilities. Mailing lists available for purchase.

*Art Marketing 101: A Handbook for the Fine Artist*, Constance Smith. North Light Books,
F & W Publications, 4700 E. Galbraith Rd., Cincinnati, OH 45236. (513) 531-2690.
(www.fwpublications.com). Also available through Art Network, PO Box 1360, Nevada City,
CA 95959. (530) 470-0862 or (800) 383-0677, e-mail: info@art .com.
(www.artmarketing.com).

*Art Marketing Handbook*, edited by Calvin J. Goodman and Florence J. Goodman.
Management Consultant in the Arts, Gee Tee Bee, 11901 Sunset Blvd., ste. 102, Los Angeles,
CA 90049. (310) 476-2622.

Art Network Press, PO Box 1360, Nevada City, CA 95959. (800) 383-0677, (530) 470-0862,
e-mail: info@artmarketing.com. (www.artmarketing.com). Artworld hotline – semi-monthly
contacts for career advancement. Resource for books, mailing lists (corporate art consultants,
reps, consultants, dealers, brokers, corporations collecting art, interior designers), art and
travel, marketing software, living artists, and an online gallery.

Artprice Annual & Falk's Art Price Index 2010 (CD-ROM). Artprice.com,
Domaine de la Source BP69, F-69270 St. Romain au Mont D'or, France. (866) 732-0826,
e-mail: info@artprice.com. (www.artprice.com).

*ArtSource Quarterly*, ArtNetwork Press, PO Box 1360, Nevada City, CA 95959.
(800) 383-0677. (www.artmarketing.com). A guide to marketing art.

Caroll Michels, Career Advisory Service for Emerging and Established Artists, 1724
Burgos Drive, Sarasota, FL 34238. (941) 927-5277, fax: (941) 927-5278,
e-mail: carollmich@aol.com. (www.carollmichels.com). Annotated mailing lists available in
printout (formatted for reproduction on labels), CD-Rom (PC and Mac) formats. Available
lisrs include Curators; Art Consultants; Curators & Art Consultants; Critics; Interior Design
& Architecture Press Contacts; International, National, and Regional Press Contacts; and New
York Area Press Contacts, formatted for reproduction on labels. *The Newsletter*, published nine
times/year with names, addresses of art consultants, resources, news, and opportunities.

Cornerstone Services, Inc., 31 South Ohioville Road, New Paltz, NY 12561. (845) 255-5722,
(www.crst.net). Mailing services, data management, and graphic design.

*Creating a Successful Craft Business*, Rogene Robbins and Robert Robbins. 2003. Allworth
Press, 10 E. 23rd St., New York, NY 10010. (800) 491-2808. (www.allworth.com).

eNR Grassroots PR Program, eNR Services, 20 Glover Ave., 2nd flr., Norwalk, CT 06850.
(888) 607-9655, (203) 846-2811, fax: (203) 846-2824, e-mail: mediaq@enr-corp.com.
(www.enr-corp.com. Local news for local media.

*Fine Art Publicity: The Complete Guide for Galleries and Artists*, Susan Abbott. 2nd ed., 2005.
Allworth Press, 10 E. 23rd St., New York, NY 10010. (800) 491-2808. (www.allworth.com).

*How to Find Art Buyers*, Nina Pratt. 1994. Succotash Press. Used copies on Amazon.com.

*How to Get Hung: A Practical Guide for Emerging Artists*, Molly Barnes. 1994. Tuttle
Publishing, member of Periplus Publishing Group, Airport Business Pk., 364 Innovation Dr.,
North Clarendon, VT 05759. (800) 526-2778, (802) 773-8930, fax: (800) 329-8885,
(802) 773-6993, e-mail: info@tuttlepublishing.com. (www.tuttlepublishing.com).

*How to Get Started Selling Your Art*, Carole Katchen. 1996. North Light Books,
F & W Publications, 4700 E. Galbraith Rd., Cincinnati, OH 45236. (800) 258-0929,
(513) 531-2690. (www.fwpublications.com). Surefire methods and expert advice that
can lead to art sales.

*How to Profit from the Art Print Market: Practical Advice for Visual Artists*, Barney Davey. 2005.
Bold Star Communications, PO Box 25386, Scottsdale, AZ 85255. (609) 499-7500,
e-mail: barney@barneydavey.com. (www.barneydavey.com, www.artprintissues.com).

*How to Sell Art, A Guide for Galleries, Dealers, Consultants and Artists' Agents*, Nina Pratt. 1992.
Succotash Press. A guide for galleries, dealers, consultants, and artists' agents. Useful for artists
unaware of the inner workings of the art world. Used copies on Amazon.com.

*How to Start and Succeed as an Artist*, Daniel Grant, Allworth Press, 10 E. 23rd St.,
New York, NY 10010. (800) 491-2808. (www.allworth.com).

*How to Survive and Prosper as an Artist: Selling Yourself Without Selling Your Soul*,
Caroll Michels. 6th ed., 2009. Henry Holt and Company, 175 Fifth Ave., New York,
NY 10010. (646) 307-5095, fax: (212) 633-0748. (www.hholt.com).

Infocus Marketing, 4245 Sigler Rd., Warrenton, VA 20187. (800) 708-LIST, fax: (866) 708-LIST, e-mail: listinfo@infocusnet.com. (www.infocuslists.com). Association list source.

*International Auction House Directory*, LTB Gordonsart, 13201 N. 35th Ave., ste. B-20, Phoenix, AZ 85029. (800) 892-4622, (602) 253-6948, fax: (602) 253-2104, e-mail: office@gordonsart.com. (www.gordonsart.com).

*Internet 101 for the Fine Artist with a Special Guide to Selling Art on eBay*, Constance Smith. 2004. ArtNetwork Press, PO Box 1360, Nevada City, CA 95959. (800) 383-0677. (www.artmarketing.com).

*Magazine and Newsletter Directory, Vol. 2, Bowker's News Media Directory 2009*. R.R. Bowker, 63 Central Ave., New Providence, NJ 07974. (888) 269-5372, (908) 285-1090. (www.bowker.com).

Mailing and Resource Lists/Career Related Books for Fine Artists, available through Caroll Michels, 1724 Burgos Drive, Sarasota, FL 34238. (941) 927-5277, fax: (941) 927-5278, e-mail: carollmich@aol.com. (www.carollmichels.com).

Mailing List Labels Packages, P O Box 1233, Weston, CT 06883. (203) 451-1592, e-mail: r.m.cellini@worldnet.att.net. Percent for Art and Art in Public Places Programs lists.

*Making a Living as an Artist*, Editors of the *Art Calendar Magazine*. 1998. The Lyons Press, Imprint of Globe Pequot Press, 246 Goose Ln., PO Box 480, Guilford, CT 06437. (203) 458-4500, customer service: (888) 249-7586, customer service fax: (800) 820-2329, e-mail: info@globepequot.com. (www.globepequot.com).

*Marketing and Buying Fine Art Online: A Guide for Artists and Collectors*, Marques Vickers. 2005. Allworth Press, 10 E. 23rd St., New York, NY 10010. (800) 491-2808. (www.allworth.com).

*Marketing Plans for Print Artists*, Sue Viders. 1999. Sue Viders, Art Marketing Consultant, 9739 Tallgrass Circle, Lone Tree, CO 80124. (800) 999-7013, e-mail: viders@worldnet.att.net. (www.sueviders.com).

MediaQ, eNR Services, 20 Glover Ave., 2nd flr., Norwalk, CT 06850. Sales: (888) 607-9101 (sales), (203) 846-2811, fax: (203) 846-2824, e-mail: info@enr-corp.com. (www.enr-corp.com). News research application giving users access to print, broadcast, and on-line content.

MediaSource Monitoring, Cision US, (Parent company of Bacon's Information), 332 S. Michigan Ave., Chicago, IL 60604. (866) 639-5087. (www.cision.com). Provides 24/7 online access to newspaper, magazine, broadcast, Internet, and blog coverage in one location.

*Newspaper Directory, Vol. 1, Bowker's News Media Directory 2009*. 2006. R.R. Bowker, 63 Central Ave., New Providence, NJ 07974. (888) 269-5372, (908) 285-1090. (www.bowker.com).

NewsWire One, eNR Services, 20 Glover Ave., 2nd flr., Norwalk, CT 06850. (800) 883-0827, e-mail: helpdesk@enr-corp.com. (www.enewsrelease.com). Targeted media list creation and press release distribution.

*Producing and Marketing Prints: The Artist's Complete Guide to Publishing and Selling Reproductions*, Sue Viders. 2nd ed., Sue Viders, Art Marketing Consultant, 9739 Tallgrass Cir., Lone Tree, CO 80124. (800) 999-7013, e-mail: viders@worldnet.att.net. (www.sueviders.com).

*Promotion for Pennies: 10 Inexpensive Ways to Self-Promote Your Artwork*, Sue Viders and
L. Diane Johnson. The National Network for Artist Placement (NNAP), 935 West Ave. 37,
Los Angeles, CA  90065. (800) 354-5348, (323) 222-4035, e-mail: NNAPnow@aol.com.
(www.artistsplacement.com).

*Self-Promotion for the Creative Person: Get the Word Out About Who You Are and What You Do*,
Lee Silber. 2001. Three Rivers Press, Imprint of Crown Publishing Group, 1745 Broadway,
New York, NY  10010. (212) 782-9000. (www.randomhouse.com).

*Selling Art 101: The Art of Creative Selling*. Robert Regis Dvorak. 2004. ArtNetwork Press,
PO Box 1360, Nevada City, CA  95959. (800) 383-0677. (www.artmarketing.com).

*Selling Art with a Higher Mind*, Barbara G. Scott. 1990. ICHOR Business Books,
Imprint of Purdue University Press, PO 388, 30 Amberwood, Oh  44805. (800) 247-6553,
fax: (419) 281-6883, e-mail: order@bookmasters.com. (www.thepress.purdue.edu,
www.bookmasters.com).

*Selling Your Crafts*, Susan Sager. Rev. ed., 2003. Allworth Press, 10 E. 23rd St., New York,
NY  10010. (800) 491-2808. (www.allworth.com).

Southern Arts Federation, 1800 Peachtree St., NW, ste. 808, Atlanta, GA  30309.
(404) 874-7244, fax: (404) 873-2148. (www.southarts.org).  Organization in partnership with
state arts agencies including Alabama, Florida, Georgia, Kentucky, Louisiana, Mississippi,
North Carolina, and Tennessee. Customized mailing lists can be generated from its database.
Southern Visual Arts Network (SEVAN), a listserv to connect members of the Southeast's
visual arts community; visit SEVAN Yahoo Group for more information.
ArtsOpportunities.org, on-line classifieds for arts community, including submission calls.

*Successful Fine Art Marketing*, Marcia Layton. 1993. Career Press, PO Box 687, 3 Tice Rd.,
Franklin Lakes, NJ  07417. (800) 227-3371, (201) 848-0310. (www.careerpress.com).

*Successful Fine Art Photography: How to Market Your Art Photography*, Harold Davis. 1992.

*Taking the Leap: Building a Career as a Visual Artist*, Cay Lang. 2nd ed., 2006.
Chronicle Books, 680 Second St., San Francisco, CA  94107. (415) 537-4283.
(www.chroniclebooks.com).

*The Art of Creating Collectors*, Zella Jackson. 1995. The Consultant Press, Limited.
Available on Amazon.com.

*The Art World Dream: Alternative Strategies for Working Artists*, Eric Rudd. 2001. Cire
Corporation, 189 Beaver St., North Adams, MA  01247. (413) 664-9550, fax: (413) 663-6662.

*The Artist's Guide to New Markets: Opportunities to Show and Sell Art Beyond Galleries*, Peggy
Hadden. 1998. Allworth Press, 10 E. 23rd St., New York, NY  10010. (800) 491-2808.
(www.allworth.com).

*The Artist's Marketing and Action Plan Workbook*, Jonathan Talbot with Geoffrey Howard.
2005. Talbot Arts, 7 Amity Rd., Warwick, NY 10990. (845) 258-4620, fax: (845) 258-4957.
(www.artistsworkbook.com).  Workbook guides reader through how to sell work and make
money, creating a personalized, step-by-step marketing and action plan.

*The Artist's Survival Manual: A Complete Guide to Marketing Your Work*, Toby Judith Klayman and Cobbett Steinberg. 2nd ed. Available on Amazon.com.

*The Fine Artist's Guide to Marketing and Self-Promotion: Innovative Techniques to Build Your Career as an Artist*, Julius Vitali. Allworth Press, 10 E. 23rd St., New York, NY 10010. (800) 491-2808. (www.allworth.com).

*The Gordon's Photography Price Annual 2010*, LTB Gordonsart, 13201 N. 35th Ave., ste. B-20, Phoenix, AZ 85029. (800) 892-4622, (602) 253-6948, fax: (602) 253-2104, e-mail: office@gordonsart.com. (www.gordonsart.com).

*TV and Radio Directory, Vol. 3, Bowker's News Media Directory 2009*. R.R. Bowker, 63 Central Ave., New Providence, NJ 07974. (888) 269-5372, (908) 285-1090. (www.bowker.com).

Video Art Productions, 5007 MacArthur Blvd., NW, Washington, DC 20016. (202) 966-9070. (www.videoartproductions.com).

*What You Do*, Lee Silber. 2001. Three Rivers Press, Imprint of Crown Publishing Group, 1745 Broadway, New York, NY 10010. (212) 782-9000. (www.randomhouse.com).

*Writing the Artist Statement: Revealing the True Spirit of Your Work*, Ariane Goodwin, Ed.D. 2002. Infinity Publishing, 1094 New Dehaven St., ste. 100, West Conshohocken, PA 19428. (877) BUYBOOK, (610) 941-9999. (www.infinitypublishing.com).

www.salestipsforartists.com, and www.talkshoe.com. Podcasts about how to promote and sell prints. Topics include "Practical Promotion – Give A Little to Get A Lot" and "The Art Biz – Who Gets How Much And Why?" by Dick Harrison, artist advisor and retired art print representative.

## Museums/Art Centers/Better College and University Galleries

AAMG (Association of Academic Museums & Galleries), Philip and Muriel Berman Museum of Art at Ursinus College, 601 E. Main St., Collegeville, PA 19426. (www.aamg-us.org). 400 member organization to promote welfare of museums and galleries associated with institutions of higher education and welfare of their staffs. General research in categorical areas.

*American Art Directory, 2010*. National Register Publishing, 890 Mountain Ave., 3rd flr., New Providence, NJ 07974. Editorial: (800) 473-7020, e-mail: NRPeditorial@marquiswhoswho.com; sales: (800) 473-7020, e-mail: NRPsales@marquiswhoswho.com. (www.americanartdir.com). Listings of national and regional art organizations; museums; libraries; associations in the US and Canada; art schools with contact data, degree programs, scholarship programs, entrance requirements, and tuition information; museums abroad; schools abroad; state directors and supervisors of art education; state arts councils; art magazines, editors, and critics; scholarships and fellowships; open exhibitions; and traveling exhibition booking agencies. Indexed by subject, personnel, and organization.

*Art Diary International: The World Art Directory*, Giancarlo Politi Editore, edited by *Flash Art Magazine*. Distributed by D.A.P./Distributed Art Publishers, Inc., 155 Ave. of the Americas, New York, NY 10013. (800) 338-2665, fax (212) 627-9484, e-mail: dap@dapinc.com. (www.artbook.com).

*Art in America Annual Guide to Museums/Galleries/Artists.* Published in August.
*Art in America,* 575 Broadway, New York, NY 10012. (212) 941-2800.
(www.artinamericamagazine.com).

*The Official Museum Directory.* National Register Publishing, 890 Mountain Ave., 3rd flr.,
New Providence, NJ 07974. (800) 473-7020, fax (908) 673-1189.
(www.officialmuseumdir.com). Published annually. Lists museums, historic sites,
planetariums, technology centers, and zoos, etc.

www.amn.org. Art Museum Network. Membership organization with links on website to
members' websites.

www.ArtCal.net. New York-area museum and gallery openings, "focusing on underknown
galleries and artists at the whim of Editors Barry Hoggard and James Wagner and assistant
editor Paddy Johnson."


## Nonprofits and Alternative Spaces

*American Art Directory 2010,* National Register Publishing, 890 Mountain Ave.,
3rd flr., New Providence, NJ 07974. Editorial: (800) 473-7020,
e-mail: NRPeditorial@marquiswhoswho.com; sales: (800) 473-7020,
e-mail: NRPsales@marquiswhoswho.com. (www.americanartdir.com). Listings of national
and regional art organizations; museums; libraries; associations in the U.S. and Canada; art
schools with contact data, degree programs, scholarship programs, entrance requirements,
and tuition information; museums abroad; schools abroad; state directors and supervisors
of art education; state arts councils; art magazines, editors, and critics; scholarships and
fellowships; open exhibitions; and traveling exhibition booking agencies. Indexed by
subject, personnel, and organization.

*Art in America Annual Guide to Museums/Galleries/Artists.* Published in August.
*Art in America,* 575 Broadway, New York, NY 10012. (212) 941-2800.
(www.artinamericamagazine.com).

Art in Embassies Program, US Department of State, 2201 C St. NW, Washington, DC
20520. (202) 647-4000. (www.aiep.state.gov). Promotes the cultural identity of America's art
and artists by borrowing original works of art by US citizens for display in US embassy
residences worldwide. Artists can submit jpeg images or URL address for consideration.

Art in General, 79 Walker St., New York, NY 10013. (212) 219-0474, info@artingeneral.org.
(www.artingeneral.org). Nonprofit contemporary arts organization in lower Manhattan.
New artwork is created and exhibited.

American Public Gardens Association (formerly American Association of Botanical Gardens
& Arboreta), 100 West 10th St., ste. 614, Wilmington, DE 19801, (302) 655-7100,
fax: (302) 655-8100. (www.publicgardens.org).

Moss Rehab Hospital, International Exhibition by Artists with Physical Disabilities,
1200 W. Tabor Rd., Philadelphia, PA 19141. (215) 456-9900. (www.einstein.edu).

Sculpture Space, 12 Gates St., Utica, NY 13502. (315) 724-8381, fax: (315) 797-6639, e-mail: info@sculpturespace.org. (www.sculpturespace.org).

*The Official Museum Directory.* National Register Publishing, 890 Mountain Ave., 3rd flr., New Providence, NJ 07974. (800) 473-7020, fax (908) 673-1189. (www.officialmuseumdir.com). Published annually. Lists museums, historic sites, planetariums, technology centers, and zoos, etc.

## Organizations/Associations

ABI (Arts Business Institute), PO Box 4850, Baltimore, MD 21211. (877) ABI-5571, fax: (877) 224-5771, e-mail: info@artsbusinessinstitute.org. (www.artsbusinessinstitute.org). Nonprofit education organization providing artists with real-world knowledge about product development, pricing, public relations, wholesaling to galleries, etc.

ACUMG (Association of College & University Museums & Galleries), Philip and Muriel Berman Museum of Art at Ursinus College, 601 E. Main St., Collegeville, PA 19426. (www.acumg.org) 400 member organization to promote welfare of museums and galleries associated with institutions of higher education and welfare of their staffs. Mailing list of 1,200 college and university professionals available on website.

Alliance of Artists Communities, 255 S. Main St., Providence, RI 02903. (401) 351-4320, fax: (401) 351-4507. (www.artistcommunities.org). Website lists residencies alphabetically, by discipline, and by region.

*American Art Directory 2010,* National Register Publishing, 890 Mountain Ave., 3rd flr., New Providence, NJ 07974. Editorial: (800) 473-7020, e-mail: NRPeditorial@marquiswhoswho.com; sales: (800) 473-7020, e-mail: NRPsales@marquiswhoswho.com. (www.americanartdir.com). Listings of national and regional art organizations; museums; libraries; associations in the US and Canada; art schools with contact data, degree programs, scholarship programs, entrance requirements, and tuition information; museums abroad; schools abroad; state directors and supervisors of art education; state arts councils; art magazines, editors, and critics; scholarships and fellowships; open exhibitions; and traveling exhibition booking agencies. Indexed by subject, personnel, and organization.

American Association of Museums, 1575 Eye St. NW, ste. 400, Washington, DC 20005. (202) 289-1818, fax: (202) 289-6578. (www.aam-us.org).

American Federation of Arts, 305 E. 47th St., 10th flr., New York, NY 10017. (212) 988-7700, fax: (212) 861-2487, e-mail: pubinfo@artweb.org. (www.afaweb.org). Organizes program of art exhibitions, publications, and educational events to benefit the museum community and enrich the public's experience and understanding of art and culture.

American Institute of Architects (AIA), 1735 New York Ave. NW, Washington, DC 20006. (202) 626-7300. (www.aia.org). Links to local chapters.

American Public Gardens Association (formerly American Association of Botanical Gardens & Arboreta), 100 West 10th St., ste. 614, Wilmington, DE 19801. (302) 655-7100, fax: (302) 655-8100. (www.publicgardens.org).

American Society of Interior Designers (ASID), 608 Massachusetts Ave. NE, Washington, DC 20002. (202) 546-3480, e-mail: asid@asid.org. (www.asid.org).

Americans for the Arts, 1000 Vermont Ave. NW, 6th flr., Washington, DC 20005 (202) 371-2830, fax: (202) 371-0424; 1 E. 53rd St., 2nd flr., New York, NY 10022. (212) 223-2787, fax: (212) 980-4857. (www.americansforthearts.org).

ANNY (Art Niche New York), 498 Broome St., New York, NY 10001. (212) 941-0130, fax: (212) 941-0138, e-mail: reginas@anny.org. (www.anny.org). Hosted by Artist's Equity and dedicated to providing a "niche" for New York artists and arts organizations.

Aperture Foundation, 547 W. 27th St., 4th flr., New York, NY 10001. (212) 505-5555, fax: (212) 598-4015. (www.aperture.org).

Art & Science Collaborations, Inc. (ASCI). 130 East End Ave., ste. 1A, New York, NY 10028. (505) 988-2994, e-mail: info@asci.org. (www.asci.org).

Art Quilt Network. (www.artquiltnetwork.com).

Artisans Center of Virginia, Willow Oak Plaza, Rte. 340 N., 801 W. Broad St., Waynesboro, VA 22980. (877) 508-6069, (540) 946-3294, fax: (540) 946-3296, e-mail: acv@netlos.net. (www.artisanscenterofvirginia.org).

Arts & Business Council of Americans for the Arts, 1000 Vermont Ave. NW, 6th flr., Washington, DC 20005 (202) 371-2830, fax: (202) 371-0424; 1 E. 53rd St., 2nd flr., New York, NY 10022. (212) 223-2787, fax: (212) 980-4857. (www.americansforthearts.org). Focuses on building stronger private-sector support for the arts.

Association of International Photography Art Dealers (AIPAD), 1767 P St. NW, ste. 200, Washington, DC 20036. (202) 986-0105, fax: (202) 986-0448, e-mail: info@aipad.com. (www.aipad.com). Produces The Photography Show.

Chicago Artists' Coalition, 70 E. Lake St., ste. 230, Chicago, IL 60601. (312) 781-0040, fax: (312) 781-0042, e-mail: info@caconline.org. (www.caconline.org).

CODA (Craft Organizations Development Association), PO Box 51, Onia, AR 72663. (870) 746-5159, e-mail: info@coda.org. (www.codacraft.org). Serves organizations with education and professional development to foster public appreciation and understanding of craft.

Handmade in America, 125 S. Lexington Ave., Asheville, NC 28801. (828) 252-0121. (www.handmadeinamerica.org). To nurture traditional and contemporary craft in Western North Carolina.

Handweavers Guild of America, 1255 Buford Hwy., ste. 211, Suwanee, GA 30024, (678) 730-0010, fax: (678) 730-0836, e-mail: hga@weavespindye.org. (www.weavespindye.org).

International Association of Art Critics (AICA), American Section, an affiliate of Association International des Critiques d'Art 15, rue Martel, F-75010 Paris. e-mail: board@aicausa.org. (www.aica-int.org).

International Fine Print Dealers Association (IFPDA), 250 W. 26th St., ste. 405, New York, NY 10001. (212) 674-6095, fax: (212) 674-6783, e-mail: ifpda@ifpda.org. (www.printdealers.com, www.ifpda.org). Produces IFPDA Print Fair. Membership directory available for nominal fee, write: 15 Gramercy Pk. S., ste. 7A, New York, NY 10003.

International Guild of Glass Artists, 27829 365th Ave., Platte, SC 57369. (458) 565-4552. (www.igga.org).

International Sculpture Center (ISC), 19 Fairgrounds Rd., ste. B, Hamilton, NJ 20077. (609) 689-1051, fax: (609) 689-1061. (www.sculpture.org). Member-supported, nonprofit to advance the creation and understanding of sculpture.

National Arts Club, 15 Gramercy Park S., New York, NY 10003. (212) 475-3424. (www.nationalartsclub.org).

National Association of Artists' Organizations (NAAO), 308 Prince St., St. Paul, MN 55101. (651) 294-0907, e-mail: info@naao.com. (www.naao.com). Service organization for artist-run organizations.

National Endowment for the Arts, 1100 Pennsylvania Ave. NW, Washington, DC 20506. (202) 682-5400, e-mail: webmgr@arts.endow.gov. (www.arts.endow.gov).

New Mexico Council on Photography, PO Box 162, Santa Fe, NM 87504. (505) 660-4085, e-mail: mickeybond505@aol.com.

Organization of Independent Artists (OIA), 45 W. 21st. St., ste. 504, New York, NY 10011. (347) 405-2422, e-mail: oiaonline@surfbest.net. (www.oia-ny.org). Support group for artists and promotes exhibition of art in public and alternative spaces in the New York City metropolitan area.

Outdoor Art Foundation, 3970 Syme Dr., Carlsbad, CA 92008. (760) 729-7076, e-mail: info@outdoorartfoundation.org. (www.outdoorartfoundation.org). Fosters outdoor public art in Carlsbad, CA.

Santa Fe Center for Photography, PO Box 2483, Santa Fe, NM 87504. (505) 984-8353. (www.visitcenter.org).

Society of American Mosaic Artists (SAMA), PO Box 428, Orangeburg, SC 29116. E-mail: info@americanmosaics.org, (www.americanmosaics.org).

Still Water, New Media Program, University of Maine, Orono. (www.newmedia.umaine.edu). Promotes network art and culture, encouraging transparency, open access to ideas and code, variability, and flexibility.

The Center for Craft, Creativity & Design, University of North Carolina, Kellogg Ctr., PO Box 1127, 1181 Broyles Rd., Hendersonville, NC 28793, e-mail: info@craftcreativitydesign.org. (www.craftcreativitydesign.org). Regional center to support and advance craft, creativity, and design in education and research and through community collaborations to demonstrate ways craft and design provide creative solutions for community issues.

The Contemporary Glass Society, c/o Broadfield House Glass Museum, Compton Dr., Kingswinford, West Midlands DY6 9NS, UK (44) 1603-507-737, fax: (44) 1603-507-737. (www.cgs.org.uk).

The Estate Project for Artists with AIDS, 330 W. 42nd St., ste. 1701, New York, NY 10036. (212) 947-6340, fax: (212) 947-6416, e-mail: estateproject@allianceforarts.org. (www.artistswithaids.org).

The National Museum of Women in the Arts, Women In The Arts and Archives on Women Artists, 1250 New York Ave. NW, Washington, DC 20005. (800) 222-7270, (202) 783-5000. (www.nmwa.org). Maintains slide registry for women artists who have had one-person museum exhibitions.

The National Network for Artist Placement (NNAP), Theatre In Progress, 935 West Ave. 37, Los Angeles, CA 90065. (800) 354-5348, (323) 222-4035, e-mail: NNAPnow@aol.com. (www.artistplacement.com). Website has directories, services, and publications to aid artists in making the transition from emerging to established artists.

The Society of American Registered Architects (SARA), 14 E. 38th St., 11th flr., New York, NY 10016. E-mail: president@sara-national.org. (www.sara-national.org).

Urban Art Network, Portland, OR. (www.urbanartnetwork.com). No office location. Dedicated to the empowerment of independent artists in the Portland, OR, area. Sponsors Street Gallery in the Pearl District on First Thursday.

Women's Caucus for Art, PO Box 1498, Canal St. Sta., New York, NY 10013. (212) 634-0007. e-mail: info@nationalwca.org, (www.nationalwca.org).

www.ArtistsRegister.com. WESTAF (Western States Arts Federation), 1743 Wazee St., ste. 300, Denver, CO 80202. (303) 629-1166. Nonprofit regional arts service organization dedicated to the arts in the West.

www.three.org/openart. The Open Art Network. Devises and promotes standards that encourage an open architecture for the Internet and digital media.


## Pastel/Watercolor

*On Location: Plein Air Painting in Pastel*, Richard McDaniel. 2005. Writer's Digest Books, F & W Publications, 4700 E. Galbraith Rd., Cincinnati, OH 45236. (513) 531-2690. (www.WritersMarket.com, www.fwpublications.com).

*Pastel Painting Techniques*, Guy Roddon. 1991. Cassell Illustrated.

*Pure Color: The Best of Pastel*, Edited by Maureen Bloomfield and Jamie Markle. 2006. North Light Books, F & W Publications, 4700 E. Galbraith Rd., Cincinnati, OH  45236. (800) 258-0929, (513) 531-2690. (www.fwpublications.com).

*Watercolor Magic*, F & W Publications, 4700 E. Galbraith Rd., Cincinnati, OH  45236. (513) 531-2690. (www.fwpublications.com).

*Watercolor, American Artist*, 770 Broadway, New York, NY  10003. (646) 654-5506, e-mail: mail@myamericanartist.com. (www.myamericanartist.com).  Quarterly.


## Periodicals

*AAA (Archives of American Art) Journal*, Archives of American Art, PO Box 37012, MRC 937, Washington, DC  20013. (202) 633-7971, fax: (202) 633-7994, e-mail: telld@si.edu. (www.aaa.si.edu). Twice yearly.

*American Art Collector*, 7530 E. Main St., ste. 105, Scottsdale, AZ  85251. (480) 425-0806, fax: (480) 425-0724. (www.americanartcollector.com).

*American Art Review*, PO Box 469116, Escondido, CA  92046. (760) 738-1178. (www.amartrev.com). Bimonthly.

*American Artist*, 770 Broadway, New York, NY  10003. (646) 654-5506, e-mail: mail@myamericanartist.com. (www.myamericanartist.com). 11 times/year.

*American Craft*, American Craft Council, 1224 Marshall St. NE, ste. 200, Minneapolis, MN 55413. (www.americancraftmag.org). Bimonthly.

*American Style*, 3000 Chestnut Ave., ste. 300, Baltimore, MD  21211. (410) 889-3093. (www.americanstyle.com). Monthly.

*Anvil Magazine*, 6690 Wentworth Springs Rd., Georgetown, CA  95634. (530) 333-2687. (www.anvilmag.com). Monthly e-zine.

*Aperture Magazine*, 547 W. 27th St., 4th flr., New York, NY  10001. (212) 505-5555, fax: (212) 598-4015. Subscription Services, PO Box 3000, Denville, NJ  07834. (866) 457-4603, e-mail: custsvc–aperture@fulcoinc.com. (www.aperture.org).

*Architectural Digest*, 6300 Wilshire Blvd., Los Angeles, CA  90048. (323) 965-3700, fax: (323) 965-4975. (www.architecturaldigest.com).  "Reader's Directory" listing of designers, architects, and galleries featured in each issue.

*Art & Antiques*, 3500 Lenox Rd., ste. 680, Atlanta, GA 30326. (770) 955-5656. 1177 Ave. of the Americas, 10th flr.,  New York, NY 10036. (212) 230-0200, fax: (212) 230-0201. (www.artandantiquesmag.com).

*Art & Auction*, 11 E. 36th St., 9th flr., New York, NY 10016. (212) 447-9555, e-mail: edit@artandauction.com. (www.artandauction.com).

*Art Guide Northwest*, 13205 Ninth Ave. NW, Seattle, WA  98177. (206) 367-6831, fax: (206) 365-0476, e-mail: btipton@artguidenw.com. (www.artguidenw.com). Guide to galleries, museums, and antiques in the Pacific Northwest.

*Art in America*, 575 Broadway, New York, NY 10012. (212) 941-2800. (www.artinmamericamagazine.com).

*Art New England*, 425 Washington St., Brighton, MA 02135. (617) 782-3008. (www.artnewengland.com).

*Art on Paper*, c/o Darte Publishing, 150 28th St., ste. 504, New York, NY 10001, (212) 675-1968, e-mail: shelly@dartepub.com. (www.dartepub.com).

*Art Papers*, Atlanta Art Papers, PO Box 5748, Atlanta, GA 31107. (404) 588-1837, fax: (404) 588-1836, e-mail: info@artpapers.org. (www.artpapers.org). Bimonthly.

*Art Times*, PO Box 730, Mt. Marion, NY 12456. (845) 246-6944, fax: (845) 246-6944, e-mail: info@arttimesjournal.com. (www.arttimesjournal.com).

*Artealdia*, American Art Corp., 905 Brickell Bay Dr., Tower II, ste. 1021 Miami, FL 33131. (305) 371-7106. (www.artealdia.com). International magazine of Latin American art.

*Artforum*, 350 Seventh Ave., New York, NY 10001, (212) 475-4000, fax: (212) 529-1257, e-mail: generalinfo@artforum.com. (www.artforum.com).

*Artist Advocate*, 224 Datura St., ste. 1015, West Palm Beach, Fl 33401, (561) 655-8778. (www.artistadvocatemagazine.com). Connecting artists with galleries.

*ARTnews*, 48 W. 38th St., 9th flr., New York, NY 10018. (212) 398-1690, e-mail: info@artnewsonline.com. (www.artnewsonline.com).

*ArtNexus*, 12955 Biscayne Blvd., ste. 410, Miami, FL 33181. (305) 891-7270, fax: (305) 891-6408, e-mail: info@artnexus.com. (www.artnexus.com). Quarterly bi-lingual (English/Spanish) focusing on Latin American art.

*ArtReview*, 3330 Pacific. Ave., ste. 404, Virginia Beach, VA 23451. (www.art-review.co.uk).

*artUS*, Foundation for International Art Criticism, 530 Molino St., ste. 212, PO Box 86187, Los Angeles, CA 90086. (213) 625-2010, fax (213) 625-2017, e-mail: artus@artext.org. (www.artext.org).

*Bomb*, aka New Art Publications, 80 Hanson Pl., ste. 703, Brooklyn, NY 11217. (866) 354-0334, (718) 636-9100, e-mail: info@bombsite.com. (www.bombsite.com). Quarterly cultural magazine focusing on new art and writing.

*Camera Arts*, PO Box 2328, Corrales, NM 87048. (800) 894-8439. (www.cameraarts.com).

*Ceramics Monthly*, 735 Ceramic Pl., ste. 100, Westerville, OH 43081. (800) 342-3594. (www.ceramicsmonthly.org).

*Common Ground Glass*, International Guild of Glass Artists, 27829 365th Ave., Platte, SC 57369. (458) 565-4552. (www.igga.org). Quarterly newsletter.

*Contact Sheet/A Journal of Contemporary Photography*, Lightwork, Robert B. Menschel Media Center, 316 Waverly Ave., Syracuse, NY 13244. (www.lightwork.org).

*Craft Arts*, Craft Arts International, PO Box 363, Neutral Bay, Sydney, NSW 2089, Australia. (61) 2-9953-8825, e-mail: subs@craftarts.com.au. (www.craftarts.com.au).

*d'ART International*, 750A St. Clair Avenue W, Toronto, Ontario M6C1B5, Canada. (416) 651-5778, e-mail: info@dartmagazine.com. (www.dartmagazine.com).

*DesignMatters*, International Interior Design Association (IIDA), 341 Merchandise Mart, Chicago, IL 60654. (888) 799-IIDA, (312) 467-1950, e-mail: iidahq@iida.org. (www.iida.org). Bi-weekly newsletter for members.

*Design Miami Magazine*, Dacra Development, 3841 NE 2nd Ave., ste. 400, Miami, FL 33137. (305) 531-8700. (www.miamidesigndistrict.net). Twice a year.

*Drawing, American Artist*, 770 Broadway, New York, NY 10003. (646) 654-5506, e-mail: mail@myamericanartist.com. (www.myamericanartist.com). Quarterly.

*Fabrik Magazine*, 269 S. Beverly Dr., ste. 1234, Beverly Hills, CA 90212, (310) 360-8333. (www.fabrikmagazine.com). Explores what drives Los Angeles's stellar creative community.

*Fiberarts*, 201 E. Fourth St., Loveland, CO 80537. Editorial: (970) 613-4679, fax: (970) 669-6117, e-mail: info@fiberarts.com; subscriptions: (800) 875-6208, (760) 291-1531, fax: (760) 738-4805, e-mail: fiberarts@pcspublink.com. (www.fiberartsmagazine.com). Covers contemporary textile art and craft.

*FineArt Magazine*, Sun Storm Arts Publishing, PO Box 404, Center Moriches, NY 11934. (631) 909-1192, e-mail: info@fineartmagazine.com. (www.fineartmagazine.com). Advertising in conjunction with coverage.

*Flash Art International*, Via Carlo Farini 68, 20159 Milano, Italy. (39) 2-6777341. (www.flashartonline.com).

*Florida Design*, 621 NW 53rd St., Boca Raton, FL 33487. (561) 997-1660. (www.floridadesign.com). "The Magazine for Fine Interior Design & Furnishings." Publishes annual "Focus on Art" issue.

*IFAR Journal*, International Foundation for Art Research, 500 Fifth Ave., ste. 935, New York, NY 10110. (212) 391-6234, fax: (212) 391-8794, e-mail: kgerg@ifar.org. (www.ifar.org).

*Interior Design Magazine*, Reed Business Information, 360 Park Ave. S., 17th flr., New York, NY 10010. (646) 746-7275, (646) 746-6400, subscriptions: (800) 900-0804, fax: (646) 746-7428, e-mail: INDNcustserv@cdsfulfillment.com. (www.interiordesign.net).

*International Artist Magazine*, International Artist Publishing, PO Box 8629, Scottsdale, AZ 85252. (877) 947-0792, fax: (480) 425-0724, e-mail: service@international-artist.com. (www.international-artist.com). Bimonthly.

*Journal of the American Veterinary Medical Association*, 1931 N. Meacham Rd., ste. 100, Schaumberg, IL 60173. (847) 925-8070, fax: (847) 925-1329, e-mail: avmjournals@avma.org. (www.avma.org). 52,000 veterinarians subscribe to this publication (an example of media that publish original artists' work).

*Landscape Architecture*, American Society of Landscape Architects (ASLA), 636 Eye St. NW, Washington, DC 20001. (888) 999-ASLA, (202) 898-2444. (www.asla.org).

*Leonardo: Art, Science & Technology*, MIT Press, 5 Cambridge Ctr., Cambridge, MA 02142. (617) 253-2889. (www.mitpress.mit.edu).

*M The New York Art World*, MBM Publications, 303 W. 42nd St., 5th flr., New York, NY 10036. (212) 956-0614. E-mail: editor@thenewyorkartworld.com.

*Modern Painters*, c/o Expediters of the Printed Word Ltd., 2323 Randolph Ave., Avenel, NJ 07001. E-mail: info@modernpainters.co.uk. (www.modernpainters.co.uk).

*New American Paintings*, Open Studios Press, 450 Harrison Ave., ste. 304, Boston, MA 02118. (617) 778-5265. (www.newamericanpaintings.com). Showcases work of emerging artists six times a year, based on juried competition.

*NY Arts Magazine*, NY Arts, 473 Broadway, 7th flr., New York, NY 10013. (212) 274-8993, fax: (212) 226-3400, e-mail: contact@nyartsmagazine.com. (www.nyartsmagazine.com). Links to NY Arts Affiliates: NY Arts Beijing Space, Art Fairs International, Broadway Gallery, World Art Media, e-Word Art Media, Art Erotica Review, and Hackers International.

*OIA Newsletter*, Organization of Independent Artists, 419 Lafayette Street, 2nd flr, New York, NY 10003. (347) 405-2422, e-mail: oiaonline@surfbest.net. (www.oia-ny.org). Support group for artists and promotes exhibition of art in public and alternative spaces in the New York metropolitan area.

*Photograph*, 64 W. 89th St., New York, NY 10024. (212) 787-0401, fax: (212) 799-3054, e-mail: info@photographmag.com. (www.photographmag.com). Bimonthly guide to photography exhibitions, private dealers, resources, and calendar of events in the US Publisher and Editor Bill Mindlin.

*Plein Air Magazine*, 224 Datura St., ste. 1015, West Palm Beach, Fl 33401. (800) 610-5771, e-mail: eric@pleinairmagazine.com. (www.pleinairmagazine.com). Devoted to fine art of outdoor painting.

*Printmaking Today*, Cello Press, 99-101 Kingsland Rd., London E2 8AG, UK (44) 20-7739-8645, e-mail: mikesims@pt.cellopress.co.uk, annedesmet@pt.cellopress.co.uk. (www.cellopress.co.uk). Quarterly International coverage.

*Sculptural Pursuit*, PO Box 749, Littleton, CO 80160. (303) 738-9892. (www.sculpturalpursuit.com).

*Sculpture*, 1633 Connecticut Ave. NW, 4th flr., Washington, DC 20009. (202) 234-0555, fax: (202) 234-2663. (www.sculpture.org).

*Sculpture Review*, 56 Ludlow St., 5th flr, New York, NY 10002. (212) 529-1763, fax: (212) 260-1732. (www.sculpturereview.com).

*Shuttle Spindle & Dyepot*, Handweavers Guild of America, 1255 Buford Hwy., ste. 211, Suwanee, GA 30024. (678) 730-0010, fax: (678) 730-0836, e-mail: hga@weavespindye.org. (www.weavespindye.org).

*SouthwestArt*, 5444 Westheimer, ste. 1440, Houston, TX 77056. (713) 296-7900, e-mail: southwestart@southwestart.com. (www.southwestart.com).

*Sunshine Artist*, Palm House, Publishing 4075 L.B., McLeod Rd,. ste. E, Orlando, FL 322811. (800) 597-2573, (407) 648-7479. (www.sunshineartist.com). Publication for art and craft show exhibitors, promoters, and patrons. Monthly.

*The Art Guide*, Div. of Harbor Publications, Inc., PO Box 883, Madison, CT 06443. (800) 524-9055, (203) 245-8009, fax: (800) 618-7244, (203) 245-7645. (www.theartguideonline.com). Distributes to 115 New York locations.

*The Art Newspaper*, 411 W. 38th St., 9th flr., New York, NY 10018. (212) 398-1690, e-mail: feedback@theartnewspaper.com. (www.theartnewspaper.com).

*The Artist's Magazine*, F & W Publications, 4700 E. Galbraith Rd., Cincinnati, OH 45236. (513) 531-2690, e-mail: TAMedit@fwpubs.com. (www.artistsmagazine.com).

*The Blacksmith's Journal*, Hoffman Publications, PO Box 1699, Washington, MO 63090. (800) 944-6134, e-mail: hpi@blacksmithsjournal.com. (www.blacksmithsjournal.com). Monthly.

*The MAG*, Artnow International Corporation, 1550 Bricknell Ave., ste. 205A, Miami, FL 33129. E-mail: themag@artnowonline.com. (www.artnowonline.com). E-zine.

*The National Mural Network Newsletter*, PO Box 40383, San Francisco, CA 94140.

*View Camera Magazine*, PO Box 2328, Corrales, NM 87048. (800) 894-8439, (505) 899-8054, fax: (505) 899-7977, e-mail: amiles@viewcamera.com. (www.viewcamera.com).

*Watercolor Magic*, F & W Publications, 4700 E. Galbraith Rd.,Cincinnati, OH 45236. (513) 531-2690. (www.fwpubs.com).

*Watercolor, American Artist*, 770 Broadway, New York, NY 10003. (646) 654-5506, e-mail: mail@myamericanartist.com. (www. myamericanartist.com). Quarterly.

*Wildlife Art News*, 1428 E. Cliff Rd. Burnsville, MN 55337. (612) 927-9056, (800) 221-6547. (www.wildlifeartmag.com).

*Workshop American Artist*, 770 Broadway, New York, NY 10003. (646) 654-5506, e-mail: mail@myamericanartist.com. (www.myamericanartist.com). Quarterly.

www.artnet.com. artnet Worldwide, 61 Broadway, 23rd flr., New York, NY 10006. (800) 4-ARTNET, (212) 497-9700, fax: (212) 497-9707. Information about artists, galleries, auctions, price database, market trends, and events.


## Photography Services

APA-Color Labs, 1451 Northside Dr. NW, Atlanta, GA 30318. (800) 543-5775, (404) 355-1355. (www.apalabs.com).

ArtTecPrints.com, 7900 San Fernando Rd., Unit A, Sun Valley, CA 91352. (800) 910-7411, e-mail: cards@ArtTecPrints.com. (www.ArtTecPrints.com). Printing on canvas, digital photos, business cards, and postcards.

colorenlargement.com, c/o Lighthouse Media, 1905 Landridge Dr., Allen, TX 75013. (469) 939-8064. (www.colorenlargement.com).

Custom Color, 2650 North Burlington Ave., Kansas City, MO 64116. (888) 605-4050. (www.customcolor.com). Slide reproductions.

Duggal, 29 W. 23rd St., New York, NY 10010. (212) 924-8100, e-mail: info@duggal.com. (www.duggal.com). Photo finishing.

Hodgson Photo Services, Black & White Photo Finishing, 206 14th St. NW, Atlanta, GA 30318. (404) 872-3686, e-mail: info@hodgsonphotoservice.com. (www.hodgsonphotoservice.com).

New Image Slide Service, Carnegie Pl., 247 Goodman St., Rochester, NY 14607.

Next Day Dupes National, 123 Lords Hwy., Weston, CT 06883. (203) 226-8404.

Next Day Dupes, 420 Broome St., New York, NY 10013. (212) 431-1508.

Noel Heberling Digital Imaging, 135 President St., Brooklyn, NY 11231. (917) 733-4640.

Overnight Prints, 1800 E. Garry Ave., Santa Ana, CA 92705. (888) 677-2000. (www.overnightprints.com).

PhotoGonia, 3338 Peachtree Rd., ste. 1703, Atlanta, GA 30326. (877) 799-9505. (www.photogonia.com). Poster-size printing on canvas and photopaper.

PowerGraphics Digital Imaging, 7097 S. State St., Midvale, UT 84047. (877) 389-8645, (801) 569-2323, fax: (469) 939-8064. (www.colorenlargement.com).

Studio Chrome Lab, 307 Seventh Ave., New York, NY 10001. (212) 989-6767. Advanced digital imaging.

The Ultimate Image Lab, 443 Park Ave. S., New York, NY 10016. (212) 683-4838. 8" x 10" copies of slides and/or digital images. Contact: Aaron Klein.


## Presentation/Promotional Materials

Archival Products, PO Box 1413, Des Moines, IA 50306. (800) 526-5640, fax: (888) 220-2397, e-mail: info@archival.com. (www.archival.com).

Ark Frames, 41 Belvidere St., Brooklyn, NY 11206. (718) 574-6862, e-mail: arkframes@mac.com, arkframes@optonline.net. Contact Levent Tuncer.

Art Display Essentials, 2 W. Crisman Rd., Columbia, NJ 07832. (800) 862-9869, (908) 496-4951, fax: (908) 496-4958. (www.artdisplay.com). Professional display racks, cases, podiums.

*Art of Displaying Art*, Lawrence B. Smith. 1998. Consultant Press.

*Art World News*, 143 Rowayton Ave., Norwalk, CT 06853. (203) 854-8566. (www.artworldnews.com). Monthly trade magazine for art and framing industry.

Artist Help Network, (www.artisthelpnetwork.com). Produced by Caroll Michels, Career Advisory Service for Emerging and Established Artists, 1724 Burgos Dr., Sarasota, FL 34238. (941) 927-5277, fax: (941) 927-5278, e-mail: carollmich@aol.com. (www.carollmichels.com). Website for fine artists organized into seven general categories: Presentation Tools; Career; Exhibitions, Commissions & Sales; Money; Legal; Creature Comforts; and other Resources.

Barronarts, 302 Butler St., Brooklyn, NY 11217. (800) 286-9179, e-mail: info@barronarts.com. (www.barronarts.com). Frames and stretchers.

bestproofreader@aol.com. Expert Proofreading and light editing for wall texts, newsletters, brochures, etc.

Canvas on Demand, 10700 World Trade Blvd., ste. 102, Raleigh, NC 27617. (800) 801-6312, e-mail: service@canvasondemand.com. (www.canvasondemand.com). Printing on canvas.

Cara Galowitz, 77 Fulton St., New York, NY 10038. (212) 619-2450, e-mail: cgalowitz@nyc.rr.com. Graphic designer specializing in museum exhibition catalogues.

Clark Cards, 115 Litchfield Ave. SE, PO Box 1155, Willmar, MN 56201. (800) 227-3658.

Color Q, 540 Richard St., Miamisburg, OH 45342. (800) 999-1007, fax: (937) 866-4101, e-mail: info@colorq.com. (www.colorq.com).

Curatorial Assistance, 113 E. Union St., Pasadena, CA 91103. (626) 577-9696, fax: (626) 449-9603, e-mail: info@curatorial.com. (www.curatorial.com). Create, produce, and manage art exhibitions and art-related projects including framing, packing and crating, exhibit design and installation, shipping and storage, and editorial and design.

Custom Color, 2650 North Burlington Ave., Kansas City, MO 64116. (888) 605-4050. (www.customcolor.com). Slide reproductions.

*Décor The Art & Framing Business Resource*, (www.decormagazine.com). Monthly trade magazine for art and the framing business.

Digital Poster Art, PO Box 40, Buffalo, NY 14207. (716) 879-0934, e-mail: digitalposterart@aol.com. (www.digitalposterart.com).

Dynacolor Graphics, PO Box 699037, Miami, FL 33269; 1182 NW 159th Dr., Miami, FL 33169. (800) 233-7990, (305) 625-8929, e-mail: mail@dynacolor.com. (www.dynacolor.com). Color postcards at good prices.

Frame Fit Co., PO Box 12727, Philadelphia, PA 19134. (800) 523-3693, (215) 288-8040, fax: (800) 344-7010, e-mail: support@framefit.com. (www.framefit.com).

Frame Masters, 1017 N. Orange Dr., Los Angeles, CA 90038. (323) 876-8371. (www.framemasters1969.com). Custom traditional frames.

Gaylord Archival Storage Materials & Conservation Supplies, PO Box 4901, Syracuse, NY 13221. (800) 448-6160, fax: (800) 272-3412. (www.gaylord.com).

Graphik Dimensions, 2103 Brentwood St., High Point, NC 27263. (800) 221-0262, fax: (336) 877-3773, e-mail: customerservice@pictureframes.com. (www.pictureframes.com).

House of Hydenryk, 601 W. 26th St., New York, NY 10001. (212) 206-9611. Fine Art Framing. (www.hydenryk.com).

Jonathan Yuen, 6 Apache Circle, Katonah, NY, 10536. (914) 232-2268, e-mail: jonathanyuen@ jonathanyuen.com. (www.jonathanyuen.com). Marketing representative, printing and promotional materials.

*Light for Art's Sake: Lighting for Artworks and Museum Displays*, Christopher Cuttle. 2007. Butterworth-Heinemann, imprint of Elsevier, Inc., 30 Corporate Dr., ste. 400, Burlington, MA 01803. (800) 545-2533, (781) 313-4700, fax: (800) 545-9935, (781) 221-1615, e-mail: usbkinfo@elsevier.com. (www.bh.com).

Light Impressions, P. O. Box 787, Brea, CA 92822. (800) 828-6216, (714) 441-4539, fax: (800) 828-5539, (714) 441-4564, e-mail: info@lightimpressionsdirect.com. (www.lightimpressionsdirect.com).

Masterpak, 145 E. 57th St., 5th flr., New York, NY 10022. (800) 922-5522, fax: (212) 586-6961, e-mail: service@masterpak-usa.com. (www.masterpak-usa.com). Packing, shipping and display materials for artists.

Metropolitan Picture Framing, 6959 Washington Ave. S., Minneapolis, MN 55439. (800) 626-3139, e-mail: info@metroframe.com. (www.metroframe.com).

Modern Postcard, 1675 Faraday, Carlsbad, CA 92008. (800) 959-8365, (760) 431-7084, fax: (760) 268-1700. (www.modernpostcard.com).

New Era Publishing, 2101 East, St. Elmo Road #110, Austin, TX 78744. (888) 928-3910. (www.newerapublishing.com).

PK Selective, 415 Mathew St., Santa Clara, CA 95050, (408) 988-1910 (www.pkselective.com). Metal plating.

Postcard Mania, 404 S. MLK Jr. Ave., Clearwater, FL 33756. (800) 628-1804, fax: (727) 442-5130, e-mail: info@postcardmania.com. (www.postcardmania.com). 5,000 postcards for $349.

Poster Print Shop, Division of Master Design, 6121 Santa Monica Blvd., Studio A, Los Angeles, CA 90038. (323) 467-5591, fax: (323) 467-5595, e-mail: info@posterprintshop.com. (www.posterprintshop.com).

*Presentation Power Tools for Fine Artists*, Renée Phillips. 2002. Manhattan Arts International, 200 E. 72nd St., 26th flr., New York, NY 10021. (212) 472-1660, e-mail: info@manhattanarts.com. (www.manhattanarts.com).

Scott Sign Systems, 7524 Commerce Pl., Sarasota, FL 34243. (800) 237-9447. (www.scottsigns.com).

Southern Tailors, 1862 Marietta Blvd. NW, Atlanta, GA 30318 (404) 367-8660, fax: (404) 367-8654. (www.southerntailors.com). Can print any image to fabric for large displays.

Tailored Lighting, 50 Bermar Pk., ste. 4a, Rochester, NY 14624. (800) 254-4487, (585) 328-2170, fax: (585) 328-2198, e-mail: phil@solux.net. (www.solux.net).

University Products, 517 Main St., Holyoke, MA 01040. (800) 628-1912, fax: (800) 532-9281, e-mail: info@universityproducts.com, custserv@universityproducts.com. (www.universityproducts.com). Archival quality materials.

Waveline Direct, 192 Hempt Rd., Mechanicsburg, PA 17055. (800) 257-8830. (717) 795-8830. (www.wavelinedirect.com). Wholesale printing.

www.4by6.com. Online postcard printing system.


## Public Art

"A Guide to Battery Park City," Hugh L. Carey, Battery Park City Authority, One World Financial Center, 24th flr., New York, NY 10281. (212) 417-2000. E-mail: info@batteryparkcity.org. (www.batteryparkcity.org). On-line guide to sculpture in Battery Park City.

Americans for the Arts' Public Network (PAN), 1000 Vermont Ave. NW, 6th flr., Washington, DC 20005 (202) 371-2830, fax: (202) 371-0424; One E. 53rd St., 2nd flr., New York, NY 10022. (212 223-2787, fax: (212) 980-4857. (www.americansforthearts.org).

www.artisthelpnetwork.com. Lists many artist resources including competitions and calls for public art projects.

Broadway Windows (NW corner of Broadway and E. 10th St., New York, NY), Washington Square East Galleries Broadway Windows, 80 Washington Square East Galleries, New York, NY 10003. (212) 998-5751, fax: (212) 998-5752, e-mail: BwayWinds@nyu.edu. (www.nyu.edu/pages/galleries). Site-specific installations in storefront windows.

CityArts, 525 Broadway, ste. 700, New York, NY 10012. (212) 966-0377, fax: (212) 966-0551, e-mail: info@cityarts.org. (www.cityarts.org). Program bringing professional artists with children and youth to create public art.

*Corporate Museums, Galleries, and Visitor's Centers: A Directory*, Victor J. Danilov. 1991. Greenwood Press, 88 Post Rd. W., Westport, CT 06881. (203) 226-3571. (www.greenwood.com).

Creative Time, 59 E. Fourth St., ste. 6E, New York, NY 10003. (212) 206-6674, fax: (212) 255-8467, e-mail: info@creativetime.org. (www.creativetime.org). Sponsor of site-specific installations.

*Dodge Reports*, McGraw Hill, 1221 Ave. of the Americas, New York, NY 10020. (212) 512-4100. (www.dodge.construction.com). Online resource for construction projects nationwide.

General Services Administration (GSA), Art In Architecture Program, 1800 F St., ste. 3300 PMB, Washington, DC 20405. Office of chief architect: (202) 501-1888. (www.gsa.gov). One half of one percent of estimated construction cost of federal buildings reserved for public art. Maintains large registry of artists interested in federal commissions.

*Going Public: A Field Guide to Developments in Art in Public Places*, Jeffrey L. Cruikshank and Pam Korza. 1988. AES Publications, Arts Extension Service, University of Massachusetts Amherst, Division of Outreach, 100 Venture Way, ste. 201, Amherst, MA 01003. (413) 545-2360, fax: (413) 577-3838, e-mail: aes@outreach.umass.edu. (www.umass.edu).

*International Directory of Sculpture Parks*, Benbow Bullock. 12 Sandy Beach, Vallejo, CA 94590. (510) 245-2242, fax: (510) 245-2252, e-mail: artnut@artnut.com. (www.artnut.com/intl.html).

Mailing List Labels Packages, PO Box 1233, Weston, CT 06883-0233. (203) 451-1592 e-mail: mllpackage@worldnet.att.net. Publishes "Mailing List Labels Packages for Percent-for Art and Art in Public Places Programs" including a Directory of Art-for-Percent and Art in Public Places Programs in the U.S., and related mailing labels, postcards, and forms. Contact: Rosemary Cellini.

Michael Ingbar Gallery of Architectural Art, 568 Broadway, New York, NY 10012. (212) 334-1100, e-mail: ingbargallery@aol.com. (www.artnet.com/michaelingbargallery.html).

MTA Arts for Transit, Metropolitan Transportation Authority, 347 Madison Ave., New York, NY 10017. (212) 972-8644. (www.mta.info/aft/about/opportunities.htm).

Outdoor Art Foundation, 3970 Syme Dr., Carlsbad, CA 92008. (760) 729-7076, e-mail: info@outdoorartfoundation.org. (www.outdoorartfoundation.org). Fosters outdoor public art in Carlsbad, CA.

Percent for Art in New York City, Dept. of Cultural Affairs, 31 Chambers St., New York, NY 10007. (212) 213-9300. (www.nyc.gov).

Percent for Art/Art in Public Places Programs, PO Box 1233, Weston, CT 06883. (203) 451-1592. Contact: Rosemary Cellini.

*Perspectives on Art in Public Places*, Publishing Center for Cultural Resources, 625 Broadway, New York, NY 10012. (212) 260-2010.

Public Art Fund, 1 E. 53rd St., New York, NY 10022. (212) 980-4575, fax: (212) 980-3610, e-mail: info@publicartfund.org. (www.publicartfund.org). Presenter of artists' projects, new commissions, and exhibitions in public spaces in New York City.

## Self-Help/Creativity

*100 Creative Drawing Ideas*, edited by Anna Held Audette. 2004. Shambhala Publications, 300 Massachusetts Ave., Boston, MA 02115. (617) 424-0030, fax: (617) 236-1563, e-mail: custserv@shambhala.com. (www.shambhala.com).

*52 Ways to Nurture Your Creativity (52 Decks)*, Lynn Gordon (author) and Karen Johnson (illustrator). 1999. Chronicle Books, 680 Second St., San Francisco, CA 94107. (415) 537-4283. (www.chroniclebooks.com).

*Affirmations for Artists*, Eric Maisel. 1996. Tarcher, Putnam Publishing Group, 375 Hudson St., New York, NY 10014. (212) 366-2000. (www.penguingroup.com).

*Art & Fear: Observations on the Perils and Rewards of Art Making*, David Bayles and Ted Orland. 2001. Image Continuum Press, PO Box 51599, Eugene, OR 97405. (541) 344-5955, fax: (541) 344-4493. (www.artandfear.com).

*Art Escapes: Daily Exercises and Inspirations for Discovering Greater Creativity and Artistic Confidence*, Dory Kanter. 2007. North Light Books, F & W Publications, 4700 E. Galbraith Rd., Cincinnati, OH 45236. (513) 531-2690. (www.fwpublications.com).

*Creative Authenticity: 16 Principles to Clarify and Deepen Your Artistic Vision*, Ian Roberts. 2004. Atelier Saint-Luc Press, PO Box 1082, Fairfield, IA 52556. (888) 333-4541. (www.ianroberts.us).

*Creativity Book: A Year's Worth of Inspiration and Guidance*, Eric Maisel. 2000. Penguin Group, 375 Hudson St., New York, NY 10014. (212) 366-2000. (www.penguingroup.com).

*Creativity for Life: Practical Advice on the Artist's Personality and Career from America's Foremost Creativity Coach*, Eric Maisel. 2007. New World Library.

*Evergreen*, Laura Stamps. Kittyfeather Press, PO Box 212534, Columbia, SC 29221. (803) 749-8579, e-mail: laurastamps@mindspring.com. A novel exploring the spiritual journey of a woman artist.

*Everyday Creative: 30 Ways to Wake Up Your Inner Artist (Cards)*, Eric Maisel. 2004. Red Wheel/Weiser, 65 Parker St., ste. 7, Newburyport, MA 01950. (800) 423-7087, fax: (877) 337-3309, e-mail: info@redwheelweiser.com. (www.redwheelweiser.com).

*Fearless Creating (Inner Workbook)*, Eric Maisel. 1995. Tarcher, Imprint of Penguin Group, 375 Hudson St., New York, NY 10014. (212) 366-2000. (www.penguingroup.com).

*Finding Water: The Art of Perseverance*, Julia Cameron. 2006. Tarcher, Imprint of Penguin Group, 375 Hudson St., New York, NY 10014. (212) 366-2000. (www.penguingroup.com).

*Finding Your Visual Voice: A Painter's Guide to Developing an Artistic Style*, Dakota Mitchell and Lee Haroun. 2007. North Light Books, F & W Publications, 4700 E. Galbraith Rd., Cincinnati, OH 45236. (513) 531-2690. (www.fwpublications.com).

*How to Avoid Making Art*, Julia Cameron. 2005. Tarcher, Imprint of Penguin Group, 375 Hudson St., New York, NY 10014. (212) 366-2000. (www.penguingroup.com).

*Inspiring Creativity: An Anthology of Powerful Insights and Practical Ideas to Guide You to Successful Creating*, Rick Benzel. 2005. Creativity Coaching Association Press. (www.creativitycoachingassociation).

*Living Out Loud*, Keri Smith. 2003. Chronicle Books, 680 Second St., San Francisco, CA 94107. (415) 537-4283. (www.chroniclebooks.com).

*Making Room for Making Art: A Thoughtful and Practical Guide to Bringing the Pleasure of Artistic Expression Back into Your Life*, Sally Warner. 1994. Chicago Review Press, 814 N. Franklin St., Chicago, IL 60610. (800) 888-4741, fax: 312-337-5110, e-mail: frontdesk@chicagoreviewpress.com. (www.chicagoreviewpress.com).

351

*No More Secondhand Art*, Peter London. 1989. Shambhala Publications, 300 Massachusetts Ave., Boston, MA 02115. (617) 424-0030, fax: (617) 236-1563, e-mail: custserv@shambhala.com. (www.shambhala.com).

*Supplies*, Julia Cameron. 2003. Tarcher, Imprint of Penguin Group, 375 Hudson St., New York, NY 10014. (212) 366-2000. (www.penguingroup.com).

*The Artist's Way: A Spiritual Path to Higher Creativity*, Julia Cameron. 10th anniversary ed., 2002. Tarcher, Putnam Publishing Group, 375 Hudson St., New York, NY 10014. (212) 366-2000. (www.penguingroup.com).

*The Artist's Muse: Unlock the Door to Your Creativity*, Betsy Dillard Stroud. 2006. North Light Books, F & W Publications, 4700 E. Galbraith Rd., Cincinnati, OH 45236. (513) 531-2690. (www.fwpublications.com).

*The Blank Canvas: Inviting the Muse*, Anna Held Audette. 1993. Shambahala Publications, 300 Massachusetts Ave., Boston, MA 02115. (617) 424-0030, fax: (617) 236-1563, e-mail: custserv@shambhala.com. (www.shambhala.com).

*The Creative License: Giving Yourself Permission To Be the Artist You Truly Are*, Danny Gregory. 2006. Hyperion Books, 77 W. 66th St., 11th flr., New York, NY 10023. Orders: Harper Collins, (800) 242-7737, fax: (800) 822-4090. (www.hyperionbooks.com).

*The New Creative Artist: A Guide to Developing Your Creative Spirit*, Nita Leland. 2006. North Light Books, F & W Publications, 4700 E. Galbraith Rd., Cincinnati, OH 45236. (513) 531-2690. (www.fwpublications.com).

*The Nine Modern Day Muses: 10 Guides to Creative Inspiration for Artists, Poets, Lovers, and Other Mortals Wanting to Live a Dazzling Existence*, Jill Badonsky. 2003. Gotham Publishing Society, PO Box 61, Village Sta., New York, NY 10014. (212) 299-3300.

*The Painter's Keys: A Seminar With Robert Genn*, Robert Genn. 1997. Educational Enterprises. Available through amazon.com.

*The Vein of Gold*, Julia Cameron. 1997. Tarcher, Imprint of Penguin Group, 375 Hudson St., New York, NY 10014. (212) 366-2000. (www.penguingroup.com).

*The View from the Studio Door: How Artists Find Their Way in an Uncertain World*, Ted Orland. 2006. Image Continuum Press, PO Box 51599, Eugene, OR 97405. (541) 344-5955, fax: (541) 344-4493. (www.artandfear.com).

*The Zen of Creative Painting: An Elegant Design for Revealing Your Muse*, Jeanne Carbonetti. 1998. Watson-Guptill Publications, 770 Broadway, New York, NY 10003. (646) 654-5500, e-mail: info@watsonguptill.com. (www.watsonguptill.com).

*The Zen of Creativity: Cultivating Your Artistic Life*, John Daido Loori. 2005. Ballantine Books, The Random House Publishing Group, 1745 Broadway, 18th flr., New York, NY 10019. (212) 782-9000. (www.randomhouse.com).

*Transitions*, Julia Cameron. 1999. Tarcher, Imprint of Penguin Group, 375 Hudson St., New York, NY 10014. (212) 366-2000. (www.penguingroup.com).

*Trust the Process*, Shaun McNiff. 1998. Shambhala Publications, 300 Massachusetts Ave., Boston, MA  02115. (617) 424-0030, fax: (617) 236-1563, e-mail: custserv@shambhala.com. (www.shambhala.com).

*Walking in this World*, Julia Cameron. 2003. Tarcher, Imprint of Penguin Group, 375 Hudson St., New York, NY  10014. (212) 366-2000. (www.penguingroup.com).

## Shipping/Crating/Packing Materials

Art Crating, 26 Van Dam, Brooklyn, NY 11222. (212) 431-8919. Crating, shipping materials, and shipping.

Art's Delivery Service, 21811 NW Seventh Ct., Pembroke Pines, FL  33029. (954) 431-6546.

Artech, 2601 First Ave., Seattle, WA 98121. (206) 728-8822, e-mail: info@artechseattle.com. (www.artechseattle.com).  Domestic and International shipping.

Artex Fine Art Services, 8712 Jericho City Dr., Landover, MD  20785. (800)-OK-ARTEX, (301) 350-5500, fax: (301) 350-5505. (www.artexfas.com).  Offices in New York: 26 West 17th Street, ste 801, New York, NY 10011, (212) 265-3111; Boston: 200 Inner Belt Rd., Somerville, MA  02143. (866) 407-9660, (617) 766-0300, fax: (617) 776-0330; Ft. Lauderdale: 2525 Davie Rd., ste. 320, Davie, FL  33317. (954) 577-5585, fax: (954) 577-5595.

Atlantic Fine Art Services, 29 Dunvegan Road, Catonsville, MD 21228. (410) 744-5040, fax (410)-744-5105, e-mail: Atlan29360@aol.com.

BrownCor International, 770 S. 70th St., Milwaukee, WI  53214. (800) 327-2278, fax: (800) 343-9228, e-mail: bccustserv@browncor.com. (www.browncor.com). Protective cushioning and other packaging materials.

Crozier Fine Arts, Inc., 525 W. 20th St., New York, NY 10011. (800) 822-ARTS, (212) 741-2024, fax: (212) 243-5209, e-mail: shipping@crozierfinearts.com, crating@crozierfinearts.com. (www.crozierfinearts.com).

Curatorial Assistance, 113 E. Union St., Pasadena, CA  91103. (626) 577-9696, fax: (626) 449-9603, e-mail: info@curatorial.com. (www.curatorial.com).  Create, produce, and manage art exhibitions and art-related projects including framing, packing and crating, exhibit design and installation, shipping and storage, and editorial and design.

D.A.D. Trucking, Inc., 76 Varick St., New York, NY 10013.  (212) 226-0054. Domestic and International. Daily scheduling for New York, New Jersey, and Connecticut.  Cross-country shuttles to California, Florida, and Chicago.

DHL. (800)-CALL-DHL. (www.dhl-usa.com).

Dun-Rite Specialized Carriers, 1561 Southern Blvd., Bronx, NY  10460. (718) 991-1100, fax: (718) 842-0994, e-mail: info@dunriteSpecialized.com. (www.dunriteSpecialized.com). Hoisting and rigging, specialized transport, and warehousing; also have private viewing room.

Federal Express, (800) GOFEDEX. (www.federalexpress.com).

Fine Art Express Incorporated, 3500 47th Ave., Long Island City, NY 11101 (718) 361-7357.

Fortress, Corporate Headquarters, 1 Design Ctr. Pl., ste. 715, Boston, MA 02210. (617) 790-3070. Storage facilities in Boston, 99 Boston St., Boston, MA 02125. (617) 288-3636, New York, 49-20 Fifth St., Long Island City, NY 11101. (718) 937-5500, Miami, 1629 NE First Ave., Miami, FL 33132. (305) 374-6161. E-mail: info@thefortress.com. (www.thefortress.com).

Frame Fit Co., PO Box 12727, Philadelphia, PA 19134. (800) 523-3693, (215) 288-8040, fax: (800) 344-7010, e-mail: support@framefit.com. (www.framefit.com).

Freight Dynamics, Inc., 3500 Holly Ln. N., ste. 30, Plymouth, MN 55447. (800) 883-8777, (763) 550-9959, fax: (763) 550-9949, e-mail: operations@freightdynamics.com. (www.freightdynamics.com). Reasonable rates.

Gaylord Bros., PO Box 4901, Syracuse, NY 13221-4901, (800) 448-6160, (www.gaylord.com). Archival packing, storage equipment, and supplies.

Hermes Freight, 139 Bay St., Staten Island, NY 10301. (718) 720-0060. Contact Len Baldassano.

International Art Transport, 54, Ave. Lenine, 94250 Gentilly, France. (33) 141 17 41 17, fax: (33) 149 85 9131. Contact: Sylvie Michel, Coordinator.

Judson Art Warehouse, 49-20 Fifth St., Long Island City, NY 11101. (718) 937-5500, fax: (718) 937-5860.

L.A. Packing, Crating and Transport, 5722 W. Jefferson Blvd., Los Angeles, CA 90016. (800) 852-9836, (323) 937-2669, fax: (323) 937-9012, e-mail: info@lapackinginc.com. (www.lapackinginc.com).

Masterpak, 145 E. 57th St., 5th flr., New York, NY 10022. (800) 922-5522, fax: (212) 586-6961, e-mail: service@masterpak-usa.com. (www.masterpak-usa.com.) Packing, shipping, and display materials for artists.

Midwest Fine Arts FAST, 2931 Abbe Rd., Lorain, OH 44054. (800) 890-3234, (440) 243-8560, fax: 243-8562. (www.midwestfinearts.com).

More Specialized Art Transportation, 145 Myer St., Hackensack, NJ 07601. (201) 678-0060.

RBA (Racine Berkow Associates), 15 W. 26th St., 12th flr., New York, NY 10010. (212) 255-2011, fax: (212) 255-2012, e-mail: rba@racineberkow.com. (www.racineberkow.com). Offices at JFK International Airport, 156-15 146 Ave., Jamaica, NY 11434. (718) 949-1200, fax: (718) 949-1309; Washington, DC, 616 N. Washington St., Alexandria, VA 22314. (703) 299-0660, fax: 703) 299-1211. International shipping agents, full services, licensed and bonded.

Red Hook Art Crating (Juggernaut Art Crating), 92 Van Dyke St., Brooklyn, NY 11231. (718) 488-0089.

Richard Wright LTD, Fine Arts Services, Division of Transpro Courier Inc., 124 Turnpike St., West Bridgewater, MA 02379. (800) 247-9744. (www.fine-arts-unlimited.com/rw.htm). Shipping, packing and crating, storage, and installation.

ShowFreight International, exhibit freight specialists. PO Box 325 Ramsey, NJ 07446. (201) 825-3680. (www.showfreightintl.com).

Southpass Transart Limited, 288 West St., New York, NY 10013. (212) 925-3067. Servicing New York and tri-state area, with scheduled trips for Florida and the Southeast.

Sterling STI, contact Julie Wrobel, Sales and Logistics Coordinator. (978) 322-2662, e-mail: jwrobel@sterlingmail.com. Very reasonable and dependable fine art shipper.

Suddath Transportation Services, 815 S. Main St., Jacksonville, FL 32207. (904) 858-1234, fax: (904) 858-1244. (www.suddathtransportation.com).

TCI, Transport Consultants International, Inc., 30 Union Ave. S., Cranford, NJ 07016, (800) 752-7002, (908) 272-6500, fax: (908) 272-6516, e-mail: bob@shippingmadesimple.com. (www.shippingmadesimple.com). Offices in Florida, 1900 S. Harbor City Blvd., ste. 218, Melbourne, FL 32901. (321) 722-0499, fax: (321) 722-0599, South Carolina, 600 Ermine Rd., Lot 587, W. Columbia, SC 29170. (803) 781-2804, fax: (803) 781-2844, and Chicago, 3435 N. Sheffield Ave., Chicago, IL 60657. (773) 755-7760, fax: (773) 755-7761. National association of fine art and antique handling companies providing national and international shipping.

The Exhibition Alliance (formerly Gallery Association of New York State), PO Box 345, Hamilton, NY 13346. (315) 824-2510, fax: (315) 824-1683, e-mail: info@exhibitionalliance.org. (www.exhibitionalliance.org). Nonprofit organizes traveling exhibitions, provides low-cost storage and insurance for members and nonmembers.

TLC (Texas Louisiana Cartage), PO Box 18439, Hattiesburg, MS 39404. (601) 261-5643, fax: (601) 261-5623, e-mail: info@tlctrucking.com. (www.tlctrucking.com).

Trimaxion Fine Arts, 29-76 Northern Blvd., Long Island City, NY 11101. (718) 784-5070, e-mail: info@trimaxion.com. (www.trimaxion.com). Crating, pedestals, fabrication, packing, viewing room, storage, trucking.

U.S.Art Company, 66 Pacella Pk. Dr., Randolph, MA 02368. (800) 872-7826, (781) 986-6500, fax: (781) 986-5595. (www.usart.com). Offices in Dallas/Fort Worth, 3250 Story Rd., ste. 104, Irving, TX 75038. (866) 898-7278, (972) 256-1122, fax: (972) 256-4433; Los Angeles, 12600 Daphne Ave., Hawthorne, CA 90250. (877) 528-7278, (323) 755-9000, fax: (323) 755-8000; New York, 37-11 48th Ave., Long Island City, NY 11101. (800) 472-5784, (718) 472-5784, fax: (718) 472-5785; Orlando, 7477 Monetry Dr., Orlando, FL 32809. (888) 802-4459, (407) 855-3444, fax: (407) 855-3950; St. Louis, 811 Hanley Industrial Ct., Brentwood, MO 63144. (866) 928-7278, (314) 918-8686, fax: (314) 918-8676; and Washington, DC, 3361 DH 75th Ave., Landover, MD 20785. (877) 508-7278, (301) 772-0225, fax: (301) 772-0227.

ULINE Shipping Supply Specialists, 2105 S. Lakeside Dr., Waukegan, IL 60085. (800) 958-5463, fax: (800) 295-5571, e-mail: customer.service@uline.com. (www.uline.com).

UniShippers, 746 E. Winchester, ste. 200, Salt Lake City, UT 84107. (800) 999-8721, (801) 487-0600, fax: (801) 487-0920. (www.unishippers.com). 269 franchise offices, with links on website.

## Tool Kit

*187 Tips for Artists: How to Create a Successful Art Career – and Have Fun in the Process!* Kathy Gulrich. 2003. Center City Publishing, 115 E. 36th St., New York, NY 10016. (212) 689-8796.

*2010 Artists & Graphic Designers Market,* edited by Mary Cox and Michael Schweer. 2006. Writer's Digest Books, F & W Publications, 4700 E. Galbraith Rd., Cincinnati, OH 45236. (513) 531-2690. (www.WritersMarket.com, www.fwpublications.com).

*A Gallery Without Walls, Revised: Selling Art in Alternative Venues,* Margaret Danielak. 2007. ArtNetwork Press, PO Box 1360, Nevada City, CA 95959. (800) 383-0677. (www.artmarketing.com).

*A Practical Guide to Consigning Art,* Tad Crawford and Susan Mellon. 3rd ed., 2008. Allworth Press, 10 E. 23rd St., New York, NY 10010. (800) 491-2808. (www.allworth.com).

*A Visual Artist's Guide to Estate Planning,* Marie Walsh Sharpe Foundation, 830 N. Tejon St., ste. 120, Colorado Springs, CO 80903. (719) 635-3220, e-mail: sharpeartfdn@quest.net. (www.sharpeartfdn.org).

Access to Health Insurance/Resources for Care (HIRC), Artist's Health Insurance Center, The Actors' Fund, National Headquarters, 729 Seventh Ave., 10th flr., New York, NY 10019. (800) 798-8447. (www.ahirc.org).

*An Artist's Guide – Making It in New York City,* Daniel Grant. 2001. Allworth Press, 10 E. 23rd St., New York, NY 10010. (800) 491-2808. (www.allworth.com).

Archives of American Art, 1285 Ave. of the Americas, 2nd flr., New York, NY 10019. (212) 399-5015, fax: (212) 307-4501. Research Ctr., 750 Ninth St. NW, ste. 2200, MRC 937, Washington, DC 20001. (202) 633-7950, fax: (202) 633-7994. (www.aaa.si.edu).

*Art and Reality: The New Standard Reference Guide and Business Plan for Actively Developing Your Career as an Artist,* Robert J. Abbott. 2nd ed., 2001. Available on Amazon.com.

*Art Licensing 101: Publishing and licensing your artwork for profit,* Michael Woodward. 2010. ArtNetwork Press, PO Box 1360, Nevada City, CA 95959. (800) 383-0677. (www.artmarketing.com).

*Art of Selling Art: Between Production and Livelihood,* Bill H. Ritchie. 1996. Used copies on Amazon.com.

*Art Office: 80+ Business Forms, Charts, Sample Letters, Legal Documents and Business Plans,* Constance Smith and Sue Viders. 2nd ed., 2007. ArtNetwork Press, PO Box 1360, Nevada City, CA 95959. (800) 383-0677. (www.artmarketing.com).

Art Sales Index, Ltd., 54 Station Rd., Egham, Surrey TW20 9LF, UK (44) 1784-473136, fax: (44) 1784-435207. (www.art-sales-index.com).

Art Solutions, 22-70 27th St., ste. 1A, Astoria, NY 11105. (718) 726-9441, fax: (718) 726-9441, e-mail: margaretoppenheimer@prodigy.net. Provenance and collections research.

*Art That Pays: The Emerging Artist's Guide to Making a Living*, Adele Slaughter and Jeff Kober. 2004. Available on Amazon.com.

*Artist Beware: The Hazards in Working with All Art and Craft Materials and the Precautions Every Artist and Craftsperson Should Take*, Michael McCann. 2005. The Lyons Press, Imprint of Globe Pequot Press, 246 Goose Ln., PO Box 480, Guilford, CT 06437. (203) 458-4500, customer service: (888) 249-7586, customer service fax: (800) 820-2329, e-mail: info@globepequot.com. (www.globepequot.com).

Artist Help Network. (www.artisthelpnetwork.com). Website for fine artists organized into seven general categories: Career; Exhibitions, Commissions, and Sales; Money; Presentation Tools; Legal; Creature Comforts; and other Resources. Produced by Caroll Michels, Career Advisory Service for Emerging and Established Artists, 1724 Burgos Dr., Sarasota, FL 34238. (941) 927-5277, fax: (941) 927-5278, e-mail: carollmich@aol.com. (www.carollmichels.com).

Artists' Equity, PO Box HG, Pacific Grove, CA 93950. E-mail: duffyart@sbcglobal.net. (www.artists-equity.org/naea.html). Mission to improve economic and working conditions of visual artists.

ArtNetwork, PO Box 1360, Nevada City, CA 95959. (800) 383-0677, (530) 470-0862, e-mail: info@artmarketing.com. (www.artmarketing.com). Resource for books, mailing lists, art and travel, marketing software, living artists, and an online gallery.

*ArtSpeak: A Guide to Contemporary Ideas, Movements, and Buzzwords*, 1945 to the Present, Robert Atkins. 2nd ed., 1997. Abbeville Press, 137 Varick St., ste. 504, New York, NY 10013. (800) 343-4499, fax: (800) 351-5073. (www.abbeville.com).

AuthorHouse (formerly 1st Books Library), 1663 Liberty Dr., ste. 200, Bloomington, IN 47403. (888) 519-5121. (www.authorhouse.com). Self publishing.

*Bottom Line*, Licensing Industry Merchandising Association, 350 Fifth Ave. New York, NY 10118. (212) 244-1944. (www.licensing.org). Quarterly licensing newsletter.

*Breaking into the Art World: How to Start Making a Living As an Artist*, Brian Marshall White. 2005. Virtualbookworm.com Publishing, Incoporated, PO Box 9949, College Station, TX 77842. (877) 376-4955. (www.virtualbookworm.com).

*Breaking Through the Clutter: Business Solutions for Women Artists and Entrepreneurs*, Judith Luther Wilder. 1999. The National Network for Artist Placement (NNAP), 935 West Ave. 37, Los Angeles, CA 90065. (800) 354-5348, (323) 222-4035, e-mail: NNAPnow@aol.com. (www.artistplacement.com).

*Business & Legal Forms for Fine Artists*, Tad Crawford. 2005. Allworth Press, 10 E. 23rd St., New York, NY 10010. (800) 491-2808. (www.allworth.com).

*Business Letters for Artists*, M. Stephen Doherty. Watson-Guptill Publications, 770 Broadway, New York, NY 10003. (646) 654-5500, e-mail: info@watsonguptill.com. (www.watsonguptill.com).

*Career Opportunities in the Visual Arts*, Richard P. Clark and Pamela Fehl, forward by Brad Holland. 2006. Ferguson Publishing Company, Imprint of Facts on File Publications, 132 W. 31st St., 17th flr., New York, NY 10001. Customer service: (800) 322-8755. (www.chelseahouse.infobasepublishing.com).

*Career Solutions for Creative People: How to Balance Artistic Goals with Career Security*, Dr. Ronda Ormont. 2001. Allworth Press, 10 E. 23rd St., New York, NY 10010. (800) 491-2808. (www.allworth.com).

*Careers in Art (Professional Career Series)*, Blythe Camenson. 2006. McGraw-Hill, 1221 Ave. of the Americas, New York, NY 10020. (212) 512-4100. (www.mcgraw-hill.com).

*Careers in Art*, Gerald F. Brommer and Joseph A. Gatto. 2nd ed., 1999. Sterling Publishing Co., 387 Park Ave. S., 5th flr., New York, NY 10016. (212) 532-7160. (www.sterlingpublishing.com).

*Caring for Your Art: A Guide for Artists, Collectors, Galleries and Art Institutions*, Jill Snyder and Maria Reidelbach. 2002. Allworth Press, 10 E. 23rd St., New York, NY 10010. (800) 491-2808. (www.allworth.com).

*Creating a Successful Craft Business*, Rogene Robbins and Robert Robbins. 2003. Allworth Press, 10 E. 23rd St., New York, NY 10010. (800) 491-2808. (www.allworth.com).

*Creative Cash: How to Profit from Your Special Artistry, Creativity, Hand Skills, and Related Know-How*, Barbara Brabec. 1998. Crown Publishing Group, Random House, 280 Park Ave., New York, NY 10017. (800) 733-3000, e-mail: crownbiz@randomhouse.com. (www.randomhouse.com).

*Do-It-Yourself QUICK-FIX TaxKit*, Barbara A. Sloan. 2010 (updated yearly) AKAS II, PO Box 123, Hot Springs National Park, AK 71902. (501) 262-2395, e-mail: askasii@aol.com. (www.akasii.com).

Fine Arts & Jewelry Division, Frenkel & Co., International Insurance Brokers, 101 Hudson St., 38th flr., Jersey City, NJ 07302. (201) 356-3400, fax: (201) 356-3431, (201) 356-3434. (www.frenkel.com).

Fine Arts Risk Management, 1530 Wilson Blvd., ste. 900, Arlington, VA 22209. (888) 812-3276, fax: (703) 312-6407, e-mail: rsalmon@nnng.com.

Franklin Covey Corporation, 2200 W. Parkway Blvd., Salt Lake City, UT 84119. (800) 819-1812 (products), (800) 360-5326 (public workshops). (www.franklincovey.com). Time management and goal planning products and seminars.

*Getting Your Act Together, Artists Resource: The Watson-Guptill Guide to Academic Programs, Artist' Colonies and Artist-in-Residence Programs, Conferences, Workshops*, Karen Chambers. Watson-Guptill Publications, Inc., 770 Broadway, New York, NY 10003. (646) 654-5500, e-mail: info@watsonguptill.com. (www.watsonguptill.com).

*Health Hazards: Manual for Artists*, Michael McCann. 5th ed., 2003. The Lyons Press, Imprint of Globe Pequot Press, 246 Goose Ln., PO Box 480, Guilford, CT 06437. (203) 458-4500, customer service: (888) 249-7586, customer service fax: (800) 820-2329, e-mail: info@globepequot.com. (www.globepequot.com).

Henderson Phillips Fine Arts Insurance, Arthur J. Gallagher & Co., Corporate Headquarters, The Gallagher Centre, 2 Pierce Pl., Itasca, IL 60143. (630) 772-3800, fax: (630) 285-4000. (www.ajg.com). Website has links to local offices.

*How to Become a Famous Artist and Still Paint Pictures*, W. Joe Innis. 2000. Backinprint.com. Order through iUniverse, 2021 Pine Lake Rd., ste. 100, Lincoln, NE 68512. (877) 288-4737, (402) 323-7800, fax: (402) 323-7824, e-mail: book.orders@iuniverse.com. (www.iuniverse.com).

*How to Escape Lifetime Security and Pursue Your Impossible Dream: A Guide to Transforming Your Career*, Kenneth Atchity. 2004. Allworth Press, 10 E. 23rd St., New York, NY 10010. (800) 491-2808. (www.allworth.com).

*How to Grow as an Artist*, Daniel Grant. 2002. Allworth Press, 10 E. 23rd St., New York, NY 10010. (800) 491-2808. (www.allworth.com).

*How to Make Money as an Artist: The 7 Winning Strategies of Successful Fine Artists*, Sean Moore. 2000. Chicago Review Press, 814 N. Franklin St., Chicago, IL 60610. (800) 888-4741, (312) 337-0747, fax: (312) 337-5110, e-mail: frontdesk@chicagoreviewpress.com. (www.chicagoreviewpress.com).

*How to Profit from the Art Print Market*, Barney Davey. 2005. Bold Star Communications, PO Box 25386, Scottsdale, AZ 85255. (602) 499-7500, e-mail: barney@barneydavey.com. (www. Artprintissues.com, www.barneydavey.com).

*How to Sell Art, A Guide for Galleries, Dealers, Consultants and Artists' Agents*, Nina Pratt. 1992. Succotash Press. A guide for galleries, dealers, consultants and artists' agents. Also useful for artists unaware of the inner workings of the art world. Used copies on Amazon.com.

*How to Survive and Prosper as an Artist: Selling Yourself Without Selling Your Soul*, Caroll Michels. 5th ed., 2001. Henry Holt and Company, 175 Fifth Ave., New York, NY 10010. (646) 307-5095, fax: (212) 633-0748. (www.hholt.com).

*I'm Here, Now What? An Artist's Survival Guide for NYC!* Amy Harrell. 2006. BookSurge Publishing, OnDemand Publishing, subsidiary of Amazon, Charleston, SC. (www.booksurge.com).

*In the Making*, Linda Weinbtraub. 2003. D.A.P./Distributed Art Publishers, 155 Ave. of the Americas, New York, NY 10013. (800) 338-2665, fax: (212) 627-9484, e-mail: dap@dapinc.com. (www.artbook.com).

*International Art Galleries: Post-War to Post-Millennium*, Luca Cerizza, Stephane Correart, Rachel Gugelberger, Barbara Hess, Sylvia Martin, Regina Schultz-Maller, Adam Szymczyk, and Jens Hoffman, edited by Uta Grosenick and Raimar Stange. 2006. Dumont Literatur und Kunst Verlag, Amsterdamer Strasse 192, D-50735 Cologne, Germany. (49) 2-21-224-1877, fax: (49) 2-21-224-1973, e-mail: info@DumontLiteraturundKunst.de. (www.DumontLiteraturundKunst.de).

*International Auction House Directory*, LTB Gordonsart, 13201 N. 35th Ave., ste. B-20, Phoenix, AZ 85029. (800) 892-4622, (602) 253-6948, fax: (602) 253-2104, e-mail: office@gordonsart.com. (www.gordonsart.com).

iUniverse, 2021 Pine Lake Rd., ste. 100, Lincoln, NE 68512. (800) 288-4677, (402) 323-7800, fax: (402) 323-7824. (www.iuniverse.com). Self publishing.

*Legal Guide for the Visual Artist*, Tad Crawford. 4th edition, 1999. Allworth Press, 10 E. 23rd St., New York, NY 10010. (800) 491-2808. (www.allworth.com).

*Licensing Art & Design*, Caryn R. Leland. 1995. Allworth Press, 10 E. 23rd St., New York, NY 10010. (800) 491-2808. (www.allworth.com).

*Licensing Photography*, Richard Weisgrau and Victor S. Perlman. 2006. Allworth Press, 10 E. 23rd St., New York, NY 10010. (800) 491-2808. (www.allworth.com).

*Living The Artists Life: A Guide to Growing, Persevering, and Succeeding in the Art World*, Paul Dorrell. 2004. Used copies on Amazon.com.

*Money Management for the Creative Person: Right Brain Strategies to Build Your Bank Account and Find the Financial Freedom to Create*, Lee T. Silber. 2002. Crown Publishing Group, Random House, 280 Park Ave., New York, NY 10017. (800) 733-3000, e-mail: crownbiz@randomhouse.com. (www.randomhouse.com).

*Opportunities in Arts & Crafts Careers*, Elizabeth Gardner. 2nd ed., 2005. Available on Amazon.com.

Prestige Art, 3909 W. Howard St., Skokie, IL 60076. (847) 679-2555, fax: (847) 679-2559, e-mail: prestige@prestigeart.com. (www.prestigeart.com). Company President Louis Shutz consults with artists on publishing and licensing of their work.

*Selling Art Without Galleries*, Daniel Grant. 2006. Allworth Press, 10 E. 23rd St., New York, NY 10010. (800) 491-2808. (www.allworth.com).

*Selling Your Crafts*, Susan Sager. Rev. 2003. Allworth Press, 10 E. 23rd St., New York, NY 10010. (800) 491-2808. (www.allworth.com).

*Success Now! For Artists: A Motivational Guide for the Artrepreneur*, Renée Phillips. 2nd ed., 2003. Manhattan Arts International, 200 E. 72nd St., 26th flr., New York, NY 10021. (212) 472-1660, e-mail: info@manhattanarts.com. (www.manhattanarts.com).

*Taking the Leap: Building a Career as a Visual Artist*, Cay Lang. 2nd ed., 2006. Chronicle Books, 680 Second St., San Francisco, CA 94107. (415) 537-4283. (www.chroniclebooks.com).

*The Art Business Encyclopedia*, Leonard Duboff. 1994. Available on Amazon.com.

*The Art World Dream: Alternative Strategies for Working Artists*, Eric Rudd. 2001. Cire Corporation, 189 Beaver St., North Adams, MA 01247. (413) 664-9550, fax: (413) 663-6662.

*The Artist in Business*, Craig Dreeszen, edited by Barbara Schaffer Bacon, John Fiscella, and Clare D. Wood. Used copies on Amazon.com.

*The Artist's Complete Health and Safety Guide*, Monona Rossol. 3rd. ed. Allworth Press, 10 E. 23rd St., New York, NY 10010. (800) 491-2808. (www.allworth.com).

*The Artist's Guide to New Markets: Opportunities to Show and Sell Art Beyond Galleries*, Peggy Hadden. 1998. Allworth Press, 10 E. 23rd St., New York, NY 10010. (800) 491-2808. (www.allworth.com).

*The Artist's Organizer*, Sue Viders and Urania Christy Target. 2007. The National Network for Artist Placement (NNAP), 935 West Ave. 37, Los Angeles, CA 90065. (800) 354-5348, (323) 222-4035, e-mail: NNAPnow@aol.com. (www.artistplacement.com).

*The Artist's Resource Handbook*, Daniel Grant. Allworth Press, 10 E. 23rd St., New York, NY 10010. (800) 491-2808. (www.allworth.com).

*The Business of Art*, Lee Caplin. 3rd ed., 1998. Used copies on Amazon.com.

*The Business of Being an Artist*, Daniel Grant. 3rd edition, 2000. Allworth Press, 10 E. 23rd St., New York, NY 10010. (800) 491-2808. (www.allworth.com).

*The Concise Oxford Dictionary of Art Terms*, Michael Clarke. 2001. Oxford University Press, USA, 198 Madison Ave., New York, NY 10016. (800) 445-9714, fax: (919) 677-1303, e-mail: custservus@oup.com. (www.oup.com/us).

*The Fine Artist's Career Guide, 2nd Edition: Making Money in the Arts and Beyond*, Daniel Grant. 2004. Available on Amazon.com.

*The Licensing Book* (monthly) and *The Licensing Report* (weekly), Adventure Publishing Group, 286 5th Ave., 3rd flr., New York, NY 10001. (212) 575-4510, fax: (212) 575-4521. (www.licensingbook.com, www.adventurepublishinggroup.com, www.adventurepub.com). Updates on new products, agreements, and properties with special section on art licensing.

*The Practical Handbook for the Emerging Artists*, Margaret Lazzari, enhanced edition, 2011. Wadsworth Publishing, Thomson Higher Education, 10 Davis Dr., Belmont, CA 94002. (800) 354-9706, fax: (800) 487-8488. (www.thomsonedu.com).

The Tony Robbins Companies, 9888 Carroll Centre Rd., San Diego, CA 92126. (800) 445-8183, customer service: (800) 488-6040). (www.tonyrobbins.com). Motivational tapes, lectures, workshops.

Video Art production, 5007 MacArthur Blvd. NW, Washington, DC 20016, (202) 966-9070. (www.videoartproduction.com).

*Why Are Artists Poor?: The Exceptional Economy of the Arts*, Hans Abbing. 2004. Amsterdam University Press (www.aup.nl), distributed by University of Chicago Press, 1427 E. 60th St., Chicago, IL 60637. (773) 702-7780, fax: (773) 702-9756. (www.press.uchicago.edu).

*Worldwide Licensing Directory*, A4 Publications Ltd., Thornleigh, 35 Hagley Rd., Stourbridge, West Midlands DY8 1QR, UK.

www.artbusiness.com. e-mail: artbusiness@artbusiness.com. Offers complete art services, art appraisals, art price data, news, articles, and market information to collectors, fine-arts professionals, and artists.

www.guild.com. The Guild, 931 E. Main St., ste. 9, Madison, WI 53703. (877) 223-4600, artists: (608) 616-2002, international: (608) 257-2590, fax: (608) 257-2690, e-mail: art-info@guild.com. Source book and website for art glass, objects and accents, art for the wall, furniture and lighting, jewelry, and accessories. Fee for inclusion.

XLibris, International Plaza II, ste. 340, Philadelphia, PA 19113. (888) 795-4274, (610) 915-5214, fax: (610) 915-0294, e-mail: info@xlibris.com. (www.xlibris.com).

## Travel

*Art Diary International: The World Art Directory*, Giancarlo Politi Editore, edited by *Flash Art Magazine*. Distributed by D.A.P./Distributed Art Publishers, Inc., 155 Ave. of the Americas, New York, NY 10013. (800) 338-2665, fax (212) 627-9484, e-mail: dap@dapinc.com. (www.artbook.com).

Artful Hotels of the World. The Humanities Exchange, 4000 Blvd. de Maisonneuve W., ste. 1409, Montréal, Québec PQ H3Z 1Jp, Canada. (514) 935-1228, fax: (514) 935-1299, e-mail: exhibitionsonline@earthlink.net. (www.humanities-exchange.org). e-mail: jgeustrace@earthlink.net. (www.artfulhotels.com). Website linking to hotels by geographical location.

Art-SITES series, Sidra Stich. Art-SITES Press, 894 Waller St., San Franciso, CA 94117. (415) 437-2456, fax: (415) 701-0633, e-mail: info@art-sites.com. (www.art-sites.com). Travel guides with emphasis on the visual arts. Volumes available for London, Northern Italy, San Francisco, Paris, Britain and Ireland, Spain, and France.

Bed & Breakfast for Art Professionals, 431 E. 12th St. (between First Ave. and Ave. A), bell 1B, New York, NY 10009. (212) 674-8535, fax: 212-533-0316, e-mail: newyorkguest@earthlink.com. Private room & bath.

City Lights Bed & Breakfast, PO Box 20355, Cherokee Sta., New York, NY 10012. (212) 737-7049, (212) 675-9351, fax: (212) 866-504-0236. (www.citylightsnewyork.com). Short-term apartment rentals in New York.

Hotel Chelsea, 222 W. 23rd St., New York, NY 10011. (212) 243-3700. (www.hotelchelsea.com).

Hotel Reservations Network. (800) 282-7613. (www.hotelreservationsnetwork.com). Nationwide booking service at 50% of published rates.

Quik Book. (800) 789-9887, (212) 779-7666. (www.quikbook.com). Hotel reservation service.

Room Exchange. (800) 846-7000. (www.roomex.net.com). Posting of rooms available worldwide for exchange.

The Marmara Manhattan, 301 E. 94th St., New York, NY 10128. (800) 621-9029), (212) 427-3100. (www.marmara-manhattan.com). Luxury extended-stay hotel.

The Roger Smith Hotel, 501 Lexington Ave. at 47th Street, New York, NY 10017. (800) 445-0277, (212) 755-1400, ext. 7499. (www.rogersmith.com). Contact: James Fox, Director of Sales.

www.amn.org Art Museum Network. Membership organization with links on website to members' websites to find out current exhibitions and events.

*Does the road wind uphill all the way? Yes, to the very end.*

CHRISTINA ROSSETTI